'This thorough and enlightening analysis will stand as the most comprehensive review of self-defense law to come forth in decades. ... [A] fascinating read for legal scholars and criminal law practitioners alike.'

Hon Virginia M Kendall, US District Court Judge (Chicago) and former Assistant US Attorney

'"[E]in großer Wurf " (a "major coup") in the area of self-defence theory and analysis [which also offers] the first perfectly accurate and comprehensive English summary of the history of, and nuanced debate over, the past and present self-defence law in Germany.'

Dr Volker Erb, Professor of Law, Johannes Gutenberg-University, Mainz, Germany

'Dr Funk in exemplary fashion examines a central question of modern political life. The result is a book that offers the most detailed comparativist study on the subject yet published.'

Daniel Polsby, Dean Emeritus, George Mason University Antonin Scalia Law School

'The book provides a thoughtful, deep, and nuanced way for the reader to think about the deadly-force controversies we face in the 21st Century.'

Joshua Dressler, Distinguished University Professor, Ohio State University

'An engaging analysis that is recommended reading for anyone with an interest in criminal law defences.'

Mark Dsouza, Deputy Director, Centre for Criminal Law, University College London

'Dr Funk's book ... offers convincing answers to many of the issues regarding self-defence's most challenging practical and theoretical questions. I find it thought-provoking and heartily recommend it.'

Boaz Sangero, Professor of Law, The College of Law and Business and The Sapir Academic College School of Law, Israel

'Dr Funk's robust and fresh approach provides a powerful analytical framework to analyse this core right that has so dominated contemporary scholarly and political debates. ... I highly recommend this book.'

Robert Leider, Assistant Professor, Antonin Scalia School of Law, George Mason University

'Dr Funk's exceptional book, truly a timely contribution to the searing national debate, offers a critically-important fresh take on self-defense's key practical, theoretical, ethical, and philosophical issues.'

Hon Bernice B Donald, US Court of Appeals for the Sixth Circuit

'This thorough and enlightening analysis will stand as the most comprehensive review of self-defense law to come forth in decades. … [A] fascinating read for legal scholars and criminal law practitioners alike.'
Hon Virginia M Kendall, US District Court Judge (Chicago) and former Assistant US Attorney

'"[E]in großer Wurf " (a "major coup") in the area of self-defence theory and analysis [which also offers] the first perfectly accurate and comprehensive English summary of the history of, and nuanced debate over, the past and present self-defence law in Germany.'
Dr Volker Erb, Professor of Law, Johannes Gutenberg-University, Mainz, Germany

'Dr Funk in exemplary fashion examines a central question of modern political life. The result is a book that offers the most detailed comparativist study on the subject yet published.'
Daniel Polsby, Dean Emeritus, George Mason University Antonin Scalia Law School

'The book provides a thoughtful, deep, and nuanced way for the reader to think about the deadly-force controversies we face in the 21st Century.'
Joshua Dressler, Distinguished University Professor, Ohio State University

'An engaging analysis that is recommended reading for anyone with an interest in criminal law defences.'
Mark Dsouza, Deputy Director, Centre for Criminal Law, University College London

'Dr Funk's book … offers convincing answers to many of the issues regarding self-defence's most challenging practical and theoretical questions. I find it thought-provoking and heartily recommend it.'
Boaz Sangero, Professor of Law, The College of Law and Business and The Sapir Academic College School of Law, Israel

'Dr Funk's robust and fresh approach provides a powerful analytical framework to analyse this core right that has so dominated contemporary scholarly and political debates. … I highly recommend this book.'
Robert Leider, Assistant Professor, Antonin Scalia School of Law, George Mason University

'Dr Funk's exceptional book, truly a timely contribution to the searing national debate, offers a critically-important fresh take on self-defense's key practical, theoretical, ethical, and philosophical issues.'
Hon Bernice B Donald, US Court of Appeals for the Sixth Circuit

Rethinking Self-Defence

The 'Ancient Right's' Rationale Disentangled

T Markus Funk

•HART•

OXFORD • LONDON • NEW YORK • NEW DELHI • SYDNEY

HART PUBLISHING

Bloomsbury Publishing Plc

Kemp House, Chawley Park, Cumnor Hill, Oxford, OX2 9PH, UK

1385 Broadway, New York, NY 10018, USA

First published in Great Britain 2021

A catalogue record for this book is available from the British Library.

Library of Congress Cataloging-in-Publication data

Names: Funk, T. Markus, author.

Title: Rethinking self-defence : the 'ancient right's' rationale disentangled / T. Markus Funk.

Other titles: Rethinking self-defense

Description: Oxford, UK ; New York, NY : Hart Publishing, an imprint of Bloomsbury Publishing, 2020. | Includes bibliographical references and index.

Identifiers: LCCN 2020028064 (print) | LCCN 2020028065 (ebook) | ISBN 9781509934171 (hardback) | ISBN 9781509934195 (ePDF) | ISBN 9781509934188 (Epub)

Subjects: LCSH: Self-defense (International law)

Classification: LCC KZ4043 .F86 2020 (print) | LCC KZ4043 (ebook) | DDC 345/.04—dc23

LC record available at https://lccn.loc.gov/2020028064

LC ebook record available at https://lccn.loc.gov/2020028065

ISBN: HB: 978-1-50993-417-1
ePDF: 978-1-50993-419-5
ePub: 978-1-50993-418-8

Typeset by Compuscript Ltd, Shannon

ACKNOWLEDGEMENTS

This book did not exactly gush out of the author's pen – or, rather, keyboard. Indeed it was more than 20 years in the making (though this time-span was marked by a considerable gap in the effort; life has a funny way of interfering with the best-laid plans). That said, the tragic events of the recent past that have ushered in widespread calls for fundamental justice reform have rendered this book's call for a transparent and comprehensive value-based dialogue very timely.

In any event, I am, and will remain, forever grateful to Jonathan Herring for his exceptional patience and invaluable insights supervising my Oxford University doctoral thesis that was the basis for this book; Jeremy Horder for agreeing to be my first supervisor; Andrew Ashworth, Andrew von Hirsch, Lucia Zedner, and Tatjana Hörnle for (in different decades) serving as my Thesis Examiners; Jeanette Otis, as well as Joan Vergados Bryson, for outstanding editing and candid feedback throughout the drafting process; Hart Publishing's Chris Harrison for his eagle-eyed review of the final manuscript; and Chin Sue Virnich for averting my many potential missteps. For their exceptionally helpful comments on various drafts of the thesis going back to the late 1990s, I also wish to thank Andrew S Boutros, Dominik Brodowski, Mark Dsouza, Joel Feinberg, George P Fletcher, Robert Leider, Daniel Polsby, Paul H Robinson, Claus Roxin, Robert Schopp, Karl Sidhu, Eberhard Schmidhäuser, and Suzanne Uniacke. I also want to specifically heap thanks upon my three best friends – my wife Kate, and my daughters Heidi and Annelise – without whose patience and love this project could have never been completed. Per course, any remaining errors are mine alone.

CONTENTS

Acknowledgements vii
Table of Abbreviations and Foreign Journals xiii
Table of Authorities xxvii
Germany Cases xxvii
US Federal Cases xxx
US State Cases xxxi
England Cases xxxix
Northern Ireland Cases xli
Scotland Cases xli
European Court of Human Rights Cases xli
German Statutes xli
US Federal Statutes xlii
US State Statutes xlii
England Statutes xliii
International Statutes xliv
Other Primary Legal Sources – Germany xliv
Other Primary Legal Sources – US xliv
Other Primary Legal Sources – International xlv
Table of Tables xlvii
Glossary of German Words and Phrases xlix

1. Setting the Stage **1**

2. Developing the 'Value-Based Model' of Self-Defence **12**
I. Early Observers of the 'Ancient Right' of Self Defence 13
II. An Introduction to Thinking of Values as Decision-Grounds 15
III. The Orthodox View: 'Two Principles in Tension' (Autonomy of the Defender v Autonomy of the Attacker) 17
IV. Advancing the Debate Through a More Value-Centric Dialogue – An Introduction to (and Preliminary Defence of) Seven Proposed Value-Based Decision-Grounds 18
A. Value #1: Reducing Overall Societal Violence by Protecting the State's Collective 'Monopoly on Force' 19
B. Value #2: Protecting the Attacker's Individual (Presumptive) Right to Life 25
C. Value #3: Maintaining the Equal Standing between People 27
D. Value #4: Protecting the Defender's Autonomy 39

E. Value #5: Ensuring the Primacy of the Legal Process 42
F. Value #6: Maintaining the Legitimacy of the Legal Order 45
G. Value #7: Deterring (Potential) Attackers..57
V. The Challenging Act of Balancing the Competing Values......................61
A. The Value-Based Model and the 'Forfeiture' of Rights.....................61
B. Considering Alternative Value-Accommodation Methods 68

3. The Scholarly Community's Surprising Neglect of Values as Self-Defence Decision-Grounds 74

I. Protecting the State's Monopoly on Force (and the Primacy of the Legal Process) 74
II. Respect for the Attacker's 'Right to Life'...76
III. Protecting Equal Standing Among People...79
IV. Protecting the Defender's Autonomy 83
V. Ensuring the Primacy of the Legal Process..85
VI. Maintaining the Legitimacy of the Legal Order..................................86
VII. Deterrence...86
VIII. Self-Defence Scholarship's Treatment of Values as Decision-Grounds...87

4. The Value-Based Model's Answer to Common Theoretical ('Hard Case') Questions 93

I. Is Self-Defence a Justification or Excuse (or Neither)? … And Why the Answer Matters..93
A. Aggressors v Passive Threats v Innocent Bystanders – The Importance of Accurate Labelling..................96
B. Mistakes: External, Internal, and Legal Justification....................98
C. 'Unreasonable' Mistakes of Fact..103
II. When Is Defensive Force 'Necessary'? 105
A. Distinguishing Self-Defence from Necessity and Duress..........106
B. The Relationship between Necessity and Imminence................108
C. Retreat and Avoiding Conflict 112
III. Proportionality of Defensive Force...114
A. Rejecting Strict Proportionality and Addressing Excessive Force 114
B. Deadly Force in Defence of Property...116
C. Responding to 'Trivial' Threats...117
IV. Necessity, Proportionality, Mistakes, and the European Convention on Human Rights 120
A. The Current Status of Positive Obligations Imposed by Article 2...121
B. Article 2 in the Self-Defence Context: Defensive Force Must Be 'Absolutely Necessary' 121

C. Article 2 in the Self-Defence Context: 'Strict Proportionality' Required 122
D. Article 2 and Deadly Force in Defence of Property 122
E. Article 2 and Mistakes 123
V. Application of the Value-Based Model to Other Challenging Cases 123
A. Innocent Attackers – The 'Standard' Case 123
B. Special Rules for 'Attacks' on the Police? 132

5. Examining German Law's Treatment of Self-Defence from a Value-Centric Perspective 134
I. Putting Germany's Self-Defence Law in Context 135
II. An Introduction to Self-Defence in Germany 136
A. The Theoretical Foundations of Self-Defence in Germany 137
B. Understanding the Arrival and Impact of 'Socio-Ethical' Limitations on Defensive Force 141
III. Subjective or Objective Standard as to Justificatory Circumstances? 144
A. Mistakes of Fact 145
B. Unknowingly Justified Defenders 146
IV. The Attack 147
A. What Interests Can Be Defended? 147
B. Need the Attacker's Conduct Be Criminal? 148
C. Special Rules for 'Attacks' on the Police? 149
D. Can Passive Conduct Constitute an 'Attack'? 150
E. Imminence 151
F. A New Definition of 'Attack'? 155
V. Defensive Conduct 156
A. Necessity 156
B. Proportionality and Excessive Force 157
C. Duty to Retreat and Avoid Conflict 159
D. Intentionally Provoked Attacks and Other Blameworthy Conduct on the Part of Defenders 161
VI. Evaluating Germany's Self-Defence Law from a Value-Centric Perspective 163

6. Examining the US Law's Treatment of Self-Defence from a Value-Centric Perspective 166
I. Putting US Self-Defence Law in Context 166
II. Subjective or Objective Standard as to the Justificatory Circumstances 169
A. Mistakes of Fact 169
B. Unknowingly Justified Defenders 170

III. The Attack 171
A. What Interests Can Be Defended? 171
B. Need the Attacker's Conduct Be Criminal? 175
C. Special Rules for Attacks on the Police? 175
D. Can Passive Conduct Constitute an 'Attack'? 177
E. Imminence 178
F. Necessity 181
G. Proportionality and Excessive Force 181
H. Duty to Retreat 182
I. Duty to Avoid Conflict 183
J. Intentionally Provoked Attacks and Other Blameworthy Conduct on the Part of the Defender 183
IV. Evaluating US Self-Defence Law from a Value-Centric Perspective 185

7. Examining the English Law's Treatment of Self-Defence from a Value-Centric Perspective 188
I. Putting England's Law of Self-Defence in Context 188
II. Subjective or Objective Standard as to the Justificatory Circumstances? 190
A. Mistakes of Fact 190
B. Unknowingly Justified Defenders 193
III. The Attack 195
A. What Can Be Defended? 195
B. Need the Attacker's Conduct Be Criminal? 195
C. Special Rules for 'Attacks' by the Police? 196
D. Can Passive Conduct Constitute an 'Attack'? 196
E. Imminence 198
IV. Defensive Conduct 202
A. Necessity 202
B. Proportionality and Excessive Force 203
C. Duty to Retreat and Avoid Conflict 206
D. Intentionally Provoked Attacks and Other Blameworthy Conduct on the Part of the Defender 208
V. Evaluating England's Self-Defence Law from a Value-Centric Perspective 209

8. Parting Observations 211

Bibliography 219
Index 239

TABLE OF ABBREVIATIONS AND FOREIGN JOURNALS

Abbreviation	Full Form
ABA Crim Just	American Bar Association Criminal Justice Magazine
ABA J	American Bar Association Journal
AC	Appeal Cases
AG	Amtsgericht [lower court]
Akron L Rev	Akron Law Review
Ala Code	Alabama Code
Alaska Stat	Alaska Statutes
Alb L Rev	Albany Law Review
All ER	All England Law Reports
Alternative LJ	Alternative Law Journal
Am Crim LR	American Criminal Law Review
Am J Bioethics	American Journal of Bioethics
Am J Juris	American Journal of Jurisprudence
Am L Rec	American Law Record
Am U L Rev	American University Law Review
Ann Rev Psychol	Annual Review of Psychology
Ariz L Rev	Arizona Law Review
Ariz Rev Stat Ann	Arizona Revised Statutes Annotated
Ariz St LJ	Arizona State Law Journal
Ark Code Ann	Arkansas Code Annotated
Ark L Rev	Arkansas Law Review

BC Int'l & Comp L Rev	Boston College International and Comparative Law Review
BC L Rev	Boston College Law Review
BU L Rev	Boston University Law Review
BayObLG	Bayerisches Oberstes Landesgericht [Bavarian Supreme State Court]
Behav Sci & L	Behavioral Sciences & the Law
Berkeley Bus LJ	Berkeley Business Law Journal
Berkeley J Crim L	Berkeley Journal of Criminal Law
Berkeley J Gender L & Just	Berkeley Journal of Gender, Law & Justice
BGH	Bundesgerichtshof [Federal Court of Justice]
BGHSt	Bundesgerichtshofes in Strafsachen [Federal Court of Justice in Criminal Matters]
British J Soc Work	British Journal of Social Work
Brook L Rev	Brooklyn Law Review
BT-Drucks	Deutscher Bundestag Drucksache [German Federal Parliament Printed Matter]
Buff Crim LR	Buffalo Criminal Law Review
Buff L Rev	Buffalo Law Review
BYU J Pub L	Brigham Young University Journal of Public Law
CA	Court of Appeal
Calif L Rev	California Law Review
Cambridge J Int'l & Comp L	Cambridge Journal of International and Comparative Law
Cambridge LJ	Cambridge Law Journal
Cambridge Student L Rev	Cambridge Student Law Review
Can JL & Juris	Canadian Journal of Law & Jurisprudence
Cardozo L Rev	Cardozo Law Review
Case W Res L Rev	Case Western Reserve Law Review

Cath U L Rev	Catholic University Law Review
CCA	Court of Criminal Appeal
CD	Commission Decision (European Human Rights Reports)
Chap L Rev	Chapman Law Review
Chi Bar Assoc Rec	Chicago Bar Association Record
Chi-Kent L Rev	Chicago-Kent Law Review
Clev St L Rev	Cleveland State Law Review
Colo Rev Stat	Colorado Revised Statutes
Colum Hum Rts L Rev	Columbia Human Rights Law Review
Colum J Gender & L	Columbia Journal of Gender and Law
Colum L Rev	Columbia Law Review
Com L League J	Commercial Law League Journal
Common L World Rev	Common Law World Review
Cong Rec	Congressional Record
Conn Gen Stat	Connecticut General Statutes
Conn L Rev	Connecticut Law Review
Cornell Int'l LJ	Cornell International Law Journal
Cornell JL & Pub Pol'y	Cornell Journal of Law and Public Policy
Cornell L Rev	Cornell Law Review
Cox CC	Cox's Criminal Cases
Cr App R	Criminal Appeal Reports
Crim Just & Behavior	Criminal Justice and Behavior
Crim Just Ethics	Criminal Justice Ethics
Crim L & Phil	Criminal Law and Philosophy
Crim L Bull	Criminal Law Bulletin
Crim LR	Criminal Law Review
Crime & Just	Crime and Justice
Dalhousie LJ	Dalhousie Law Journal

Del Code Ann	Delaware Code Annotated
Dick L Rev	Dickinson Law Review
Drake L Rev	Drake Law Review
Drexel L Rev	Drexel Law Review
Duke LJ	Duke Law Journal
ETS	European Treaty Series
ECHR	European Convention on Human Rights
ECtHR	European Court of Human Rights
Edinburgh L Rev	Edinburgh Law Review
EHRR	European Human Rights Reports
Emory Int'l L Rev	Emory International Law Review
Emory LJ	Emory Law Journal
ER	English Reports
Ethics	Ethics
Eur J Criminology	European Journal of Criminology
EWCA Civ	England and Wales Court of Appeals (Civil Division)
EWCA Crim	England and Wales Court of Appeals (Criminal Division)
EWHC (Admin)	England and Wales High Court (Administrative Division)
FBI L Enforcement Bull	FBI Law Enforcement Bulletin
Fla L Rev	Florida Law Review
Fla St U L Rev	Florida State University Law Review
Fla Stat	Florida Statutes
Fla Stat Ann	Florida Statutes Annotated
Fordham L Rev	Fordham Law Review
Fordham Urb LJ	Fordham Urban Law Journal
GA Res	General Assembly Resolution

GA	Goltdammer's Archiv für Strafrecht [Goltdammer's Archive for Criminal Law] (Germany)
Ga L Rev	Georgia Law Review
GC	General Chamber
Geo LJ	Georgetown Law Journal
Geo Mason L Rev	George Mason Law Review
Geo Wash L Rev	George Washington Law Review
Grundgesetz	German Constitution
Global Jurist Frontiers	Global Jurist Frontiers
Harv CR-CL L Rev	Harvard Civil Rights-Civil Liberties Law Review
Harv J on Legis	Harvard Journal on Legislation
Harv JL & Gender	Harvard Journal of Law & Gender
Harv L Rev	Harvard Law Review
Harv Women's LJ	Harvard Women's Law Journal
Hastings Bus LJ	Hastings Business Law Journal
Hastings LJ	Hastings Law Journal
Haw Rev Stat	Hawaii Revised Statutes
HL	House of Lords
Hofstra L Rev	Hofstra Law Review
Hous Bus & Tax LJ	Houston Business and Tax Law Journal
Ill Comp Stat	Illinois Compiled Statutes
Ind LJ	Indiana Law Journal
Int'l J Const L	International Journal of Constitutional Law
Int'l JL Pol'y & Fam	International Journal of Law, Policy and the Family
Int'l Theory	International Theory
Iowa L Rev	Iowa Law Review

Isr L Rev	Israel Law Review
J Am Inst Crim L & Criminology	Journal of the American Institute of Criminal Law and Criminology
J Applied Psychol	Journal of Applied Psychology
J Comp L	Journal of Comparative Law
J Contemp Legal Issues	Journal of Contemporary Legal Issues
J Crim L	Journal of Criminal Law
J Crim L & Criminology	Journal of Criminal Law and Criminology
J Disp Resol	Journal of Dispute Resolution
J Econ Literature	Journal of Economic Literature
J Eur Tort Law	Journal of European Tort Law
J Fam Psychol	Journal of Family Psychology
J Hum Resources	Journal of Human Resources
J Interpersonal Violence	Journal of Interpersonal Violence
J Legis	Journal of Legislation
J on Eur Hist L	Journal on European History of Law
J Phil	Journal of Philosophy
J Pol Econ	Journal of Political Economy
J Prac Ethics	Journal of Practical Ethics
J S Afr L	Journal of South African Law
J Soc & Soc Welfare	Journal of Sociology and Social Welfare
J Tort L	Journal of Tort Law
JL & Econ	Journal of Law and Economics
JL & Pol	Journal of Law & Politics
JL & Soc Challenges	Journal of Law & Social Challenges
JL Econ & Pol'y	Journal of Law, Economics & Policy
JL Soc'y	Journal of Law in Society
JR	Juristische Rundschau [Legal Review] (Germany)

Jura	Jura [Law] (Germany)
Jurid Trib	Juridical Tribune
Just Q	Justice Quarterly
JZ	Juristen Zeitung [Lawyers Newspaper] (Germany)
Kan Stat Ann	Kansas Statutes Annotated
KB	King's Bench
Ky LJ	Kentucky Law Journal
L Annals Titu Maiorescu U	Law Annals of Titu Maiorescu University
LQR	Law Quarterly Review
La L Rev	Louisiana Law Review
La Stat Ann	Louisiana Statutes Annotated
Law & Contemp Probs	Law and Contemporary Problems
Law & Dev Rev	Law and Development Review
Law & Ethics Hum Rts	Law and Ethics of Human Rights
Law & Hum Behav	Law and Human Behavior
Law & Phil	Law and Philosophy
Law & Pol'y	Law and Policy
Law & Soc'y Rev	Law and Society Review
LS	Legal Studies
Lewis & Clark L Rev	Lewis & Clark Law Review
LG	Landgericht [regional court] (Germany)
Man LJ	Manitoba Law Journal
Md L Rev	Maryland Law Review
MDR	Monatsschrift für Deutsches Recht [Monthly Journal for German Law]
Me Crim Code	Maine Criminal Code
Me Rev Stat	Maine Revised Statutes
Melb J Int'l L	Melbourne Journal of International Law

Mich L Rev	Michigan Law Review
Minn L Rev	Minnesota Law Review
Miss C L Rev	Mississippi College Law Review
Mo L Rev	Missouri Law Review
Mo Rev Stat	Missouri Revised Statutes
MLR	Modern Law Review
Monash U L Rev	Monash University Law Review
Monist	Monist
Mont Code Ann	Montana Code Annotated
MPC	Model Penal Code
N Ill U L Rev	Northern Illinois University Law Review
NC Gen Stat	North Carolina General Statutes
NC L Rev	North Carolina Law Review
NH Rev Stat Ann	New Hampshire Revised Statutes Annotated
NJ Rev Stat	New Jersey Revised Statutes
NJ Stat Ann	New Jersey Statutes Annotated
NY Penal Law	New York Penal Law
NYU J Legis & Pub Pol'y	New York University Journal of Legislation and Public Policy
NYU L Rev	New York University Law Review
NYU Rev L & Soc Change	New York University Review of Law and Social Change
NZ L Rev	New Zealand Law Review
Nat'l L Sch India Rev	National Law School of India Review
Neb L Rev	Nebraska Law Review
Neb Rev Stat	Nebraska Revised Statutes
New Crim LR	New Criminal Law Review
New LJ	New Law Journal
NI	Northern Ireland Law Reports

NJW	Neue Juristische Wochenschrift [New Legal Weekly] (Germany)
Nomos	Nomos [Law] (United States)
Notre Dame JL Ethics & Pub Pol'y	Notre Dame Journal of Law, Ethics & Public Policy
Notre Dame L Rev	Notre Dame Law Review
Nottingham LJ	Nottingham Law Journal
NStZ	Neue Zeitschrift für Strafrecht [New Journal for Criminal Law] (Germany)
Nw U L Rev	Northwestern University Law Review
Ohio St J Crim L	Ohio State Journal of Criminal Law
Ohio St LJ	Ohio State Law Journal
Okla L Rev	Oklahoma Law Review
OLG	Oberlandesgericht [higher regional court] (Germany)
Or L Rev	Oregon Law Review
Or Rev Stat	Oregon Revised Statutes
Osgoode Hall LJ	Osgoode Hall Law Journal
OJLS	Oxford Journal of Legal Studies
Pa Cons Stat	Pennsylvania Consolidated Statutes
Pac LJ	Pacific Law Journal
Pace L Rev	Pace Law Review
PC	Privy Council
Penn St Int'l L Rev	Penn State International Law Review
Phil & Pub Aff	Philosophy & Public Affairs
Phil Issues	Philosophical Issues
Phil Rev	Philosophical Review
Phil Stud	Philosophical Studies
Police Q	Police Quarterly
Polish Pol Sci YB	Polish Political Science Yearbook

Pravnik	Pravnik [Lawyer] (Slovenia)
Proc Aristotelian Soc'y	Proceedings of the Aristotelian Society
Psychol Pub Pol'y & Law	Psychology, Public Policy, and Law
QB	Queen's Bench
Queen's LJ	Queen's Law Journal
RI Gen Laws	Rhode Island General Laws
RG	Reichsgericht [Federal Court of Justice 1879–1944] (Germany)
RGSt	Reichsgericht in Strafsachen [Federal Court of Justice in Criminal Matters] (Germany)
Rutgers U L Rev	Rutgers University Law Review
S Afr LJ	South African Law Journal
S Cal Interdisc LJ	Southern California Interdisciplinary Law Journal
S Cal L Rev	Southern California Law Review
S Cal Rev L & Soc Just	Southern California Review of Law and Social Justice
San Diego L Rev	San Diego Law Review
Santa Clara L Rev	Santa Clara Law Review
SC(J)	Session Cases, High Court of Justiciary
Seton Hall L Rev	Seton Hall Law Review
Soc Probs	Social Problems
Social Phil & Pol'y	Social Philosophy and Policy
St Louis-Warsaw Transatlantic LJ	Saint Louis-Warsaw Transatlantic Law Journal
St Mary's LJ	St. Mary's Law Journal
Stan L & Pol'y Rev	Stanford Law and Policy Review
Stan L Rev	Stanford Law Review
Stellenbosch L Rev	Stellenbosch Law Review
StGB	Strafgesetzbuch [German Criminal Code]

Suffolk Transnat'l L Rev	Suffolk Transnational Law Review
Sw U L Rev	Southwestern University Law Review
Tenn L Rev	Tennessee Law Review
Tex Code Ann	Texas Code Annotated
Tex L Rev	Texas Law Review
Tex Penal Code	Texas Penal Code
Tex Penal Code Ann	Texas Penal Code Annotated
Tex Rev L & Pol	Texas Review of Law and Politics
Tex Tech L Rev	Texas Tech Law Review
Tex Wesleyan L Rev	Texas Wesleyan Law Review
Theoretical Inquiries L F	Theoretical Inquiries in Law Forum
U Chi L Rev	University of Chicago Law Review
U Chi Legal F	University of Chicago Legal Forum
U Cin L Rev	University of Cincinnati Law Review
U Colo L Rev	University of Colorado Law Review
U Det Mercy L Rev	University of Detroit Mercy Law Review
U Ill L Rev	University of Illinois Law Review
U La Verne L Rev	University of La Verne Law Review
U Louisville L Rev	University of Louisville Law Review
U Md LJ Race Religion Gender & Class	University of Maryland Law Journal of Race, Religion, Gender and Class
U Miami L Rev	University of Miami Law Review
U Mich JL Reform	University of Michigan Journal of Law Reform
U Pa J Const L	University of Pennsylvania Journal of Constitutional Law
U Pa L Rev	University of Pennsylvania Law Review
U Pac L Rev	University of the Pacific Law Review
U Pitt L Rev	University of Pittsburgh Law Review
U Rich L Rev	University of Richmond Law Review

U St Thomas JL & Pub Pol'y	University of St. Thomas Journal of Law and Public Policy
U Tas L Rev	University of Tasmania Law Review
U Toronto LJ	University of Toronto Law Journal
UC Davis L Rev	University of California-Davis Law Review
UC Irvine L Rev	University of California-Irvine Law Review
UNSW LJ	University of New South Wales Law Journal
USF L Rev	University of San Francisco Law Review
UCL J L & Juris	University College London Journal of Law and Jurisprudence
UCLA L Rev	University of California-Los Angeles Law Review
UMKC L Rev	University of Missouri-Kansas City Law Review
Utah Code Ann	Utah Code Annotated
Utah L Rev	Utah Law Review
Utrecht L Rev	Utretcht Law Review
Va J Crim L	Virginia Journal of Criminal Law
Va J Int'l L	Virginia Journal of International Law
Va L Rev	Virginia Law Review
Val U L Rev	Valparaiso University Law Review
Vand L Rev	Vanderbilt Law Review
W St U L Rev	Western State University Law Review
Wake Forest JL & Pol'y	Wake Forest Journal of Law & Policy
Wake Forest L Rev	Wake Forest Law Review
Wash L Rev Online	Washington Law Review Online
Wash Rev Code	Revised Code of Washington
Wash U JL & Pol'y	Washington University Journal of Law & Policy
Wash U Juris Rev	Washington University Jurisprudence Review

Washburn LJ	Washburn Law Journal
Wayne L Rev	Wayne Law Review
WLR	Weekly Law Reports
Wm & Mary J Race Gender & Soc Just	William & Mary Journal of Race, Gender, and Social Justice
Wm & Mary L Rev	William & Mary Law Review
Women's Rts L Rep	Women's Rights Law Reporter
Yale L & Pol'y Rev	Yale Law & Policy Review
Yale LJ	Yale Law Journal
ZStW	Zeitschrift Für Die Gesamte Strafrechtswissenschaft [Journal of the Complete Criminal Science] (Germany)

TABLE OF AUTHORITIES

Germany Cases

[1890] 21 RGSt 168 .... 138, 147–48
[1890] 21 RGSt 189 .... 144, 153
[1895] 27 RGSt 44 148
[1906] 35 RGSt 403 147
[1918] 53 RGSt 132 151
[1919] 54 RGSt 196 .... 144, 146
[1920] 55 RGSt 82 .... 4–5, 69–70, 137–38, 152, 156
[1920] 55 RGSt 167 147
[1921] 56 RGSt 259 146
[1926] 60 RGSt 261 145–46
[1926] 60 RGSt 273 147
[1927] 61 RGSt 216 151
[1928] 72 RGSt 305 149
[1930] 64 RGSt 101 .... 144, 153
[1931] 65 RGSt 159 151
[1933] 67 RGSt 337 151–52
[1935] 69 RGSt 265 147
[1935] 69 RGSt 308 .... 137, 157–58
[1938] 72 RGSt 57 .... 137, 150, 156
[1952] BGH 2 StR 8/50 145
[1952] BGH 2 StR 105/51 145
[1952] BGH 3 StR 217/52 .... 148, 155, 160
[1953] BGH 3 StR 151/53 .... 144, 146, 148
[1958] BGH NJW 1405 150
[1962] BayObLG NJW 1782 147
[1962] BGH JR 186 160
[1962] BGH NJW 308 .... 146, 160
[1963] BayObLG NJW 824 .... 144, 150, 153, 158–59
[1965] BayObLG MDR 65 159
[1965] BGH GA 147 156
[1966] AG Bensberg NJW 733 143
[1966] OLG Stuttgart NJW 745 148
[1968] BGH GA 182 137
[1968] BGH NJW 1885 137
[1969] BGH GA 23 .... 137, 156

[1969] BGH GA 117 .... 145, 161
[1969] BGH NJW 802 161
[1972] BGH 2 StR 679/71 .... 139, 156, 158, 162–63
[1972] BGH MDR 16 146
[1973] BGH NJW 255 151
[1975] BGH MDR 194 160
[1975] BGH NJW 62 161
[1975] BGH NJW 1161 148
[1976] BGH JR 335 161
[1979] BGH NJW 2053 151
[1980] BGH GA 67 147
[1980] BGH NJW 1806 146
[1982] BGH 3 StR 375/82 157
[1983] BGH 4 StR 703/82 146
[1984] BGH JZ 507 161
[1984] BGH JZ 529 161
[1984] BGH NJW 986 161
[1985] BayObLG NJW 2600 .... 144, 153, 157
[1985] BGH JR 113 161
[1988] LG München NJW 1860 .... 146, 157
[1989] BGH NJW 3027 156
[1989] BGH 1 StR 741/88 153
[1989] BGH 4 StR 2/89 163
[1991] BayObLG JZ 936 150
[1991] BayObLG NJW 2031 148
[1991] BGH NJW 503 162
[1991] BGH 2 StR 535/91 151
[1992] BGH 4 StR 464/92 157
[1992] OLG Karlsruhe NJW 1329 147
[1993] BGH 3 StR 354/93 163
[1994] BGH NJW 871 162
[1994] OLG Düsseldorf NJW 1971 .... 145, 147, 157
[1995] BGH NJW 973 .... 151, 156
[1995] BGH 4 StR 294/95 .... 141, 164
[1995] OLG Stuttgart NJW 2646 159
[1996] BGH NJW 2315 163
[1996] BGH 5 StR 432/95 .... 156, 164
[1998] BGH 4 StR 114/98 .... 152, 156
[2000] BGH 3 StR 331/00 .... 136, 146, 156
[2001] BGH 1 StR 48/01 .... 153, 157
[2002] BGH 3 StR 490/01 156
[2002] BGH 3 StR 503/01 152
[2003] BGH 1 StR 403/02 .... 146, 158
[2003] BGH 2 StR 529/02 157

[2003] BGH 3 StR 153/03 161
[2003] BGH 3 StR 458/02 157
[2003] BGH 3 StR 483/02 ..... 153, 155
[2003] BGH 4 StR 267/02 136
[2005] BGH 1 StR 99/05 152
[2005] BGH 2 StR 237/05 161–62
[2007] BGH 5 StR 404/06 151
[2010] BGH 1 StR 351/10 157
[2010] BGH 2 StR 454/09 158
[2010] BGH 2 StR 483/10 163
[2011] BGH 2 StR 375/11 157
[2012] BGH 2 StR 311/12 ..... 153, 155, 157
[2012] BGH 4 StR 197/12 ..... 146, 153, 156, 162–63
[2013] BGH 1 StR 449/13 ..... 153, 157
[2013] BGH 4 Str 347/13 156–57
[2013] BGH 4 StR 551/12 ..... 144, 146
[2014] BGH 1 StR 630/13 ..... 157, 161–62, 164
[2014] BGH 5 StR 134/14 ..... 147, 156–57
[2015] BGH 1 StR 606/14 136
[2015] BGH 2 StR 473/14 161–62
[2015] BGH 3 StR 84/15 157
[2015] BGH 3 StR 199/15 ..... 144, 146
[2015] BGH 5 StR 397/15 152
[2016] BGH 1 StR 597/15 164
[2016] BGH 2 StR 523/15 ..... 138, 141, 143, 161
[2016] BGH 4 StR 235/16 ..... 144–45, 151–52
[2016] BGH 5 StR 138/16 ..... 152, 156–57
[2016] BGH 5 StR 564/15 ..... 153, 156–57
[2017] BGH 1 StR 486/16 151–53
[2017] BGH 1 StR 588/16 ..... 146, 151–52
[2017] BGH 2 StR 118/16 155–56
[2017] BGH 2 StR 188/17 ..... 137, 151, 156–57
[2017] BGH 2 StR 219/16 156–57
[2017] BGH 2 StR 252/17 156–57
[2017] BGH 3 StR 622/17 ..... 137, 142, 147, 159
[2017] BGH 4 StR 35/17 ..... 144–45, 151, 157
[2017] BGH 4 StR 197/17 157
[2017] BGH 4 StR 635/16 ..... 151–52, 157
[2018] BGH NStZ 69 136
[2018] BGH 1 StR 208/18 ..... 136, 163
[2018] BGH 4 StR 107/18 138
[2018] BGH 4 StR 214/18 143
[2018] BGH 4 StR 242/18 143
[2018] BGH 5 StR 421/18 ..... 152, 156

[2018] OLG Zweibrücken 42 .... 141, 144, 146, 158
[2019] BGH 1 StR 363/18 .... 144, 147, 156
[2019] BGH 1 StR 585/18 152
[2019] BGH 4 StR 456/18 .... 146, 161–63
[2019] LG Dortmund 39Ks 8/14 .... 138, 160
[2019] LG Muenster 123 .... 144, 156, 158, 161

US Federal Cases

Acers v United States, 164 US 388 (1896) 169, 178
Addington v United States, 165 US 184 (1897) 169
Allen v United States, 164 US 492 (1896) 182
Beard v United States, 158 US 550 (1895) 169, 174
Brookhart v Janis, 384 US 1 (1966) 66
Caleshu v SC Merrill Lynch, 737 F Supp 1070 (ED Mo 1990) 120
Collado v City of New York, 2019 WL 3996735 (SDNY Aug 23, 2019) 176
Costello v Town of Warwick, 2008 WL 1752486 (2nd Cir Apr 17, 2008) 176
Deere v Calderon, 890 F Supp 893 (CD Cal 1995) 4
Frisby v Schultz, 487 US 474 (1988) 166
Gourko v United States, 153 US 183 (1894) 183
Graham v Connor, 490 US 386 (1989) 176
Gregg v Georgia, 428 US 153 (1976) 51
JDB v North Carolina, 564 US 261 (2011) 170
Johnson v Zerbst, 304 US 458 (1938) 66
Kopf v Skyrm, 993 F2d 374 (4th Cir 1993) 176
Lloyd v Jefferson, 53 F Supp 2d 643 (D Del 1999) 169
McDonald v Chicago, 561 US 742 (2010) 1
Neevel v Herns, 2018 WL 6441071 (WD Wis Dec 7, 2018) 168
Rosemond v United States, 134 S Ct 1240 (2014) 167
Rowe v United States, 164 US 546 (1896) 169, 182–83
Stansbury v California, 511 US 318 (1994) 170
Stillwagon v City of Delaware, 175 F Supp 874 (SD Ohio 2016) 169–70, 176, 181
Stillwagon v City of Delaware, 274 F Supp 3d 714 (SD Ohio 2017) 171
Taylor v United States, 414 US 17 (1973) 66
Thompson v United States, 155 US 271 (1894) 183
Thornburgh v American College of Obstetricians & Gynecologists, 106 S Ct 2169 (1986) 118
United States v Acosta-Sierra, 690 F3d 1111 (9th Cir 2012) 109
United States v Blodgett, 513 F Supp 1056 (D Mont 1981) 54
United States v Carlson, 547 F2d 1346 (8th Cir 1976) 66
United States v Fokker Servs BV, 818 F3d 733 (DC Cir 2016) 52
United States v Gulley 29 F App'x 228 (6th Cir 2002) 59
United States v Haynes, 143 F3d 1089 (7th Cir 1998) 178

United States v Herbert, 26 F Cas 287 (DC Crim Ct 1856) 166
United States v Jennings, 855 F Supp 1427 (MD Pa 1994) 109
United States v Lopez, 913 F3d 807 (9th Cir 2019) 130
United States v Oakie, 12 F3d 1436 (8th Cir 1993) 109
United States v Oakie, 61 F3d 894 (3d Cir 1995) 109
United States v Ortiz, 927 F3d 868 (5th Cir 2019) 103
United States v Peterson, 483 F2d 1222 (DC Cir 1973) 181
United States v Ramirez, 537 F3d 1075 (9th Cir 2008) 216
United States v Reynolds, 235 US 133 (1914) 59
United States v Skinner, 667 F2d 1306 (9th Cir 1982) 182
United States v Travers, 28 F Cas 204 (CCD Ma 1814) 166
Wallace v United States, 162 US 466 (1896) 168, 172, 183

US State Cases

Alexander v Commonwealth, 508 SE2d 912 (Va Ct App 1999) 174
Alexander v Commonwealth, 531 SE2d 567 (Va 2000) 174
Ammons v State, 102 So 642 (Fla 1924) 170
Armstrong v State, 143 P 870 (Okla Crim App 1914) 173
Babcock v People, 22 P 817 (Colo 1889) 181
Bailey v People, 130 P 832 (Colo 1913) 174
Barkley v State, 213 SW 642 (Tex Crim App 1919) 172
Bell v City of Albany, 436 SE2d 87 (Ga Ct App 1993) 176
Bellcourt v State, 390 NW2d 269 (Minn 1986) 185
Bloom v State, 58 NE 81 (Ind 1900) 172
Bolyard v Commonwealth, 397 SE2d 894 (Va Ct App 1990) 182
Bond v Baltimore & OR Co, 96 SE 932 (W Va 1918) 168
Bosler v Modern Woodmen of Am, 160 NW 966 (Neb 1916) 170
Bostic v State, 10 So 602 (Ala 1892) 174
Boykin v People, 45 P 419 (Colo 1896) 132
Bozeman v State, 104 SE 640 (Ga 1920) 172
Bray v State, 78 So 463 (Ala Ct App 1918) 173
Brown v State, 18 SW 1051 (Ark 1892) 174
Burch v State, 696 A2d 443 (Md Ct App 1997) 168
Calloway v State, 262 P 696 (Okla Crim App 1928) 170
Camarillo v State, 82 SW3d 529 (Tex Ct App 2002) 171
Carpenter v State, 36 SW 900 (Ark 1896) 173
Castro v State, 2014 WL 5020052 (Tex Ct App Oct 8, 2014) 170
Chapman v Commonwealth, 15 SW 50 (Ky Ct App 1891) 172
In re Christian S, 872 P2d 574 (Cal 1994) 168
Coleman v State, 320 A2d 740 (Del 1974) 169
Commonwealth v Alexander, 383 A2d 887 (Pa 1978) 171
Commonwealth v Caterino, 678 A2d 389 (Pa Sup Ct 1996) 127

Commonwealth v Donahue, 20 NE 171 (Mass 1889)....172
Commonwealth v Emmons, 43 A2d 568 (Pa 1945).... 81, 174
Commonwealth v Fowlin, 710 A2d 1130 (Pa 1998)....185
Commonwealth v Haddock, 704 NE2d 537 (Mass App Ct 1999)....174
Commonwealth v Hammond, 953 A2d 544 (Pa Super Ct 2008)....183
Commonwealth v Helm, 402 A2d 500 (Pa 1979)....179
Commonwealth v Hourigan, 12 SW 550 (Ky Ct App 1889)....184
Commonwealth v Mayfield, 585 A2d 1069 (Pa Super Ct 1991)....167
Commonwealth v Naylor, 553 NE2d 542 (Mass 1990)....185
Commonwealth v Niemic, 696 NE2d 117 (Mass 1998)....182
Commonwealth v O'Neil, 641 NE2d 702 (Mass 1997)....184
Commonwealth v Samuel, 590 A2d 1245 (Pa 1991)....185
Commonwealth v Schulze, 2017 WL 665633 (Penn Ct CP Feb 17, 2017)....182
Corn v Rivera, 108 A3d 779 (Pa 2014)....182
Crawford v State, 17 SE 628 (Ga 1893)....172
Dabney v State, 21 So 211 (Ala 1897)....184
Darling v State, 225 SW 328 (Ark 1920)....172
Dearborn v State, 420 SW3d 366 (Tex Ct App 2014)....174
Dodson v Commonwealth, 167 SE 260 (Va 1933)....168
Dooley v State, 268 So 3d 880 (Fla Ct App Apr 3, 2019)....182
Driggers v United States, 95 P 612 (Okla 1908)....173
Dryer v State, 53 P2d 700 (Okla Crim App 1936)....172
Drysdale v State, 10 SE 358 (Ga 1889)....184
Duncan v State, 6 SW 164 (Ark 1887)....182
Easterling v State, 267 P2d 185 (Okla Crim App 1954)....179
Elizondo v State, 487 SW3d 185 (Tex Crim App 2016)....184
Ellison v State, 410 A2d 519 (Del Super Ct 1979)....177
Estep v Commonwealth, 4 SW 820 (Ky Ct App 1887)....174
Fertig v State, 75 NW 960 (Wis 1898)....172
Fielder v State, 683 SW2d 565 (Tex Ct App 1985)....178
Fielder v State, 756 SW2d 309 (Tex Crim App 1988)....178
Fisk v State, 71 P2d 499 (Okla Crim App 1937)....170
Fleming v State, 604 So 2d 280 (Miss 1992)....171
Floyd v State, 36 Ga 91 (Ga 1867)....181
Foreman v State, 257 NW 237 (Neb 1934)....167
Forrester v State, 4 SW2d 966 (Tex Crim App 1927)....170
Fortenberry v State, 55 Miss 403 (Miss 1877)....178
Fosbinder v Svitak, 20 NW 866 (Neb 1884)....172
Foster v Shepherd, 101 NE 411 (Ill 1913)....174
Frank v State, 68 NW 657 (Wis 1896)....184
Freeney v State, 59 SE 788 (Ga 1907)....174
Gaines v Commonwealth, 14 SE 375 (Va 1892)....184
Gallery v State, 17 SE 863 (Ga 1893)....170
Gann v State, 383 SW2d 32 (Tenn 1964)....185

Garnett v State, 632 A2d 797 (Md 1993) ... 95
Geralds v State, 647 NE2d 369 (Ind Ct App 1995) ... 174
Gibson v State, 8 So 98 (Ala 1890) ... 184
Gilbert v Commonwealth, 506 SE2d 543 (Va Ct App 1998) ... 185
Goodall v State, 1 Or 333 (Or 1861) ... 178
Goshen v People, 44 P 503 (Colo 1896) ... 172
Gunn v State, 365 NE2d 1234 (Ind Ct App 1977) ... 99
Haire v State, 393 P3d 1304 (Wyo 2017) ... 182
Harbour v State, 37 So 330 (Ala 1904) ... 181
Hardin v State, 49 SW 607 (Tex Crim App 1899) ... 168
Harold v State, 67 So 761 (Ala Ct App 1915) ... 174
Hayner v People, 72 NE 792 (Ill 1904) ... 174
Hicks v State, 984 A2d 246 (Md Ct Spec App 2009) ... 177
Hill v State, 143 So 3d 981 (Fla Ct App 2014) ... 175
Humphrey v State, 966 SW2d 213 (Ark 1998) ... 170
Hunt v State, 16 So 753 (Miss 1895) ... 182
Hunter v State, 128 SW2d 1176 (Tex Crim App 1939) ... 184
Jackson v Commonwealth, 36 SE 487 (Va 1900) ... 184
Jenkins v State, 942 So 2d 910 (Fla 2d DCA 2006) ... 167
Johnson v State, 23 SW 7 (Ark 1893) ... 182
Johnson v State, 829 SE2d 652 (Ga Ct App 2019) ... 185
Jordan v State, 146 SW 881 (Tex Crim App 1912) ... 175
Kelton v State, 160 SW 342 (Tex Crim App 1913) ... 175
Kennard v State, 28 So 858 (Fla 1900) ... 183–84
Lancy v State, 361 SE2d 841 (Ga Ct App 1987) ... 168
Langley v State, 373 So 2d 1267 (Ala Crim App 1979) ... 179
Latham v State, 46 SW 638 (Tex Crim App 1898) ... 175
Lawson v State, 41 SE 993 (Ga 1902) ... 175
Lovett v State, 11 So 550 (Fla 1892) ... 170
Lynn v Commonwealth, 499 SE2d 1 (Va Ct App 1998) ... 182, 184
Matthews v State, 58 SW 86 (Tex Crim App 1900) ... 183
May v People, 6 P 816 (Colo 1885) ... 170
May v State, 460 So 2d 778 (Miss 1984) ... 179
McDonald v State, 14 SW 487 (Tenn 1890) ... 169
McDonald v State, 346 NE2d 569 (Ind 1976) ... 185
McKee v State, 372 P2d 243 (Okla Crim App 1962) ... 181
Miller v Comm'r of Corr, 105 A3d 294 (Conn App Ct 2014) ... 183
Mobley v State, 2019 WL 290063 (Md Ct App Jan 15, 2019) ... 168
Montgomery v Commonwealth, 36 SE 371 (Va 1900) ... 172
Mornes v State, 2018 WL 3751351 (Tex Ct App Aug 8, 2018) ... 174
Moyers v State, 197 SE 846 (Ga 1938) ... 172
Nabors v State, 25 So 529 (Ala 1899) ... 169
Nash v State, 84 SW 497 (Ark 1904) ... 183
Nelson v State, 2019 WL 3955049 (Miss Aug 22, 2019) ... 168, 170

Nygren v State, 616 P2d 20 (Ala 1980) 179
Oldacre v State, 72 So 303 (Ala 1916) 172
Paz v State, 852 P2d 1355 (Ida 1993) 168
People v Aris, 215 Cal App 3d 1178 (Cal Ct App 1989) 178
People v Armstrong, 653 NE2d 17 (Ill App Ct 1995) 185
People v Battle, 129 Cal Rptr 3d 828 (Cal App 2011) 179–80
People v Beasley, 778 P2d 304 (Colo Ct App 1989) 185
People v Bennett, 80 NW 9 (Mich 1899) 170
People v Bigford, 2016 WL 10736071 (Mich Cir Ct, May 16, 2006) 178
People v Brady, 232 Cal Rptr 3d 220 (Cal Ct App 2018) 170
People v Button, 39 P 1073 (Cal 1895) 170
People v Camacho, 2015 WL 8551831 (Cal Ct App Dec 11, 2015) 174
People v Cebalos, 526 P2d 241 (Cal 1974) 81
People v Coughlin, 35 NW 72 (Mich 1887) 173
People v Culton, 92 Cal App 3d 113 (Cal Ct App 1979) 171
People v Curtis, 450 P2d 33 (Cal 1969) 177
People v Dillon, 180 NE2d 503 (Ill 1962) 179
People v Donguli, 28 P 782 (Cal 1891) 170
People v Emerson, 62 P 1069 (Cal 1900) 170
People v Emick, 103 AD2d 643 (NY App Div 1984) 179–80
People v Gonzales, 71 Cal 569 (1887) 183
People v Hecker, 42 P 307 (Cal 1895) 172, 174, 182
People v Hess, 687 P2d 443 (Colo 1984) 177
People v Humphrey, 921 P2d 1 (Cal 1996) 178
People v Jaramillo, 183 P3d 665 (Colo Ct App 2008) 172
People v Kelly, 322 NE2d 527 (Ill App Ct 1975) 99
People v Khachaturyan, 2019 WL 4296870 (Cal Ct App Sept 11, 2019) 170
People v Lenkevich, 229 NW2d 298 (Mich 1975) 182
People v Matthews, 30 Cal Rptr 2d 330 (Cal Ct App 1994) 170
People v Mayfield, 928 P2d 485 (Cal 1997) 182
People v McGraw, 2019 WL 1922855 (Cal Ct App Apr 30, 2019) 169
People v Newcomer, 50 P 405 (Cal 1897) 181
People v Nguyen, 61 Cal 4th 1015 (Cal 2015) 178
People v Pappas, 383 NE2d 1190 (Ill App Ct 1978) 99
People v Reed, 695 P2d 806 (Colo Ct App 1984) 179
People v Scott, 349 P3d 1028 (Cal 2015) 182
People v Stevens, 858 NW 2d 98 (Mich Ct App 2014) 178
People v Surber, 2017 WL 281760 (Cal Ct App Jan 23, 2017) 174
People v Tomlins, 107 NE 496 (NY 1914) 174
People v Tyson, 2019 WL 3852432 (Cal Ct App Aug 16, 2019) 167
People v Vargas, 2018 WL 6188255 (Cal Ct App Nov 28, 2018) 182
People v Villarreal, 604 NE2d 923 (Ill 1992) 177
People v Wafer, 907 NW2d 584 (Mich 2018) 168
People v White, 409 NE2d 73 (Ill App Ct 1980) 99

People v Wilburn, 2019 WL 1746844 (Mich Ct App, Apr 18, 2019) 169
People v Wilkins, 2018 WL 4091012 (Cal Ct App Aug 28, 2018) 179
People v Williams, 88 NE 1053 (Ill 1909) 169
People v Williams, 115 Cal App 3d 446 (1981) 171
Petty v State, 216 SW 867 (Tex Crim App 1919) 184
Phillips v Jamieson, 16 NW 318 (Mich 1883) 172
Porter v State, 148 A3d 1 (Md Ct Spec App 2016) 179
Porter v State, 166 A3d 1044 (Md Ct App 2017) 168, 180
Priser v State, 2019 WL 3216805 (Ala July 17, 2019) 170–71
Rauck v State, 11 NE 450 (Ind 1887) 172
Redd v State, 25 SE 268 (Ga 1896) 169
Reid v State, 425 SE2d 315 (Ga Ct App 1992) 182
Rodriguez v State, 641 SW2d 669 (Tex Ct App 1982) 170
Rodriguez v State, 710 SW2d 60 (Tex Crim App 1986) 170
Russell v State, 122 So 683 (Ala 1929) 172
Sams v United States, 721 A2d 945 (DC 1998) 183
Scales v State, 11 So 121 (Ala 1892) 181
Shipp v Landry, 147 So 3d 721 (La Ct App 2014) 174
Shorter v People, 2 NY 193 (NY Ct App 1849) 169
Smith v State, 41 NE 595 (Ind 1895) 181
Smith v State, 965 SW2d 509 (Tex Crim App 1998) 184
Sparks v Commonwealth, 20 SW 167 (Ky Ct App 1885) 173
Spiegel's House Furnishing Co v Indus Comm'n, 123 NE 606 (Ill 1919) 174
State v Abeyta, 901 P2d 164 (NC 1995) 182
State v Alberico, 861 P2d 192 (NM 1993) 179
State v Allery, 682 P2d 312 (Wash 1984) 178
State v Baker, 441 SE2d 551 (NC 1994) 80
State v Ballou, 40 A 861 (RI 1898) 184
State v Barrett, 442 P3d 492 (Kan 2019) 168, 182
State v Baxendale, 370 P3d 813 (NM Ct App 2016) 173
State v Beltz, 388 P3d 93 (Kan 2017) 182
State v Berkley, 19 SW 192 (Mo 1892) 169
State v Bethune, 99 SE 753 (SC 1919) 170
State v Bingman, 745 P2d 342 (Mont 1987) 185
State v Blane, 116 P 660 (Wash 1911) 172
State v Bougneit, 294 NW2d 675 (Wis 1980) 184
State v Bowens, 501 A2d 577 (NJ Super Ct 1985) 168
State v Bowens, 532 A2d 215 (NJ 1987) 168
State v Bowers, 2019 WL 3679665 (SC Ct App Aug 7, 2019) 185
State v Bristol, 84 P2d 757 (Wyo 1938) 183
State v Cable, 22 SW 953 (Mo 1893) 182
State v Cadotte, 42 P 857 (Mont 1895) 169
State v Campos, 921 P2d 1266 (NC 1996) 182
State v Cardenas, 380 P3d 866 (NM Ct App 2016) 168

State v Carothers, 594 NW2d 897 (Minn 1999)....182
State v Carter, 713 A2d 255 (Conn Ct App 1998)....170
State v Ciaccio, 112 So 486 (La 1927)....172
State v Clifford, 17 NW 304 (Wis 1883)....169
State v Collins, 893 P2d 217 (Kan 1995)....182
State v Conally, 3 Or 69 (Or Cir Ct 1869)....174
State v Cook, 802 SE2d 575 (NC Ct App 2017)....171
State v Copley, 828 SE2d 35 (NC Ct App 2019)....168
State v Craig, 514 P2d 151 (Wash 1973)....184
State v Cross, 26 NW 62 (Iowa 1885)....184
State v Dephenbaugh, 145 SE 634 (W Va 1928)....184
State v Doherty, 98 P 152 (Or 1908)....181
State v Dooley, 26 SW 558 (Mo 1894)....172
State v Doris, 94 P 44 (Or 1908)....184
State v Edgerton, 69 NW 280 (Iowa 1896)....172
State v Ellis, 186 P3d 245 (2008)....176
State v Evans, 28 SW 8 (Mo 1894)....183
State v Felton, 329 NW2d 161 (Wis 1983)....180
State v Flory, 276 P 458 (Wyo 1929)....168
State v Friesz, 898 NW2d 688 (ND 2017)....183
State v Gagnon, 567 NW2d 807 (ND 1997)....167
State v Gallegos, 719 P2d 1268 (NM Ct App 1986)....179
State v Gartland, 694 A2d 564 (NJ 1997)....182
State v George, 249 P3d 202 (Wash App 2011)....169
State v Gheen, 41 SW3d 598 (Mo Ct App 2001)....181
State v Glowacki, 630 NW2d 392 (Minn 2001)....183
State v Gordon, 89 SW 1025 (Mo 1905)....184
State v Graham, 195 NW2d 442 (Minn 1972)....185
State v Gray, 77 SE 833 (NC 1913)....169, 173
State v Green, 110 SE 145 (SC 1921)....172
State v Green, 318 NJ Super 361 (App Div 1999)....171
State v Grott, 2019 WL 1040681 (Wash Ct App March 5, 2019)....184
State v Guido, 191 A2d 45 (NJ 1963)....180
State v Harris, 222 NW2d 462 (Iowa 1974)....168
State v Harrod, 15 SW 373 (Mo 1891)....169
State v Harvey, 828 SE2d 481 (NC 2019)....168
State v Havican, 569 A2d 1089 (Conn 1990)....168
State v Hawkins, 23 P 475 (Or 1890)....184
State v Herriges, 455 NW2d 635 (Wis Ct App 1990)....167
State v Hodges, 716 P2d 563 (Kan 1986)....178
State v Holbrook, 188 P 947 (Or 1920)....172
State v Howell, 53 P 314 (Mont 1898)....172
State v Hundley, 693 P2d 475 (Kan 1985)....178
State v Irabor, 822 SE2d 421 (NC App 2018)....182

State v Isbell, 524 SW3d 90 (Mo Ct App 2017) 170
State v Ivicsics, 604 SW2d 773 (Mo Ct App 1980) 174
State v Jackson, 936 P2d 761 (Kan 1997) 184–85
State v Jacobson, 2018 WL 4395018 (Minn Ct App 2018) 182
State v Johnson, 2019 WL 1125924 (Wash Ct App March 12, 2019) 169
State v Jones, 7 SE 296 (SC 1888) 169
State v Kane, 335 NJ Super 391 (App Div 2000) 171
State v Keeter, 174 SE 298 (NC 1934) 170
State v Kelly, 478 A2d 364 (NJ 1984) 179
State v Kennedy, 85 SE 42 (NC 1915) 184
State v Kindred, 49 SW 845 (Mo 1899) 168
State v Koss, 551 NE2d 970 (Oh 1990) 178
State v Lea, 485 SE2d 874 (NC Ct App 1997) 182
State v Lee, 67 SE 141 (SC 1910) 184
State v Lee, 811 SE2d 562 (NC 2018) 168
State v Leidholm, 334 NW2d 811 (ND 1983) 53, 178, 180
State v Lewis, 717 A2d 1140 (Conn 1998) 185
State v Lynch, 436 So 2d 567 (La 1983) 179
State v Maney, 138 SE 441 (NC 1927) 175
State v Manns, 37 SE 613 (W Va 1900) 173
State v Marfaudille, 92 P 939 (Wash 1907) 174
State v Marr, 765 A2d 645 (Md Ct App 2001) 180
State v Marsh, 490 P2d 491 (Or 1971) 184
State v Marshall, 573 NW2d 406 (Neb 1998) 170
State v Martin, 666 SW2d 895 (Mo Ct App 1984) 179
State v Matuu, 2017 WL 4339427 (Haw Ct App Sept 29, 2017) 171–72
State v McCracken, 166 P 1174 (NM 1917) 173
State v Metcalfe, 212 NW 382 (Iowa 1927) 172
State v Meyers, 781 P2d 700 (Kan 1989) 185
State v Middleham, 17 NW 446 (Iowa 1883) 174
State v Mills, 69 A 841 (Del 1908) 173
State v Mize, 340 SE2d 439 (NC 1986) 184
State v Norman, 378 SE2d 8 (NC 1989) 180
State v Nunn, 356 NW2d 601 (Iowa Ct App 1984) 179
State v Parks, 183 P 433 (NM 1919) 170
State v Parnoff, 186 A3d 640 (Conn 2018) 179
State v Peacock, 40 Ohio St 333 (Ohio 1883) 174
State v Pellegrino, 577 NW2d 590 (SD 1998) 174
State v Pendleton, 567 NW2d 265 (Minn 1997) 174
State v Peou, 579 NW2d 471 (Minn 1998) 185
State v Perkins, 91 A 265 (Conn 1914) 173
State v Peterson, 857 A2d 1132 (Md Ct Spec App 2004) 180
State v Pisciotta, 968 SW2d 185 (Mo Ct App 1998) 130
State v Pollard, 900 NW2d 175 (Minn Ct App 2017) 168

State v Potter, 244 SE2d 397 (NC 1978)....184
State v Reece, 349 P3d 712 (Utah 2015)....182
State v Reeves, 636 NW2d 22 (Iowa 2001)....179
State v Richardson, 511 P2d 263 (Idaho 1973)....177
State v Rider, 1 SW 825 (Mo 1886)....184
State v Sadler, 26 So 390 (La 1899)....169
State v Salary, 343 P3d 1165 (Kan 2015)....179
State v Scott, 43 NW 62 (Minn 1889)....184
State v Silva, 2019 WL 3311168 (Utah Jul 23, 2019)....168
State v Sims, 431 P3d 288 (Kan 2018)....182
State v Smith, 30 P 679 (Mont 1892)....173
State v Smith, 71 P 973 (Or 1903)....170
State v Smith, 807 A2d 500 (Conn App Ct Oct 22, 2002)....176
State v Sterrett, 25 NW 936 (Iowa 1885)....169–70
State v Stone, 880 P2d 1296 (Mont 1994)....185
State v Sullivan, 50 NW 572 (Iowa 1879)....178
State v Sullivan, 383 P3d 574 (2016)....184
State v Taylor, 44 SW 785 (Mo 1898)....173
State v Terry, 128 A3d 958 (Conn App Ct 2015)....183
State v Thomas, 423 NE2d 137 (Ohio 1981)....178
State v Thompson, 13 So 392 (La 1893)....182
State v Usher, 111 NW 811 (Iowa 1907)....170
State v Walker, 59 SE 878 (NC 1907)....167
State v Williams, 815 SW2d 43 (Mo Ct App 1991)....185
State v Winters, 2004 WL 899732 (Wash Ct App Apr 27, 2004)....178
State v Zorn, 100 SW 591 (Mo 1907)....168
Stewart v State, 1 Ohio St 66 (Oh 1852)....181
Storey v State, 71 Ala 329 (Ala 1882)....172–73
Swanner v State, 58 SW 72 (Tex Crim App 1900)....184
Thompson v State, 85 NW 62 (Neb 1901)....173
Townsend v Briggs, 34 P 116 (Cal 1893)....172
Treadway v State, 144 SW 655 (Tex Crim App 1912)....178
Trogdon v State, 32 NE 725 (Ind 1892)....170
Truelove v State, 2010 WL 8231393 (Miss Dec 20, 2010)....171
Viliborghi v State, 43 P2d 210 (Ariz 1935)....174
Wade v State, 724 So 2d 1007 (Miss Ct App 1998)....183
Wade v State, 748 So 2d 771 (Miss 1999)....183
Wallace-Bey v State, 172 A3d 1006 (Md Ct App 2017)....180
Washington v State, 263 SE2d 152 (Ga 1980)....174
Washington v State, 997 NE2d 342 (Ind 2013)....171
Watkins v State, 613 A2d 379 (Md 1992)....181
Watts v State, 885 NE2d 1228 (Ind 2008)....185
Webb v State, 801 SW2d 529 (Tex Crim App 1990)....171
Wells v State, 141 SW 96 (Tex Crim App 1911)....174

West v State, 617 P2d 1362 (Okla Crim App 1980)....181
Whitten v State, 16 SW 296 (Tex Ct App 1891)....173
Willis v State, 61 NW 254 (Neb 1894)....174
Wilson v State, 11 So 556 (Fla 1892)....173
Wilson v State, 36 SW 587 (Tex Crim App 1896)....183
Young v State, 104 NW 867 (Neb 1905)....169, 174
Zimmerman v State, 114 So 3d 446 (Fla Dist Ct App 2013)....7

England Cases

Albert v Lavin [1981] 1 All ER 628 (QB)....191, 199
Albert v Lavin [1982] AC 546 (HL)....103
Beckford v R [1987] 3 All ER 425 (PC)....194
Beckford v The Queen [1988] AC 130 (PC)....188, 192, 199, 203
Blackburn v Bowering [1994] 1 WLR 1324 (CA)....202, 204
Dakin's Case [1828] 168 ER 999....191
DPP v Bailey [1995] 16 Cr App R 257....188
DPP v Morgan [1975] 2 All ER 347 (HL)....191–92
Marsh v DPP [2015] EWHC 1022 (Admin)....209
Oraki v DPP [2018] EWHC 115 (Admin)....196
Palmer v R [1971] AC 814 (PC)....202–03, 205
Palmer v R [1971] 1 All ER 1077 (PC)....203
R (Bennett) v Coroner [2007] EWCA Civ 617....133, 192
R (Collins) v Secretary of State for Justice [2016] EWHC 33 (Admin)....189, 205
R v Ahluwalia [1992] 4 All ER 889 (CA)....200–01
R v Bird [1985] 1 WLR 816....207
R v Bowen [1996] 4 All ER 837 (CA)....203
R v Brittain, No 3431/C/84, December 6, 1984 transcript....208
R v Canns [2005] EWCA Crim 2264....192
R v Charlton [2003] EWCA Crim 415....201
R v Cheeseman [2019] EWCA Crim 149....188–89, 194, 205
R v Chuong [2013] EWCA Crim 1716....204
R v Clegg [1995] 2 WLR 80 (HL)....205
R v Coley [2013] EWCA Crim 223....193
R v Conway [1989] QB 290, 297....130
R v Dadson [1850] 4 Cox CC 358....193–95
R v Day [2015] EWCA Crim 1646....205
R v Deana [1909] 2 Cr App R 75 (CA)....203
R v Dudley and Stephens [1884] 14 QB 273....197–98
R v Duffy [1949] 1 All ER 932 (CA)....200
R v Faraj [2007] EWCA Crim 1033....192, 204
R v Fennell [1971] 1 QB 428....199
R v Goode [2014] EWCA Crim 90....192

R v Goodwin (Anthony) [2018] EWCA Crim 2287 201
R v Graham [1982] 1 All ER 801 (CA) 203
R v Harvey [2009] EWCA Crim 469 .... 204, 209
R v Hasan [2005] 2 AC 467 .... 108, 130
R v Hayes [2011] EWCA Crim 2680 189
R v Hinchcliffe [1823] 168 ER 998 203
R v Hitchens [2011] EWCA Crim 1626 .... 188, 195, 205
R v HM Coroner for East Kent ex p Spooner [1987] 88 Cr App R 10 197
R v Howe and Bannister [1987] AC 417 (HL) 197
R v Huntley [1852] 175 ER 497 .... 203, 206
R v Ibrahim [2014] EWCA Crim 121 .... 192, 204
R v Keane [2010] EWCA Crim 2514 .... 188, 209
R v Knock [1877] 14 Cox CC 1 194
R v Lobell [1957] 1 QB 547 188
R v Martin (Anthony) [2001] EWCA Crim 2245 .... 8, 188, 192, 206
R v McGrath [2010] EWCA Crim 2514 (CA) 188, 209
R v McInnes [1971] 3 All ER 295 (CCA) 205, 207
R v Morris [2014] 1 WLR 16 192
R v Mula [2013] EWCA Crim 1293 204
R v O'Brien [2004] EWCA Crim 2900 .... 188, 208
R v O'Grady [1987] QB 995 193
R v Odgers [1843] 174 ER 355 206–07
R v Owino [1995] Crim L Rev 743 203
R v Oye [2013] EWCA Crim 1725 192
R v P&O European Ferries (Dover) Ltd [1990] 93 Cr App R 72 197
R v Press and Thompson [2013] EWCA Crim 1849 204
R v Rashford [2005] EWCA Crim 3377 209
R v Ray [2017] EWCA Crim 1391 .... 189, 205, 207
R v Renouf [1986] 1 WLR 522 (CA) 188
R v Riddell [2017] EWCA Crim 413 .... 194, 204
R v Robinson [2017] EWCA Crim 923 .... 188, 192, 204
R v Rose [1884] 15 Cox CC 540 .... 191, 199, 203
R v Scarlett [1994] 98 Cr App R 290 203
R v Semini [1948] 1 KB 405 207
R v Smith [1837] 171 ER 441 195
R v Taj [2018] EWCA Crim 1743 193–94
R v Thornton [1992] 1 All ER 306 (CA 1991) 200
R v Weston [1879] 14 Cox CC 346 191
R v Wheeler [1968] 52 Cr App R 28 (CA) 188
R v Whyte [1987] 3 All ER 416 (CCA) 199
R v Williams (Gladstone) [1984] 78 Cr App R 276 .... 192, 203
R v Williams (Gladstone) [1987] 3 All ER 411 (CA) 191, 194, 203
R v Wilson [2006] EWCA Crim 1880 192
R v Wilson [2019] EWCA Crim 1882 203

R v Yaman [2012] EWCA Crim 1075 194
Re A (Conjoined Twins: Surgical Separation) [2001] 2 WLR 480 198
Sharman v Coroner [2005] EWHC 857 (Admin) 196
Shaw (Norman) v R [2002] 1 Cr App R 10 204
Wheeldon v CPS [2018] EWHC 249 (Admin) 196

Northern Ireland Cases

R v Browne [1973] NI 96 208

Scotland Cases

Owens v HM Advocate [1946] SC(J) 119 199

European Court of Human Rights Cases

Bubbins v United Kingdom [2005] 41 EHRR 24 .... 123, 132
Da Silva v United Kingdom [2016] 63 EHRR 12 123
Gul v Turkey [2002] 34 EHRR 28 123
HLR v France [1998] 26 EHRR 29 121
Kelly v United Kingdom [1993] 16 EHRR 20 123
LCB v United Kingdom [1998] ECtHR 108 121
Makaratzis v Greece [2005] 41 EHRR 49 123
McCann v United Kingdom [1996] 21 EHRR 97 .... 123, 132
McCann v United Kingdom [2016] 21 ECtHR 97 GC 121
Oneryildiz v Turkey [2005] 41 EHRR 20 121–22
Osman v United Kingdom [1998] ECtHR 101 121
Putintseva v Russia [2012] ECtHR 820 122
Stewart v United Kingdom [1984] 7 EHRR 453 132
Stubbings v United Kingdom [1997] 23 EHRR 213 121

German Statutes

Entwurf Eines Strafgesetzbuchs E 1962, BT-Drucks. IV/650 (1962) [1962 Draft Criminal Code] 158
StGB § 16 146
StGB § 32 .... 136, 142, 155, 159
StGB § 32(1) 142
StGB § 32(2) 142
StGB § 33 .... 137, 146, 159

StGB § 34 .... 151, 155
StGB § 35(1) 154
StGB § 211 154

US Federal Statutes

18 USC § 1111 54
Model Penal Code (Am. Law Inst., Proposed Official Draft 1962) 185
Model Penal Code § 3.04 167
Model Penal Code § 3.04(1) 180
Model Penal Code § 3.04(2)(b) 81, 167
Model Penal Code § 3.09 176

US State Statutes

18 Pa Cons Stat § 505 (2019) 109
18 Pa Cons Stat § 508(a) (2019) 176
720 Ill Comp Stat 5/7-5 (2019) 176
Ala Code § 13A-3-23 (2019) 171
Ala Code § 13A-3-27(b) (2019) 175–76
Alaska Stat § 11.81.370(a) (2019) 176
Ariz Rev Stat Ann § 13-404 (2019) 180
Ariz Rev Stat Ann § 13-410(C) (2019) 175–76
Ark Code Ann § 5-2-610(b) (2019) 176
Colo Rev Stat § 18-1-704(3)(b) (2019) 185
Colo Rev Stat § 18-1-707(2) (2019) 175–76
Colo Rev Stat § 18-1-901(3)(p) (2019) 171
Conn Gen Stat § 53a-22(c) (2019) 176
Del Code Ann tit 11, § 464 (2019) 180
Fla Stat § 776.05(3) (2019) 176
Fla Stat Ann § 776.012(2) (2019) 182
Haw Rev Stat § 703-300 (2019) 172
Haw Rev Stat § 703-304 (2019) 171
Haw Rev Stat § 703-307(3) (2019) 176
Haw Rev Stat § 707-700 (2019) 171
Kan Stat Ann § 21-5227(a) (2019) 176
La Stat Ann § 14:20(A) (2019) 176
Me Crim Code § 2(23) (2019) 171
Me Rev Stat tit 17-A, § 107(2) (2019) 176
Mo Rev Stat § 563.046(3) (2019) 176
Mont Code Ann § 45-3-102 (2019) 176
NC Gen Stat § 15A-401(d)(2)(a-b) (2019) 176

NH Rev Stat § 625:11 (2019) ... 127
NH Rev Stat Ann § 627:5(11) (2019) ... 176
NJ Rev Stat § 2C:11-1(b) (2019) ... 171
NJ Stat Ann § 2C:3-7(b)(2) (2019) ... 176
NJ Stat Ann §§ 2C:3–4(a) (2019) ... 109
NY Penal Law § 35.15(2) (2019) ... 183
NY Penal Law § 35.15(2)(a)(ii) (2019) ... 132
NY Penal Law § 35.30(1) (2019) ... 175–76
Neb Rev Stat § 28-1412(3) (2019) ... 176
Or Rev Stat § 161.239 (2019) ... 176
Pa Cons Stat § 2301 (2019) ... 171
RI Gen Laws § 12-7-8 (2019) ... 176
RI Gen Laws § 12-7-9 (2019) ... 176
Tex Code Ann § 39-11-611 (2019) ... 171
Tex Penal Code art 1105, subd 8 ... 173
Tex Penal Code § 9.31 (2019) ... 109
Tex Penal Code § 9.31(b)(4)(A) (2019) ... 185
Tex Penal Code § 9.31(b)(4)(B) (2019) ... 185
Tex Penal Code § 9.32 (2019) ... 109
Tex Penal Code Ann § 9.32(a)(2)(B) (2019) ... 171
Tex Penal Code Ann § 9.42(3)(A) (2019) ... 116
Tex Penal Code Ann § 9.51 (2019) ... 175–76
Utah Code Ann § 76-2-404 (2019) ... 176
Wash Rev Code § 9A.16.040(3) (2019) ... 176

England Statutes

Coroners and Justice Act 2009 ... 199
Coroners and Justice Act 2009, § 54 ... 201, 208
Coroners and Justice Act 2009, § 54(1) ... 201, 208
Coroners and Justice Act 2009, § 54(2) ... 201, 208
Coroners and Justice Act 2009, § 54(4) ... 201, 208
Coroners and Justice Act 2009, § 54(5) ... 201, 208
Coroners and Justice Act 2009, § 54(6) ... 201, 208
Coroners and Justice Act 2009, § 54(7) ... 208
Coroners and Justice Act 2009, § 56 ... 208
Crime and Courts Act 2013 ... 8, 189
Criminal Damage Act 1971 ... 188
Criminal Justice and Immigration Act 2008, § 76 ... 188–89, 193
Criminal Justice and Immigration Act 2008, § 76(1)(A) ... 188
Criminal Justice and Immigration Act 2008, § 76(3) ... 189, 192, 194
Criminal Justice and Immigration Act 2008, § 76(4) ... 192, 194
Criminal Justice and Immigration Act 2008, § 76(5) ... 193

Criminal Justice and Immigration Act 2008, § 76(5)(A) 189, 204
Criminal Justice and Immigration Act 2008, § 76(6) 189
Criminal Justice and Immigration Act 2008, § 76(6)(A) 189, 208
Criminal Justice and Immigration Act 2008, § 76(7) 199, 202–04
Criminal Justice and Immigration Act 2008, § 76(8) 189
Criminal Law Act 1967, § 3 188
Criminal Law Act 1967, § 3(1) 195
Legal Aid, Sentencing and Punishment of Offenders Act 2012 189
Offences Against the Person Act 1861, § 20 207
Police Act 1996, § 89(2) 196
Police and Criminal Evidence Act 1984 ('PACE'), § 24A 196
Serious Crime Act 2015, § 76(1) 131, 201–02

International Statutes

Criminal Code of the Argentine Nation, art 34(6) 14
Brazilian Penal Code, art 23 14
Criminal Law of the People's Republic of China, art 20 14
Egyptian Penal Code, art 56 14
Indonesian Penal Code, art 49(1) 14
Japanese Penal Code, art 36(1) 14
The Permanent Constitution of the State of Qatar, art 39 14
Swedish Penal Code, ch 24, § 1 14
Turkish Criminal Code, art 25 14
Criminal Code of Ukraine, art 36 14

Other Primary Legal Sources – Germany

Grundgesetz, art 1 141
Grundgesetz, art 2 141
Grundgesetz, art 103 142
Grundgesetz, art 103(2) 142

Other Primary Legal Sources – US

131 Cong Rec H317-03 (daily edn 6 Feb 1985) 15
133 Cong Rec H3066-04 (daily edn 5 May 1987) 15

Other Primary Legal Sources – International

Council of Europe, European Convention for the Protection of Human Rights and Fundamental Freedoms (ECHR), Nov 4, 1950, ETS No 005,
art 1 .... 22, 40, 43, 85
art 2 .... 21–22, 29, 49, 58, 75, 121, 123, 133
art 2(2) 122, 132
art 5 .... 21, 26, 29, 49, 58
art 6 .... 22, 49
art 8 .... 22, 40, 49
art 11 .... 22, 40, 49
art 13 .... 22, 29, 43, 49, 85
Council of Europe, European Convention for the Protection of Human Rights and Fundamental Freedoms (ECHR), Mar 20, 1953, ETS No 009, art 1 22
Council of Europe, European Convention for the Protection of Human Rights and Fundamental Freedoms (ECHR), Sept 16, 1953, ETS No 046, art 2 22
Council of Europe, European Convention for the Protection of Human Rights and Fundamental Freedoms (ECHR), Nov 22, 1984, ETS No 117, art 2 56
GA Res 217 (III) A, Universal Declaration of Human Rights (Dec 10, 1948) (UN Declaration),
art 1 .... 21, 26, 29, 49, 58
art 2 .... 21, 26, 29, 49
art 3 .... 21–22, 75, 49, 58, 75
art 6 .... 21, 26, 43, 49, 85
art 7 .... 21, 26, 29, 43, 49, 85
art 8 .... 21, 43, 49, 85
art 10 .... 21, 49
art 11 .... 21, 43, 49, 85
art 12 .... 21, 29, 40, 49
art 13 .... 21, 40, 49
art 17 .... 21, 29, 49
art 20 .... 21, 40, 49
art 21 .... 21, 29
art 22 .... 21, 40, 49
art 29 .... 21, 29, 32, 40–41, 49, 51, 58

TABLE OF TABLES

Table 1	Test of the Value-Centric Position (Key)	71
Table 2	Non-Culpable Threat	72
Table 3	Culpable Threat	111
Table 4	Innocent Threat	124
Table 5	Overview of Comparative, International Value-Based Models	217

GLOSSARY OF GERMAN WORDS AND PHRASES

German Word/Phrase	English Translation
Chapters I–IV	
Die sozialethischen Einschränkungen der Notwehr	Socio-ethical limitations on self-defence
Kommentar	Commentary
Vorbemerkung	Introductory comment
Die Notwehr	Self-defence
Festschrift	Commemorative
Notwehr als Menchenrecht – Zugleich eine Kritik der Entscheiduing des LG Frankfurt am Main im 'Fall Daschner'	Self-defence as a human right – and a concurrent critique of the Frankfurt at the Main National Court's ruling in the 'Case Daschner'
Die Erforderlichkeit der Notwehrhandlung	The necessity of the self-defensive action
Der Allgemeine Teil des Strafrechts in der aktuellen Rechtsprechung	The General Part of the Criminal Law [as interpreted/set forth] in the contemporary jurisprudence
Notwehr und Proportionalität	Self-defence and proportionality
Gewaltmonopol	[The state's][1] monopoly on force
Strafrecht Allgemeiner Teil. Grundlagen. Der Aufbau der Verbrechenslehre	General Part of the criminal law. Foundations. Constructing the doctrine of crime [criminalization]
Die Friedenspflicht der Bürger und das Gewaltmonopol des Staates'	The citizen's obligation to act peacefully and the state's monopoly on force

[1] Note that brackets are added in part to facilitate translational clarity by providing context for the usage of certain German terms.

Rechtsstaat Und Gewaltmonopol (Recht Und Staat in Geschichte Und Gegenwart)	The constitutional state and the [state's] monopoly on force (the history and present [relationship between] law and the state
Störung des Gegenseitigkeitsverhältnisses	Upsetting the equal standing [between people]
Die Intersubjektive Begründung und Begrenzung der Notwehr	Intersubjective foundation of, and limitations to, self-defence
Legalitätsprinzip	Principle of legality [requiring German prosecutors, following the 'the principle of compulsory prosecution,' to press charges whenever they have sufficient evidence to support a conviction]
Gleichordnung	Equal standing/order
Die Angriffsverursachung bei der Notwehr	The reasons for [or provocation of] defensive conduct in self-defence doctrine
Notstand und Notwehr	Necessity and self-defence
Strafrecht, Allgemeiner Teil	Criminal law, the General Part
Überlegungen zur tödlichen Notwehr bei nicht lebensbedrohlichen Angriffen	Considerations/Thoughts concerning deadly defensive force in the context of non-life-threatening attacks

Ch. V (German Chapter)

Abschreckung	Deterrence
Strafgesetzbuch or '*StGB*'	German criminal code
Gewaltmonopol	The state's monopoly on force
Die 'Sozialethische Einschränkungen' des Notwehrrechts	The 'socio-ethical limitations' to the right of self-defence
Notwehr und Notwehrexzess	Self-defence and excessive force in self-defence
Gerechtfertigt	Justified
Duldungspflicht	Obligation to absorb a certain amount of harm/injury [in the context of certain attacks otherwise giving rise to the right to exercise self-defence]

Güterproportionalität	Proportionality between the harm inflicted and the harm threatened
Rechtsordung	Legal order
Systematischer Kommentar zum Strafgesetzbuch, Band 1	Systematic commentary on the penal code, Volume 1
Das Strafrecht des Deutschen Volkes	The criminal law of the German people
Der Allgemeine Teil des Deutschen Strafrechts	The General Part of the German criminal law
Rechtsbewährungsprinzip	Principle of law-protection [protecting the empirical inviolability of the legal order]
Die Begründung der Notwehr	The reasons [justification] for self-defence
das Recht muss dem Unrecht nicht weichen	The right need not yield to the wrong
Schneidigkeit/Schärfe	Harshness Severity [of Germany's self defence law]
Schutzwehr/Gegenwehr	Resistance [to force/an attack]/purely defensive force
Archiv des Criminalrechts	Archives of the Criminal Law
Strafgesetzbuch	German criminal code
Lehrbuch des deutschen Strafrechtes	Textbook of the German Criminal Law
Notwehr und Nothilfe: Zum Prinzip der Abwehr Rechtwidriger Angriffe	Self-defence and emergency aid: On the principle of defending against unlawful attacks
Trutzwehr	Counter-attack [the use of offensive force to neutralise or limit an attack]
Individualrechtliche begründung	Personal protection justification [for self-defence]
dualistische Begründung	Dualistic justification
Individualinteresse/Schutzprinzip	The law's interest in allowing self-defence to protect the individual's autonomy/rights

Strafrecht Nach Logisch-Analytischer Methode	Criminal law using [following] a logical-analytical method
Über die Wertstruktur der Notwehr	On the value-structure of self-defence
Notrecht des Staates aus staatlicher Rechtsnot	State emergency law on the basis of the state's legal need/emergency
Deutsche Straftheorie	German criminal law theory
Bundesgerichtshof	German Federal Court of Justice [highest court in the system of ordinary jurisdiction]
Störung des Gegenseitigkeitsverhältnises	Violation of equal standing [between people]
Strafgessetzbuch: Leipziger Kommentar	German Criminal Code: Leipzig Commentary [a text viewed by many as providing the most complete and comprehensive coverage of currently-applicable German criminal law]
Die Geeignetheit der Verteidigungshandlung bei der Notwehr – Strittiges in der aktuellen Diskussion	The appropriateness/suitability of self-defensive action – Controversial [issues] in the contemporary discussion
sozialethische Einschränkungen	Socio-ethical limitations/limits
Mindestsolidarität	Minimal solidarity [between people]
Pflicht zur Rücksichtsnahme or *Nachsicht gegenüber Rechtsgenossen*	Expectation that citizens exhibit a level of tolerance toward each other
Not Kennt Kein Gebot	Necessity/Emergency knows no rules
Die Grenzgebiete Zwischen Notstand und Notwehr	The border areas between emergency and self-defence
Die gebotene Verteidigung gegen provozierte Angriffe. Überlegungen aus Anlass der neusten Rechtsprechung des Bundesgerichtshofs zur Notwehrprovokation'	The required defence against provoked attacks. Considerations on the occasion of the latest case law/rulings from the [German] Federal Court of Justice on self-defence provocation
Prinzipientheorie der Notwehreinschränkungen'	Principle-based theory of the limtiations on self-defence
Normalfall	Typical/standard case

Grundgesetz für die Bundesrepublik Deutschland	Basic law of the Federal Republic of Germany
Legalitätsprinzip'	The principle of compulsory prosecution [requiring prosecutors to press charges whenever they have sufficient evidence to support a conviction]
geboten	Appropriate [defensive force]
erforderlich	Necessary [defensive force]
Schranken	Limitations [on defensive force]
krasses Missverhältnis	… in cases of gross disproportion (*krasses Missverhältnis*) …
Grenzen der Strafbarkeit im Notwehrrecht	Limits of criminal liability in self-defence law
Gesamtes Strafrecht	All/Comprehensive [German] criminal law
Effective Selbstverteidigung und Notwehrrecht	Effective self-defence and self-defence law/doctrine
Notwehr bei Auseinandersetzungen in engen persönlichen Beziehungen	Self-defence in the context of disputes involving close personal relationships
Zur Einschränkung des Notwehrrechts bei der Verteidigung von Sachgütern	On limiting the right to self-defence in [the context of] the defence of property
Gebotensein' und 'Erforderlichkeit' der Notwehr	Appropriateness and Necessity in [the context of] self-defence
Erforderlichkeit der Abwehrhandlung, Gebotensein der Notwehrhandlung; Provokation und Rechtsmissbrauch; Notwehrexzess	Necessity of the defensive act, appropriateness of the defensive act; provocation and abuse of rights
Verteidigungswillen	Defensive will
Das Deutsche Strafrecht	The German Criminal Law
Vorsatz und Risiko	Intent and risk
Zum Stande der Lehre vom personalen Unrecht	On the state of the teaching on/concerning personal injustice

Festschrift für Hans Welzel zum 70. Geburtstag am 25. März 1974	Commemorative publication for Hans Welzel's 70th birthday on March 25, 1974
Motivbündel	Bundle/collection of motives
Erlaubnistatbestandsirrtümer	Mistakes regarding/concerning justificatory facts
Putativnotwehrexzess	Putative excessive force
Irrtum über Tatumstände	Errors/mistakes about factual circumstances
Notwehr gegen Notwehr	[On the prohibition against exercising] self-defence against self-defence
Die deutschsprachige Strafrechtwissenshcaft nach der Strafrechtsreform im Spiegel des Leipziger Kommentars und des Wiener Kommentars'	The German-language study of the criminal law in the context of the criminal law reform of the Leipzig Commentary and the Vienna Commentary
Zum Verteidigungswillen bei der Notwehr	On the defensive will in the context of self-defence
Das Strafgesetzbuch für den Norddeutschen Bund	The North German Confederation's Criminal Code
Lehrbuch des Deutschen Strafrechts	The textbook of the German criminal law
Rechtswidriger Angriff	[The] unlawful attack
Umwelt und Recht	Environment and law
Das Strafgesetzbuch für das Deutsche Reich	The German Reich's criminal code
Praxiskommentar	Practice/practitioner commentary
Rechtfertigung und Entschuldigung	Justification and excuse
wesentliche Förmlichkeiten	Essential formalities [basic requirements set out by the law]
Hoheitsträger	Sovereign/authorities
hoheitlicher Eingriff	Intrusion by the authorities [in a citizen's activities]
öffentliches Recht	Public law

Polizeirecht	The law governing the police and policing
Spaltungslösung	Solution through cleaving [in the context of excessive force, preventing officers acting pursuant to police law from being found liable, but nevertheless leaving open the possibility of discipline and requests for compensation when the officer exceeds the authority provided by police law/regulations]
Begründung und Grenzen der Nothilfe	Justification of, and limits on, emergency aid
Grenzen privater nothilfe	Limits/boundaries on private emergency aid
Notwehr gegen Unterlassen	Self-defence against inaction [or failures to act]
rechtfertigender Notstand	Justifying necessity
gegenwärtig	Imminent/present
Effizienzlösung	Efficiency solution [when a later use of defensive force will, objectively speaking, be futile or more problematic/difficult]
Die Rechtswidrigkeit des Angriffs in den Notwehrbestimmungen	The illegality of the attack in the context of the self-defence requirements/laws
Die Notwehr im System der Notrechte	Self-defence in [the context of] the system of emergency rights
Mannstoppwirkung	The effectiveness of stopping/immobilizing the attacker
Bundesgerichtshof	[German] Federal Court of Justice
Haustyrannenfall	The [Federal Court of Justice] case of the 'family tyrant' [domestic abuser]
mit Heimtücke	By stealth
entschuldigenden Notstand	Excusable necessity

Angriff	Attack
Gefahr	Danger
Präventiv-Notwehr	Anticipatory self-defence
Erfolgsunrecht	Unjust/wrongful outcome
Handlungsunrecht	Unjust/wrongful behaviour
Prinzip des überwiegenden Interesses	The principle of the overriding interest [in the self-defence context, the principle that the potential harm defended against must be greater than the harm inflicted]
erforderlich	Necessary
Grundsatz der möglichsten Schonung des Angreifers	Principle of the most gentle available treatment of the attacker [the concept that the person exercising self-preferential force must use the least amount of force necessary to thwart the attack]
mildeste Mittel/mildeste Abwehrmittel	Least harmful defensive means
Notwehr Gegen Verschuldete Angriffe'	Self-defence against culpable attacks
Trutzwehr	Counter-attack
Schutzwehr	Purely defensive force
zugespitzte Situation	Exacerbated situation
Güterproportionalität/Abwägung der betroffenen Rechtsgüter	Proportionality/the principle that the defensive force deployed be proportional to the harm threatened by the attacker
Stufenlehre	The teaching of gradation/escalation [in the context of the use of firearms for self-defense, the law's expectation that a defender, when possible, will first use lesser/escalating force prior to using a fiream]
Abwägung der betroffenen Rechtsgüter	Weighing of the competing goods

grobes or krasses or unerträgliches Missverhältnis	[Cases of] gross/unacceptable disproportion [between the harm threatened and the defensive force used]
provoziert	Provoked
Das Strafrecht des deutschen Mittelalters	The criminal law of the German Middle Ages
Merkmal Der Gegenwärtigkeit in Notwehrrech Bei Neuen Konfliktmustern Aus Rechtsvergleichender Sicht	Characteristics of [the] imminence [requirement] in the self-defence in new conflict patterns [viewed] from a comparative perspective
misbillingendes Vorverhalten	Disapproved of prefatory activity
Zur Einschränkung der Notwehrbefugnis	On/concerning the limitation of self-defence
riskante Schonung	Risky care [the concept of having to exercise less forceful defensive force even if that creates/presents a greater risk of harm to the defender]
Garantenpflicht/Garantenstellung	Guarantee obligation [the concept that the defender can in some contexts be considered to be the guarantor of the attacker – such as in cases of attacks by close family members]
Rücksichtsnahmeverpflichtung	Obligation to be considerate [an obligation that the defender in some circumstances must exercise special care/consideration in the context of her use of self-preferential force]
Kein Recht zur Beweisvernichtung nach einem potentiellen Selbstbedienungsladendiebstahl	No right to destroy evidence after a potential theft from a self-service store
Absichtsprovokation	Purposeful provocation [intentional, calculated provocation by the defender solely for the purpose of later being able to claim self-defence after the attacker 'rises to the bait']

Vorsatzprovokation	Intentional provocation [involving situations, such as those involving recklessness, that have not yet crossed over to the level of *Absichtsprovokation*, but where a person considers it to be possible that a situation of self-defence may follow from his actions, and accepts that this may happen]
Eingeschränkte Notwehr unter Ehegatten	Limited self-defence in situations involving spouses.
Nothilfe gegen provozierte Angriffe	Emergency aid against/to thwart provoked attacks
sozialethisch zu missbilligen	Socially unacceptable [conduct]
Dreistufenlehre/ Dreistufentheorie	Three-level [progression] theory

1

Setting the Stage

The 'ancient right'[1] of self-defence is a topic on which academics, legislators, judges, media legal experts, and laymen alike have strongly held – and often strongly divergent – views. It is among the handful of criminal law areas that has received substantial academic (and public) attention. What is more, the current conversations about over-policing, violence, and self-preferential force have once again brought to the forefront the challenges inherent in setting boundaries between the state's claimed 'monopoly on force' and the individual's right to deploy self-preferential violence against an attacker. In the wake George Floyd's brutal killing, this topic for good reason has assumed a central role as society considers how the criminal justice system operates, and where reform is most needed.

Some scholars, including Schopp, Erb, Engberg, and Kates, have advocated what can be fairly characterised as 'tough on crime' approaches that would more broadly authorise deadly force in defence of the defender's 'personal domain.'[2] Certain legislators and others in the public square who similarly favour a broad authorisation for defensive force, in turn, advocate for strict 'stand-your-ground' and 'castle doctrine' laws grounded almost exclusively on protecting the autonomy of the individual defender. Supporters of these harder-edged views argue for

[1] Johnson describes the right of self-defence as 'undergird[ing] our basic thinking about fundamental rights and duties,' as a 'building block of our culture,' and a 'backstop of our civilization.' See NJ Johnson, 'Self-Defense' (2006) 2 *Journal of Law, Economics & Policy* 187, 196. See also B Porat, 'Lethal Self-Defense against a Rapist and the Challenge of Proportionality: Jewish Law Perspective' (2013) 26 *Columbia Journal of Gender & Law* 123, 124–25; MF Wilson, 'System of Self-Redress' (1879) 7 *American Law Record* 577, 583; Plato, 'The Laws' in E Hamilton and H Cairns (eds), *The Collected Dialogues of Plato* (New Jersey, Princeton University Press, 360 BC/1961) 1429; *McDonald v Chicago*, 561 US 742, 767n 15 (2010).

[2] Note that the focus here is largely on using self-preferential force to *kill* the attacker. This limitation was selected because the use of deadly force against a real or putative attacker involves the irremediable killing of another to save oneself. It, therefore, is the most challenging type of defensive force to justify. Put another way, if deadly defensive force can be justified in a particular circumstance, then so, too, can resorting to lesser levels of force. See generally, F Leverick, *Killing in Self-Defence* (Oxford, Oxford University Press, 2006) 4. This book, moreover, will largely (though not exclusively) focus on *self*-defence, rather than defence of *others* – or private defence more generally – because self-preferential force is the most problematic in light of the inherent self-interest involved when one opts to save one's own life at the expense of another's. That said, much of what is written here will also be generally useful as an analytical lens through which to assess a broader range of defensive force situations, including those situations in which the quantum of self-preferential force falls short of the deadly. In those situations, similar – though not necessarily overlapping or identical – value-judgment will be implicated.

their respective positions when assessing highly-controversial examples, such as George Zimmerman's claimed right to self-defence in his deadly encounter with Trayvon Martin; Texas retiree Joe Horn's shotgun killing of two men he suspected of burglarising his neighbour's home; and Travis McMichael's taking of Ahmaud Arbery's life while trying to effect a purported 'citizen's arrest' after Arbery allegedly trespassed on a Georgia construction site.

On the other side of this debate stands the balance of prominent contemporary academics, including Ashworth, Fletcher, and Leverick, who call for a more 'pacifist' and 'humanitarian' account of self-defence. They, for example, would deny deadly force in defence of property or to ward off 'mere' serious bodily injury (as opposed to death). And somewhere in the middle we find the law of self-defence as the majority of jurisdictions enact it and enforce it (and, for that matter, as most members of the public will likely find consistent with their own moral standards, intuitions, and expectations).[3]

Considering the normative distance between these positions, an important assumption tested here is that value-judgements (whether expressed or not) permeate self-defence doctrine, generally, and individual self-defence decisions, specifically. In fact, it is the general absence of a more transparent and comprehensive value-centric approach/language shared among experts in the field that informs the inquiry at the very heart of this book.[4] As the in-the-public-consciousness examples noted at the outset demonstrate, the lack of a truly value-centric self-defence dialogue has resulted in a weak methodology for meaningfully tackling a critical criminal justice issue in a manner that is transparent, democratic, and sustainable. In the face of the various recent – and deeply unfortunate – high-profile incidents referenced above, thoughtful people within and outside of the halls of academia have had occasion to pause and think more deeply about the central subject of this book, namely, self-defence's underlying rationale. More specifically, the hypothesis tested here, from what is conceded is a generally Anglo-American perspective, is that a broader and more explicit

[3] As we will see, today's fashionable pacifist-leaning position, close to representing contemporary scholarly orthodoxy, diverges significantly from the law in the subject jurisdictions and elsewhere (though, oddly, that reality is rarely recognised in the literature, perhaps illustrating that academicians on occasion lose sight of and ignore – and in some instances no doubt do not care about – the distinction between what they wish the law was and what it actually is). Deviating from the mainstream among self-defence theorists, most jurisdictions do not require a 'wrongful' attack, do not strictly require retreat, and do not limit justifiable self-defence to deadly threats. The 'libertarian' position, on the other hand, is also in tension with what is seen in the 'real world.' For example, most jurisdictions require citizens to defer to public authorities for their protection when possible and do forbid deadly force in defence of property. See generally VF Nourse, 'Self-Defense and Subjectivity' (2001) 68 *University of Chicago Law Review* 1235, 1272–74 ('[N]either the libertarian nor the pacifist can claim to have won the debate about self-defence. Neither theoretical position actually describes the law of self-defense.').

[4] For a discussion of the importance of transparency in democratic criminal justice systems, see generally R Simmons, 'The Role of the Prosecutor and the Grand Jury in Police Use of Deadly Force Cases: Restoring the Grand Jury to Its Original Purpose' (2017) 65 *Cleveland State Law Review* 519, 531–32; S Bibas, 'Transparency and Participation in Criminal Procedure' (2006) 81 *New York University Law Review* 911, 961.

consideration of the values[5] potentially implicated when a person elects to engage in the self-preferential use of force will (1) improve the transparency and quality of the decision-making, and, relatedly, (2) diminish the corrosive role of hidden normativity.

But it is also important to recognise that the assessment of decision-making 'quality' undertaken here does not rely on individual normative evaluations of end-states or social outcomes, nor does it require universal convergence on the seven values that will be proposed here. Rather, the inquiry concerns the application of self-defence rules in terms of whether developing a common analytical and value-explicit language encourages and facilitates more nuanced, focused decision-making. To the extent this book reveals that a value-explicit approach permits a justice system to reach self-defence decisions in a more democratic, logical, and policy-based manner – and, relatedly, to identify and narrow areas of dispute, leaving less room for hidden normativity (spoiler alert – these questions will be answered in the affirmative) – then the prediction concerning 'quality' is deemed confirmed. Further, if there is disagreement (and it is hard to imagine there will not be) about what values should be included, and what relative weights should be accorded them, then that does not highlight some sort of *deficiency* in the proposed approach. To the contrary, it *reaffirms* the importance of initiating such a long-overdue, value-focused discussion. Like virtually everything else in the law – from debates about qualified immunity protections for the police, eminent domain and cyber-stalking, to abortion rights, war crimes, and drug legalisation – disagreement about the relative weighing of implicated/competing interests is part and parcel of legal discourse and decision-making. So why should self-defence be any different? What is needed to make such a debate valuable, however, is a shared analytical language as a point of departure. For otherwise those involved in the discussion will miss the opportunity for a productive exchange; they will instead fall prey to the increasingly common (and unfortunate) tendency to speak at, and past, each other.

Although a significant amount of scholarly ink has been spilled on the various technical and instrumental aspects of self-defence, curiously, there has been little scrutiny given to the core questions of how, when, and why values should influence self-defence outcomes. The approach proposed here is premised on the considered view that justice systems, when confronted with self-defence claims, must always balance various competing interests (and values), including procedural justice and the need to shore up the justice system's legitimacy and creditworthiness; the role of equal standing between citizens; everyone's presumptive "right to life;" the primacy of the legal process; general and specific deterrence; and the state's

[5] A few words on nomenclature may be appropriate at this early stage. In academic literature, the terms 'principles' and 'values' are often conflated. See generally PA Alces, 'Regret and Contract Science' (2000) 89 *Georgetown Law Journal* 143, 156–61. That conflation is, in fact, understandable, as the two terms share much in common. The decision here is to default to the term 'value,' however, because it has become a legal colloquialism commonly used by commentators (though some alternatively refer to 'self-defense factors,' see, eg, C Kopacz and E Penick, 'Double-Edge Sword of Victim Survival: Imperfect Self Defense' (2015) 29 *Chicago Bar Association Recommendations* 32, 34).

historical claim to a monopoly on force. But, as we shall see, to date, the scholarly discussion, legislative debate, and judicial decision-making has overlooked this broader array of competing values, focusing instead on technical and instrumental interests, or, to the extent discussed at all, on only one or two narrow values. As a result, justice systems from the outset have been limited in their abilities to persuasively, transparently, and justly decide cases, and, relatedly, determine the appropriate emphasis the legal system places (and should place) on state power.

In the context of this work's baseline focus on whether, when, and how values function as self-defence decision-grounds,[6] consider the 1920s case involving a youthful German fruit thief and an older orchard-owning farmer armed with a shotgun and accompanied by his dog.[7] The German Supreme Court ruled that the farmer, who shot and seriously injured the youth as he was fleeing with his friends and a bag of fruit, acted properly in defence of his property. The Court justified this outcome by noting that the farmer was protecting a legally recognised personal interest (his fruit), thus putting the farmer's actions within the penumbra of self-defence.[8] More specifically, the Court found that the farmer had used justified, potentially deadly force because shooting the youth was the *only way* the farmer could stop the youth from running away with the illegally picked fruit.[9]

Even though the tangible interest protected was only a bag of fruit, and the potential cost was the young man's life, it is fair to say that the ruling was in line with the then-prevalent systemic value-judgement that a criminal should never be permitted to 'get away' with his crime (thus, in the language of the day, avoiding an outcome that would impermissibly force the 'right' to 'yield' to the 'wrong').[10] The holding, moreover, reflected the largely unbounded notion that a person, once he knowingly became a criminal threat to the other's lawful interests, forfeited

[6] The term 'decision-ground,' as used here, distinguishes values actually implicated in a particular self-defence scenario ('value-based decision-grounds') from those that are not. Put another way, when a value provides a reason for deciding a self-defence case one way or the other, it becomes a 'decision-ground.' See generally *Deere v Calderon*, 890 F Supp 893, 897 (CD Cal 1995).

[7] [1920] 55 RGSt 82, 83 (Sept 20, 1920), discussed in C-F von Scherenberg, *Die Sozialethischen Einschränkungen der Notwehr* (Bern, Peter Lang AG, 2009) 22–23.

[8] As discussed in ch 5(IV)(A), German law has always interpreted the 'self' to include property and other personal interests beyond mere bodily integrity.

[9] 55 RGSt 82, 83–84.

[10] Ibid at 85–86. See also H Rosenau, 'Notwehr und Notstand' in H Satzger and W Schluckebier (eds), *Strafgesetzbuch: Kommentar*, vol 4 (Heymanns Verlag GmbH, 2019) side-note 2; T Fischer, '§ 32 Vorbemerkungen' in *Strafgesetzbuch* (Heymanns Verlag GmbH, 2019) side-note 2; V Erb, 'Notwehr und Notstand' in B von Heintschel-Heinegg (ed), *Münchner Kommentar zum Strafgesetzbuch, Band 1* (Beck CH, 2017) side-notes 12–18. [Note that German textbooks typically refer to 'Vorbemerkung' and 'Randnote' – the former refers to sections providing 'introductory comment,' and the latter to the 'side-note' or 'margin-note' accompanying the particular section; for consistency's sake, this book will throughout refer to 'Vorbemerkung' and 'side-note.'] As will be explained in subsequent chapters, this outcome is no longer possible under today's reinterpretation of the statutory German law of self-defence. It, moreover, would also likely violate Article 2 of the European Convention on Human Rights, which provides, among other things, that '[e]veryone's right to life shall be protected by law.' See chs 4(IV) & 5(II)(B).

the full array of rights the justice system otherwise accorded him. Such a culpable actor, it was argued, could not expect an innocent victim to subjugate his interests (no matter how trivial) to the 'attacker's' physical welfare. Nor could the culpable actor expect the legal system to permit him to violate the law without (in this case privately-initiated) repercussion.

As the Court put it, 'where the right is to be protected against the wrong,' it is inappropriate to ask the defender, acting in the urgency of the moment, to concern himself with avoiding disproportionate damage to the attacker's interests'.[11] The Court also noted that a contrary ruling would preclude all deadly force in defence of property (an outcome the Court apparently considered untenable).[12] The German Supreme Court, in delivering this ruling, therefore explicitly rejected the notion that self-defence cases required any 'weighing' of competing values. To the contrary, it held that there was only *one* outcome-determinative systemic value or goal, namely, ensuring the primacy of the 'right' over the 'wrong.'[13]

A person who today reviews this holding may understandably be unpersuaded – or even offended – by it.[14] The underlying reasons for this rejection, in turn, provide insights into the values, as well as their relative accommodation, that those reviewing the case consider prerequisite to justified self-preferential force.

Let us use the German Supreme Court's value-monistic approach to set up a short (and, hopefully, illustrative) thought experiment to demonstrate the importance values play in how we think about self-defence cases. As you read about the German Supreme Court's ruling, what was your initial/intuitive response? Did the decision strike you as fair or unfair? (My operating assumption is that, for most readers, the German Court got it wrong. But either way, on what do you base this decision?) Can you jot down a list of core reasons for why and how you reached the conclusion you did? Phrased differently, what, specifically, makes the German farmer's conduct right or wrong, legal or illegal, for each of us?

As the chief proponent of the approach proposed here, I will predict that most readers will have noted a number of reasons that reflect their discrete and deeply personal (and, yet, probably not completely overlapping or otherwise fully converging) value judgements, many of which can be slotted under some or all of the seven values proposed later. The near-certainty that there will be distance between different readers' responses, moreover, simply underscores the deeper point that self-defence assessments, like all other areas of the law, require us to deploy our own moral and ethical compasses, largely informed by our respective upbringings and life experiences. And those compasses, of course, are not always calibrated identically.

This brief exercise has hopefully nudged you, the reader, towards the conclusion that most of us can, with relative ease, rely on our intuitions to evaluate

[11] 55 RGSt 82, 85–86.
[12] Ibid at 85.
[13] Ibid at 86–87.
[14] As noted, today's 'socioethical limitations' would preclude such an outcome. See ch 5(II)(B).

the justness of purported instances of self-defence. And that is what legislators, scholars, judges, and law enforcers are already doing, and not only in the context of self-defence cases (though some perhaps might argue that our intuitive evaluations, in fact, drive, and cause us to reconstruct, value-judgments, not the other way around). The challenge, of course, is that intuitions are inherently personal, residing largely in our subconscious; this is a point made by this book's repeated references to 'hidden normativity' characterising our thinking about self-defence. To be understood, and to facilitate a rational discussion, however, the basis for a person's intuition must be explained and justified. And this becomes even more true as the facts of a particular case become more morally cloudy and challenging.

Consider that, on a macro-morality-level, the German Court's ruling can be said to elevate the farmer's interests over those of the broader community to such an extent that an individual like him can be said to become an alienated being, lacking responsibilities or obligations to his fellow man (other than to not improperly invade another's personal sphere).[15] Of course, the counter-argument is that the German Court in fact got it right – and that any contrary ruling would unjustifiably leave private property unprotected in the absence of law enforcement, and, in so doing, would foster the 'tyranny of the criminal class.'

Both sides of this debate will be analysed and put to the test. But central to our undertaking is a recognition that, by merely proclaiming a categorical rule ('the right need never yield to the wrong') and then strictly applying that rule to the facts of the case, the German Court, for no good stated reason, omitted what will be argued are other equally important value-based decision-grounds.[16] As noted, these grounds, summarised and defended in Chapter 2, include the systemic, collective interest in reducing overall violence and protecting the state's monopoly on force; protecting the fruit thief's individual right to life on humanitarian grounds; safeguarding the equal standing between the farmer and the fruit thief; ensuring the primacy of the legal process; avoiding decisions that could lead to an erosion of the criminal justice system's moral credibility (and, thus, legitimacy); and deterrence.[17]

Putting these abstract concepts into an additional real-world framework, the division of public sentiment concerning self-defence's core function was also in evidence when, on a rainy April day in 2012, 28-year-old Neighbourhood Watch Captain George Zimmerman shot and killed 17-year-old Florida teenager

[15] See generally J Rawls, 'The Basic Liberties and Their Priority' in SM McMurrin (ed), *The Tanner Lectures on Human Values III* (Cambridge, Cambridge University Press, 1982) 3, 46–63. See also GS Alexander, 'Intergenerational Communities' (2014) 7 *Law & Ethics Human Rights* 21, 29; MJ Sandel, *Democracy's Discontent: America in Search of a Public Philosophy* (Cambridge, Mass, Harvard University Press, 1996) 15; SJ Heyman, 'Foundations of the Duty to Rescue' (1994) 47 *Vanderbilt Law Review* 673, 742; B Neuborne, 'Ghosts in the Attic: Idealized Pluralism, Community and Hate Speech' (1992) 27 *Harvard Civil Rights-Civil Liberties Law Review* 371, 375–81.

[16] See ch 5(II).

[17] See ch 2(IV)(A)–(G).

Trayvon Martin.[18] After informing the 911 operator that there was a 'real suspicious guy' in his neighbourhood (a neighbourhood that had recently suffered from a spate of break-ins), Zimmerman began to chase the unarmed, but physically more imposing, Martin, ultimately fatally shooting him following a scuffle. Zimmerman, invoking Florida's 'Stand Your Ground' law, claimed he lawfully shot Martin in self-defence.[19] Family and friends of the slain Martin, on the other hand, portrayed Zimmerman as a vindictive, racist man chasing the unrealised dream of being in law enforcement.[20]

Following a three-week trial, the jury acquitted Zimmerman of murder. The jury rejected the prosecutor's argument that Zimmerman had deliberately pursued Martin and instigated the fight in order to be able to claim self-defence.[21] In handing down this verdict, the jury sparked a national debate about both race and self-defence.[22]

But notably absent from both the public debate and the Court's legal analysis was a discussion of how Zimmerman's role in instigating the deadly confrontation impacted the state's interest in protecting the equal concern and reciprocal respect among people. Similarly undiscussed was whether and how Zimmerman's conduct threatened the state's interest in protecting Zimmerman's *and* Martin's individual autonomous rights, whether the ruling allowed self-defence to become a substitute for the legal process, whether the result from a collective perspective failed to properly protect the state's monopoly on force, and what specific or general deterrent impact Zimmerman's conduct might have. That said, this failure to examine more closely these normative questions is not entirely surprising, given that the jury was simply applying the jury instruction to the facts as it found them. Addressing, and assessing, questions of value, however, is something that, as detailed at the end of this book, should take place not only in legislatures and code-drafting rooms, but that must also be institutionalised as part of jury instructions.

In another highly charged case, Ahmaud Arbery, a 25-year-old black man, was being chased by white armed residents of a South Georgia neighbourhood, Gregory

[18] See generally *Zimmerman v State*, 114 So3d 446 (Fla Dist Ct App 2013); CNN Library, 'Trayvon Martin Shooting Fast Facts' *CNN* (5 June 2013) www.cnn.com/2013/06/05/us/trayvon-martin-shooting-fast-facts/index.html; CKY Lee, 'Making Race Salient: Trayvon Martin and Implicit Bias in a Not Yet Post-Racial Society' (2013) 91 *North Carolina Law Review* 1555, 1612.

[19] *Zimmerman*, 114 So3d at 446.

[20] See generally DL Hutchinson, 'Continually Reminded of Their Inferior Position: Social Dominance, Implicit Bias, Criminality, and Race' (2014) 46 *Washington University Journal of Law & Policy* 23, 93–94; MA Franks, 'I Am/I Am Not: On Angela Harris's Race and Essentialism in Feminist Legal Theory' (2014) 102 *California Law Review* 1053, 1062–64. As this book will discuss in ch 6(II), the concept of 'reasonable fear' is central in US self-defence cases. Zimmerman carrying a firearm while Martin was unarmed and Zimmerman's mixed martial arts training were major challenges Martin was able to overcome.

[21] See L Alvarez and C Buckley, 'Zimmerman Is Acquitted in Trayvon Martin Killing' *NY Times* (New York, 13 July 2013) A1. For a discussion of the duty to retreat and avoid conflict under US law, see ch 6(III)(H) & (I).

[22] See Lee (n 18) 1567, citing K Thompson and J Cohen, 'Trayvon Martin case: Poll finds stark racial divide' *Washington Post* (10 April 2012) A3.

McMichael and his son Travis McMichael. In the video that appeared prior to the arrest of the McMichaels, the unarmed Arbery can be seen initially ducking to the right when he sees Travis McMichael aim his shotgun at him after McMichael exited his white pickup truck and tried to effect what, as of this writing, appears to be a legally defective citizen's arrest (Gregory McMichael meanwhile was in the bed of the truck). Arbery comes around the passenger side of the truck and is moving towards McMichael when McMichael discharges his shotgun twice into Arbery at short range, killing him. Under Georgia law, there is a good argument that Arbery's effort to disarm the threatening McMichael was justified self-defence. In the media furor that followed the tragic shooting, however, Arbery's apparently lawful exercise of self-defence, and the logical progression that justified his ultimately doomed effort to disarm the threatening younger McMichael, was almost treated as an after-thought. Rather, the wisdom of Georgia's citizen's arrest laws tended to receive the most attention. Indeed, as of this writing, it is the McMichaels who are claiming self-defence against Arbery (even though Georgia generally prevents the initial wrongful aggressor from cloaking himself with this justification). Any careful attempts to understand Arbery's conduct, or the tragic interaction between Rayshard Brooks and Atlanta police officer Garrett Rolfe outside of a Wendy's restaurant, from a value-based perspective, in short, have been thus far left by the wayside.

The broader system's failure to discuss these key issues serves to highlight this book's core concern that, by following the prevailing analytical practices, legislators, courts, and fact-finders are missing the opportunity to render more all-considerations-included outcomes. Such a deeper, value-centric discussion, it will be argued, serves to minimise the impact of hidden and undemocratic individualised normativity. In contrast, we today permit obscured, individual value judgements by, as relevant here, legislators, judges, and jurors, undue room to expand and undermine transparency and the rule of law, and, in many cases, become outcome-determinative.

For a final, stage-setting illustration of the underlying assumption examined here – namely, that in the absence of a value-explicit dialogue we allow hidden normative judgements about values to drive self-defence decisions – consider the highly publicised English case of eccentric Norfolk farmer Tony Martin. Martin was convicted in The Crown Court at Norwich and given a life sentence.[23] He had used an illegally possessed pump-action shotgun to shoot and kill unarmed 16-year-old burglar Fred Barras, and to seriously injure Barras' accomplice, Brendan Fearon.[24]

[23] See I Dobinson and E Elliot, 'A Householder's Right to Kill or Injure an Intruder Under the Crime and Courts Act 2013: An Australian Comparison' (2014) 78 *Journal of Criminal Law* 80, 83–84.

[24] Martin's conviction was subsequently reduced to manslaughter on appeal because of Martin's purported diminished capacity. See *R v Martin* [2001] EWCA Crim 2245.

The fact that Martin's attackers had extensive criminal records caused politicians – reflecting the type of public sentiment at times expressed in the Trayvon Martin case – to advocate for reform of England's self-defence law.[25] The suggestion was that, because an after-the-fact analysis of Barras' background established that Barras was a 'career criminal,' his right to life somehow deserved lesser legal protection. (This 'they had it coming' position also finds supporters in corners of the public and political classes who weighed in on the controversial 1980s US case involving 'subway vigilante' Bernhard Goetz, which will be discussed later).

This argument, however, sounds less in self-defence and more in punishment or societal vengeance. Missing was a recognition that Martin's decision not to retreat and not to avoid conflict implicated a broader, more inclusive array of values than articulated in the public discourse, legal commentary, or judicial decision-making.[26]

These real-life examples, taken from the subject jurisdictions, provide insights not only into the public's perception of what a 'right' or 'just' outcome is, but also into how different value-informed assessments can yield very different results. For example, while the English legal system jailed the farmer for using excessive force to protect his property, the German Court lauded the German farmer as a defender not only of his property, but, in fact, of the entire legal order.

To help gauge the current level of (in)attention paid to values as decision-grounds, Chapter 3 examines the extent to which scholars proposing comprehensive theories of self-defence engage (or, more to the point, do *not* engage) in explicitly value-informed assessments of self-defence doctrine and decision-making. The survey reveals that the scholarly debate surrounding self-defence, rather than reflecting a comprehensively value-centric approach, to a fault focuses more narrowly on the 'technical' legal aspects of self-defence to determine whether and when instances of defensive force should be encouraged, authorised, merely tolerated, or outlawed. And those few commentators who have treated values as self-defence decision-grounds usually anchor their analysis on only one or two narrow values, such as the attacker's right to life, or, on the opposite side of the value continuum, the defender's right to protect her autonomy. This relative neglect of values is both surprising and disappointing.

The assumption tested here posits that, by focusing on facts, designing tactics, and treating self-defence instrumentally to advance certain goals, justice systems lose the opportunity to benefit from a deeper conversation about jurisprudential matters of value, moral principles, and fundamental human rights. It, at the outset, is recognised, however, that debates concerning the relative importance of a defender's 'autonomy' versus an attacker's 'humanity' (and intermediate

[25] See generally C Dyer and A Travis, 'Hague's law: the whole truth and nothing but?' *The Guardian* (26 April 2000, 20:34 EDT) www.theguardian.com/politics/2000/apr/27/uk.thatcher.

[26] England's contemporary treatment of the duties to avoid conflict and to retreat is discussed in ch 7(IV)(C).

variants thereof) have been carrying on in one form or another for hundreds of years.[27] And we are far from having a dispositive 'winner' in sight. So, while hoping to find *the* answer to this long-standing debate could fairly be considered overly ambitious, the still quite striving goal here is to test the value-based model's central belief that there are, in fact, benefits to encouraging a more value-centric, comprehensive dialogue about the roles values play when assessing doctrinal issues, as well as an individual's use of self-preferential force in the face of a perceived threat.

True, there surely will be lively disagreement over what values matter (and why). But it bears repeating that, rather than undermining the purpose of the value-based model we are testing, this observation simply serves to *reinforce* its central tenet that an open and explicit debate about normative judgements is the core advantage of the more openly value-informed approach proposed here. Put another way, the mere act of recognising that we may fundamentally disagree on, say, how much protecting the equal standing between people is a value worth recognising (and how much weight to give it if recognised) can only improve the quality of the self-defence debate.

As this summary foreshadows, this book covers considerable ground. And yet, the value-explicit approach we are testing does not rely on establishing that the particular values detailed in the value-based model are the *only* ones that could possibly be included. Nor will it be contended that the proposed value-based model represents the only reasonable way of conceptualising, ordering, or prioritising the implicated values.

Criminal law, after all, is a notoriously untidy collection of proscriptions and corresponding moral judgements (and this is true regardless of geography and jurisdiction).[28] While it is true that there exists a considerable volume of scholarship at some level dedicated to synthesising the relationship between moral and legal patterns in self-defence and other contexts,[29] this book will demonstrate that there is no emerging accord on the 'values driving criminal law.' In the end, then, and important to the testing of the proposed value-centric dialogue, this book seeks to introduce the value-based model as a reasonably defensible – and important – jumping-off point for a rational and transparent discussion of the patinaed topic of self-defence.

[27] See generally H Lesch, 'Die Notwehr' in G Widmaier et al (eds), *Festschrift für Hans Dahs* (Schmidt, Dr Otto 2005) 81, 90–93. See also P Bónis, 'The Self-Defense in the Tripartitum and the European ius commune' (2014) 5 *Journal on European History of Law* 80, 81 ('The issue of the legitimate self-defense has been one of the most debated question[s] in criminal law for centuries.').

[28] See generally CB Hessick, 'Motive's Role in Criminal Punishment' (2006) 80 *Southern California Law Review* 89, 128–30; JL Diamond, 'The Myth of Morality and Fault in Criminal Law Doctrine' (1996) 34 *American Criminal Law Review* 111, 118–27; RG Singer, 'The Resurgence of Mens Rea: III – The Rise and Fall of Strict Criminal Liability' (1989) 30 *Boston College Law Review* 337, 407–08. See also D Ormerod and K Laird, *Smith, Hogan, and Ormerod's Criminal Law* 15th edn (Oxford, Oxford University Press, 2018) 5–12.

[29] See generally ch 3.

In summary, to test the value-centric position first introduced in this stage-setting chapter, Chapter 2 proposes the 'value-based model' of self-defence. This model serves as a template facilitating a deeper exploration of the value-based approach by demonstrating how a value-centric approach might operate. With this value-based template in place, Chapter 3 conducts the aforementioned thematic literature review. The primary purpose of this literature review is to determine whether the value-based model holds up to scrutiny and, in fact, provides something 'extra' that usefully goes beyond the existing scholarship in the field. Chapter 4, in turn, relies on the value-based template to provide a sound point of departure for addressing some of the central theoretical questions that have long challenged the self-defence debate. To further test the hypothesis, Chapters 5–7 deploy the value-based approach to critically evaluate the self-defence laws in Germany, the US, and England, respectively, with particular attention paid to whether and how these jurisdictions examine values in their self-defence legislation and decision-making. As the events of recent history have vividly illustrated, the time has come for a broad dialogue about the values animating criminal justice reform, generally, and this foundational criminal justice defence, specifically.

2

Developing the 'Value-Based Model' of Self-Defence

A small club of prominent theorists, including Ashworth, Erb, Fletcher, Leverick, and Sangero, are among the relatively few who, at some level at least, have examined whether and how questions of value should impact the broader self-defence debate.[1] Leverick, for example, views protecting the 'right to life' as the only relevant decision-ground.[2] Erb similarly invokes the basic right to life. He, however, reaches exactly the opposite conclusion than Leverick. Erb argues that, because allowing a person to use deadly force to protect his right to life against potentially deadly threats is an 'imperative human right requirement,' any narrowing of the authorisation must be carefully scrutinised.[3] Sangero, on the other hand, believes certain 'factors' (primarily the defender's autonomy, the attacker's culpability, and harm to the 'social-legal order') explain the underlying 'rationale' of self-defence law.[4] While these scholars do discuss values as providing the rationale justifying self-defence, we will demonstrate that even their commendable accounts are too limited.

As outlined above, this book in part tests the value-based model's position that a more detailed accounting of the underlying values believed to provide a rationale for self-defence facilitates a more transparent and rational discussion concerning 'appropriate' self-defence outcomes. The proposed value-centric approach minimises the hidden normativity characterising much of the past and present self-defence discourse among legislators, scholars, judges, and the public.[5] This transparency, in turn, is designed to enhance the community's acceptance of the decision-making.[6]

[1] For a more detailed discussion of their respective approaches, see ch 3.

[2] F Leverick, *Killing in Self-Defence* (Oxford, Oxford University Press, 2006) viii.

[3] V Erb, 'Notwehr als Menchenrecht – Zugleich eine Kritik der Entscheiduing des LG Frankfurt am Main im "Fall Daschner"' (2005) 25 *Neue Zeitschrift für Strafrecht* 593, 594.

[4] See B Sangero, *Self-Defence in Criminal Law* (Oxford, Hart Publishing, 2006) 90–106 [hereinafter Sangero, *Self-Defence*]. See also B Sangero, 'A New Defense for Self-Defense' (2006) 9 *Buffalo Criminal Law Review* 475 [hereinafter Sangero, 'New Defense'].

[5] See generally E Chemerinsky, 'Getting Beyond Formalism in Constitutional Law: Constitutional Theory Matters' (2001) 54 *Oklahoma Law Review* 1, 1–7.

[6] The openness and accessibility of the government are, after all, said to be essential elements of liberal democratic theory and are consistent with modern Western political values. See generally M Fenster, 'The Opacity of Transparency' (2006) 91 *Iowa Law Review* 885, 894–902; J Rawls, *Justice as Fairness: A Restatement* (Cambridge, Mass, Harvard University Press, 2001) 781.

To test this claim, we will construct the 'value-based model' of self-defence. The value-based model is, as noted, intended to provide a basis for critical analysis of the different legal systems and theoretically challenging scenarios. By first identifying a set of values believed to lie at the heart of the self-defence doctrine, and then analysing when and how, depending on the underlying operative facts, each value 'matters' (that is, becomes a 'decision-ground'), this book seeks to offer a uniquely useful perspective from which to assess the self-defence questions that for centuries have challenged those who have considered them.

I. Early Observers of the 'Ancient Right' of Self-Defence

Certain 'core' offences – such as murder, assault, and similar offences against persons, as well as property crimes such as fraud or theft – are typically the first (and often the only) crimes listed if a person were to survey society at large on the topic of 'what is – and should be – criminal.' The centrality of the first category of 'original' victim-based crimes against persons was, in the eighteenth-century language of Blackstone, traced to the violation of the 'sacredness' of the body.[7]

To Blackstone's thinking, even the most incidental non-consensual and unjustified contact is unlawful, for 'every man's person being sacred, and no other having a right to meddle with it, in any the slightest manner.'[8] And even today, the availability of self-defence as a legal defence limiting (or eliminating) criminal liability, up to and including for murder, has been accorded what can safely be described as bedrock status.[9] Indeed, most philosophers, lawyers, and laymen alike – regardless of ideology, geography, or legal tradition – have accepted the concept of self-preferential defensive force to ward off threats.[10]

By way of further example of 'historical' conceptions of self-defence, John Locke's oft-cited view was that a person who demonstrates a 'settled design upon another man's life, puts him in a state of war with him against whom he had declared such an intention.'[11] For Thomas Hobbes, in turn, the right to act on the

[7] 4 Bl Comm 270.

[8] 3 Bl Comm 120. See also B Hooker, 'The Elements of Well-Being' (2015) 3 *Journal of Practical Ethics* 15, 35; RG Frey, 'Moral Standing, the Value of Lives, and Speciesism' in R Shafer-Landau (ed), *The Ethical Life* 4th edn (New York, Oxford University Press, 2017) 283, 289.

[9] That self-defence is, in general terms at least, so well-settled is unusual. The list of controversial criminal law concepts is long and includes necessity and duress as defences to murder, international double jeopardy, various legal privileges (including attorney-client, doctor-patient, spousal, and reporter), and extraterritorial jurisdiction.

[10] See generally TA Green, 'The Jury and the English Law of Homicide 1200–1600' (1976) 74 *Michigan Law Review* 413.

[11] J Locke, *Second Treatise on Government* (1689) ch XVI. See also TE Holland, 'Introduction' in G Da Legnano, *Tractatus De Bello, De Represaliis et de Duello* (Andesite Press, 2015/1917) 278 (discussing Milanese scholar Giovanni da Legnano and quoting him as finding that 'self-defense proceeds from natural law, and not from positive law, civil or canon'); C De Pisan, *The Book of Fayettes of Armes and of Chyvalrye* (Oxford, Oxford University Press, 1932) 211 ('[A] man in deffense is permitted to hurt another', since 'Iuste defense' was 'preuyleged.').

motive of self-preservation was the most essential of the rights of man. As he put it in *Leviathan*, there are 'some rights which no man can be understood by any words or other signs to have abandoned or transferred, [chief among them] the right of resisting them that assault him by force.'[12] Indeed, Hobbes' view of the right to self-defence is so firmly rooted in the law and morality that it prevails even against the otherwise untouchable sovereign so that, if the sovereign lawfully comes to kill a subject, that subject has a lawful right to resist.[13] (Note that a Hegelian critique of the Hobbesian account of the natural state of humans is that it is intrinsically human to recognise the humanity in others and to acknowledge their recognition of our humanity.[14])

Alberico Gentili, Professor of Civil Law at Oxford, in 1598 similarly wrote that self-defence:

> is a necessary right; for what can be done against violence, says Cicero, without resort to violence? This is the most generally accepted of all rights. All laws and all codes allow the repelling of force by force. There is one rule which endures forever, to maintain one's safety by any and every means.[15]

More than 400 years later, David Gauthier picked up these rights-based arguments. He suggested that:

> [a] legal system which failed to recognise the right, which failed to recognise the justification each person has to act in her own protection in the light of imminent danger, could have no valid claim on the allegiance or obedience of those it sought to bring within its sway.[16]

But even beyond Anglo-American jurisprudence, using force, up to and including deadly force, to defend yourself is among the least controversial legal topics (though the 'when's' and 'how's' are of course always hotly disputed – which, indeed, is this book's central point of departure).[17] Even self-described pacifists have accepted the justifications advanced in favour of self-defensive force.[18]

[12] T Hobbes, *Leviathan* (London, Penguin Classics, 1982/1651) ch XIV, para 8.

[13] Ibid ch XXI, para 12.

[14] GW Hegel, *Phenomenology of Spirit* (Cambridge, Cambridge University Press, 2019/1807) paras 178–96. This conception is consistent with the Aristotelian understanding that humans are fundamentally political (and thus social) animals who by nature identify other humans as being human like oneself. T Irwin, *Aristotle, Nicomachean Ethics* 2nd edn (Oxford, Oxford University Press, 1999) 10–11.

[15] C Phillipson, 'Introduction' to Alberico Gentili, *De Iure Belli Libri Tres*, vol II (William S. Hein & Company, 1995) ch 13, 58–59 (citing Marcus Tullius Cicero, *On Invention, Book II* (84 BC) ch 22); 4 Bl Comm 1–3, 143, 176, 183–85 (discussing the 'natural right of resistance and self preservation, when the sanctions of society and laws are found insufficient to restrain the violence of oppression').

[16] D Gauthier, 'Self-Defense and the Requirement of Imminence' (1996) 57 *University of Pittsburgh Law Review* 615, 616.

[17] See, eg, Criminal Code of the Argentine Nation, art 34(6); Brazilian Penal Code, art 23; Criminal Law of the People's Republic of China, art 20; Egyptian Penal Code, art 56; Indonesian Penal Code, art 49(1); Japanese Penal Code, art 36(1); The Permanent Constitution of the State of Qatar, art 39; Swedish Penal Code, c 24, § 1; Turkish Criminal Code, art 25; Criminal Code of Ukraine, art 36.

[18] See C Ryan, 'Self-Defense, Pacifism and the Possibility of Killing' (1983) 93:3 *Ethics* 508, 510 (arguing that problem of self-defence for the pacifist is not problem of whether self-defence is permissible, but rather of why it is permissible).

II. An Introduction to Thinking of Values as Decision-Grounds

As noted above, and as elaborated on later, self-defence rulings and legislative enactments regrettably are rarely accompanied by discussions concerning the broader spectrum of values at play when self-preferential force is exercised, let alone by a deeper examination of how the criminal justice system should react when identified values come into conflict. So when members of the US Congress, in support of a call for law reform, argue that US subway vigilante Bernhard Goetz 'is the victim and the symbol of twin horrors in this Nation: rampant crime in the cities and gun control laws which do not allow the innocent to protect themselves,'[19] they do not explain (and themselves may not have sought to identify and understand) the deeper value-judgements driving their views. Rather, the implicit assertion, highlighting the noted concerns over hidden normativity,[20] is that drafting more permissive self-defence laws, or more laxly enforcing the existing defensive force authorisations, will deter criminal attacks and ensure that wrong-doers 'get what they deserve.'

But what tends to be surprisingly absent from such pro-liberalisation arguments is a recognition that any changes to self-defence law require challenging trade-offs in terms of values. Making self-defence more readily available, for example, may also encourage vigilantism, increase overall societal violence, and undermine the very goals of most modern criminal justice systems. And so when framed in the context of the value-based model, broadening the self-defence justification potentially threatens to: undermine the state's traditional monopoly on force; reduce protection of the (presumptive) right to life possessed by even culpable attackers; deprive purported attackers of the right to due process that is said to form the cornerstone of modern, pluralistic legal systems; allow self-preferential force to become a substitute for the legal process; and potentially conflict with widely held standards of right and wrong, thereby harming the criminal justice system's own legitimacy.[21]

[19] 133 Cong Rec H3066-04 (daily edn 5 May 1987) (statement of Rep Marlene). See also 131 Cong Rec H317-03 (daily edn 6 Feb 1985) (statement of Rep Mica) (discussing 'statistics on a national survey that indicated that 45 to 50 percent of all of the people in the United States agree with what Bernard [sic] Goetz did').

[20] See generally CKY Lee, *Murder and the Reasonable Man: Passion and Fear in the Criminal Courtroom* (New York, New York University Press, 2003) 33–43, 65–66; AG LeFrancois, 'The Act of Judging and the Performance of Being Earnest: Responding to Professor Chemerinsky's Informalism' (2001) 54 *Oklahoma Law Review* 26, 32.

[21] A few additional words on terminology may be appropriate. First, although the term 'wronging' is often given a broader meaning in moral and legal evaluation, for our purposes the term refers to actions that reflect an intentional disregard for another's equal standing as a citizen. 'Autonomy,' on the other hand, is given a fairly expansive definition consistent with the term's usage in legal decisions and scholarly writings; an individual's autonomy, so defined, comprises all of that person's legally recognised interests, including his concrete interests and his sovereignty. Autonomy is thus synonymous with self-determination and is restricted when a person is prevented from acting in accordance with

On the other hand, those, like Leverick, who would significantly limit the right to self-defence may also: define the state's monopoly on force overly broadly; fail to recognise that the culpable attacker's right to life is only presumptive; pay insufficient attention to the moral asymmetry between culpable, less-culpable, and innocent 'attackers'; undervalue the importance of protecting the defender's autonomy; threaten to damage the criminal justice system's moral authority and legitimacy; and significantly reduce self-defence's (general and specific) deterrent impact. The reality that different people will take different positions on these values reinforces, rather than devalues, the benefit of a more value-centric dialogue. What is more, and as we shall see, any theory of self-defence that for no good reason leaves these values unexamined is fatally flawed.

Turning back to Leverick, she believes the right to life (or, more specifically, the *attacker's* right to life) demands that only a deadly attack justifies deadly force, and that any other outcome threatens the criminal justice system's moral authority.[22] Schopp, on the other hand, concludes that the defender's right to autonomy justifies killing the attacker to defend far more than only the defender's life, lest the public lose respect for a law that unduly (from his perspective) limits defensive force.[23] It will be contended that these accounts, while they do discuss self-defence from a value-centric perspective, for no persuasive reason are overly limited in the scope of values they consider. And their bottom-line answers, consequently, leave themselves unnecessarily open to criticism.

Per Golding, legal rulings

> have to be supported by justifying reasons …. If values enter into a judicial justification, they do not do so as personal predilections. The values must have some purchase on the community to which they are addressed.[24]

What is needed, then, is, first, an accounting of those values providing a reasonable (though, as noted, not necessarily the only) rationale for self-defence; second, a means of determining when and how these values in certain circumstances can

his lawful action-plans. Any unjustified threat to an individual's bodily integrity, property, or right to act – or to refrain from acting – therefore constitutes a threat to that individual's autonomous sphere of self-determination. See generally A Brudner, 'The Ideality of Difference: Toward Objectivity in Legal Interpretation' (1989–1990) 11 *Cardozo Law Review* 1133, 1184–86, 1205–10; John Rawls, *A Theory of Justice* (Cambridge, Mass, Harvard University Press, 1971) 209–10.

[22] See Leverick (n 2) 151.

[23] See RF Schopp, *Justification Defenses and Just Convictions* (Cambridge, Cambridge University Press, 1998) 83–84. For a criticism of this approach, see TM Funk, 'Justifying Justifications' (1999) 19 *OJLS* 631. See also Erb (n 3) 596–97 (noting the normative difference between innocent and culpable attackers).

[24] M Golding, 'A Note on Discovery and Justification in Science and Law' in JR Pennock and JW Chapman (eds), *Justification: Nomos XXVIII* (1986) 124, 138. See also RRM Verchick, 'Culture, Cognition, and Climate' [2016] *University of Illinois Law Review* 969, 977; DM Kahan and D Braman, 'Cultural Cognition and Public Policy' (2006) 24 *Yale Law and Policy Review* 149, 150, cited in TS Aagaard, 'Environmental Harms, Use Conflicts, and Neutral Baselines in Environmental Law' (2011) 60 *Duke Law Journal* 1505, 1562; RK Greenstein, 'The Three Faces of ORPP: Value Clashes in the Law' (1993) 54 *Louisiana Law Review* 95, 121–23.

become decision-grounds; and third, an understanding of how the values are accommodated when they come into conflict.

III. The Orthodox View: 'Two Principles in Tension' (Autonomy of the Defender v Autonomy of the Attacker)

The public and academic debate over the cases of Tony Martin, Treyvon Martin, Bernhard Goetz, and the German fruit thief illustrate the importance of answering the question of how a given self-defence outcome serves to protect (1) the autonomy of the defender[25] versus (2) the autonomy of the (culpable or innocent[26]) attacker. Theories of personal autonomy, developed by philosophers Immanuel Kant[27] and Georg Hegel,[28] and interpreted by criminal theorists, such as George Fletcher,[29] support the orthodox view that these are, in fact, the two core autonomy-based *principles* in tension. And so the question becomes whether the justice system's resolution of a particular case strikes the proper balance between these two competing principles by, for example, vindicating individual autonomy, reducing violence, and treating people as ends rather than as means.[30]

This book recognises that identifying these two guiding principles in tension with each other in self-defence cases is important. But this only marks the *starting point* of the value-centric inquiry. The principle of protecting the defender and the principle of protecting the attacker are, after all, little more than abstract concepts.[31] They must be given substantive normative content and concrete

[25] Because the term 'victim' can be read to imply a culpable attack, this book will instead generally use the more neutral term 'defender.'

[26] The terms 'culpability' and 'innocence' in this book refer to legal culpability. As discussed in ch 2(IV)(F)(i) & (ii), however, moral and legal culpability ideally are co-extensive and overlapping in criminal justice systems grounded on the conventional public morality.

[27] See I Kant, *The Metaphysics of Morals* (Cambridge, Mass, Hackett Publishing, 1991) 56–60. See also M Pawlik, 'Die Notwehr nach Kant und Hegel' (2002) 114 *Zeitschrift Für Die Gesamte Strafrechtswissenschaft* 259, 274.

[28] See G Hegel, *Philosophy of Right* (New York, Dover Publications, 1952) 89–90.

[29] See GP Fletcher, *Rethinking Criminal Law* (New York, Oxford University Press, 1978) 855–64 [hereinafter Fletcher, *Rethinking*], discussed in M Kremnitzer and K Ghanayim, 'Proportionality and the Aggressor's Culpability in Self-Defense' (2004) 39 *Tulsa Law Review* 875, 892; GP Fletcher, 'Proportionality and the Psychotic Aggressor: A Vignette in Comparative Criminal Theory' (1973) 8 *Israel Law Review* 367, 371 [hereinafter Fletcher, 'Proportionality'].

[30] See generally S Kershnar, 'Forfeiture Theory and Symmetrical Attackers' (2017) 36 *Criminal Justice Ethics* 224, 224–45; JA Hessbruegge, *Human Rights and Personal Self-Defense in International Law* (New York, Oxford University Press, 2016) 266. See also E Gellner, *Conditions of Liberty: Civil Society and Its Rivals* (London, Penguin Books, 1994) 28–29; GP Fletcher, *A Crime of Self-Defense: Bernhard Goetz and the Law on Trial* (New Jersey, Prentice Hall, 1988) 24; J Dressler, 'Rethinking Heat of Passion: A Defense in Search of a Rationale' (1982) 73 *Journal of Criminal Law & Criminology* 421, 454; Fletcher, 'Proportionality' (n 29) 377.

[31] See generally WN Gemmill, 'Criminal Procedure' (1912) 3 *Journal of the American Institute of Criminal Law & Criminology* 566, 586.

meaning in order to be analytically useful. What follows, therefore, is an attempt to bridge this rationale gap through the value-based model of self-defence. The enumerated individual values can be fairly conceptualised as standing behind, and providing analytical content to, the two (defender v attacker) macro-principles.

IV. Advancing the Debate Through a More Value-Centric Dialogue – An Introduction to (and Preliminary Defence of) Seven Proposed Value-Based Decision-Grounds

Did the young subway riders by whom Goetz felt threatened, or the youthful German thief who attempted to make away with the farmer's fruit, simply 'forfeit' their right to have the justice system protect their lives? Did they, through their conduct, step outside of the law's protection? Advancing the position that, say, the principle of protecting the defender in these cases outweighed the principle of protecting the attacker rings hollow when not buttressed by supporting analysis.[32] Per the position we are testing, the two principles[33] said to be in tension in self-defence cases are in fact only given meaning and weight by the values that inform them (and, once identified, the next step of determining their relative priority is, as discussed in Chapter 2(V)(B), even more challenging).

The hoped-for benefit of the value-based model's focus on: protecting the state's monopoly on force (value #1); protecting the individual attacker's (presumptive) right to life (value #2); maintaining the equal standing between people (value #3); protecting the defender's autonomy (value #4); ensuring the primacy of the legal process (value #5); maintaining the legitimacy of the legal order (value #6); and deterring attackers (value #7) is not that the model in all cases dictates a particular balance or accommodation between the values. Rather, the model will achieve its transparency-enhancing objective if it offers a reasonable, defensible starting point for determining what is in fact 'at stake' in different self-defence scenarios. The core belief we are assessing, after all, is whether the self-defence discussion is enhanced by carefully tracing the landscape of implicated values; justifying why certain values should, under the facts of the case, receive more weight than others; and determining whether the balance of values can be said to reasonably justify treating the conduct as self-defence.

It is recognised that the seven values discussed in this chapter could of course be organised differently. For example, reducing overall societal violence (value #1),

[32] See generally Golding (n 24) 138, cited in E Chemerinsky, 'Rationalizing the Abortion Debate: Legal Rhetoric and the Abortion Controversy' (1982) 31 *Buffalo Law Review* 107, 129–32. See also D Sandomierski, 'Tension and Reconciliation in Canadian Contract Law Casebooks' (2017) 54 *Osgoode Hall Law Journal* 1181, 1230–32.

[33] For a short comment on terminology, see n 5 in ch 1.

ensuring the primacy of the legal process (value #5), maintaining the legitimacy of the legal order (value #6), and general deterrence (a component of value #7) could be grouped together as tending to reflect broader *collective or societal* interests. On the other hand, protection of the attacker's individual (presumptive) right to life (value #2), maintaining the equal standing between persons (value #3), protecting the defender's autonomy (value #4), and specific deterrence (the other component of value #7) could be grouped together as tending to safeguard *personal or individual* interests. Alternatively, the values could be grouped by those *authorising* defensive force (primarily values #3, #4, and #7) and those tending to *restrict* defensive force (primarily values #1, #2, and #5 – value #6's focus on maintaining the legitimacy of the legal order tends to function more like a 'swing value,' in that normative judgements to a greater extent will impact whether it authorises or restricts values). That said, for present purposes the view is that, even though such alternative groupings can be justified, the order selected here defensibly serves its hypothesis-testing function.

A. Value #1: Reducing Overall Societal Violence by Protecting the State's Collective 'Monopoly on Force'

Summary Justification for Including This Value:

Reducing overall societal violence, generally, and preventing unjustified attacks on citizens' rights, specifically, are fairly described as twin goals of most modern criminal justice systems (though there, as discussed, and depending on one's perspective, can certainly be other ones, including punishing the deserving and instrumentally protecting the goals valued by the state). In that sense, then, value #1 recognises the *collective* objective of seeking to minimise societal violence.

To help set the analytical stage, it is assumed that all citizens, including culpable attackers, have a fundamental right to life, and, further, that when possible (and appropriate) this right to life should be protected. Relatedly, and from a more statist, collectivist perspective, in a modern pluralistic society, the state in the main aims to advance such interpersonal violence reduction through its default monopoly on legitimate force.

But a state must erect guardrails around its right (and, practically speaking, ability) to prevent actors from exercising self-preferential force. Indeed, it is entirely reasonable to say that a person's right to life is – and, indeed, as a practical matter, must be – conditioned on his conduct (more on this below when we discuss waiver versus forfeiture). More specifically, engaging in conduct that renders the person an 'unjustified threat' to another should limit the state's interest in fully extending all available legal protection to the attacker. And this, it will be argued, is even more so when the person's conduct is culpable.

The approach outlined here, however, treats only serious conduct as justifying the state's decision to effectively suspend a person's all-things-being-equal basic right to be free from intrusion into his personal sphere (such intrusions including, at the extreme end, death and serious bodily injury) unless and until that person no longer poses such a serious and unjustified threat.[34]

Tension with, or Support for, the Other Values:[35]

Reducing overall violence by protecting the state's monopoly on legitimate force, as defined here, is an inherently *collective* value that recognises the systemic, societal interest in violence reduction and the state's role in achieving this end. In contrast, value #2 (protecting the individual attacker's presumptive right to life) is an *individual* value focused on protecting the individual and personal right not to be killed. Because the collective interest of the state reflected in value #1 is omnipresent (in the sense that the modern state will, when able to do so, want to resolve disputes through its enforcement mechanisms, an interest also directly reflected by value #5 – ensuring the primacy of the legal process), it by necessity will tend to in all cases function as a decision-ground that, all other things being equal, tends to be antagonistic to the private use of force. It, for example, will most frequently find itself in direct tension with the more defender-focused values of maintaining the equal standing between people (value #3) and protecting the autonomy of the defender (value #4). On the other hand, the collective interests this value represents tend to find support in value #5 (ensuring the primacy of the legal process) and value #6 (maintaining the legitimacy of the legal order). Whether protection of the individual attacker's presumptive right to life (value #2) or general and specific deterrence (value #7) are in tension, or aligned, with this collective state interest will largely depend on the particular factual scenario (and is particularly subject to normative weighting – after all, one could also reasonably take the position that the state's collective interest in violence reduction is not, in fact, antagonistic to the private use of force; indeed, one can take the position, as the German law does,[36] that the private

[34] Note that ch 2(V)(A) advances an explanation for why it is reasonable to accept the position that by becoming an 'unjust threat,' the 'attacker' to some extent correspondingly 'forfeits' her right to non-interference. As discussed, this book will try to bridge the analytical gaps traditional 'forfeiture-of-rights' theory has left open by introducing the concept of 'waiver' of the right to non-interference. It will be contended that this addition allows us to distinguish between those who 'waive' their right to non-interference (by knowingly/culpably initiating the threatened attack), and those who 'forfeit' their right to non-interference (by unwittingly/non-culpably becoming a threat).

[35] As discussed below in ch 2(V), it is conceded that assigning any particular 'relative weight' to competing interests is inherently a normative judgement, rather than a quasi-scientific determination. In addition, seeking to balance basic individual human rights (like the right to life) against more collective interests (like reduction in crime) is jurisprudentially challenging. But it nevertheless is important for this undertaking to arrive at *a* reasonable way (though, as noted in ch 1 above, not necessarily *the only* way) of accommodating the seven identified values when they come into conflict. In furtherance of this end, the book, therefore, must consider how each value tends to (prior to the introduction of specific fact scenarios) find itself supporting, or in tension with, the other six values.

[36] See discussion at ch 5.

use of force in the absence of state protection actually is, through both general and specific deterrence (value #7), supportive of the state's collective interest in violence-reduction).

Limitations:

This value, in contrast to some of the others, will be implicated to varying extents in virtually all self-defence cases. The extent to which this value-as-decision-ground lends weight to either the principle of protecting the defender or the principle of protecting the attacker, however, will be in large part determined by the weight accorded to the six other values discussed immediately below and on the evaluator's perspectives on the moral and functional legitimacy of the state's claimed monopoly on force. For those values and perspectives moderate, on a sliding scale, the violence-reduction value, providing guidance concerning who should be protected in a conflict-of-rights situation.

Most will recognise the legitimate state interest in trying to reduce overall violence (and, in general terms at least, the importance of protecting the state's default monopoly on legitimate force).[37] Indeed, reducing interpersonal violence in this manner can be said to ensure certain fundamental human rights,[38] principally

[37] See generally R Pest, 'Die Erforderlichkeit der Notwehrhandlung' in F Stam and A Werkmeister (eds), *Der Allgemeine Teil des Strafrechts in der aktuellen Rechtsprechung* (Baden-Baden, Nomos Verlagsgesellschaft, 2019) 137; L Greco, 'Notwehr und Proportionalität' [2018] GA 665, 670 (defining self-defence as an exception to the state's monopoly on force ('*Gewaltmonopol*'); the citizen who defends the legal order is thus operating as a surrogate of the state). See also H Lesch, 'Die Notwehr' in G Widmaier et al (eds), *Festschrift für Hans Dahs* (Schmidt, Dr Otto 2005) 87. Max Weber advanced the position that the state alone has the right to use or authorise the use of physical force, and that this represents a defining characteristic of the modern state. See M Weber, 'Politics as a Vocation' in HH Gerth and CW Mills (eds), *From Max Weber: Essays in Sociology* (London, Taylor and Francis, 1919/1946) 78. That said, some scholars have diverged from Weber, following the tradition set by Thomas Hobbes and arguing that ideal of the monopoly of violence concerns not only its control, but also its use. Viewed from this perspective, the state alone can legitimately wield violence *except* in cases of immediate self-defence. See generally R Poscher, 'The Ultimate Force of the Law: On the Essence and Precariousness of the Monopoly on Legitimate Force' (2016) 29 *Ratio Juris* 311, 313–14.

[38] With regard to the fundamental human rights that will be discussed herein in the context of each of the seven articulated values, this book in this chapter will primarily focus on specific articles in the 1948 United Nations Universal Declaration of Human Rights: Art 1 (all humans are born free and equal in dignity and rights, endowed with reason and conscience, and should act towards one another in a spirit of brotherhood), Art 2 (equal rights and freedoms for all), Art 3 (equal right to life, liberty, and security), Art 6 (equal recognition as a person before the law), Art 7 (right to equality and equal protection), Art 8 (right to effective remedy by competent national tribunals for violations of fundamental rights), Art 10 (right to fair and public hearing in the determination of rights or criminal guilt), Art 11 (presumption of innocence), Art 12 (right to legal protection against arbitrary interference with privacy, family, home, or correspondence), Art 13 (right to freedom of movement), Art 17 (right to own property), Art 20 (freedom of association), Art 21 (will of the people is basis of government's authority), Art 22 (right to economic, social, and cultural rights indispensable for dignity and free development of personality), and Art 29 (free and full development of personality in a community also involves reciprocal duties; laws should be limited to securing basic rights and freedoms and ensuring morality, public order, and general welfare in a democratic society). See GA Res 217 (III) A, Universal Declaration of Human Rights (Dec 10, 1948) [hereinafter UN Declaration]. This book will also throughout this chapter consider specific articles and protocols in the 1953 (effective date) European Convention on Human Rights: Art 2 (right to life and state's obligation to secure this right), Art 5 (right to liberty and

protecting every citizen's (presumptive) right to life.[39] While this value, therefore, may be less controversial, it still must be examined to ensure that it, indeed, should be treated as a decision-ground in self-defence cases.[40]

The notion that self-defence law is an appropriate exception to the state's so-called 'monopoly on force' derives from the belief that citizens have a right against the state for protection from wrongful aggression.[41] (Though the counter-argument, discussed in particular in the context of value #4, of course is that this analysis turns self-defence upside down; self-defence is, in fact, a non-derivative 'inherent right' – and, indeed, a human right – deriving from natural law, rather than something the state 'grants' its citizens.)[42] So citizens collectively give up the right to use force as they wish in return for the state's protection. The predominant (though, as discussed later, not exclusive) contemporary perspective is that, because of practical difficulties in providing around-the-clock protection, the state must in turn grant citizens the right of self-defence (and defence of others) when state protective force is unavailable.[43] As Kadish frames it:

> [T]he individual does not surrender his fundamental freedom to preserve himself against aggression by the establishment of the state authority, [for such a surrender would only be rational if it] 'yields a quid pro quo of greater, not lesser, protection against aggression than he had before.'[44]

security of person), Art 6 (right to a fair trial), Art 8 (right to respect for one's private and family life), Art 11 (right to freedom of association), and Art 13 (right to an effective remedy for rights violations). See Council of Europe, European Convention for the Protection of Human Rights and Fundamental Freedoms [hereinafter ECHR], Nov 4, 1950, ETS No. 005, as well as Protocol 1's Art 1 (right to peaceful enjoyment of possessions) (ECHR, Mar 20, 1953, ETS No. 009) and Protocol 4's Art 2 (freedom of movement) (ECHR, Sept 16, 1953, ETS No. 046).

[39] See generally UN Declaration (n 38), Art 3; ECHR (n 38), Art 2. See also K Kühl and M Heger, 'Vorbemerkung' in *Strafgesetzbuch: Kommentar* § 32 (Heymanns Verlag GmbH, 2018) side-note 11a; C Roxin, *Strafrecht Allgemeiner Teil. Grundlagen. Der Aufbau der Verbrechenslehre, Bd. I*, § 15 (Beck CH, 2006) side-note 4; Erb (n 3) 596–97. But see UNCHR (Sub-Commission), 'Prevention of Human Rights Violations Committed with Small Arms and Light Weapons' (2006) UN Doc. A/HRC/Sub.1/58/27 (prepared by Barbara Frey), www.smallarmssurvey.org/fileadmin/docs/N-Instruments/2006-UNGA-Prevention%20of%20human%20rights%20violations.pdf [hereinafter UNCHR 'Small Arms'] (concluding that the 'principle of self-defence' is not a broadly recognised human right).

[40] While the 'system' has an overall interest in reducing all kinds of violence (through, say, policing, education, judicial reform, etc), the state's monopoly on force as discussed here is focused more narrowly on minimising acts of interpersonal violence. See generally Weber (n 37) 77, 78 (defining the state as 'a human community which claims the monopoly of the legitimate use of force within a given territory'). But see CW Morris, *An Essay on the Modern State* (Cambridge, Cambridge University Press, 2002) 288–295 (arguing that states neither have nor seek a monopoly on legitimate force because they authorise a wide range of private violence both for personal reasons, including self-defence, and on behalf of the state, such as to prevent crime).

[41] See generally JQ Whitman, 'Between Self-Defense and Vengeance/Between Social Contract and Monopoly of Violence' (2004) 39 *Tulsa Law Review* 901, 902, cited in KK Ferzan, 'Self-Defense and the State' (2008) 5 *Ohio State Journal of Criminal Law* 449, 463.

[42] See generally DB Kopel, et al 'The Human Right of Self-Defense' (2007) 22 *Brigham Young University Journal of Public Law* 43.

[43] S Kadish, 'Respect for Life and Regard for Rights in the Criminal Law' (1976) 64 *California Law Review* 871, 884, discussed in R Segev, 'Fairness, Responsibility and Self-Defense' (2005) 45 *Santa Clara Law Review* 383, 446–47.

[44] Ibid at 885.

The logic, then, is that because the use of defensive force is only licensed or derived from the state, the state can (and, in fact, must) place reasonable limits on its use through, for example, the necessity and proportionality requirements.[45]

The principle of protecting even the culpable attacker can, indeed, be considered one of the most persuasive examples demonstrating the criminal law's desire to reduce *all* violence.[46] For if the law concerned itself solely with value #4 (protecting the defender's autonomy), then even the most trivial infringement would authorise the defender to use all defensive force, up to and including deadly force, necessary to ward off that 'threat.'

The apparent tension between the state's monopoly on force and the below-discussed value of protecting the individual defender's autonomous interests (#4) is eased when one properly understands self-defence as in a back-up or fail-safe to state power, available where protection by the state authorities is not reasonably and equally accessible. In that sense, it has been argued that self-defence functions as a *subsidiary* right.[47] Setting aside those situations in which the state authorises private citizens to use force on its behalf (for example the *posse comitatus*[48]), it is secondary to the state's use of force through its security apparatus (as relevant here, the police); only when the police are unavailable is self-preferential force said to be 'necessary' as an *exception* to the state's monopoly on force.[49] The state's obligation to protect individual rights thus creates a *default* priority for state force as a means of thwarting attacks (when available and effective).[50] The value, therefore, is opposed to private 'punishment,' but not the defence of private interests. As Nourse puts it:

> This is manifested nowhere more clearly than the standard requirement of defences that the state be unavailable – a requirement that demands deference to the state's monopoly on violence. For example, the doctrine of self-defence insists that the threat be so imminent as to prevent lawful recourse and often emphasises this fact by requiring retreat.[51]

In fact, limiting defensive force to that which is *necessary* under the facts, and that which is *not disproportionate* considering the totality of the circumstances,

[45] See generally D Sweeney, 'Standing Up to Stand Your Ground Laws: How the Modern NRA-Inspired Self-Defense Statutes Destroy the Principle of Necessity, Disrupt the Criminal Justice System and Increase Overall Violence' (2016) 64 *Cleveland State Law Review* 715, 727; DL Creach, 'Partially Determined Imperfect Self-Defense: The Battered Wife Kills and Tells Why' (1982) 34 *Stanford Law Review* 615, 627–29. See also M Dsouza, *Rationale-Based Defences in Criminal Law* (Oxford, Hart Publishing, 2017) 47, 53–56 ('[C]onstituent elements [including the right to protect one's life] mark the boundaries of the positive guidance that can be given by any moral criminal law.').

[46] See generally Erb (n 3) 593–94. See also T Fischer, '§ 32 Vorbemerkungen' in *Strafgesetzbuch* (Heymanns Verlag GmbH, 2019) ch I side-notes 13–15b.

[47] See Lesch (n 37) 111–12; Fischer (n 46) side-note 35.

[48] J K Elsea, *The Posse Comitatus Act and Related Matters: The Use of the Military to Execute Civilian Law* (Version 7, Congressional Research Service R42659, 2018).

[49] See T Rönnau and K Hohn, '§ 32 Notwehr' in G Cirener et al (eds), *Strafgesetzbuch: Leipziger Kommentar, Band 3* (Berlin, De Gruyter, 2019) side-note 183–84.

[50] See ibid. See also Kühl and Heger (n 39) side-note 11a.

[51] V Nourse, 'Reconceptualizing Criminal Law Defenses' (2003) 151 *University of Pennsylvania Law Review* 1691, 1725.

can, as discussed below, be said to recognise basic human solidarity. At the same time, these requirements also preserve the collectivist interest of ensuring that self-preferential force does not become an alternative to (or otherwise improperly undermine) the state's default obligation to protect its citizens, lest they use available force to protect themselves.[52]

At this point, a few words of clarification may be in order. The criminal justice system's common (and necessary) response to unjustified private violence is that agents of the law have the ability to apply force against those who transgress criminal proscriptions.[53] This 'legal violence,' then, is fundamentally anti-violent because its ultimate aim is to reduce the level of overall violence in society.[54] In this respect, law has a negative relation to violence; by countering violence, law contributes to social order.[55]

Sceptics of this collectivist position, like Schopp, counterpose that the attacker, and particularly the culpable attacker, deserves no quarter. They claim that the criminal law must, therefore, not concern itself with protecting such an attacker's purported rights.[56] Rather, the focus must more narrowly be on whether the defensive force was in fact necessary.[57]

Assume, for example, that Andrew knowingly takes Victor's matches from a restaurant table and is just about to drive away. A self-defence law grounded exclusively in the principle of protecting the defender (and that ignores the state's interest in reducing overall violence) would permit Victor, the owner of the matches, to use deadly force if that was the only way for Victor to ensure the safe return of his property.[58]

But even supporters of such uncompromising positions are likely to agree that there must be *some* limits on self-defence. Whether these limits are based on the law's recognition of empathy and the basic human solidarity between people, the notion that unfettered defensive force amounts to an abuse of the right, or more functional limiting concepts such as 'necessity' and 'proportionality,' there is general agreement that some boundaries on defensive force are both appropriate

[52] See generally J Isensee, 'Die Friedenspflicht der Bürger und das Gewaltmonopol des Staates' in G Müller and K Eichenberger (eds), *Staatsorganisation und Staatsfunktionen im Wandel: Festschrift für Kurt Eichenberger zum 60 Geburtstag* (Duncker & Humblot, 1982) 23; D Merten and G Arzt, *Rechtsstaat Und Gewaltmonopol (Recht Und Staat in Geschichte Und Gegenwart)* (1975) 33.

[53] See N Sales, 'Regulating Cyber-Security' (2013) 107 *Northwestern University Law Review* 1503, 1521.

[54] See H Schwirck, 'Law's Violence and the Boundary Between Corporal Discipline and Physical Abuse in German South West Africa' (2002) 36 *Akron Law Review* 81, discussing R Cover, 'Violence and the Word' (1986) 95 *Yale Law Journal* 1601, 1605–17. See also L Sytnichenko, 'Otfried Höffe's Theory of Social Justice' (2015) 44 *Polish Political Science Yearbook* 23, 28.

[55] See generally G Binder, 'Victims and the Significance of Causing Harm' (2008) 28 *Pace Law Review* 713, 727.

[56] See Schopp (n 23). See also ch 2(IV)(D) (discussing Schopp's perspectives on the value of protecting the defender's autonomy).

[57] See Schopp (n 23) 84. For an analysis and criticism of this approach, see Funk (n 23) 631. See also Erb (n 3) 596–97 (noting the normative difference between innocent and culpable attackers).

[58] See generally Schopp (n 23) 83–84.

and required.[59] By developing these boundaries of self-defence,[60] and in so doing helping define the role of citizens and the state, the defence functions as a means of allocating the permission to use violence between the state and the individuals who comprise it.[61]

B. Value #2: Protecting the Attacker's Individual (Presumptive) Right to Life

Summary Justification for Including This Value:

While value #1 concerned society's *collective* interest in minimising interpersonal violence by protecting the state's monopoly on force, value #2 focuses on the attacker's *individual*, personal right to life. The central (and largely uncontroversial) limitations on self-defence – namely necessity, imminence, and proportionality – apply to both culpable and non-culpable attackers. These near-universally recognised restrictions demonstrate that protecting the attacker, and even a culpable one, in fact deserves treatment as an important stand-alone value. And while few values will generate as much disagreement as value #2, the very fact that different observers will want to add or take weight away from this value underscores how important the normative assessment of this value is to self-defence outcomes (and why the proposed value-centric dialogue aids transparent decision-making).

Tension with, or Support for, the Other Values:

The notion of protecting attackers (and, in particular, culpable attackers) is likely to generate disagreement between those who bring into the debate very different normative judgements about the extent to which defensive force should be authorised, generally, and to what extent culpable offenders deserve protection, specifically. Those (like Schopp) who can be expected to accord more weight to warding off the imputation of unequal standing between people (value #3), protecting the defender's autonomy (value #4), and deterrence (value #7) will likely be the most sceptical about the inclusion of this value as a stand-alone decision-ground. After all, why should the culpable attacker acting outside of the law's bounds formally receive state protection? On the other hand, those (like Leverick) who focus more narrowly on reducing overall violence by protecting the state's monopoly on force (value #1) and ensuring the primacy of the legal process (value #5) can be expected to place

[59] See generally Rönnau and Hohn (n 49) side-notes 225–29.

[60] See generally Sweeney (n 45) 715, 727; Creach (n 45) 615, 627–29. See also Dsouza (n 45) 47, 53–56 ('[C]onstitutent elements [including the right to protect one's life] mark the boundaries of the positive guidance that can be given by any moral criminal law.').

[61] See generally Ferzan (n 41) 460–61. See also Whitman (n 41) 901, 902, cited in Ferzan (n 41) 463; Kadish (n 43) 871, 884, discussed in Segev (n 43) 383, 446–47.

more weight on this value when compared to the other more 'pro-defender' values.[62]

Limitations:

While we will discuss the value of protecting the defender's broad autonomy (value #4), the instant value's interest in protecting the attacker's presumptive 'right to life' is framed in terms of protecting the attacker from *death*. This asymmetry (the defender's broader autonomy interests versus the attacker's narrower right to life) is intentional. It reflects that this book is explicitly focused on deadly self-preferential force.[63] Additionally, it is consistent with the position (discussed in the forfeiture context in Chapter 2(V)(A)) that culpable attackers are *presumptively entitled to less relative protection* than moral innocents.

According to Leverick, 'in a legal system that holds the equality of life to be a fundamental value, the aggressor has a right to life just as the victim does.'[64] And this claim is surely defensible. Protecting the attacker (even the culpable one) is, in fact, part and parcel of modern self-defence law.[65]

Consider, for example, the aforementioned doctrinal necessity and imminence limitations. They, as noted,[66] play an important part in preserving the state's monopoly on force and are central to the subject jurisdictions' self-defence laws. Additionally, and unless overridden or outweighed by other values, these guardrails around self-preferential force also help secure the *individual* attacker's right to due process of law.[67] For, wherever one believes the line must be drawn, few are likely to disagree that the criminal law must also at some level consider the well-being of the *source* of the threat to the defender, namely, the well-being of the attacker.[68] In fact, notions of basic human solidarity and respect for fundamental human rights arguably compel this conclusion.[69]

It may be argued, of course, that there is no such thing as a legally or morally recognised systemic interest in protecting the attacker; or that describing this

[62] See ch 2(IV)(C)(i) for a discussion concerning how the values might alternatively be grouped as tending to protect the attacker versus the defender.

[63] See text of n 2 in ch 1.

[64] Leverick (n 2) 45, citing Ryan (n 18) 510.

[65] See generally FP Hubbard, 'The Value of Life: Constitutional Limits on Citizens' Use of Deadly Force' (2014) 21 *George Mason Law Review* 623, 646; SE Henderson and K Sorensen, 'Search, Seizure, and Immunity: Second-Order Normative Authority and Rights' (2013) 32 *Criminal Justice Ethics* 108, 114.

[66] See ch 2(IV)(A).

[67] See R Leider, 'Taming Self-Defense: Using Deadly Force to Prevent Escapes' (2018) 70 *Florida Law Review* 971, 1002.

[68] See generally Hubbard (n 65) 646.

[69] See generally UN Declaration (n 38) Art 1 (all humans born free and equal in dignity and rights, endowed with reason and conscience, and should act towards one another in a spirit of brotherhood), Art 2 (equal rights and freedoms for all); Art 3 (equal right to life, liberty, and security); Art 6 (equal recognition as a person before the law); Art 7 (right to equality and equal protection); ECHR, Nov 4, 1950, ETS No. 005 (n 38) Art 5 (right to liberty and security of person).

interest as a 'value' overstates the case. The weakness of such positions, as examined in Chapter 2(IV)(B), is that there are persuasive value-based arguments for treating protection of even culpable attackers as something the criminal justice system (presumptively) values. Even the culpable attacker's welfare must be considered, because even the culpable attacker is a human who does not under all circumstances forfeit his complete entitlement to human concern and respect on account of his misbehaviour. As Kahan and Braman, discussing the contemporary law's humanist commitment, frame it:

> The self-conscious refusal of contemporary doctrine to license deadly force to protect nonvital affronts … expresses the 'supreme value of human life' recognised by any civilized system of law.[70]

In the modern democratic tradition, ethical, social, and political thought is anchored to the idea of equality of people under the law, and the worth of even the criminal human.[71] This position is based on the assumption that, all other things being equal (and they, by definition, are *not* always equal in self-defence cases), two human lives, as human lives, are similarly valuable.[72] If this were not so, then all culpable attacks, regardless of how trivial, could be met with deadly force (bringing to mind the case of the youthful fruit thief discussion from Chapter 1). But this is not the law in any known contemporary jurisdiction. That said, and as discussed immediately below, what most of the scholarship concerning itself with the defender's right to life largely ignores is that this is and must be a *presumptive* right. And, as we shall see, there are more reasons for this presumption to be overcome than Leverick and others acknowledge.

C. Value #3: Maintaining the Equal Standing between People

> *Summary Justification for Including This Value:*
>
> An ordered society is said to require an equal concern, and reciprocal respect, for rights between and among citizens. Building on this foundation, culpable attackers, like criminals/victimisers more generally, uniquely threaten not only to *harm* their victims, but through their threatened attack additionally

[70] DM Kahan and D Braman, 'The Self-Defensive Cognition of Self-Defense' (2008) 45 *American Criminal Law Review* 1, 9.

[71] See generally B-V Ikejiaku, 'International Law, the International Development Legal Regime and Developing Countries' (2014) 7 *Law & Development Review* 131, 139–40; EH Pfuhl, Jr., 'Humanistic Criminology: Future Prospects' (1985) 12 *Journal of Sociology & Social Welfare* 604, 625–26; J Delaney, 'Towards a Human Rights Theory of Criminal Law: A Humanistic Perspective' (1978) 6 *Hofstra Law Review* 831, 857–58. See also AT Knapp, 'Law's Revolutionary: James Wilson and the Birth of American Jurisprudence' (2014) 29 *Journal of Law and Politics* 189, 234–35.

[72] See generally Igor Primoratz, *Justifying Legal Punishment* (Humanities Press International, 1989) 158–99, 161–66. See also Hubbard (n 65) 646.

threaten their victims with a unique *wrong* by effectively disrespecting the victim's right to equal standing in the public and private spheres. Particularly in cases involving culpable attackers, self-preferential force exercised in self-defence allows the defender to most immediately repel the attack (thwarting the threatened *harm*). The defender's force also puts himself in a position to maintain the equal standing between himself and his attacker by protecting his personal domain (thwarting the threatened *wrong*). In this sense, then, self-defence permits individuals to be sovereign by allowing them to not only assert rights, but to also recognise those same rights in others. But self-defence also renders them subject in the sense that they must obey the laws they, as a collective, impose on their fellow humans.

Tension with, or Support for, the Other Values:

Warding off the imputation of unequal standing inherent in culpable attacks can be understood as a value ancillary to protecting the defender's autonomy (value #4) and is also generally aligned with deterrence (value #7). On the other hand, violence reduction (value #1), protection of the attacker (value #2), and ensuring the primacy of the legal process (value #5) are, all other things being equal, generally antagonistic to this more defender-centric value. Maintaining the legitimacy of the legal order (value #6), moreover, finds itself in an unusual posture with respect to this value, because cases in which maintenance of equal standing is under- or over-weighted can yield results potentially threatening to the legal order's moral legitimacy.

Limitations:

Because this decision-ground is necessarily based on thwarting a *culpable* attacker's attempted imposition of unequal standing, it is not implicated in the case of non-culpable/innocent aggressors. This is so because, without a culpable attack, the attacker through his actions does not threaten to disrespect or discount the defender's right to equal standing. Such an attacker may threaten a *harm* but is not threatening a *wrong*.

i. The Importance of Equal Standing – And the Unique Threat Posed by Culpable Attacks

Unlike the collective value of overall violence-reduction and protection of the monopoly on force (value #1), and the individual value of protecting even the culpable attacker's right to life (value #2), the instant value of ensuring the equal standing between people (and, relatedly, recognising the unique threat culpable attacks pose) may to some be less self-explanatory. Indeed, it is likely the most controversial of the values set forth here, in part because it stands in tension with most of the other values and protects an interest that not everyone considers equally important.

Those other values have a tendency to *limit* a defender's exercise of self-preferential force. This value, in contrast, when implicated through culpable attacks, has the characteristic of *expanding* a defender's all-other-things-equal right to exercise self-defence. That said, and as with the other values, its individual impact on whether defensive force should be justified must be measured on a relative sliding scale.[73] As discussed in Chapter 2(IV)(A) and (B), controlling social harm and evaluating conduct on the basis of relative culpability can, in fact, be said to be the criminal law's central organising principles (or at least so one hopes).[74]

Relatedly, we will assume general (though not universal)[75] agreement that the criminal law furthers the preservation of fundamental human rights[76] by requiring individuals to maintain relationships of restraint.[77] As a result, the criminal law can be said to, in the main, aim to punish and deter those who knowingly violate these relationships of restraint.[78] Put another way, and assuming the accuracy of these foundational assumptions, the criminal law at its core focuses on the *attitudes* a criminal defendant expresses toward rights and related proscriptions.[79] And so a person who controls her conduct in a manner designed to avoid violating rights and proscriptions conveys respect for them, whereas a person who opts to not conform her conduct in this manner conveys disrespect.[80] In this sense, then, 'respecting' rights and proscriptions means according another person's rights sufficient value when compared to one's own interests, and, relatedly, taking the steps necessary to avoid engaging in actions in pursuit of one's own interests that are likely to violate another's rights.

While perhaps controversial in some circles, it is posited here that these are fairly basic, and perhaps even minimal, expectations we fairly can impose on others in a civilised society. As Bottoms and Tankebe writing in the context of procedural justice put it, 'citizens who have deliberately chosen the path of obedience might

[73] More on this in ch 2(V), below.

[74] See generally J Horder, *Ashworth's Principles of Criminal Law* 8th edn (Oxford, Oxford University Press, 2016) 1–3, 53–58; A Simester and A von Hirsch, *Crimes, Harms, and Wrongs: On the Principles of Criminalisation* (Oxford, Hart Publishing, 2011) 3–31.

[75] See ch 2(IV)(F).

[76] See generally UN Declaration (n 38) Arts 1, 2, 7, 12, 17, 21, 22, and 29; ECHR, Nov 4, 1950, ETS No. 005 (n 38) Arts 2, 5, and 13.

[77] See generally BB Sendor, 'The Relevance of Conduct and Character to Guilt and Punishment' (1996) 10 *Notre Dame Journal of Law, Ethics & Public Policy* 99, 124; BB Sendor, 'Restorative Retributivism' (1994) 5 *Journal of Contemporary Legal Issues* 323, 363 [hereinafter Sendor, 'Restorative Retributivism'].

[78] See generally Sendor, 'Restorative Retributivism' (n 77); BB Sendor, 'Mistakes of Fact: A Study in the Structure of Criminal Conduct' (1990) 25 *Wake Forest Law Review* 707. See also Rönnau and Hohn (n 49) side-notes 66–68, 71.

[79] See generally J Dressler, *Understanding Criminal Law* § 9.01(B) (London, LexisNexis, 1995); BB Sendor, 'Crime as Communication: An Interpretive Theory of the Insanity Defense and the Mental Elements of Crime' (1986) 74 *Georgia Law Journal* 1371, 1393–94. See also D Ormerod and K Laird, *Smith, Hogan, and Ormerod's Criminal Law* 15th edn (Oxford, Oxford University Press, 2018) 10–12 (noting that criminal conduct can be 'wrongful without being harmful'). *Cf* ch 2(IV)(F)(ii)(b) (discussing 'regulatory' and strict liability offences).

[80] See generally Sendor, 'Restorative Retributivism' (n 77) 323; Rönnau and Hohn (n 49) side-notes 66–68, 71. See also J McMahan, 'Self-Defense and the Problem of the Innocent Attacker' (1994) 104 *Ethics* 252, 261 (contending that culpable attackers are liable to more defensive harm).

well be resentful if and when they observe a blatant lack of obedience to law, or an absence of self-restraint ….'[81] Erb similarly comments that attacks by innocents, such as children or individuals operating under a mistake, do not knowingly elevate their interests over those of their victims. Culpable attackers, in contrast, threaten to impose what effectively is unequal standing on their victims.[82]

It follows that laws embodying what later will be described as the 'fully expressed public morality'[83] not only enable individuals to make universal *demands*, but also carry with them corresponding reciprocal *obligations*. So my demand that I not be harmed inherently carries with it the obligation that I not harm anyone else.[84] Rousseau articulated a similar notion of reciprocity:

> [I]t is in order that we may not fall victims to an assassin that we consent to die if we ourselves turn assassins …. The rights one recognises in others one can demand in others; but we cannot demand from others what we refuse to respect. It is a practical impossibility.[85]

[81] A Bottoms and J Tankebe, 'Beyond Procedural Justice: A Dialogic Approach to Legitimacy in Criminal Justice' (2012) 102 *Journal of Criminal Law & Criminology* 119, 138.

[82] V Erb, 'Notwehr und Notstand' in Bernd von Heintschel-Heinegg (ed), *Münchner Kommentar zum Strafgesetzbuch, Band 1* (Beck CH, 2017) side-note 209. But see Rönnau and Hohn (n 49) side-note 72 (describing recognition of reciprocity in the context of equal standing – *störung des Gegenseitigkeitsverhältnisses* – as dangerous, and commenting that, while it may be a justifiable consideration in the context of intentional attacks, self-defence is also available for unintentional and morally involuntary attacks).

[83] The use of the term 'public' morality here is meant to recognise that, while most people have their own *private* morality, the *malum in se* (ie, wrong because morally blameworthy) core of democratic criminal justice systems, as applied by the courts and police, is the product of *society* acting out of broad social consensus to criminalise conduct that threatens harm to others and is 'substantially wrongful.' See generally F Picinali, 'Innocence and Burdens of Proof in English Criminal Law' (2014) 13 *Law Probability & Risk* 243, 256; AD Miller, 'Two Theories of Criminal Justice' (1981) 79 *Michigan Law Review* 904. But see B Levin, 'The Consensus Myth in Criminal Justice Reform' (2018) 117 *Michigan Law Review* 259, 281–83. *Malum prohibitum* (ie, wrong only because criminalised) offences, in contrast, do not typically draw the same public approbation. Such offences include 'regulatory' or 'pre-emptive' criminal proscriptions that have little to do with willed anti-social conduct (to wit, 'wronging'), but rather are aimed at changing conduct for other instrumental reasons. See generally SG Mayson, 'Collateral Consequences and the Preventative State' (2015) 91 *Notre Dame Law Review* 301, 332. The focus is on defining and declaring a set of 'pre-existing [public] wrongs' resulting in formal, public, and punitive measures through the criminal process. See A Duff, 'A Criminal Law We Can Call Our Own' (2017) 111 *Northwestern University Law Review* 1491, 1496–1501. See also A Duff, *The Realm of Criminal Law* (Oxford, Oxford University Press, 2018) 52–91. But see MM Dempsey, 'Public Wrongs and the "Criminal Law's Business" – When Victims Won't Share' in Rowan Cruft et al (eds), *Crime, Punishment, and Responsibility: The Jurisprudence of Anthony Duff* (Oxford, Oxford University Press, 2011) 254–72 (disagreeing with Duff's approach and focusing on the reasons that apply to the conduct of criminal justice officials, rather than on values that are threatened by a defender through her criminal conduct). For a comprehensive critique of the trend of 'over-criminalising' conduct for regulatory reasons, see AJ Ashworth, 'Is the Criminal Law a Lost Cause?' (2000) 116 *LQR* 225.

[84] See generally Erb (n 3) 595–96 (contending that culpable individuals 'choose' to expose themselves to defensive force). But for a view that the criminal law is best envisioned as being a branch of public or administrative law lacking such a distinct moral basis, see, eg, T Skolnik, 'Homelessness and the Impossibility to Obey the Law' (2016) 43 *Fordham Urban Law Journal* 741, 744–63; V Chiao, 'Ex Ante Fairness in Criminal Law and Procedure' (2012) 15 *New York Criminal Law Review* 277, 279–90; M Thorburn, 'Justifications, Powers, and Authority' (2008) 117 *Yale Law Journal* 1070, 1097–1109; SB Young, 'The Moral Basis of American Law: An Hypothesis' (2004–2005) 82 *University of Detroit Mercy Law Review* 649, 651–55.

[85] J-J Rousseau, *The Social Contract* (London, Penguin Books, 1762/1947) 28.

When other competent individuals who claim similar rights to be absolute ends recognise one's equal standing (and equal right to non-interference), then that right becomes an objective reality, as opposed to a mere subjective claim.[86] As Leoni, defending Rousseau's position, observed:

> [I]t is no nonsense to presume that every criminal would admit and even request condemnation for other criminals in the same circumstance [because] there is a 'common will' on the part of every member of a community to hinder and eventually punish certain kinds of behavior that are defined as crimes in that society.[87]

We can thus say that individuals are sovereign in the sense that they are able to assert rights and recognise the same rights in others; but individuals are also subject, in the sense that they must obey the laws which they themselves collectively make and cannot fairly complain if and when they are held to account for their failure to do so. In fact, lessons learned in everyday life teach that a person can, to varying levels, show direct or implied hostility towards a particular right by intentionally violating – or recklessly, carelessly, or negligently disregarding – it. By so doing, that person conveys the viewpoint that he does not consider others' rights to be sufficiently important, when compared to the offender's own competing interests.

An example taken from everyday life might help illustrate this dynamic. Consider something as relatively benign as getting rudely cut off in morning traffic by a reckless driver. For many or most, such an action will trigger anger and frustration explainable not by any concrete delay or other quantifiable 'injury.' Rather, the reckless driver demonstrates *disrespect* towards the other drivers by thoughtlessly elevating his interests in getting through traffic above everyone else's decision to patiently wait in a queue of cars. (In fact, even in cases of criminal negligence, an interpretive assessment of the objective facts shows some – though admittedly a reduced – level of disregard towards the interests of others).[88]

Consider another example. If Andrew intentionally hits Victor with a bat as part of a robbery, Andrew rather obviously conveys disrespect to Victor's legitimate, legally recognised interests in his physical integrity, right to be free from pain, and interest in maintaining equal standing. Andrew, through his conduct, thus knowingly and predictably subjects himself to criminal sanction. On the other hand, if Andrew intentionally hits Victor with a bat because Andrew reasonably, but incorrectly, believes Victor is about to launch an attack on him, then Andrew's

[86] See ibid at 139–41.

[87] B Leoni, *Freedom and the Law* 3rd edn (Indianapolis, Liberty Fund, 1991) 136.

[88] See generally ibid. See also P Arenella, 'Convicting the Morally Blameless: Reassessing the Relationship Between Legal and Moral Accountability' (1992) 39 *UCLA Law Review* 1511, 1535–44; J Hampton, 'Correcting Harms Versus Righting Wrongs: The Goal of Retribution' (1992) 39 *UCLA Law Review* 1659; J Hampton, 'Forgiveness, Resentment and Hatred and the Retributive Idea' in JG Murphy and J Hampton, *Forgiveness and Mercy* (Oxford, Oxford University Press, 1988) 35, 111–61; N Lacey, *State Punishment: Political Principles and Community Values* (London, Routledge, 1988) 176. See also H Morris, 'Persons and Punishment' in H Morris, *On Guilt and Innocence: Essays in Legal Philosophy and Moral Psychology* (1976) 36.

act does not signal such a disrespect for Victor's rights. If, however, Andrew is acting recklessly with his bat and 'accidentally' hits Victor, then Andrew's reckless conduct still conveys a lack of respect for Victor's interests (though the type of disrespect is normatively distinguishable from the first robbery scenario).

Finally, in those jurisdictions that reject criminalisation of negligent conduct, if Andrew hits Victor with a bat out of mere negligence, he will not be viewed as having met the threshold condition of exhibiting behaviour departing below the norm of respect necessary for a criminal conviction. Andrew, therefore, likely could defeat a prosecutor's criminal charges by presenting a failure-of-proof defence and showing the absence of the required *mens rea*/mental element, or he could seek to present an excuse defence. (That said, Andrew may still be the subject of Victor's civil lawsuit).

'Traditional' or 'core' criminal liability, indeed, cannot exist without such norm violation (though it can be fairly pointed out that many contemporary 'regulatory' offences are not based on true moral blame).[89] In this sense, then, human desire is to make moral judgements universal.[90] There, indeed, can be practical value in giving formal legal expression to this human desire.[91] The criminal justice system effectively expresses condemnation by punishing wrongdoers, and allows society to gain practical benefits from doing so. These practical benefits include the system's communicative value (moral condemnation of the action and the individual signalled by a criminal conviction and possible general deterrence), as well as potential criminal confinement (resulting in specific deterrence, as well as incapacitation).[92]

Applying these conceptions of rights to the criminal law, 'traditional' or 'core' criminal liability can be said to employ the sanction uniquely at the criminal law's disposal, namely, individualised moral blame.[93] As Ormerod and Laird put it, in

[89] Note that the criminal justice systems in the subject jurisdictions (as opposed to in our 'model' system) contain thousands of 'regulatory' criminal proscriptions that have little or nothing to do with willed antisocial conduct (to wit, 'wronging'), but rather are aimed at changing conduct for other instrumental reasons. For a comprehensive critique of the trend of over-criminalising conduct for regulatory reasons, see Ashworth (n 83) 225.

[90] See generally DE Soles, 'Four Concepts of Loyalty' (1993) 8 *International Journal of Applied Philosophy* 43; A Buchanan and R Powell, 'The Limits of Evolutionary Explanations of Morality and Their Implications for Moral Progress' (2015) 126 *Ethics* 1; A Oldenquist, 'Loyalties' (1982) 79 *Journal of Philosophy* 173.

[91] See generally Lon L Fuller, *The Morality of Law* (New Haven, Yale University Press, 1964) 33–91, 95–106.

[92] See generally J Habermas, *Faktizität und Geltung Beiträge zur Diskurstheorie des Rechts und Des Demokratischen Rechtsstaats* (Suhrkamp, 1992) 29. For the English translation, see J Habermas, *Between Facts and Norms: Contributions to a Discourse Theory of Law and Democracy* (Oxford, Polity Press, 1996), quoted in UK Preub, 'Communicative Power and the Concept of Law' (1995) 17 *Cardozo Law Review* 1179, 1189.

[93] See generally B Vogel, 'The Core Legal Concepts and Principles Defining Criminal Law in Germany' in M Dyson and B Vogel (eds), *The Limits of Criminal Law: Anglo-German Concepts and Principles* (Cambridge, Intersentia, 2018) 26. See also UN Declaration (n 38) Art 29 (standing for legislative minimalism, in that laws should be limited to securing basic rights and freedoms).

contrast with civil law, conduct that is criminal *traditionally* (though, as discussed, not always)[94] involves a 'public wrong' (reflecting the important role the public has in defining and punishing crimes), as well as a 'moral wrong.'[95]

With this foundational discussion in place we can now close the loop on culpability and equal standing. Assuming a given legal system defines certain threatened knowing and intentional physical contact, such as assault or battery, as morally blameworthy, it will also conclude that the conduct signals an impending substantive break in the above-described relationship of restraint. A system focused on maintaining equality in this sense will, consequently, permit a person threatened with such a criminal attack to repel it by using necessary and appropriate defensive force (because after-the-fact systemic punishment is ill-suited at undoing – and, indeed, may not be calibrated to undo – the attacker's imposition unequal standing).[96] Some 'attacks,' such as those committed by individuals operating under a reasonably mistaken belief that they are acting properly, or by mental incompetence, in contrast, do not signify such a break in the relationship of restraint and do not threaten the equal standing of the defender and the attacker.[97]

Lessons learned in everyday life teach that a person can show hostility or disrespect toward another's right by intentionally, recklessly, or carelessly violating or otherwise disregarding it.[98] By so doing, that person conveys the viewpoint that he does not consider others' rights to be sufficiently important when compared to the

[94] See generally ch 2(IV)(F).

[95] Ormerod and Laird (n 79) 5–12. See also M Osiel, 'The Banality of Good: Aligning Incentives Against Mass Atrocity' (2005) 105 *Columbia Law Review* 1751, 1772; A Duff, *Punishment, Communication and Community* (New York, Oxford University Press, 2001) 143–45, cited in J Bronsther, 'Torture and Respect' (2019) 109 *Journal of Criminal Law & Criminology* 423, 430; RHS Tur, 'Justifications of Reverse Discrimination' in M Stewart (ed), *Law, Morality and Rights* (Dordrecht, Springer, 1983) 259, 274 ('[T]he "fault principle" is the basis … of the criminal law of at least the western world.'). But see PH Robinson, 'Imputed Criminal Liability' (1984) 93 *Yale Law Journal* 609, 658 (noting situations like strict criminal liability 'in which furtherance of the utilitarian goal of deterrence disregards principles of culpability'), cited in AJ Sepinwall, 'Faultless Guilt: Toward a Relationship-Based Account of Criminal Liability' (2017) 54 *American Criminal Law Review* 521, 523 n 4.

[96] See generally A Duff, *Answering for Crime: Responsibility and Liability in the Criminal Law* (Oxford, Hart Publishing, 2007) 11, 51–52; A Duff, 'Punishment, Citizenship and Responsibility' in H Tam (ed), *Punishment, Excuses and Moral Development* (Taylor & Francis, 1996) (contending that punishment should aim to alter the moral sentiments of offenders, rather than simply giving offenders an external/prudential reason for desistence).

[97] See generally Schopp (n 23) 71–83; S Macedo, 'What Self-Governing Peoples Owe to One Another: Universalism, Diversity, and the Law of Peoples' (2004) 72 *Fordham Law Review* 1721, 1725–38; RF Schopp, 'Reconciling Irreconcilable Capital Punishment Doctrine as Comparative and Noncomparative Justice' (2001) 53 *Florida Law Review* 475, 516 [hereinafter Schopp, 'Reconciling']; SR Munzer, *New Essays in the Legal and Political Theory of Property* (Cambridge, Cambridge University Press, 2010) 167. See also RF Schopp, 'Multiple Personality Disorder, Accountable Agency, and Criminal Acts' (2001) 10 *Southern California Interdisciplinary Law Journal* 297, 319 [hereinafter Schopp, 'MPD'] ('The criminal justice system of a liberal society protects equal standing and individual self-determination by proscribing and punishing conduct that violates protected rights and interests.').

[98] See generally Rönnau and Hohn (n 49) side-notes 70–71. See also G Lamond, 'Core Principles of English Criminal Law' in Dyson and Vogel (n 93) 26.

offender's own competing interests.[99] And, so, when a given legal system defines certain knowing and intentional physical contact, such as assault or battery, as morally blameworthy, it will also find that the conduct signifies a substantive break in the above-described relationship of restraint.[100]

Character theorists, in fact, would contend that such an insufficient concern for the interests of others is in itself a blameworthy character trait[101] (though a counter-argument is that this defines the principle domain of criminal law too broadly[102]). And so innocent actors merely err as to the scope of the victim's rights, whereas culpable aggressors who threaten a wrong deny the victims their right to respect.[103] Innocent 'attackers,' in short, do not break the relationship of restraint and do not threaten the equal standing of the defender and the attacker.[104]

For societies to function, then, members of the community must share an organised set of basic attitudes concerning the rights of others – those who knowingly disregard these attitudes are not only liable to receive criminal punishment, but they also expose themselves to the possibility of resistance by those whom they attempt to victimise. To the extent that an attacker acts culpably, he is threatening not only a harm, but he is also threatening a wrong, in that he has disrespected the defender's autonomy and the defender's right to make self-directed decisions.

Laws embodying and reflecting the conventional public morality allow individuals to make universal demands, but also carry with them corresponding obligations. My demand that I not be harmed thus carries with it the obligation that I not harm anyone else. By engaging in criminal behaviour, the individual differentiates himself from the social group; through his wronging of others, the criminal puts himself in a unique position in the group that implies superiority over the other members of the group. No longer an equal, he subjugates his victims, while elevating himself. 'The rights one recognises in others one can demand in others; but we cannot demand from others what we refuse to respect. It is a practical impossibility.'[105]

[99] See generally P Ramsay, 'The Responsible Subject as Citizen: Criminal Law, Democracy and the Welfare State' (2006) 69 *MLR* 29, 45–49; EJ Weinrib, 'Restitutionary Damages as Corrective Justice' (2000) 1 *Theoretical Inquiries in Law Forum* 1, 29; R Eckstein, 'Towards a Communitarian Theory of Responsibility: Bearing the Burden for the Unintended' (1991) 45 *University of Miami Law Review* 843, 844–48.

[100] See generally Rönnau and Hohn (n 49) side-notes 64, 68–73; Lamond (n 98) 26.

[101] Consider in this context the choice-based theories proposed in CO Finkelstein, 'Responsibility for Unintended Consequences' (2005) 2 *Ohio State Journal of Criminal Law* 579. See also M Moore and H Hurd, 'Punishing the Awkward, the Stupid, the Weak, and the Selfish: The Culpability of Negligence' (2011) 5 *Criminal Law & Philosophy* 147.

[102] See, eg, A Duff, 'Choice, Character, and Criminal Liability' (1993) 12 *Law & Philosophy* 345.

[103] See A Brudner, 'Agency and Welfare in the Penal Law' in S Shute et al (eds), *Action and Value in Criminal Law* (Oxford, Oxford University Press, 1996) 32.

[104] See generally Rönnau and Hohn (n 49) side-notes 66–68, 71; Macedo (n 97) 1721, 1725–38; Schopp, 'Reconciling' (n 97) 475, 516; Munzer (n 97) 167; Schopp (n 23) 71–83. See also Schopp, 'MPD' (n 97) 297, 319 ('The criminal justice system of a liberal society protects equal standing and individual self-determination by proscribing and punishing conduct that violates protected rights and interests.'). *Cf* H Frowe, *Defensive Killing* (Oxford, Oxford University Press, 2014) 1–2.

[105] Rousseau (n 85) 28.

If, as argued here, the mutual recognition and acceptance of individual rights is a prerequisite to a functioning legal system and to the development of personal identity and self-fulfilment, then self-defence, along with law enforcement protection, serves to safeguard the individual by preventing unjustified threats against, or intrusions into, his personal domain. The personal sphere, after all, allows one to develop one's personality, and it is believed that individuals develop basic human faculties, such as choice and reasoned decision, only through the exercise of their own autonomy.[106] The right to be free from attacks, then, is central to a liberal society and to the individual's personal development, and self-defence law recognises and protects such freedom in the absence of police protection or other means of avoiding the attack. To the extent that a more non-democratic legal order de-emphasises and disregards the importance of the citizens' personal domain, that order can be expected to more strictly limit the availability of self-defence.

Innocent actors, at bottom merely err as to the scope of the victim's rights. Not so with culpable aggressors. They threaten a wrong by denying the victims their right to respect. By in this manner denying the conceptual basis of rights and of personality as an end, the culpable wrongdoer threatens a unique type of damage to the victim and that precludes him from demanding a precisely proportionate response.

Consider a case in which Andrew knowingly steps onto Victor's land without Victor's consent. We would say that Andrew is subject to criminal prosecution for trespass (and may under certain circumstances have to face defensive force).[107] This is so not because Andrew harmed Victor in any meaningful way, other than perhaps by crushing a few blades of grass. Prosecution, instead, is appropriate because Andrew's conduct reflected a conscious disregard for Victor's right to decide who can step on his land, and the trespass therefore amounts to a wrong.

Assume, finally, that the fully culpable Andrew burglarises Victor's house and steals the stamp collection Victor has painstakingly put together over the years, and has invested his entire life's savings in. It is clear that Andrew's conduct infringes on Victor's autonomy in the sense that Victor's concrete interests are harmed by the theft of his stamp collection, and that Victor is deprived of his discretionary competence in that he no longer is able to decide what to do with the stamp collection. There is indeed a near-universal feeling among victims of crime that they have not only been physically injured or deprived of their property, but that they have also in a sense been 'violated' because another person intentionally violated the victim's personal domain and disrespected the victim's equality and right to non-interference. It is no defence, moreover, for Andrew to claim that he will later

[106] See W Kargl, 'Die Intersubjektive Begründung und Begrenzung der Notwehr' (1998) 110 *Zeitung der Allgemeinen Deutschen Strafrechtswissenschaft* 38, 57–60; FA Hayek, *The Fatal Conceit: The Errors of Socialism* (London, Taylor & Francis, 1988) 62–64 (discussing the impact of the state's respect for the personal domain). See also Leoni (n 87) 93.

[107] Note, however, that under English law the trespass is not a crime, but rather a civil wrong.

sell Victor's stamp collection and give the substantial proceeds to needy children, because, even if Andrew's motives are 'pure,' the theft still manifests Andrew's disrespect of Victor's equal standing and, therefore, wrongs Victor. Wronging as the gravamen of crime may, in short, not be justified on the basis of putative consequential benefits to society or the individual. Of course, the extent of the defensive force authorised will depend on how one assesses the other implicated values – but those like Schopp favouring deadly force in defence of property will almost necessarily have to accord this value significant weight (while those opposing it will tend to devalue it).

Adapting a line of argument developed by Dsouza, and consistent with Lockean notions on the conduct-guiding norms underlying the criminal law,[108] Andrew's disrespect of Victor's property reflects defective 'norm-reasoning' (a disregard for the normative guidance provided by the criminal law – as distinct from 'functional reasoning,' which concerns a person's exercised capacity to observe facts, and, therefrom, reach reasoned factual conclusions and judgements).[109] A person who acts pursuant to poor norm-reasoning acts, either because she inculcates contrary normative values or because she simply opts to ignore them. Either way, she invites blame because she displays an inappropriate attitude towards the normative guidance the law gives all citizens.[110] Character theorists would contend that such an insufficient concern for the interests of others is in itself a blameworthy character trait[111] (though a counter-argument is that this defines the principle domain of criminal law too broadly[112]).

In short, it can be said that a society without self-defence would effectively make the abstract ordering of legal possessions impossible, for all actions within the personal domain would largely be conditioned on whether someone else has a greater interest in (and ability to simply take) the object or benefit. By denying the conceptual basis of rights and of personality as an end, the wrongdoer denies his *own* right to respect, and threatens a unique type of damage to the victim that precludes him from demanding a precisely proportionate response.

There, moreover, is a near-universal feeling among crime victims that they have not only been physically injured or deprived of their property, but that they have also in a sense been emotionally 'violated' because another person intentionally dishonoured the victim's personal domain and disrespected the victim's equality and right to non-interference. In fact, considerable empirical evidence establishes

[108] J Locke, *Two Treatises of Government and a Letter Concerning Toleration* (New York, Dover Publications, 1690/2003) 136–37, 141, 154–55.

[109] See Dsouza (n 45) 24–33. For a more instrumental account of the criminal law that is not based on public condemnation or wronging, but, rather, on the criminal law's 'constitutive function' to condemn structural inequality – described as 'character flaws' of given communities – such as racist violence, gay-bashing, etc, see Dempsey (n 83) 269–70 (defining 'wrongs' as actions that 'the polity must condemn if it is to transform itself').

[110] Dsouza (n 45) 26.

[111] Consider in this context the choice-based theories proposed in Finkelstein (n 101) 579; Moore and Hurd (n 101) 147.

[112] See, eg, Duff (n 102) 345.

that, once victimised, individuals tend to feel vulnerable and become particularly fearful of future victimisation, lending additional support for the claim that culpable attacks pose a unique threat.[113]

But a word of caution is in order. It is important to reiterate that, while an attacker's culpability has the above-stated normative significance, the mere presence of culpability does not allow the victim to 'punish' or exert his 'revenge' (either individually or 'on behalf of society').[114] An attacker's culpability, rather, can be said to be relevant only in the sense that it changes the basic *nature of the threat*; in essence, the culpable attacker is threatening a harm, and he is *also* threatening the defender a wrong that (1) reduces the criminal law's interest in protecting the attacker from a subsequent intrusion into the attacker's personal domain and (2) increases the law's interest in protecting the defender.[115] By threatening such a unique wrong, then, the morally culpable attacker poses a threat to the equal standing of his putative victim which, in turn, shifts the relative, sliding-scale balance of interests and more broadly authorises self-preferential defensive force.[116]

ii. Why Protection of the Socio-Legal Order Is not Treated as a Separate Value

This may be an appropriate point at which to explain why, in this book, I elected to not treat protection of the socio-legal order as an independently cognisable value. It is true that a number of scholars, including Sangero and Kremnitzer,[117]

[113] For some of the long-term effects of criminal victimisation, see generally AJ Lurigio and PA Resick, 'Healing the Psychological Wounds of Criminal Victimization: Predicting Postcrime Distress and Recovery' in AJ Lurigio et al (eds), *Victims of Crime, Problems, Policies, and Programs*, vol 25 (Thousand Oaks, Sage Publications, 1990) 50, 57 (discussing studies showing that burglary victims had a greater tendency to report vulnerability, fear, sleep disturbances, and repetitive thoughts about the victimisation). See also K Rhoades, 'Choice & Trafficking' (2018) 64 *St Louis Business Journal* 30; M Coyle, 'The Transformative Potential of the Truth and Reconciliation Commission: A Skeptic's Perspective' (2017) 95 *Canadian Bar Review* 767, 775; LN Henderson, 'The Wrongs of Victim's Rights' (1985) 37 *Stanford Law Review* 937, 957 ('The intrusiveness of [core] crimes threatens and denies a victim's "personhood," subjecting the victim to devastating psychological consequences.'); B Bettelheim, *Surviving and Other Essays* (London, Thames & Hudson, 1979) 28. See also KF Ferraro, *Fear of Crime: Interpreting Victimization Risk* (Albany, New York University Press, 1995) 120.

[114] See generally Pest (n 37) 144; R Lorca, 'The Presumption of Punishment: A Critical Review of Its Early Modern Origins' (2016) 29 *Canadian Journal of Law and Jurisprudence* 385, 398 n.57.

[115] The *mens rea* justifying criminal punishment under the paradigm advanced here, therefore, is intention or reckless advertence to the excessive risk. While negligent individuals may be liable in tort, they are inappropriate for criminal liability because they cannot be said to have disrespected another's equal standing or to have imputed inequality. See generally Rönnau and Hohn (n 49) side-notes 66–68, 71. This threatened wrong, moreover, lends weight to the argument that third parties have a corollary right to get involved and use force against the attacker in order to protect the defender; that said, and as noted at the outset, the exercise of force to protect third parties it outside of the scope of this book.

[116] See generally Rönnau and Hohn (n 49) side-notes 226–27 (discussing advantages – and disadvantages – of a 'flexible' approach to identifying the limits of self-defence).

[117] See M Kremnitzer, 'Proportionality and the Psychotic Aggressor: Another View' (1983) 18 *Israel Law Review* 178, 181–91, discussed in Sangero, 'New Defense' (n 4) 527–28 ('I agree with Kremnitzer

have followed the German approach[118] of treating protection of the legal order as an independent factor, value, or principle. Sangero, for example, echoes the German approach in that he believes that 'the justification of private defence … is based on the social interest of protection of the public order in general and the legal system in particular.'[119]

While I am certainly not taking the position that protection of the legal order is irrelevant, I maintain that this concept of protecting (or enforcing) 'the law' is already sufficiently accounted for elsewhere in the value-based model. Specifically, the present subsection (value #3) explicitly grounds the value of warding off the imputation of lesser standing on the criminal actor's inherent disrespect for the legally recognised rights of his victim (and authorises the defender to use force to prevent this imputation). Value #1, in turn, seeks to promote collective violence-reduction by limiting individual self-defence to those cases in which the state, through its law enforcement organs, is unable to protect the person being attacked.[120] Value #4, moreover, authorises force to protect the defender's legally recognised right to autonomy,[121] value #6 seeks to avoid outcomes that could undermine the perceived moral legitimacy of the legal order,[122] and value #7 concerns deterring future violations of the law.[123] Considering this back-drop, the interests reflected in these four free-standing values infuse the concept of 'protection of the socio-legal order' with its substance.[124] While I, therefore, recognise that it is possible to try to unify these different legal-order-protecting interests under one umbrella term, the position advanced is that those interests are dispersed throughout these different values. Developing 'protection of the socio-legal order' as a separate value is, therefore, not necessary in this analytical framework.

that the protection of the socio-legal order is immense[ly] important for the justification of private defense.'). See also K Ghanayim and MS-A Wattad, 'Reconsidering the Grounds and the Causing Conditions for the Necessity Defense: Between Justification and Excuse – A Comprehensive Study' (2017) 86 *University of Missouri at Kansas City Law Review* 111, 138; L Levanon, 'Criminal Punishment as a Restorative Practice' (2015) 18 *New York Criminal Law Review* 537, 568; NM Omichinski, 'Applying the Theories of Justifiable Homicide to Conflicts in the Doctrine of Self-Defense' (1987) 33 *Wayne Law Review* 1447, 1459–60, citing Fletcher, *Rethinking* (n 29) 869.

[118] See generally ch 5(II)(A).

[119] Sangero, *Self-Defence* (n 4) 67. See also ch 5(II). This perspective finds support in communitarian and civic republican literature (two closely related, though not entirely overlapping, schools of thought) which emphasises that civic virtue is a republic's lifeblood; without a citizenry that is ready and willing to take an active part in defending the government (and, relatedly, the rule of law), even a mixed constitution will fail. See generally R Dagger, 'Communitarianism and Republicanism' in GF Gaus and C Kukathas (eds), *Handbook of Political Theory* (Thousand Oaks, Sage Publications, 2014) 170–71.

[120] See ch 2(IV)(A).

[121] See ch 2(IV)(D).

[122] See ch 2(IV)(F).

[123] See ch 2(IV)(G). While, as noted, values #2, #3, and #4 concern private/relational harm against the victim, the society's more general right to remain free from violence are most directly addressed in this value (value #7) as well as in value #1.

[124] See, eg, Fletcher, *Rethinking* (n 29) 869 ('[T]he autonomy of the individual is identified with the sanctity of the Legal Order.'). See also Sangero, *Self-Defence* (n 4) 68 (discussing, in the context of 'protection of the socio-legal order,' self-defence's impact on 'deterring offenders and preventing offences').

D. Value #4: Protecting the Defender's Autonomy

Summary Justification for Including:

This Value: Related to the concept of safeguarding the equal standing between people is the value of protecting the defender's autonomy.[125] An individual's exercise of autonomous rights (including the right to self-directed action, to a personal sphere, and to own property) can be instrumentally closely related to his pursuit of self-fulfilment. The personal sphere, in turn, allows one to develop one's personality. The modern liberal state accords free people equal standing in the public sphere (see value #3) and, relatedly, strives to ensure that people have a private domain of non-public life in which they are given the opportunity to exercise their own comprehensive moral doctrines, and to develop their own conceptions of the good.

Tension with, or Support for, the Other Values:

Protection of the defender's autonomy arguably is the primary function of self-defence. That said, a defender's interest in protecting her autonomy is not absolute and must at times yield to the competing interests of reducing overall societal violence by protecting the state's monopoly on force (value #1), protecting the attacker's presumptive right to life (value #2), and ensuring the primacy of the legal process (value #5). In contrast, maintaining the equal standing between people (value #3) and deterrence (value #7) tend to mutually support this value. Maintaining the legitimacy of the legal order (value #6), on the other hand, can once again be negatively impacted by an under- or over-weighting of the instant value.

Limitations:

Protecting equal standing (value #3) is only implicated in the context of *culpable* attackers. In contrast, protecting the defender's autonomy (admittedly a bit of a catch-all term that is defined here as including the defender's legally protected private sphere, personal sovereignty, personal domain, and right to non-interference) can apply to both culpable *and* non-culpable attackers – though this book contends that a culpable attack poses a greater, normatively distinguishable threat to a defender's autonomy than an innocent one.

As the term '*self*-defence' implies, protecting the threatened defender's autonomy grounds self-defence.[126] That said, and as recognised both by the violence-reducing

[125] In fact, some could argue that the discussion of protecting the autonomy of defenders should be subsumed within the preceding approach towards safeguarding the equal standing of citizens, *see* ch 2(IV)(C), since individual autonomy can be said to be part and parcel of equal standing. While that argument has some appeal, the decision made here is to give them separate treatment since protection of the defender's autonomy can be said to be a sufficiently distinct value as to justify such individualised treatment.

[126] See Sangero, *Self-Defence* (n 4) 67–73. As noted, while the Value-Based Model has broad application and could be used to address defence of others' situations, a full analysis of defence of others is outside of the scope of the instant undertaking.

function of self-defence (value #1) and the understanding that even culpable attackers have a right to life (value #2), life in modern society necessarily entails that citizens must at times tolerate certain intrusions into their autonomy in order to advance broader welfarist objectives.[127] If, as argued here, the mutual recognition and acceptance of individual rights is a prerequisite to a functioning legal system, then self-defence must safeguard the individual by preventing *unjustified* (as determined by weighting this value against the others) threats against, or intrusions into, his personal domain when equally effective state protection is unavailable.[128]

i. The Personal Domain Is Important …

Continuing the discussion started in Chapter 2(IV)(C) with value #3 (ensuring equal standing among individuals), an ordered modern society must afford some room for individual expression within each person's personal domain.[129] Without such a protected personal domain 'we are thrown back on the sort of structure found in the mob, in which everybody is free to express himself against some hated object of the group.'[130] Raz agrees that 'the promotion and protection of personal autonomy are the core of the liberal concern for liberty.'[131] The UN has in fact long recognised personal autonomy as a fundamental human right.[132]

Nozick posits that only a person who has the ability to shape his own life in accordance with some overall plan, has – or can strive for – a meaningful life.[133] A liberal state must, therefore, accord free people generally equal standing in the public sphere (value #3), but as reflected by value #4 must also ensure that people have a private, autonomous domain of non-public life.[134]

My description of this value, and its focus on the defender's personal autonomy, is not, however, meant to devalue the attacker's legitimate interests. Instead, the

[127] See generally Erb (n 82) side-note 87; RM Ackerman, 'Communitarianism and the Roberts Court' (2017) 45 *Florida State University Law Review* 59, 87. See also GP Fletcher, 'Domination in the Theory of Justification and Excuse' (1996) 57 *University of Pittsburgh Law Review* 553, 556.

[128] See generally GP Fletcher, 'The Nature of Justification' in S Shute et al (eds), *Action and Value in Criminal Law* (Oxford, Oxford University Press, 1993) 175, 181; GP Fletcher, 'Punishment and Self-Defense' (1989) 8 *Law & Philosophy* 201, 210, 213–15.

[129] *Cf* R Washburn, 'The Decline of Authority' (1927) 32 *Commercial Law League Journal* 229, 230.

[130] G H Mead, *Mind, Self, and Society* (Chicago, University of Chicago Press, 1967) 221.

[131] J Raz, *The Morality of Freedom* (Oxford, Oxford University Press, 1986) 203–04.

[132] See generally UN Declaration (n 38) Arts 12, 13, 20, 22, and 29; ECHR, Nov 4, 1950, ETS No. 005 (n 38) Arts 1, 8, and 11. See also Kargl (n 106) 57–60; W von Humboldt, *The Limits of State Action* (Indianapolis, Liberty Fund, 1993) 12–13; Hayek (n 106) 62–64 (discussing the impact of the state's respect for the personal domain); Leoni (n 87) 93; Mead (n 130) 221.

[133] R Nozick, *Anarchy, State, and Utopia* (New York, Ingram Publisher Services, 1974) 31. See generally Rönnau and Hohn (n 49) side-note 64.

[134] See generally Rawls (n 6) 139, discussed in A Ripstein, 'Tort Law in Liberal State' (2007) 1 *Journal of Tort Law* 1, 9. See also B Ackerman, *Social Justice in the Liberal State* (New Haven, Yale University Press, 1981) 11–12, 347–378.

value more narrowly focuses on safeguarding the defender's rights.[135] One impact of unjustified attacks (whether culpable or non-culpable) is that they breach the sphere of autonomy enjoyed by everyone – and culpable attacks, as noted above, also uniquely threaten the broader legal order.[136]

ii. … But Autonomy Cannot Be Absolute

The position advanced immediately above is that a person's autonomous sphere has value and is, therefore, something the criminal law must protect (including through law relating to self-defence). That said, like all rights, the right to autonomy is not limitless.

Raz has noted the difficulties with the positions taken by 'pure individualists,' such as Kant and Nozick, who he believes ignore the reciprocal reasonable limitations on autonomy.[137] The UN in its Universal Declaration of Human Rights has similarly observed that, in the context of development of individual personality, '[e]veryone has duties to the community.'[138] Indeed, paying taxes, driving to the speed limit, appearing for jury duty, and countless other restrictions on our autonomous activities demonstrate that, in modern liberal democracies (and, for that matter, in non-modern society), our individual desires must frequently yield to broader social interests.[139]

It would, therefore, be odd if self-defence was the only area of human endeavour where a person was permitted to ignore all other societal considerations and could act in a purely self-interested and self-directed manner without regard for the attendant external costs of such action.[140] Stated differently, while self-defence obviously plays the herein-discussed important role in ordered society, the criminal law must provide even the fully culpable attacker's autonomy with some (albeit reduced) level of protection because the law concerns itself with protecting the

[135] See generally RF Schopp, 'Verdicts of Conscience: Nullification and Necessity as Jury Responses to Crimes of Conscience' (1996) 69 *Southern California Law Review* 2039, 2070; J Feinberg, *Harm to Self* (New York, Oxford University Press, 1986) 52–70. See also J Nedelsky, *Law's Relations: A Relational Theory of Self, Autonomy, and Law* (New York, Oxford University Press, 2013) 19–27.

[136] See generally Rönnau and Hohn (n 49) side-notes 64–66; C Fehr, 'Self-Defence and the Constitution' (2017) 43 *Queen's Law Journal* 85, 96–98; Sangero, 'New Defense' (n 4) 552–53; Omichinski (n 117) 1459–60.

[137] Raz (n 131) 273–74. See also A Ripstein, *Force and Freedom: Kant's Legal and Political Philosophy* (Cambridge, Mass, Harvard University Press, 2009) 399.

[138] See generally UN Declaration (n 38) Art 29.

[139] See generally CV Ward, 'Restoring Fairness to Campus Sex Tribunals' (2018) 85 *Tennessee Law Review* 1073, 1105–08; Erb (n 82) side-note 215; T Dagan, 'The Currency of Taxation' (2016) 84 *Fordham Law Review* 2537, 2558–59. *Cf* JS Mill, *On Liberty and Utilitarianism* (New York, Bantam Doubleday Dell Publishing Group, 1993) 143–50, discussed in J Chapman, 'Doomsday: A Look at the Ethical Issues Behind the Government's Coercive Powers in Response to a Public Health Nightmare' (2008) 9 *Journal of Law and Social Challenges* 24, 35–37.

[140] See generally SD Smith, 'Is the Harm Principle Illiberal' (2006) 51 *American Journal Of Jurisprudence* 1, 4–14; CR Sunstein and RH Thaler, 'Libertarian Paternalism Is Not an Oxymoron' (2003) 70 *University of Chicago Law Review* 1159, 1167–71; JS Mill, *On Liberty and Other Writings* (Cambridge, Cambridge University Press, 1989) 11.

well-being of *all* people.[141] That said, it is recognised that there will be disagreement on precisely where the boundary should be drawn (indeed, the resolution of this core challenge is what the value-based model seeks to make more explicit). As the thematic literature review in Chapter 3 illustrates, even though the value of protecting the defender's autonomy is almost universally recognised, there is far less agreement on how it should function when in tension with competing values (and, for that matter, on what values are in fact 'competing').

E. Value #5: Ensuring the Primacy of the Legal Process

Summary Justification for Including This Value:

Due process is the cornerstone of modern, pluralistic legal systems. And, as noted, self-defence must not become a substitute for the legal process, lest it undermine the primacy of the legal process. Consistent with value #1, the system's interest in due process signals that, in the type of conflict-of-rights situation created in self-defence scenarios, the state should, if possible, determine guilt or innocence, administer punishment, and determine restitution. And even in the case of morally innocent attackers who would not be appropriate for criminal sanction, or situations where only property rights are at issue, systemic interests lean in favour of letting the courts (in such cases, the civil courts) resolve disputes and affix blame. Consequently, instances of private use of self-preferential force should be carefully circumscribed.

Tension with, or Support for, the Other Values:

This value supports the proposition that, all other things being equal, societies prefer to have disputes settled in court, rather than through the exercise of self-preferential force. As such, this value is most closely aligned with protection of the state's monopoly on force (value #1), protection of the individual attacker (value #2), and maintenance of the legitimacy of the legal order (value #6). Warding off the imputation of unequal standing (value #3), protection of the defender (value #4), and deterrence (value #7) are, all other things being equal, more likely to be antagonistic to, and therefore in tension with, this value.

Limitations:

This value is only implicated in cases where (1) resort to the legal process is a realistic possibility and (2) the rights threatened are generally compensable. That is, in those cases where the attacker threatens death or serious bodily injury, resort to the legal process is unable to prevent or remedy the damage. In such cases, this decision-ground carries far less weight.

[141] See generally Leverick (n 2) 3; Erb (n 82) side-notes 217–23. *Cf* Creach (n 45) 672 ('Self-defense represents legally sanctioned vigilante action.').

As observed with value #1 (collective violence-reduction/monopoly on force), in a liberal society, law and (unsanctioned and unjustified) private violence are often viewed as presumptively antagonistic (though as our discussion of German law will show, and common sense teaches, there certainly can be situations in which private violence is, in fact, supportive of the respect for, and adherence to, the law).[142] Law serves to minimise violence in society while concurrently striving to be no more coercive than necessary.[143] Unjustified and unsanctioned violence, on the other hand, is disruptive and undermines organised society and threatens the legal order. This is one reason that having the ability to resort to the available legal process to resolve disputes is considered a fundamental human right – and why necessity should not be the only limitation on a defender's exercise of self-preferential force.[144] This value (like the collective interest in minimising violence (value #1) and the individual attacker's right to life (value #2)) is, therefore, in tension with the preceding value's focus on the defender's autonomy (value #4). For if the defender's autonomy were the only interest of concern, then a defender would, in fact, be permitted to deploy all force necessary to prevent any intrusion into it.

i. Another Argument against Unfettered 'Self-Help'

Based on the foregoing discussion, I will assume relatively broad agreement that society has a powerful collective interest in thoughtfully circumscribing the situations in which citizens are permitted to use private violence against each other (though disagreement over the precise boundaries will, as noted, surely persist). The criminal justice system, for example, must delicately balance the citizen's right to safety (and the use of self-defence to ensure protection of the defender's autonomy (value #4)) against its commitment to maintaining a stable society that punishes only after affording the accused due process, and that does not tolerate vigilante law enforcement or acts of revenge that threaten to undermine the legitimacy of the legal order (generally, values #5 and #6).[145]

To the extent possible, then, the justice system must promote the resolution of disputes in the courts. Vigilantism and similar unauthorised 'self-help'

[142] See generally JY Kim, 'The Rhetoric of Self-Defense' (2008) 13 *Berkeley Journal of Criminal Law* 261, 290; Whitman (n 41) 903; A Sarat and T Kearns, 'A Journey Through Forgetting: Toward a Jurisprudence of Violence' in A Sarat and TR Kearns (eds), *The Fate of Law* (Ann Arbor, University of Michigan Press, 1993) 209, 212; Cover (n 54) 1613. See also ch 2(IV)(C)(ii) (discussing why the value-based model does not treat protecting the socio-legal order as a stand-alone value).

[143] See generally Schwirck (n 54) 81.

[144] See generally UN Declaration (n 38) Arts 6, 7, 8, and 11; ECHR, Nov 4, 1950, ETS No. 005 (n 38) Arts 1 and 13.

[145] See generally HL Hart, *The Concept of Law* (Oxford, Oxford University Press, 1994) 1 (providing a comprehensive discussion of the function of the law); L Nader, 'The Anthropological Study of Law' in P Sack and J Aleck (eds), *Law and Anthropology* (New York, New York University Press, 1992) 3 (same, but from an anthropological perspective); H Kantorowicz, *The Definition of Law* (Octagon Press Ltd, 1980) 1 (same, but discussing the law's function).

crime-control options, in contrast, seek to wrest from the liberal state – that has not authorised private violence in aid of ensuring law-abidingness – the authority to punish and condemn, and threaten to incrementally push society toward non-democratic lawlessness.[146]

ii. Why Ensuring the Primacy of the Legal Process and Maintaining the Legitimacy of the Legal Order Are Not Coextensive Values

One may wonder why ensuring the primacy of the legal process (value #5) is not subsumed within the to-be-discussed value-based decision-ground of maintaining the legitimacy of the legal order (value #6). The answer is that the value of maintaining the legitimacy of the legal order, as it will be defined here, is only implicated in cases when the defensive conduct under consideration, or the proposed limitation of such conduct, is so far outside the bounds of the fully expressed public morality[147] that it threatens to undermine the law's very moral authority in the sense of public respect.[148] Such cases will necessarily (one hopes) be relatively rare – but, nevertheless, it is a particularly important value to consider in self-defence cases given the unusually intense amount of public scrutiny they often receive.[149]

As noted, ensuring primacy of the legal process seeks to reasonably avoid self-help options by presumptively relying on the judicial forum to adjudicate disputes, address losses to person or property, and impose punishment. In this sense, this value is in most direct tension with the value of protecting the defender's

[146] See generally D Markel, 'Retributive Justice and the Demands of Democratic Citizenship' (2012) 1 *Virginia Journal of Criminal Law* 1, 33; S Uniacke, 'Self-Defense and Natural Law' (1991) 36 *American Journal of Jurisprudence* 73, 79. See also K Bilz, 'The Puzzle of Delegated Revenge' (2007) 87 *Boston University Law Review* 1059, 1101; W Gossett, 'The Rule of Law or the Defiance of Law' (1969) 55 *American Bar Association Journal* 823, 824.

[147] More fully articulated in ch 2(IV)(F)(ii).

[148] See generally SE Clark et al, 'Legitimacy, Procedural Justice, Accuracy, and Eyewitness Identification' (2018) 8 *UC Irvine Law Review* 41, 61–66; Bottoms & Tankebe (n 81) 120; TR Tyler and J Fagan, 'Legitimacy and Cooperation: Why Do People Help the Police Fight Crime in Their Communities?' (2008–09) 6 *Ohio State Journal of Criminal Law* 231, 233; TR Tyler, 'Procedural Justice, Legitimacy, and the Effective Rule of Law' (2003) 30 *Crime & Justice* 283, 283–357 [hereinafter Tyler, 'Procedural Justice']; TR Tyler, 'Trust and Law Abidingness: A Proactive Model of Social Regulation' (2001) 81 *Boston University Law Review* 361, 378 [hereinafter Tyler, 'Trust and Law Abidingness']; TR Tyler, *Why People Obey the Law* (New Haven, Yale University Press, 1990) 20–26, 161–65 [hereinafter Tyler, *Obey*]. See also S Kadish, 'Some Observations on the Use of Criminal Sanctions in Enforcing Economic Regulations' (1963) 30 *University of Chicago Law Review* 423, discussed in J Coffee, 'Hush: The Criminal Status of Confidential Information After McNally and Carpenter and the Enduring Problem of Overcriminalization' (1988) 26 *American Criminal Law Review* 121, 148.

[149] See generally M E Castillo, 'Florida's Stand Your Ground Regime: Legislative Direction, Prosecutorial Discretion, Public Pressures, and the Legitimization of the Criminal Justice System' (2016) 42 *Journal of Legislation* 101, 101–02 https://heinonline.org/HOL/P?h=hein.journals/jleg42&i=90.

autonomy interests (value #4). So if the above-described (and below-analysed) German farmer recognised one of our youthful fruit thieves or otherwise had the ability to use the legal process to seek the return of, or compensation for, the stolen fruit, then his decision to shoot the thieves in order to guarantee that his apples are not stolen would be further undermined (including because the force under these circumstances was not 'necessary' to ensure that he was not permanently deprived of the fruit, even though it was necessary to prevent the instant attack on his property). Because in liberal democracies the criminal justice system is responsible for punishment,[150] instances of claimed self-defence must be carefully scrutinised to confirm that legal process options were not reasonably available.

F. Value #6: Maintaining the Legitimacy of the Legal Order

i. Summary Justification for Including This Value

A longer-term, and frequently discussed, objective of a functioning criminal justice system is that the populace respects it and considers it legitimate. A criminal justice system's proscriptions and defences can, sociologically speaking at least, be fairly described as the formal embodiment of a set of elementary moral values (usually those of the group dominant in political authority) in an official edict. These values, in turn, are reinforced with exceptions (defences) and an official penal sanction. A functioning justice system must, therefore, embody widely held moral standards of right and wrong (that is, it must reflect – or at least come close to reflecting – what has already been termed the 'fully expressed public morality').[151] As procedural justice theory teaches, a justice system that in this manner enjoys popular support is able to more effectively draw on the stigmatic effect of conviction to reinforce basic moral standards and encourage compliance.

[150] See generally AE Addae, 'Challenging the Constitutionality of Private Prisons: Insights from Israel' (2019) 25 *William & Mary Journal of Race, Gender, and Social Justice* 527, 549–52; Markel (n 146) 38–43, discussed in D Gray, 'Retributivism, Confrontation, and the Death Penalty: Some Skepticism About Dan Markel's Skepticism' (2018) 51 *Texas Technical Law Review* 1, 11; PH Robinson, 'The Ongoing Revolution in Punishment Theory: Doing Justice as Controlling Crime' (2010) 42 *Arizona State Law Journal* 1089, 1089–90.

[151] 'Public morality,' as used herein, refers to the moral and ethical standards enforced in a society, whether through law enforcement, social pressure, or otherwise. See generally RP George, 'The Concept of Public Morality' (2000) 45 *American Journal of Jurisprudence* 17, 19; HL Hart, 'Social Solidarity and the Enforcement of Morality' (1967) 35 *University of Chicago Law Review* 1, 1–13; JR Gusfield, 'Moral Passage: The Symbolic Process in Public Designations of Deviance' (1967) 15 *Social Problems* 175, 175–88. The concept of violations of the criminal law reflecting successive levels of substantive and procedural societal condemnation is discussed by, among others, R Schopp in his book *Justification Defenses and Just Convictions* (n 23) 30–31 (discussing the 'fully-articulated conventional morality').

Of course, universal acceptance is not (and, realistically, probably cannot be) the hallmark of effective legislative efforts. But to the extent the community perceives the law as noticeably deviating from its shared (and publicly recognised) conceptions of bedrock 'justice,' the law's moral credibility will be undercut. The result is a diminution of the law's legitimacy (in the sense of moral authority) and, derivatively, its ability to effectively fulfil its crime-control and conduct-guiding functions. Stated differently, when the justice system accepts laws or enforcement actions that corrosively clash with the fully expressed public morality on basic issues of right and wrong, the entire justice system may suffer.

Placing these more generalised observations in the self-defence framework, to maintain the criminal law's moral authority and corresponding popular legitimacy, the justice system's range of permissible defensive force outcomes must not drastically deviate from the community's perceptions of 'just results.' For even though political liberalism may be premised on a plurality of reasonable moral doctrines, there is a limit to what a free democratic regime bound by the majority principle can tolerate.

ii. Tension with, or Support for, the Other Values

Maintaining the legitimacy of the legal order is another value that can be viewed (and weighted) very differently depending on one's perspective. And so those who tend to place greater significance on the equal standing between people (value #3), protecting the defender (value #4), and deterrence (value #7) can be expected to object to outcomes that they consider too deferential toward collective violence reduction (value #1), protection of the attacker (value #2), and ensuring the primacy of the legal process (value #5). Of course, the same is true in the opposite direction. But while disagreement with outcomes is unavoidable, reaching results that shake people's fundamental confidence in the moral legitimacy of the legal order are the ones that implicate value #6.

iii. Limitations

This decision-ground is, as noted, only implicated in the relatively rare cases where the contemplated outcome is so at odds with the fully expressed public morality that it threatens to erode the criminal law's popular legitimacy. An example of such a rare case could be if the courts, say, adopted a Schoppian approach and authorised deadly force to defend against a teenager threatening trivial property interests. Alternatively, the legislature could follow Leverick's lead by making deadly defensive force unavailable in cases of serious bodily injury or rape at the hands of a culpable attacker because of a narrow focus on value #2 (protecting the attacker's right to life). Unlike the other values, then, maintaining the legitimacy of the legal order is framed in terms of *avoiding* certain outcomes (that is, avoiding erosion of the justice system's popular authority).

iv. Legitimacy and Procedural Justice

Trust and legitimacy, both central to ensuring the moral authority of the law,[152] dominate contemporary discussions of procedural justice.[153] Social psychology has produced extensive literature on the central concept that, to be considered *legitimate*, the public must collectively believe that 'authorities, institutions, and social arrangements are appropriate, proper, and just.'[154] To be *effective*, on the other hand, 'legal rules and decisions must be obeyed.'[155] The procedural justice perspective is that, when compared to punishment, deterrence, or other external incentives, internalised feelings of legitimacy and trust are more potent and longer lasting.[156] As Tyler frames it, the public's 'law-related behaviour [is] powerfully influenced by people's subjective judgements' about the system's fairness.[157] And so, when the system is viewed as achieving unfair results, '[t]his undermines [the legal order's] legitimacy.'[158]

Identifying an agreed-upon definition of 'legitimacy' is challenging.[159] Sociologists and psychologists focus on people's attitudes towards authority.[160]

[152] Raz (n 131) 400–01.

[153] See generally Clark et al (n 148) 61–66; S Cody and A Koenig, 'Procedural Justice in Transnational Contexts' (2018) 58 *Virginia Journal of International Law* 1, 8–11; EJ Miller, 'Encountering Resistance: Contesting Policing and Procedural Justice' [2016] *University of Chicago Legal Forum* 295, 356; K Murphy et al, 'Motivating Compliance Behavior Among Offenders: Procedural Justice or Deterrence?' (2016) 43 *Criminal Justice & Behavior* 102, 103; Bottoms and Tankebe (n 81) 120; J Jackson et al, *Just Authority?: Trust in the Police in England and Wales* (Cullompton, Taylor & Francis, 2012) 1; Tyler and Fagan (n 148) 233; Tyler, 'Procedural Justice' (n 148) 283–357; Tyler, 'Trust and Law Abidingness' (n 148) 378; Tyler, *Obey* (n 148) 20–26, 161–65. Perceived 'procedural injustice,' in contrast, has been said to contribute to increased public support for violent self-help mechanisms, including vigilante violence. See generally J Tankebe, 'Self-Help, Policing, and Procedural Justice: Ghanaian Vigilantism and the Rule of Law' (2009) 43 *Law & Society Review* 245, 270. Note that the term 'procedural justice' is a broad concept that encompasses both the quality of decision-making and outcomes, as well as the more process-based quality of treatment. See Bottoms and Tankebe (n 81) 145. This book will focus on the former (outcomes) more than on the latter (procedure).

[154] TR Tyler, 'Psychological Perspectives on Legitimacy and Legitimation' (2006) 57 *Annual Review of Psychology* 375, 375–400. See also Cody and Koenig (n 153) 9–11; M Boone and M Kox, 'Neutrality as an Element of Perceived Justice in Prison: Consistency Versus Individualization' (2014) 10 *Utrecht Law Review* 118; I Loader and R Sparks, 'Unfinished Business: Legitimacy, Crime Control, and Democratic Politics' in J Tankebe and A Liebling (eds), *Legitimacy and Criminal Justice: An International Exploration* (Oxford, Oxford University Press, 2013) 105–26; LB Solum, 'Procedural Justice' (2004) 78 *Southern California Law Review* 181, 265.

[155] TR Tyler, 'Public Mistrust of the Law: A Political Perspective' (1998) 66 *University of Cincinnati Law Review* 847, 856.

[156] See Miller (n 153) 356; Tyler, 'Procedural Justice' (n 148) 283–84. See also M Dyson and B Vogel, 'Reflections on Criminal Law in England and Germany' in Dyson and Vogel (n 93) 563–64.

[157] Tyler, 'Procedural Justice' (n 148) 284.

[158] Ibid at 287; R Sparks et al, *Prisons and the Problem of Order* (Oxford, Oxford University Press, 1996) 2, discussed in Bottoms and Tankebe (n 81) 121, 131–32.

[159] See generally D Beetham, *The Legitimation of Power* (MacMillan Education, 2013) 34 (discussing differences between the legal, philosophical, and sociological meanings of 'legitimacy'). See also Bottoms and Tankebe (n 81) 124–32; J Raz, *Between Authority and Interpretation: On the Theory of Law and Practical Reason* (Oxford, Oxford University Press, 2009) 128; M Weber, *Economy and Society: An Outline of Interpretive Sociology* (Berkeley, University of California Press, 1978) 53–56, 215.

[160] Bottoms and Tankebe (n 81) 129. See also Beetham (n 159) 20; Tyler, 'Procedural Justice' (n 148) 307–08; Weber (n 159) 31–36.

From this perspective, legitimacy, rather than being dictated by a single transaction, 'is more like a perpetual discussion, in which the content of the power-holders' later claims will be affected by the nature of the audience response.'[161]

Normative legitimacy, on the other hand, is a moral and political concept. It is intertwined with the idea that the legal authority has a right – indeed, a moral right – to regulate conduct or issue directives, and requires that the process is (morally or politically) fair or just or lawful.[162] Legal legitimacy, which can be considered a species of normative legitimacy, requires that authority be exercised according to legally valid rules.[163] Finally, democratic legitimacy requires an authority that allows its subjects to participate in the decision-making process and that also is genuinely responsive to their interests.[164]

Procedural justice, as discussed here in the main, concerns itself with sociological and psychological creditworthiness (that is, how people *feel* about authorities and the broader criminal justice system) rather than democratic or normative legitimacy (which focuses on whether the authority's actions are, in fact, lawful or responsive or justified). Social science research has, in fact, raised doubts about the once-popular notion that legislators can effectively deter crime purely by manipulating the universe of criminal proscriptions or by increasing punishment.[165]

Value #6's more modest goal, then, is to avoid self-defence cases that discourage three desirable and interlinked general behaviours among the public, namely, compliance with the law, cooperation with legal authorities, and support for the empowerment of the law.[166] And, to this point, research has consistently demonstrated that '[t]he loss of popular legitimacy for the criminal justice system produces disastrous consequences for the system's performance. If citizens do not trust the system, they will not use it.'[167]

[161] Bottoms and Tankebe (n 81) 129.

[162] See, eg, Joseph Raz, 'Legitimate Authority' in *The Authority of Law* (2009) 3–4. *See also* Miller (n 153) 358; Bottoms and Tankebe (n 81) 131–32.

[163] See Miller (n 153) 356.

[164] Ibid at 357.

[165] E Osborne, *Self-Regulation and Human Progress: How Society Gains When We Govern Less* (Palo Alto, Stanford University Press, 2018) ch 2.

[166] See Tyler, 'Procedural Justice' (n 148) 290, 310–18.

[167] See M Moore, 'Legitimizing Criminal Justice Policies and Practices' [1997] 66 *FBI Law Enforcement Bulletin* 14, 17, quoted in Tyler, 'Procedural Justice' (n 148) 292–97 (discussing research on procedural justice). See also Bottoms and Tankebe (n 81) 154–55, 160–68 (discussing legitimacy studies and calling for more empirical work); R Hollander-Blumoff, 'The Psychology of Procedural Justice in the Federal Courts' (2011) 63 *Hastings Law Journal* 127, 134–37, cited in P Foohey, 'Jevic's Promise: Procedural Justice in Chapter 11' (2018) 93 *Washington Law Review Online* 128, 142 (canvassing procedural justice research); R Hollander-Blumoff and Tom R Tyler, 'Procedural Justice and the Rule of Law: Fostering Legitimacy in Alternative Dispute Resolution' [2011] *Journal of Dispute Resolution* 1, 3–4 (examining research about the effects of people's perceptions of procedural justice); J Darley et al, 'Enacting Justice: The Interplay of Individual and Institutional Perspectives' in MA Hogg and J Cooper (eds), *The Sage Handbook of Social Psychology* (Thousand Oaks, Sage Publications, 2003) 458–76; D Beetham, *The Legitimation of Power* (Amherst, Prometheus Books, 1991) 3–114; M Hoffman, 'Moral Internalization: Current Theory and Research' in L Berkowitz (ed) *Advances in Experimental Social Psychology*, vol 10 (San Diego, Elsevier Science Publishing, 1977) 85, 85–133.

Perceived *injustice* in a self-defence outcome, in short, can seriously (though typically only incrementally) undermine the perceived trustworthiness of the broader criminal justice system.[168] And this can lead to the justice system rendering itself unable to safeguard the fundamental human rights discussed throughout this chapter.[169]

v. *The Value-Based Model's Eight Stages of Condemnation Lead to the 'Fully Expressed Public Morality'*

The discussion that follows addresses the ongoing debate over whether self-defence should be considered a justification or excuse (or neither).[170] Specifically, this book will deconstruct, from an Anglo-American procedural perspective, how a person can be said to violate the 'fully expressed public morality.' This, in turn, will help us better understand the procedural justice view that widely rejected self-defence decisions can adversely impact the broader public's view of the legitimacy of the legal order. The analysis, moreover, offers additional reasons for why maintaining the legitimacy of the legal order (value #6) deserves a place within the value-based model of self-defence.

a. Additional Comments on Condemnation and the Criminal Justice System

Criminal justice systems punish by inflicting hard treatment on those who provably failed to abide by certain rules or commands relating to proscribed conduct.[171] Self-defence outcomes that are broadly rejected as immoral threaten to incrementally erode the justice system's moral credibility, undermine compliance with the law, and reduce cooperation with legal authorities.[172] And, to this point, research has consistently demonstrated that '[t]he loss of popular legitimacy for the criminal justice system produces disastrous consequences for the system's performance. If citizens do not trust the system, they will not use it.'[173]

[168] Cody and Koenig (n 153) 24; M Van Craen and WG Skogan, 'Trust in the Belgian Police: The Importance of Responsiveness' (2015) 12 *European Journal of Criminology* 129, 145; Tankebe (n 153) 252; D De Cremer and TR Tyler, 'The Effects of Trust in Authority and Procedural Fairness on Cooperation' (2007) 92 *Journal of Applied Psychology* 639, 640.

[169] See, eg, UN Declaration (n 38) Arts 1, 2, 3, 6, 7, 8, 10, 11, 12, 13, 17, 20, 22, and 29; ECHR, Nov 4, 1950, ETS No. 005 (n 38) Arts 2, 5, 6, 8, 11, and 13.

[170] See generally G Gaggioli, 'Human Rights and Personal Self-Defense in International Law' (2017) 18 *Melbourne Journal of International Law* 460, 464. For a fuller discussion of this topic, see ch 4(I).

[171] See generally HM Hart, Jr., 'The Aims of the Criminal Law' (1958) 23 *Law & Contemporary Problems* 401, 403–05.

[172] See Tyler, 'Procedural Justice' (n 148) 290, 310–18.

[173] See Moore (n 167) 17, quoted in Tyler, 'Procedural Justice' (n 148) 292–97 (discussing research on procedural justice). See also Bottoms and Tankebe (n 81) 154–55, 160–68 (discussing legitimacy studies and calling for more empirical work); Hollander-Blumoff (n 167) 134–37, cited in Foohey (n 167) 142 (canvassing procedural justice research); Hollander-Blumoff and Tyler (n 167) 3–4 (examining research about the effects of people's perceptions of procedural justice); Darley (n 167) 458–76; Beetham (n 167) 3–114; Hoffman (n 167) 85–133.

But understanding the meaning of a conviction on a deeper level requires analysis beyond the observation that the criminal justice system 'condemns' that conduct and that bad outcomes can erode respect for the system. To provide additional clarity on these modalities of operation, this book endeavours to (in summary form) deconstruct the criminal conviction. Specifically, it will be suggested that an individual must pass through the eight distinct stages of legal (as well as, consequently, moral) evaluation before he can be punished criminally as (1) a fully culpable actor who (2) has violated the integrated set of provisions that constitute the criminal law.

In brief, the first such stage is institutional, in that the criminal justice system *defines* certain *conduct* as condemnable. The second through eight stages, on the other hand, are applied by the prosecutor, judge, or jury in the process of allocating institutional condemnation to a *particular defendant*.[174] The position tested here is whether, to deserve criminal punishment in a liberal criminal justice system, a defendant must pass through *all eight* evaluative stages.

b. Stage One: Defining the Partially Expressed Public Morality

Legislators (and, to a lesser extent, the courts) are charged with the task of creating offence definitions that designate certain conduct as 'criminal.'[175] They, in so doing, transform a broad prohibitory norm ('thou shall not kill') into a specific offence definition with action (*actus reus*) and, typically, state-of-mind (*mens rea* – 'the actor is not guilty unless the mind is guilty')[176] elements. These offence definitions thus seek to capture the blameworthiness of the overall conduct resulting in criminally punishable harm (such as 'first-degree homicide').

The institutional actors can in this sense be said to represent, reinforce, and maintain what this book has described as the 'partially expressed public morality.'[177] Criminal conduct, after all, is 'conduct which, if duly shown to have taken place, will incur a formal and solemn pronouncement of the moral condemnation of the community.'[178] The 'morality' contained in the offence definition is

[174] It is of course possible to think of, and order, the stages differently, but the classification and ordering in this subchapter fairly reflects the actual procedural and conceptual operation of the criminal law.

[175] See generally RF Wright, 'Public Defender Elections and Popular Control over Criminal Justice' (2010) 75 *Missouri Law Review* 803, 825; PH Robinson, 'Fair Notice and Fair Adjudication: Two Kinds of Legality' (2005) 154 *University of Pennsylvania Law Review* 335, 376.

[176] Examples include 'malice aforethought,' 'knowingly,' 'wilfully,' 'recklessly,' and (sometimes) 'criminally negligently.'

[177] Relatedly, Schopp has extensively discussed the 'conventional morality.' See RF Schopp, 'Sexual Predators and the Structure of the Mental Health System: Expanding the Normative Focus of Therapeutic Jurisprudence' (1995) 1 *Psychology, Public Policy, and Law* 161, 166. Schopp's analysis has, in fact, at some level inspired the approach detailed here.

[178] Hart (n 171) 405. See also PH Robinson and JM Darley, 'Testing Competing Theories of Justification' (1998) 76 *North Carolina Law Review* 1095, 1107; GK Gardner, '*Bailey v Richardson* and the Constitution of the United States' (1953) 33 *Boston University Law Review* 176, 193.

therefore described here as 'public,' because it, in a functioning justice system, is shaped by broad public support, typically develops 'organically' over the years,[179] and is designed to represent widely held moral standards of right, wrong, evil, and good.

By labelling certain conduct 'criminal,' then, the justice system, as conceived here, at a bedrock level[180] expresses widely accepted (and thus 'conventional') moral standards within the given society.[181] Note, however, that the partially expressed public morality as defined herein only addresses those (core) aspects of morality that are commonly perceived as falling within the public jurisdiction, and that are, therefore, properly subject of the criminal law.[182]

Moving from the general to the specific, and accepting for present purposes the assumptions laid out above, individual offence definitions seek to account for these rather abstract prohibitory norms by providing citizens with more specific behavioural directives.[183] By criminalising murder, for instance, the legal order expresses the conventional moral standard that unjustified killing is condemnable. A fully culpable attacker deserving punishment under this understanding of the criminal law is consequently always condemned for having violated the partially expressed public morality represented by the offence definition because that, after all, is where the inquiry starts.[184] (This is not to deny, of course, that many of

[179] See FA Hayek, *The Constitution of Liberty* (Chicago, University of Chicago Press, 1990) 148–61; JC Carter, *The Provinces of Written and Unwritten Law* (Whitefish, Kissinger Publishing, 2010/1889) 11–12. See also A Klein, 'Criminal Law and the Counter-Hegemonic Potential of Harm Reduction' (2015) 38 *Dalhousie Law Journal* 447, 462–63.

[180] Note that this minimalist understanding of what should be criminalised finds support in, among other places, the UN Declaration of Human Rights. See generally UN Declaration (n 38) Art 29. See also Ormerod and Laird (n 79) 8 (contending that conduct should only be criminalised when it protects individual autonomy or 'those social arrangements necessary to ensure that individuals have the capacity and facilities to exercise their autonomy').

[181] See generally J Chalmers and F Leverick, 'Fair Labelling in Criminal Law' (2008) 71 *MLR* 217, 245; J Gardner, 'The Mark of Responsibility' (2003) 23 *OJLS* 157; DL Bazelon, 'The Morality of the Criminal Law' in Thomas Morawetz (ed), *Criminal Law* (New York, New York University Press, 1991) 5; Hart (n 171) 404–05.

[182] In this sense, the conventional *social* morality does not overlap completely with the conventional *public* morality. The social morality addresses aspects of the citizens' social life, such as courtesy to strangers and helpfulness to neighbours and the elderly, which are not properly the subject of criminal legislation. See generally O Bakircioglu, 'The Contours of the Right to Self-Defence: Is the Requirement of Imminence Merely a Translator for the Concept of Necessity' (2008) 72 *Journal of Criminal Law* 131, 131, 152–53; Schopp (n 135) 2079–80; *Gregg v Georgia*, 428 US 153, 181 (1976). But see Dempsey (n 83) 269–70 (contending that the criminal justice system should also seek to redress communal 'character flaws' such as racism, patriarchal violence, structural inequalities, and homophobia). In any event, a full treatment of whether the criminal law can and should be employed as an instrument for such aspirational undertakings is beyond the scope of this book.

[183] See generally RF Schopp, 'Justification Defenses and Just Convictions' (1993) 24 *Pace Law Journal* 1233, 1270.

[184] Recall from our prior discussion that the conventional public morality allows us to delineate those wrongs that are criminal from the universe of wrongs. This is why intentional breach of contract, eg, is not criminalised even though it involves the intentional disregard for another's rights and equal standing. See ch 2(IV)(F).

today's criminal codes frequently are replete with largely regulatory provisions that bear what can be characterised as a faint relation to conduct meriting broader moral condemnation.[185])

c. Stage Two: The Prosecutor Decides to Bring Charges

Though this step may appear pro forma, prior to deciding to file formal charges, diligent prosecutors will have carefully examined the facts of the case, analysed the legal basis for bringing charges, and listened to defence counsel 'pitch' them on what (reduced) charges, if any, are most appropriate.[186] This second level of condemnation, thus, can be said to occur at the level of *specific* application. Indeed, US and English prosecutors have considerable, and often overlooked, discretion in deciding whether to prosecute offences that are 'on the books'[187] (where the principle of legality, in contrast, requires German prosecutors, following 'the principle of compulsory prosecution,' to press charges whenever they have sufficient evidence to support a conviction).[188] Prosecutors, moreover, not only select the specific charges that will be filed, but they also determine what penalties to request from the court.[189] The mere act of filing the charges, then, initiates the first (though still only partially expressed) defendant-specific aspect of public/systemic condemnation.

d. Stage Three: Establishing the Defendant's Mental Fitness to Proceed

Moving through the procedural and substantive steps, consider next mental competency. In the US, before a defendant can plead or be tried criminally, the judge must determine that the defendant is mentally fit to plead and to take part in his trial.[190] An individual whose mental condition renders him unable to understand the proceedings against him is not mentally fit to plead or proceed to trial and

[185] See generally G Lamond, 'What Is a Crime' (2007) 27 *OJLS* 609; SP Green, 'Moral Ambiguity in White Collar Criminal Law' (2004) 18 *Notre Dame Journal of Law, Ethics & Public Policy* 501, 501–03.

[186] A reasonable argument is that there should be an intermediate step, namely, a step at which the police or other law enforcement personnel either arrest the individual (in reactive cases) or otherwise recommend to the prosecutor that the person be prosecuted. Because this 'police discretion' step is handled so differently from jurisdiction to jurisdiction, for the sake of simplicity, this book will essentially roll this activity – which also clearly has a condemnatory flavour to it – into the prosecutorial decision to bring charges.

[187] See generally WH Simon, 'The Organization of Prosecutorial Discretion' in M Langer and D Sklansky (eds), *Prosecutors and Democracy – A Cross-National Study* (Cambridge, Cambridge University press, 2017) 176, 177; DK Brown, 'Democracy and Decriminalization' (2007) 86 *Texas Law Review* 223, 256–60.

[188] See generally M Manikis and P Grbac, 'Bargaining for Justice: The Road Toward Prosecutorial Accountability in the Plea Bargaining Process' (2017) 40 *Manitoba Law Journal* 85, 88; JH Langbein, 'Controlling Prosecutorial Discretion in Germany' (1974) 41 *University of Chicago Law Review* 439, 467. See also discussion at ch 5(II)(B).

[189] See generally *United States v Fokker Servs BV*, 818 F3d 733, 738 (DC Cir 2016).

[190] See generally Horder (n 74) 157.

must (if possible) first have his competency restored.[191] At a later stage (the sixth stage), the fact-finders determine whether the defendant is excused; but note that excuses presuppose wrongdoing on the defendant's part.[192] At this early second stage, in contrast, no such wrongdoing is presupposed, but, rather, the defendant – who may or may not be guilty of the crimes charged – is found mentally fit to plead and/or to take part in his trial. This stage, therefore, is not truly condemnatory. Instead, it is more akin to a required procedural step that may remove some quantum of stage one and stage two condemnation from those who have been declared incompetent.

e. Stage Four: The Fact-Finder Determines that this Particular Defendant Violated the Offence Definition

When a prosecutor decides to prosecute a case, a judge declines to find the defendant incompetent or to dismiss the charges, and the fact-finder (whether judge or jury) thereafter convicts the defendant, the fact-finder reaffirms the stage-one institutional condemnation. In addition, the fact-finder determines that the defendant standing in the well of the court in fact *is* guilty of violating the particular offence definition. The fourth condemnatory stage thus focuses on the conduct of a specific defendant and shares more in common with the cognitive process of fact-finding than with imposition of moral value-judgement.[193]

The fact-finder at this stage in effect says that the *system* appropriately criminalised and condemned the certain type of conduct as violating the partially expressed public morality (that is, there was no jury nullification (in the US) or perverse verdict (in England) or, in theory at least, 'judicial nullification' when the judge is the fact-finder (in all three subject jurisdictions)). The fact-finder additionally conveys that this *particular* defendant is guilty of the crime charged. That is, the fact-finder determines that the prosecutor met her burden of proving beyond a reasonable doubt that the defendant engaged in the criminal proscription's action (*actus reus*) and state-of-mind (*mens rea*)[194] elements. The defendant, therefore, can pass through this fourth stage as having violated the partially expressed public morality represented by the offence definition.

Of course, if the defendant made a *mistake* as to the circumstances, this may vitiate his *mens rea*. In such cases, the defendant operated based on an incorrect

[191] Ibid.

[192] See *State v Leidholm*, 334 NW2d 811, 814–15 (ND 1983); Fischer (n46) side-note 14; A Brudner, 'Constitutionalizing Self-Defense' (2011) 61 *University of Toronto Law Journal* 867, 893; D Husak, 'A Liberal Theory of Excuses' (2005) 3 *Ohio State Journal of Criminal Law* 287, 291.

[193] See generally S Klinger, 'Youth Competence on Trial' [2007] *New Zealand Law Review* 235, 240.

[194] Some criminal proscriptions, such as statutory rape, are strict liability offences that do not contain a *mens rea* element requiring proof that the defendant had the degree of belief or wilful disregard as to the existence of certain facts or circumstances that are typically required in criminal cases. See T Dupree, 'You Sell Molly, I'll Sell Holly: Prosecuting Sex Trafficking in the United States' (2018) 78 *Louisiana Law Review* 1025, 1046–47.

assumption of fact, rather than for a *prima facie* criminal purpose. For example, assume Victor and Andrew (who do not know each other) are having dinner at the same restaurant. Unbeknownst to both, the waiter slips a powerful hallucinogenic into Andrew's drink, causing Andrew to develop an ungovernable fury against Victor. Andrew grabs a steak knife from the table and chases Victor, cornering Victor. Victor grabs his own steak knife to defend himself but is unsuccessful in the combat that ensues – Andrew stabs Victor to death. Andrew's conduct was involuntary (despite being the initial aggressor); he, therefore, lacks the *mens rea* for murder.[195]

f. Stage Five: The Defendant Was Not Justified

Justification defences (including self-defence)[196] become relevant at the fifth stage, where the actor who violated an offence definition without having a justification for doing so is condemned. The discussion at the first stage drew attention to the fact that an offence definition merely contains the partially expressed public morality; the offence definition describes a general category of conduct proscribed at the institutional level (but this only tells part of the story). To establish that a defendant violated the *fully expressed* public morality of a liberal society by wronging or attempting to wrong another, the prosecutor must not only show that the defendant's conduct satisfies the offence definition, but he must also refute any claim made by the defence that the defendant's conduct fell into a subset of generally proscribed behaviour that is exempt from condemnation and punishment because it was justified as, say, self-defence.[197]

If the fact-finder concludes that the conduct occurred under justifying circumstances that create such an *exception* to the broader proscription contained in the offence definition, then the defendant cannot be condemned as having violated the fully expressed public morality.[198] An act initially perceived as wrongful from the 'outsider's' perspective as violating the partially expressed public morality contained in the offence definition may, therefore, in fact be legally

[195] See generally JD Brooks, 'Deadly-Force Self-Defense and the Problem of the Silent, Subtle Provocateur' (2015) 24 *Cornell Journal of Law & Public Policy* 533, 549. *Cf* SH Kadish, 'Excusing Crime' (1987) 75 *California Law Review* 257, 259 (distinguishing 'genuine human actions' and 'mere events … which happen to involve a human body'); RC Hauhart, 'The Involuntary Action Defense to a Criminal Indictment' (1984) 11 *Northern Kentucky Law Review* 321, 350 (taking the position that the *actus reus* requires the 'determination of the actor'). For a discussion of whether a mistake of fact may also undermine the *actus reus*, see ch 4(I)(B)(iv).

[196] See ch 4(I).

[197] See generally B Sangero, 'Heller's Self-Defense' (2010) 13 *New Criminal Law Review* 449, 456–57; *United States v Blodgett*, 513 F Supp 1056, 1060 (D Mont 1981). *Cf* 18 USC § 1111 (defining murder as 'unlawful killing').

[198] See generally Fletcher, *Rethinking* (n 29) 457. *See also* Kühl and Heger (n 39) side-note 2; K Greenawalt, *Conflicts of Law and Morality* (New York, Oxford University Press, 1989) 286. For more on justifications versus excuses, see ch 4(I).

permissible (though not necessarily laudatory) from a more fully informed all-things-considered perspective.

While it of course is possible that Anglo-American prosecutors, knowing that the defendant can make a strong self-defence case, may decide not to charge the defendant in the first place, or may drop charges upon such a realisation, the reason that justifications are part of the fifth condemnatory stage is that a defendant's stage-five condemnation is a prerequisite to violating the fully expressed public morality.[199] An offence description such as 'it is illegal to intentionally kill another person' accordingly only represents the partially expressed public morality. 'It is illegal to intentionally kill another person, *except* when the killing occurs in the course of actual self-defence,' in contrast, represents the fully expressed public morality, for it also contemplates potential justifications that create exceptions to the prohibitory norm expressed by the offence definition.[200]

g. Stage Six: The Defendant Is Not Excused

The discussion so far has sought to demonstrate that justified conduct creates an *exception* to the proscription contained in the offence definition, and that using force in self-defence consequently does not infringe on the attacker's rights because it does not in a legal sense *wrong* him. An excused defendant, in contrast, actually *does* violate the offence definition; he, however, does so under circumstances that make punishment inappropriate because the defendant's conduct cannot be morally attributed to him.[201] Stated differently, offence definitions require *action-plans*; excuses, in contrast, function *retrospectively* to undermine the required relation between the proscribed conduct and the actor's pursuit of his action-plan with regard to the offence.[202] A conviction and subsequent punishment hence condemn the defendant as one who transgressed the fully expressed public morality as an accountable agent by systemic standards, and who, therefore, is morally blameworthy for the wrong he inflicted or intended to inflict.[203]

The conclusion reached here is that self-defence can only provide a justification.[204] It cannot excuse, for the excused actor, unlike the justified actor, in fact violated the fully expressed public morality. We would not, after all, say

[199] See generally RA Hillman, 'The Rhetoric of Legal Backfire' (2002) 43 *Boston College Law Review* 819, 859; E D'Arcy, *Human Acts* (Oxford, Oxford University Press, 1963) 81.

[200] In this context, consider studies showing the disjunct between public views on self-defence and existing and proposed statutes. See, eg, KC Oleson and JM Darley, 'Community Perceptions of Allowable Counterforce in Self-Defense and Defense of Property' (1999) 23 *Law & Human Behaviour* 629.

[201] See generally MN Berman and IP Farrell, 'Provocation Manslaughter as Partial Justification and Partial Excuse' (2011) 52 *William & Mary Law Review* 1027, 1045–46.

[202] See generally Schopp (n 183) 1277.

[203] See generally G Lamond, 'Coercion and the Nature of Law' (2001) 7 *Legal Theory* 35, 52–53; Schopp (n 23) 29; S Uniacke, *Permissible Killing: The Self-Defence Justification of Homicide* (Cambridge, Cambridge University Press, 1994) 137–41.

[204] See ch 4(I).

'unlawful killing is wrong except when the killer is insane.' Rather, we say 'unlawful killing is wrong, but we will not criminally condemn and punish actors who were insane when they killed.'[205]

h. Stage Seven: The Defendant Is Sentenced

Because the sentencing of defendants is so fact-specific, there is little benefit to be had from attempting to detail which defendants might or should receive what sentences. That said, any discussion of condemnation by the fully expressed public morality is incomplete without recognising that the judicial officer's act of imposing a sentence completes the condemnatory cycle. It can also serve to either enhance the level of condemnation applied to an individual (through a harsh sentence and/or a harsh assessment of the defendant and her conduct), or it can diminish the level of condemnation (through a light sentence or a statement by the judicial officer that somehow minimises the defendant's moral blameworthiness).

i. Stage Eight: The Conviction Is Upheld on Appeal and Becomes Final

The final step in the subject jurisdictions is that a reviewing body determines that the proscription is lawful (eg, the law is constitutional), the charges were properly filed, the defendant had a fair trial, and the sentencing was lawful.[206] While in many cases the public may have already reached their conclusion following the conviction and may not wait for the appeal, from a technical perspective one cannot say that a defendant was condemned by the fully expressed public morality unless and until his conviction has gone through the process provided and was found to have been just.

j. 'Unjust' Self-Defence Outcomes as Threats to the Broader Justice System

Self-defence almost by definition governs how people act in a time of crisis, exempting certain behaviours from criminal liability. As discussed above in Chapter 2(IV)(F)(i), self-defence outcomes are uniquely susceptible to sharply diverging from what the broader public may intuitively consider acceptable and just.[207] When self-defence outcomes drastically (and consistently) diverge from a

[205] While some actors are excused because their incompetency prevents them from being legally accountable for their actions, others did not apply their capacities to their selection of an action-plan due to reasonably mistaken beliefs that render them internally, but not externally, justified. For a more detailed discussion, see ch 4(I)(B).

[206] See also ECHR, Nov 22, 1984, ETS No. 117 (n 38) Protocol 7, Art 2 (providing for the right to appeal in criminal matters).

[207] See generally JV Robert and JW de Keijser, *Democratising Punishment: Sentencing, Community Views and Values* (2014); PH Robinson and JM Darley, 'Intuitions of Justice: Implications for Criminal Law and Justice Policy' (2007) 81 *Southern California Law Review* 1, 31. See also J Bowers and PH Robinson, 'Perceptions of Fairness and Justice: The Shared Arms and Occasional Conflicts

community's shared intuitions of justice (in the form of the fully expressed public morality), one impact is that the law's moral credibility risks being undercut.[208]

G. Value #7: Deterring (Potential) Attackers

Summary Justification for Including This Value:

Systemically deterring crime is for good reason generally (though not universally) considered a central function of the criminal justice system. When a particular defender uses force to thwart an attack, she clearly imposes an immediate, and potentially significant, cost on the attacker that makes wrongdoing riskier. The greater the scope of self-defence permitted against attackers, the higher the likelihood that potential (and, in particular, *culpable*) attackers will be deterred from engaging in the kind of conduct that authorises defensive force.

Tension with, or Support for, the Other Values:

Successful general deterrence tends to support value #1's interest in minimising violence and protecting the state's monopoly on force. And authorising deadly force to defend a culpable attack on a trivial interest might in fact deter attacks (value #7), serve to provide maximum protection to the defender's autonomy (value #4), and ward off the imputation of lesser standing in the case of a culpable attacker (value #3). But such disproportionate force (and I say this with a recognition that others may not reach the same normative conclusion as to 'disproportion') also undermines the value of maintaining the primacy of the legal process (value #5), provides almost no protection for the attacker (value #2), and may yield results deemed unacceptable by the public so that it harms the legitimacy of the legal order (value #6).

Limitations:

This admittedly more controversial decision-ground, like safeguarding the equal standing between citizens (value #3), is only implicated when the attacker is culpable. If, on the other hand, the attacker is not culpable because she, for example, is operating under an honest and reasonable mistake (that is, she does not know she is threatening both a wrong and a harm), then the attacker by definition cannot be deterred by the availability of self-defence. (Of course, if the attacker is acting recklessly, carelessly, negligently, etc, then this analysis might change).

of Legitimacy and Moral Credibility' (2012) 47 *Wake Forest Law Review* 211, 217; PH Robinson et al, 'The Disutility of Injustice' (2010) 85 *NYU Law Review* 1940, 2026; J Nadler, 'Flouting the Law' (2005) 83 *Texas Law Review* 1399, 1417; JA Blumenthal, 'Who Decides? Privileging Public Sentiment About Justice and the Substantive Law' (2003) 72 *University of Missouri at Kansas City Law Review* 1, 9; DM Kahan, 'Social Influence, Social Meaning, and Deterrence' (1997) 83 *Virginia Law Review* 349, 351.

[208] Rönnau and Hohn (n 49) side-notes 231–33.

The final value considered here is deterrence.[209] Indeed, this value in many ways can be viewed as buttressing the other values (and the fundamental human rights they represent and protect[210]). This book, moreover, for ease of reference generally refers to the two standard species of deterrence (general deterrence and specific deterrence[211]) interchangeably, despite their admitted differences, which will be discussed immediately below.

Broadly speaking, deterrence is divided into two categories.[212] *General* deterrence is indirect, in that it focuses on general prevention of crime by sending a 'message' to the universe of potential bad actors.[213] *Specific* deterrence, in contrast, focuses on the individual in question; its intent is to discourage her from future criminal acts by instilling an understanding of the adverse consequences of criminality.[214] So, while general deterrence strategies focus on future group behaviours by impacting potential criminals' rational decision-making processes, specific deterrence focuses on directing the threat of punishment or negative consequences to known individuals in order to prevent those persons from committing crimes in the future.[215]

i. General Deterrence and Self-Defence

Elaborating on the above, when applied to self-defence, the theory grounding general deterrence leads to the reasonable assumption[216] that more permissive

[209] See generally Rönnau and Hohn (n 49) side-notes 66–67; Kremnitzer and Ghanayim (n 29) 886; DM Farrell, 'The Justification of General Deterrence' (1985) 94 *Philosophical Review* 367, 369–73, discussed in TB Randles, 'Soft-Served Deserts: Soft Retributivism as a Free Will-Independent Alternative for the Criminal Justice System' (2018) 67 *Catholic University Law Review* 495, 506. See also Erb (n 82) side-note 4. But see DP Rosenbaum, 'Community Crime Prevention: A Review and Synthesis of the Literature' (1988) 5 *Justice Quarterly* 323, 336 ('Clearly, deterrence (whether specific or general) and self-defense are separate objectives.').

[210] Both general and specific deterrence, eg, can be said to protect the right to life and the equality between people. See generally UN Declaration (n 38) Arts 1, 3, and 29; ECHR, Nov 4, 1950, ETS No. 005 (n 38) Arts 2 and 5.

[211] See generally KD Tomlinson, 'An Examination of Deterrence Theory: Where Do We Stand' (2016) 80 *Federal Probation Journal* 33, 34.

[212] See generally PH Robinson and JM Darley, 'The Role of Deterrence in the Formulation of Criminal Law Rules: At Its Worst When Doing Its Best' (2003) 91 *Georgia Law Journal* 949, 992–95 (discussing these factors), cited in D Crump, 'Deterrence' (2018) 49 *St Mary's Law Journal* 317, 320; I Ehrlich, 'Participation in Illegitimate Activities: A Theoretical and Empirical Investigation' (1973) 81 *Journal of Political Economy* 521, 535.

[213] See generally M Bagaric and P Isham, 'A Rational Approach to the Role of Publicity and Condemnation in the Sentencing of Offenders' (2019) 46 *Florida State University Law Review* 239, 247–48; A Pathinayake, 'Should We Deter Against General Deterrence' (2018) 9 *Wake Forest Journal of Law & Policy* 63, 78.

[214] See generally M Bagaric et al, 'Trauma and Sentencing: The Case for Mitigating Penalty for Childhood Physical and Sexual Abuse' (2019) 30 *Stanford Law & Policy Review* 1, 43.

[215] See generally RE Wagner, 'Corporate Criminal Prosecutions and Double Jeopardy' (2019) 16 *Berkeley Business Law Journal* 205, 218; M Ferrante, 'Deterrence and Crime Results' (2007) 10 *New Criminal Law Review* 1, 61. See also AF Popper, 'In Defense of Deterrence' (2011) 75 *Albany Law Review* 181, 203.

[216] It must be conceded that this proposition, to the best of the author's knowledge, has not been (and perhaps cannot be) empirically tested with reliable/conclusive results. See generally R Paternoster,

self-defence laws will generally deter crime. The logic is that individuals will be more likely to 'think twice' before engaging in criminal conduct of the type that could invoke the right of the victim to exercise self-defence.[217] Thus, there is a claimed benefit when self-defence laws and enforcement approaches create in the potential criminal's mind the worry that his criminal behaviour is likely to result in tangible and immediate negative consequences.[218]

But do criminals in fact act sufficiently rationally to render the deterrence argument persuasive? There is substantial support for the view that criminals, as a group, are not typically characterised by highly rational future planning.[219] Instead, research has shown that criminals tend to more commonly act on impulse and behave opportunistically; in fact, violent attackers in particular tend to least carefully weigh the pros and cons of their attacks. As the court put it well in *United States v Gulley*:

> Many of the offenders that we see commit what we would consider almost irrational crimes. They're impulsive, they have difficulty controlling their impulses, and they exercise poor judgement. That's a characteristic of their lives.[220]

Of course, there are also those who advance the idea that criminals in the main act instrumentally rationally.[221]

'Decisions to Participate in and Desist from Four Types of Common Delinquency: Deterrence and the Rational Choice Perspective' (1989) 23 *Law & Society Review* 7, 8 n 1 (noting that deterrence theory has received 'scant research attention').

[217] See generally Rönnau and Hohn (n 49) side-notes 66–67.

[218] See generally J Garcia, 'Defending Self-Defense: Why Florida Should Follow the Eleven States That Already Allow for Campus Carry' (2018) 31 *St Thomas Law Review* 89, 103–05; OG Hatch, 'The Brady Handgun Prevention Act and the Community Protection Initiative: Legislative Responses to the Second Amendment' [1998] *Birmingham Young University Law Review* 103; JR Lott, Jr. and DB Mustard, 'Crime, Deterrence, and Right-To-Carry Concealed Handguns' (1997) 26 *JLS* 1, 1 (finding that 'allowing citizens to carry concealed weapons deters violent crimes'), cited in A Winkler, 'Is the Second Amendment Becoming Irrelevant' (2018) 93 *Indiana Law Journal* 253, 264 n 55. But see Lesch (n 37) 86–87, 106 (taking the position that deterrence should not play a role in self-defence analysis).

[219] See generally PH Robinson and JM Darley, 'Does Criminal Law Deter? A Behavioural Science Investigation' (2004) 24 *OJLS* 173, 178–81 (reviewing evidence that suggests that criminals do not behave rationally), cited in AT Azmat, 'What Mistake of Law Just Might Be: Legal Moralism, Liberal Positivism, and the Mistake of Law Doctrine' (2015) 18 *New Criminal Law Review* 369, 397 (2015). *Cf* CNW Keckler, 'Life v. Death: Who Should Capital Punishment Marginally Deter?' (2006) 2 *Journal of Law & Economics* 51, 77 n 61 (contending that 'even highly abnormal offenders act rationally to avoid arrest').

[220] *United States v Gulley*, 29 F Appx 228, 230 (6th Cir 2002). See also A Chalfin and J McCrary, 'Criminal Deterrence: A Review of the Literature' (2017) 55 *Journal of Economic Literature* 5; W Brookbanks and R Ekins, 'The Case Against the "Three Strikes" Sentencing Regime' [2010] *New Zealand Law Review* 689, 708; TM Funk, 'A Mere Youthful Indiscretion? Reexamining the Policy of Expunging Juvenile Delinquency Records' (1996) 29 *University of Michigan Journal of Law Reform* 885, 929; *United States v Reynolds*, 235 US 133, 150 (1914) (Holmes, J, concurring).

[221] See, eg, LE Dervan, 'White Collar Overcriminalization: Deterrence, Plea Bargain, and the Loss of Innocence' (2013) 101 *Kentucky Law Journal* 723, 739–40; A Driggers, 'Raj Rajaratnam's Historic Insider Trading Sentence' (2012) 49 *American Criminal Law Reporter* 2021, 2036; Keckler (n 219) 77 n 61; DM Kreps, *A Course in Microeconomic Theory* (New Jersey, Princeton University Press, 1990) 19–22.

But in the final analysis, harbouring some doubts about the precise efficacy of deterrence does not serve to negate this value. For there is scant support for the proposition that specifically, and perhaps also generally, deterring crime is an impact entirely divorced from the availability of self-defence. (And if this were ever to change, a system so persuaded can simply decide to accord less weight to the value of deterrence.)

Turning to this value's limitations, here, too, the culpability of the attacker plays a crucial role in determining whether the value is considered a decision-ground. If an individual is not culpable (to wit, is not following an intentional and voluntary action-plan that either involves posing a criminal threat to someone, or, alternatively, that demonstrates disregard for another's rights via recklessness, carelessness, or perhaps even negligence), then changing the nature or amount of defensive force available can be expected to have little or no impact on that attacker's behaviour.[222] A young child or mentally incompetent attacker who mistakenly thinks that the person he is attacking is a tree, for example, will not change his conduct, regardless of the amount of defensive force potentially coming his way (though it might make a more rational potential attacker more careful about his conduct).

ii. *Specific Deterrence and Self-Defence*

Vindicating the rights of defenders by permitting defensive force entails the imposition of costs on an attacker – and that is true whether the deterrent effect is focused on the general public or on an individual person. Specific deterrence, as relevant here, potentially impacts those individual actors who have faced such defensive force in the past and who, it is hoped, have 'learned their lesson' (or are learning it in the moment when the force has or is about to be applied to them). Most of the arguments made, and limitations noted above concerning general deterrence, also apply to specific deterrence. The reason for including this short discussion, then, is to simply recognise that there are two types of deterrence potentially at play.[223] The value of deterrence, moreover, is largely in harmony with the value of protecting the defender (value #4) and ensuring the equal standing between individuals (value #3). But, at some level at least, it is in general tension with the remaining values.

[222] See generally Rönnau and Hohn (n 49) side-notes 66–67; MY Ewert, 'One Strike and You're Out of Public Housing: How the Intersection of the War on Drugs and Federal Housing Policy Violated Due Process and Fair Housing Principles' (2016) 32 *Harvard Journal on Racial & Ethnic Justice* 57, 77 n 130.

[223] For a deeper discussion about proportionality and excessive force, see ch 4(III).

V. The Challenging Act of Balancing the Competing Values

By way of brief recap, we thus far have proposed a template, dubbed the 'value-based model,' that is anchored on the seven values that collectively represent one perspective on self-defence's underlying rationale. The objective of the exercise was to test the core claim that a more value-centric dialogue facilitates a more transparent, quality-enhancing understanding of self-defence's underlying rationale.[224] And, in fact, the analysis up to this point has provided initial support for this position (subject to testing in subsequent chapters) and demonstrated that values do, and should, matter in self-defence cases. Further, we have had an opportunity to discuss the general tensions and conflicts between the values. Building on this understanding, we can now turn to the challenging question of how values as decision-grounds should be ordered or balanced, and how conflicts between them might be resolved when they conflict or 'clash.'

But prior to this more fine-grained discussion of how to approach accommodating values in different self-defence scenarios, we must address the foundational question of whether and when an attacker can be said to 'forfeit' her right to life (which is antecedent to the discussion over what constellation of value-weighting might justify such a forfeiture). The position advanced here is that the distinction between the attacker's threatening harm versus wrong – and the related distinction between 'waiving' and 'forfeiting' rights – provides a (and, perhaps, the most) persuasive explanation of what happens when rights 'clash.' In fact, I – admittedly somewhat immodestly – believe this new waiver-versus-forfeiture distinction in critical respects advances what has become the somewhat stagnant traditional forfeiture theory analysis.

A. The Value-Based Model and the 'Forfeiture' of Rights

As discussed below, a number of commentators, including Leverick, Sangero, Uniacke, and Thomson, have endorsed the position that a person's right to life is ultimately conditioned on conduct. But this common-sense observation merely initiates the analysis because, in order to infuse the position with content, one at a minimum must understand what types of conduct create what kinds of 'gaps' to, or limitations on, a person's conditional right to life.

[224] See ch 2.

i. Rights Theory

Rights theorists Uniacke,[225] Leverick,[226] Sangero,[227] Thomson,[228] Rodin,[229] and others broadly maintain that the right to self-defence is not a right grounded merely on the passive right not to be killed. Rather, they contend that it is a moral right that affirmatively authorises the defender's self-preferential conduct. They point to what they describe as the moral asymmetry between the defender and the attacker and use that as the basis for justifying the resulting 'forfeiture' (either conditional or unconditional) of the attacker's right to life and to non-interference. Dressler, in fact, goes so far as to reject forfeiture theory entirely because he considers the killing of a wrongdoer 'morally insignificant.'[230]

One challenge faced by such a broad conception of forfeiture is that, once forfeited, the attacker's right to life can be said to be forfeited even after the immediate threat subsides. To address this concern, Uniacke and Leverick[231] argue in favour of a narrower conception of forfeiture. Uniacke's notion of 'temporary forfeiture' refers to a 'right lost … due to some crime or fault, breach … or neglect of contract or rules on the part of the person who forfeits.'[232] She also draws on the concept derived from forced choice theory that a person posing an 'unjust threat' *temporarily* loses her right to non-interference. This loss-of-right situation continues only as long as the culpable or innocent attacker 'for no good reason' poses the threat.[233]

The position advanced here is that a theory of forfeiture provides the most – and, indeed, the only – persuasive avenue for justifying self-defensive killing. Alternative methods proffered to explain self-defence fall short of the mark. For example, Wallerstein claims that the right to life cannot be forfeited – even temporarily.[234] Yet in her final analysis, she contends that when a defender uses deadly force against an aggressor 'he has justifying circumstances and does not violate the aggressor's right to life and does not wrong him.'[235] In the absence of some type of forfeiture theory, this final step in Wallerstein's analysis appears incomplete because killing an innocent attacker certainly violates his right to life – indeed, it extinguishes it.

[225] See Uniacke (n 203) 213.

[226] See Leverick (n 2) 166.

[227] See Sangero, *Self-Defence* (n 4) 39, 44, 88.

[228] See JJ Thomson, 'Self-Defense' (1991) 20 *Philosophy & Public Affairs* 283, 299.

[229] See D Rodin, *War and Self-Defense* (Oxford, Oxford University Press, 2003) 88–89.

[230] See J Dressler, 'Battered Women and Sleeping Abusers: Some Reflections' (2006) 3 *Ohio State Journal of Criminal Law* 457, 465–66, discussed in V Bergelson, 'Justification or Excuse – Exploring the Meaning of Provocation' (2009) 42 *Texas Technical Law Review* 307, 316. But see DN Husak, 'Partial Defenses' (1998) 11 *Canadian Journal of Law & Jurisdiction* 167, 170.

[231] Leverick (n 2) 66.

[232] Uniacke (n 203) 201.

[233] Ibid.

[234] S Wallerstein, 'Justifying the Right to Self-Defense: A Theory of Forced Consequences' (2005) 91 *Virginia Law Review* 999, 1032.

[235] Ibid at 1031.

ii. Forced Choice Theory[236]

Forced choice theory postulates that when an attacker 'forces' a defender into a position where the defender has no option but to make a choice between lives, the attacker loses the right to complain that his life is the one in jeopardy.[237] The defender, thus, faces a ('forced') choice between sustaining a deadly injury or killing the attacker. In contrast, the attacker, who under the theory is able to stop his attack at any time and thereby avoid harm to anyone, does not face a similar forced choice.[238]

For commentators like Wasserman, the very justification[239] of self-defence is deeply rooted in this 'critical asymmetry between the present aggressor and his victim.'[240] Viewed from this perspective, forced choice theory applies to all self-defence cases. The manifest challenge to forced choice theory, however, is that it does not substantively distinguish between culpable and non-culpable threatened attacks. Instead, it simply assumes *all* attackers are culpable and, therefore, are making a deliberate decision to 'force' the defender's hand to either kill or absorb the attack.[241] This presumption, however, is also the theory's fatal defect, because the difference between culpable and non-culpable attackers is, in fact, absolutely critical.[242]

Any comprehensive theory of self-defence must address – and distinguish – *culpability*-based conceptions of responsibility (morally intentional actors), on the one hand, and *causally-based* conceptions of responsibility (morally unintentional actors), on the other.[243] By fixating on the defendant rather than the act, forced choice theory tends to blur the lines between excuse and justification – and, for reasons discussed in Chapter 4(I), this is a valuable distinction worth maintaining.

iii. Answering the Gateway Questions: Can Rights Ever Be 'Forfeited' by an Innocent Attacker?

Kasachkoff critiques forfeiture theory by not unreasonably questioning whether an attacker's right to life can ever be 'forfeited' when the attacker is non-culpable.[244]

[236] Note that forced choice theory is also discussed in some detail below at ch 2(V)(A)(ii).

[237] See generally Erb (n 3) 596–97; D Wasserman, 'Justifying Self-Defense' (1987) 16 *Philosophy & Public Affairs* 356, 371; P Montague, 'Self-Defense and Choosing Between Lives' (1981) 40 *Philosophical Studies* 207, 211, 216.

[238] See Wallerstein (n 234) 1010–11. See also S Dimock, 'Criminalizing Dangerousness: How to Preventively Detain Dangerous Offenders' (2015) 9 *Criminal Law & Philosophy* 537, 551–52; KK Ferzan, 'Culpable Aggression: The Basis for Moral Liability to Defensive Killing' (2012) 9 *Ohio State Journal of Criminal Law* 669, 688–89.

[239] The book concedes that the term 'justification' is normative and has no preordained meaning; thus, a 'correct' approach cannot be discovered through theorising.

[240] Wallerstein (n 234) 1027. See also Kim (n 142) 281; Segev (n 43) 432–33.

[241] See generally Wasserman (n 237) 364.

[242] *Cf* Erb (n 3) 597 (distinguishing between culpable and innocent attackers).

[243] See generally Rönnau and Hohn (n 49) side-note 68.

[244] T Kasachkoff, 'Killing in Self-Defense: An Un-Questionable or Problematic Defense?' (1998) 17 *Law & Philosophy* 509, 519.

He contends that forfeiture must be linked to fault because blameless persons cannot be said to 'deserve' to lose their lives.[245] Uniacke, in response, argues that forfeiture is based purely on the *conduct* of the aggressor, rather than on any notion of the aggressor's *fault*.[246] That is, it is only by becoming an 'unjustified immediate threat to the life of another' that a person forfeits his right to life.[247] And while Schopp does not formally use the language of forfeiture, his culpability-based analysis appears to track the same concept:

> By engaging in a criminal law violation of the victim's sovereignty, the aggressor steps outside the domain of central, self-regarding life decisions within which he can claim a right to freedom from interference. The victim's exercise of defensive force against the aggressor does not, therefore, violate his right to self-determination.[248]

Schopp, consequently, believes that the attacker has a right against non-interference that could be forfeited, for his 'right to self-determination never extended to actions that intrude into the [defender's] protected domains.'[249] But, while Schopp frames his analysis from the perspective of a presumptively morally culpable attacker threatening a 'criminal law violation,' is the morally innocent attacker really seeking to 'intrude' on the defender's right to self-determination or equal standing?[250] For the reasons set forth below, I believe the approaches developed by scholars such as Kasachkoff, Uniacke, and Schopp have merit. But it is hoped that, by introducing an alternative (and overdue) way of understanding forfeiture that directly addresses the innocent versus culpable attacker conundrum, we can advance a considerably more robust forfeiture argument.

iv. The Value-Based Model's Approach to the 'Forfeiture' of Rights – Introducing the Concept of 'Waiver'

Adopting Uniacke's and Thomson's approaches, Leverick concludes that:

> It is acceptable to kill an aggressor because the aggressor, in becoming an unjust immediate threat to the life of another that cannot be avoided by reasonable means, *temporarily forfeits her right to life*, at least as long as these conditions remain in force.[251]

Leverick's quasi-Hohfeldian 'claim-right' point of departure,[252] however, is, as noted, considerably hampered by the bluntness of the term 'forfeiture.' Under the

[245] T Kasachkoff, 'Comment and Reply to Suzanne Uniacke's "A Response to Two Critics"' (2000) 19 *Law & Philosophy* 635, 639.

[246] S Uniacke, 'In Defense of "Permissible Killing": A Response to Two Critics' (2000) 19 *Law & Philosophy* 627, 629.

[247] Ibid.

[248] Schopp (n 23) 75–76.

[249] Ibid at 78.

[250] Farrell argues that notions of distributive justice allow us to allocate harm to an unjust aggressor. See generally Farrell (n 209) 372.

[251] Leverick (n 2) 2 (emphasis added).

[252] See WN Hohfeld, 'Some Fundamental Legal Conceptions as Applied in Judicial Reasoning' (1913) 23 *Yale Law Journal* 16–59.

orthodox view, an attacker 'forfeits' his rights as a result of his 'wrongful' conduct; this implies a form of open-ended punishment or penalty.[253] Dsouza in fact faults forfeiture theory because it, in the self-defence context, 'carries with it punitive undertones and suggests some element of fault on the part of the person suffering the defensive action.'[254] Leverick similarly allows that a forfeiture-based account of self-defensive killing is 'likely to be controversial' because 'of the term's association with fault, penalty, or punishment.'[255]

The position proposed here seeks to overcome these challenges by replacing the notion of blanket forfeiture with a more fine-grained analysis which distinguishes between (morally) intentional and unintentional actors.[256] This new approach deploys this bifurcation to blunt – and, in fact, perhaps overcome – the traditional arguments advanced against the concept of forfeiture of rights.

It has been recognised that there can be a '*conditional forfeiture*' or '*temporary suspension of rights*,' either of which apply to innocent defenders who, because they pose unjust threats of *harm*, forfeit their right to non-interference conditioned on their being a continued threat.[257] As Simons, discussing Bergelson, puts it, conditional forfeiture is 'a special kind of forfeiture, involving a conditional right to life, where the actor loses the right if he becomes an unjust immediate threat.'[258]

Building on this concept of forfeiture conditioned on conduct, we here introduce the concept of '*conditional waiver*' to describe culpable attackers who knowingly pose a threat of both harming and *wronging*, thereby waiving their right to non-interference.[259] While Simons contends that self-defence 'involves (involuntary) forfeiture'[260] (presumably in the sense that the forfeiture being imposed is unchosen by the attacker), the position developed here is that knowing and intentional attackers are, in fact, morally blameworthy.[261] The natural consequence of

[253] See generally Thomson (n 228) 261. See also Leverick (n 2) 67; W Kaufman, 'Is There a Right to Self-Defense?' (2004) 23 *Criminal Justice Ethics* 20, 25–29; Schopp (n 23) 75–76.

[254] Dsouza (n 15) 66–67. See also J Herring, 'Law and the Relational Self' 714–15 (MS on file with author) (discussing the various traditional arguments against forfeiture theory).

[255] Leverick (n 2) 67. See also Kaufman (n 253) 25–29; Schopp (n 23) 75–76; Thomson (n 228) 261.

[256] Erb, eg, recognises this distinction in the self-defence context, contending that the 'duty of interpersonal solidarity' is greater with innocent attackers. See Erb (n 3) 596.

[257] One way of conceptualising this is thinking of the waiver or forfeiture as opening a gap in the attacker's otherwise inviolable personal domain. This gap remains open so long as the individual continues to pose such a threat, and, because the availability of self-defence is limited by the value-based model's decision-grounds, the gap, once created, does not result in unconditional and open-ended forfeiture.

[258] KW Simons, 'The Relevance of Victim Conduct in Tort and Criminal Law' (2005) 8 *Buffalo Criminal Law Review* 541, 544 n 9. See also C Elliott, 'Interpreting the Contours of Self-Defence Within the Boundaries of the Rule of Law, the Common Law and Human Rights' (2015) 79 *Journal of Criminal Law* 330, 339; S Krause, 'Killing in Defence of Property: A Constitutional Approach' [2012] *Journal of South African Law* 469, 477.

[259] The notion that the normative culpability/responsibility of the attacker is relevant to the defender's ability to exercise defensive force (and what amount of defensive force the defender can utilise) finds support in some of the German scholarship. See, eg, Lesch (n 37) 91.

[260] Simons (n 258) 544 n 9.

[261] See generally Vogel (n 93) 43–44; RE Wagner, 'Corporate Criminal Prosecutions and the Exclusionary Rule' (2016) 68 *Florida Law Review* 1119, 1123. *Cf* KL Bell, 'Toward a New Analysis of the Abortion Debate' (1991) 33 *Arizona Law Review* 907, 927.

launching a morally blameworthy attack is that the conduct creates in the defender the right to resort to lawful defensive force, which, in turn, justifies imputing the intent to conditionally *waive* the attacker's right to non-interference.[262]

The decision to in this manner bifurcate the traditional omnibus term 'forfeiture' also responds to critics, such as Kasachkoff, by recognising the considerable normative asymmetry between those who threaten to merely harm, and those who threaten to both harm *and* wrong.[263] And so while 'forfeiture' traditionally refers to the simple *loss* of a particular right,[264] waiver includes conduct-inferred *knowing and intentional relinquishment* or abandonment of a known right.[265] When an individual engages in a criminal attack on another, she knows (or can be imputed to know) that she, through her conduct, has knowingly relinquished her right to non-interference in her autonomous sphere of self-determination.[266] Innocent attackers, in contrast, by definition do not know of the wrongfulness of their conduct. They, therefore, at worst can be said to forfeit some of their ability to claim an absolute right to non-interference because the defenders cannot be expected to always subjugate their own substantive interests to those of the attacker (whether innocent or otherwise).

v. Bridging the 'Culpable' Versus 'Innocent' Divide Through the Concept of 'Waiver' of Rights

The instant analysis, in short, endorses, and in fact is grounded on, the argument that, by becoming what Uniacke has aptly termed an 'unjust threat,'[267] the attacker creates a morally distinctive asymmetry between himself and the person whom he is threatening.[268] Per Uniacke, individuals cannot be said to possess unconditional human rights; rather, they have rights that are *conditioned* on their behaviour (that is, on their not wronging *or* harming another).[269]

[262] See generally *Taylor v United States*, 414 US 17, 20 (1973) (finding implied waiver of right to be present during trial when defendant absconded). See also A Rose, 'Forfeiture of Confrontation Rights Post-Giles: Whether a Co-Conspirator's Misconduct Can Forfeit a Defendant's Right to Confront Witnesses' (2011) 14 *NYU Journal of Legislation & Public Policy* 281, 293–94; *United States v Carlson*, 547 F2d 1346, 1358 (8th Cir 1976).

[263] See ch 2(IV)(C).

[264] See generally D Alm, 'Self-Defense, Punishment and Forfeiture' (2013) 32 *Criminal Justice Ethics* 91, 99.

[265] See generally *Johnson v Zerbst*, 304 US 458, 464 (1938). See also LS Rulli, 'Seizing Family Homes from the Innocent: Can the Eighth Amendment Protect Minorities and the Poor from Excessive Punishment in Civil Forfeiture' (2017) 19 *University of Pennsylvania Journal of Constitutional Law* 1111, 1159; *Brookhart v Janis*, 384 US 1, 4 (1966).

[266] See generally *Taylor*, 414 US at 20; Rose (n 262) 293–94.

[267] It is important to note that this term does not rely on a negative moral judgement about the attacker, but instead is based entirely on the attacker's status as threatening an actual unjustified invasion of the defender's personal domain.

[268] See generally E Aloyo, 'Just Assassinations' (2013) 5 *International Theory* 347, 359; Uniacke (n 203) 75–81.

[269] Uniacke (n 203) 157–58. See generally HL Hart, 'Are There Any Natural Rights?' in A Quinton (ed), *Political Philosophy* (Oxford, Oxford University Press, 1967) 53. See also T McConnell, 'The Nature and

Uniacke, in line with philosophers like Grotius and Pufendorf, however, also maintains that the moral or criminal culpability of the 'unjustified threat' is irrelevant. Grotius similarly described as 'innocent' or 'unoffending' those who do not create a dangerous situation that threatens an unjust injury. And Pufendorf, like Grotius who equates 'innocent' with 'unoffending' (in the sense of not creating a dangerous situation threatening an unjust injury),[270] implied that self-defence against insane or reasonably mistaken – and therefore morally innocent – aggressors is justifiable: '[I]t is enough that the other have no right to attack or kill me, and there be on my side no obligation to die in vain.'[271] While the person posing the threat may be morally innocent, the threat he is posing is therefore nonetheless 'unjust' in the sense that there is no objectively good reason warranting it. The defender need not tolerate it.[272]

This argument supports a right of self-defence against moral innocents, such as madmen, sleepwalkers, and those labouring under a mistake, who pose an immediate and identifiable threat. Such actors threaten the defender's autonomy with harm the defender cannot be legally required to absorb.[273] Once an actor through his actions – either voluntary or involuntary, culpable or blameless – becomes an immediate unjust threat to another, his right to non-interference in his personal domain is either conditionally waived or forfeited (depending on the culpability of the attacker) to an extent compatible with the implicated decision-grounds. The right to non-interference, moreover, remains forfeited until he ceases to be such a threat.

The position taken here is generally in accord in terms of some self-defence *outcomes*. But it critically differs in terms of the rationale and practical *implications*. A significant point of departure is that the above approach pays insufficient attention to the exceptionally significant normative distinction between culpable and innocent threats.[274] In so doing, this popular approach to the forfeiture of

Basis of Inalienable Rights' (1984) 3 *Law & Philosophy* (1984) 25, 28; H Bedau, 'The Right to Life' (1968) 52 *Monist* 550, 568 (adopting a forfeiture theory in the case of culpable aggressors: '[T]he offender, by violating the life or liberty or property of another, has lost his own right to have his life, liberty, or property respected.'), discussed in SP Green, 'Castles and Carjackers: Proportionality and the Use of Deadly Force in Defense of Dwellings and Vehicles' [1999] *University of Illinois Law Review* 1, 20–21.

[270] Hugo Grotius, *On the Rights of War and Peace* (Charleston, Nabu Press, 2009) 62.

[271] S von Pufendorf, *De Officio Hominis et Civis Juxta Legem Naturalem Libri Duo*, vol 2 (Palala Press, 2015/1927) 31.

[272] See generally Rönnau and Hohn (n 49) side-notes 64, 68–73; Krause (n 258) 478; J Horder, 'Redrawing the Boundaries of Self-Defence' (1995) 58 *MLR* 431, 435–38; Uniacke (n 146) 95; JJ Thomson, *Rights, Restitution, and Risk: Essays in Moral Theory* (Cambridge, Mass, Harvard University Press, 1986) 42–46. For an analogous discussion of morally innocent actors in tort law, see JL Coleman, *Risks and Wrongs* (Cambridge, Cambridge University Press, 1992) 332. For a criticism of Coleman's argument, see A Walen, 'Consensual Sex Without Assuming the Risk of Carrying an Unwanted Fetus; Another Foundation for the Right to an Abortion' (1997) 63 *Brooklyn Law Review* 1051, 1098–1100. See also Uniacke (n 203) 157–58.

[273] See generally J McMahan, 'Self -Defense Against Morally Innocent Threats' in PH Robinson et al (eds), *Criminal Law Conversations* (New York, Oxford University Press, 2011) 385–406; Lesch (n 37) 103.

[274] See generally Segev (n 43) 392 n 27.

rights conundrum fatally overlooks that not all attacks are created equally. To the contrary, morally distinguishable attacks require morally defensible responses.

Moving from the general to the specific, while threats of harm from innocents threaten defenders with concrete losses (see value #4), threats of wrong posed by culpable attackers *additionally* threaten to impute lesser standing to the defender (value #3) (as well as, to a more diffuse extent, to everyone else who has refrained from engaging in criminal conduct). Similarly, the concept that all individuals owe each other a basic obligation of 'human solidarity' (and, thus, the responsibility to refrain from harming others when possible) can reasonably be interpreted more strictly in the context of morally innocent attackers who do not threaten the imputation of lesser standing (value #3).[275] Parting from Uniacke's approach, then, the theory introduced here draws a sharp distinction between culpable and innocent threats – that is, between wrongs implicating waiver and harms implicating forfeiture – on the basis of their normative/qualitative differences. These differences, in turn, affect the relative weights accorded to the value-based model's decision-grounds that provide content to the macro principles of 'protecting the defender' and 'protecting the attacker.' This distinction between waiver and forfeiture of an attacker's rights allows us to meaningfully distinguish between culpable and non-culpable threats, thereby overcoming the deficiencies in Uniacke's and Leverick's conception of the undifferentiated 'aggressor' posing an 'unjust and immediate threat.'

B. Considering Alternative Value-Accommodation Methods

The discussion thus far has demonstrated that culpable attackers are most appropriately viewed as waiving their right to non-interference, whereas non-culpable attackers are best conceived of as merely forfeiting the right. With this analysis in hand, we can proceed to the important discussion of how the values implicated in self-defence cases should be ordered, or accommodated, in those cases where they come into friction or outright conflict. Put another way, the discussion concerning the general *existence* of forfeiture and waiver sets the stage for an examination of how the implicated values become decision-grounds that justify *individual instances* of forfeiture or waiver.

Recall that, if the value-centric position we are testing holds, in cases of purported self-defence, the value-based model will serve to enhance the discussion by making more explicit (a) *what* decision-grounds are at play, (b) the *extent* to which the implicated decision-grounds are at play, and (c) the necessary *sliding-scale accommodation* between conflicting decision-grounds. This, it is hoped, will facilitate more transparent and balanced decision-making. That said, it is also

[275] See generally Lesch (n 37) 103–04 (retreat and avoiding conflict, and absorbing minor harm, appropriate in such cases; contending that resulting damage to a defender's property must be covered by the state). See also ch 2(IV)(C).

conceded that any 'balancing approach,' including the one proposed here, has inherent challenges. Assigning any particular relative weight to competing interests, after all, requires the application of normative judgements, rather than the reaching of quasi-scientific determinations.[276] In addition, there are some jurisprudential challenges implicated when seeking to balance basic individual human rights (such as the right to life) against more collective interests (such as reduction in crime).[277]

But we will for now set those issues aside because, while interesting, the fact that all 'balancing' efforts are open to some level of critique is not fatal to our undertaking. For when the right of a defender to use self-preferential force clashes with, say, the right of an attacker to be free from harm, the conflict between them must somehow be resolved by reference to established legal principles (and, central here, to the recognised interests/values driving them). This orientation toward principles, while not free from doubt, aids judges and other fact-finders in their efforts to determine which right takes priority, and under what circumstances.[278] If the value-centric position we are testing holds, then a more transparent approach to taking account of the conflicting demands between rights will help narrow (though not eliminate) the scope of conflicts between rights.[279]

i. Single Value Approach

One could argue that a system based entirely on a *single* decision-ground avoids inconsistency and potential abuse. German law, as introduced in Chapter 1, in the early part of the last century broadly endorsed such a single-value system. The German view was that 'the right must not have to yield to the wrong,' and that the defender therefore was only limited by necessity.[280] Similarly, Leverick has largely (though, as we shall see, not exclusively) focused on the 'equality of [the attacker's] life' as the critical decision-ground dictating outcomes.[281] And Schopp, in turn, has built his model around protecting the autonomy of the defender.[282] The difficulty with such single-value systems, however, is that, while it is true that

276 See generally L Zedner, 'Securing Liberty in the Face of Terror: Reflections from Criminal Justice' (2005) 32 *Journal of Law & Society* 510, 510–11. See also I Pavic, 'Human Dignity in the Context of Prison Privatization' (2018) 8 *Jurisdiction Tribunal* 6, 14; N Petersen, 'Avoiding the Common-Wisdom Fallacy: The Role of Social Sciences in Constitutional Adjudication' (2013) 11 *International Journal of Constitutional Law* 294, 299–300.

277 See generally R Dworkin, 'Rights as Trumps' in J Waldron (ed), *Theories of Rights* (Oxford, Oxford University Press, 1985) 153, cited in C Michaelsen, 'Reforming Australia's National Security Laws: The Case for a Proportionality-Based Approach' (2010) 29 *University of Tasmania Law Review* 31, 35.

278 See generally G Beck, 'The Idea of Human Rights Between Value Pluralism and Conceptual Vagueness' (2007) 25 *Penn State International Law Review* 615, 630.

279 See ibid. See also G Beck, 'The Moral Void at the Heart of Human Rights Adjudication' (2013) 8 *Journal of Comparative Law* 237, 238–40; LK Klein, 'Rights Clash: How Conflicts Between Gay Rights and Religious Freedoms Challenge the Legal System' (2010) 98 *Georgia Law Journal* 505, 519.

280 See, eg, 55 RGSt 82, 83.

281 See discussion in ch 3(III).

282 See discussion in ch 3(IV).

they provide comfortable and convenient bright-line answers to most questions, they also, for no objectively good reason, ignore competing values.

Consider the aforementioned German fruit thief example. The 'traditional' German approach permitted the Prussian farmer to use deadly force to ensure that the youthful thief was not able to make off with his fruit because the 'wrong' must never yield to the 'right.' The German Supreme Court, in delivering this ruling, made no effort to analyse (or, for that matter, even recognise the existence of) any competing interests that might be at stake. And this was so despite the obvious reality that, as detailed in Chapter 2(V), there are, in fact, such other competing interests. The exclusion of the other decision-grounds from consideration, however, at a minimum called for an explanation. But none was forthcoming. Instead, the German Court simply re-stated the categorical rule and strictly applied it to the facts of the case.[283] Clearly, the single-value approach inadequately explains self-defence's underlying rationale.

ii. Simple Priority Approach

Alternatively, one could use a *simple priority approach* allowing the value most directly at play to dictate the self-defence outcome.[284] While employing such a more open-textured tactic may be preferable to the competing single-value approach, this solution likewise requires the decision-maker to, for no good reason, ignore other impacted values.[285]

iii. The Proposed Weighted Value Approach

As already mentioned, it at the outset is accepted that the identified values do not have self-evident weights. As such, any 'balancing' of values is inherently challenging. As Zedner puts it:

> Typically, conflicting interests are said to be 'balanced' as if there were a self-evident weighting of or priority among them. Yet rarely are the particular interests spelt out, priorities made explicitly, or the process by which a weight is achieved made clear …. Although beloved of constitutional lawyers and political theorists, the experience of criminal justice is that balancing is a politically dangerous metaphor unless careful regard is given to what is at stake.[286]

[283] 55 RGSt 82, 85. See also ch 5(II).

[284] See generally N Croquet, 'Implied External Limitations on the Right to Cross-Examine Prosecution Witnesses: The Tension Between a Means Test and a Balancing Test in the Appraisal of Anonymity Requests' (2010) 11 *Melbourne Journal of International Law* 27, 63–64; R Alexy, 'Constitutional Rights, Balancing, and Rationality' (2003) 16 *Ratio Juris* 131, 134; DB Wexler, 'Justice, Mental Health, and Therapeutic Jurisprudence' (1992) 40 *Cleveland State Law Review* 517, 520.

[285] See generally PH Robinson, 'Hybrid Principles for the Distribution of Criminal Sanctions' (1987–1988) 82 *Northwestern University Law Review* 19, 29.

[286] Zedner (n 276) 510–11. See also J Habermas, 'Reply to Symposium Participants, Benjamin N Cardozo School of Law' in M Rosenfeld and A Arato (eds), *Habermas on Law and Democracy Critical*

Recall that the core claim tested here is whether consideration of a broader array of values operating as decision-grounds will improve the transparency/quality of self-defence decision-making. The proposed numerical assignments that follow are designed to broadly illustrate (1) that different fact-scenarios appropriately require one to consider different values as decision-grounds; (2) that consideration of these values, and their relative weighting, improves the transparency of decision-making; and (3) that such a value-centric discussion lays the groundwork for the challenging task of determining a reasonable accommodation of the different values when the defender's and attacker's interests conflict.

Put another way, the illustration that follows is designed to help test the value-centric position. But it is not meant to suggest that the value-based model (or, for that matter, any similar model) will yield precise and fully defensible self-defence outcomes in all cases.[287] With these points and limitations in mind, we, for illustrative purposes, will assign numerical values to different fact scenarios.

Table 1 Test of the Value-Centric Position (Key)

Weight	Meaning
1	Decision Ground Favours Protecting *Defender*
0	Decision Ground Not Pertinent
−1	Decision Ground Favours Protecting *Attacker*

To demonstrate the application of value quantification to a hypothetical in the self-defence context, consider the case of hallucinating and mentally incompetent Andrew who is threatening to slap Victor as Victor is sitting on a park bench. Andrew, in fact, believes Victor to be a fly. Assume further that Victor's only means of avoiding the minor battery is by using deadly force against Andrew. To understand whether such deadly force should be sanctioned, this book must examine how the facts of this particular case would be evaluated under the value-based model of self-defence.

The scenario just described leaves undisturbed the presumption that both parties have a fundamental, individual right to life deserving protection (values #2 and #4), and that the state has the related collective interest in reducing interpersonal violence (as reflected in value #1). The harm posed by the attack, moreover, is not so severe as to be non-compensable (and could be resolved in

Exchanges (Berkeley, University of California Press, 1998) 430, discussed in R Alexy, 'Balancing, Constitutional Review, and Representation' (2005) 3 *International Journal of Constitutional Law* 572, 573; TA Aleinikoff, 'Constitutional Law in the Age of Balancing' (1987) 96 *Yale Law Journal* 943, 1001–05.

[287] See generally J Herring and C Foster, 'Welfare Means Relationality, Virtue and Altruism' (2012) 32 *Legal Studies* 480, 484 (commenting that balancing tests can inaccurately lend a 'quasi-scientific credibility'); M Kagan, 'Dubious Deference: Reassessing Appellate Standards of Review in Immigration Appeals' (2012) 5 *Drexel Law Review* 101, 161 (same); Zedner (n 276) 510–11 (noting that, in the typical 'balancing test,' 'rarely are the particular interests spelt out, priorities made explicitly, or the process by which a weight is achieved made clear').

court, implicating value #5), and the use of deadly force to avert it is, therefore, disproportionate to the interest threatened. The incompetent Andrew, moreover, is unable to conform his conduct to the strictures of the law and is not attempting to elevate his interests above those of the victim. Deterrence (value #7) and maintaining equal standing between people (value #3) are, therefore, also not implicated.[288] While Andrew's act clearly threatens Victor's autonomy (value #4), it, moreover, is not the type of 'most serious' (culpable) conduct implicating equal standing (resulting in the complete 'forfeiture' of Andrew's right to non-interference discussed in Chapter 2(V)(A)).

Turning to maintaining the legitimacy of legal order (value #6), not authorising Victor to use lethal force to avoid a slap will not cause the public to lose respect for, or confidence in, the criminal justice system (indeed, authorising such force against the hallucinating Andrew will likely pose a greater threat to this value). Finally, ensuring the primacy of the legal process (value #5) also counsels against authorising deadly force because the relatively minor harm can, as necessary, be civilly compensated.

Considering all the values at play, then, Victor's right to autonomy and non-interference in this case should on balance yield to the justice system's interest in protecting the hallucinating, non-culpable Andrew:

Table 2 Non Culpable Threat

Nature of Threat: Non-culpable threat from insane Andrew
Seriousness of Threat: Low (slap on the face)
Defensive Force: Deadly force

Decision Ground	**Weight**	**Summary of Reasoning**
Value #1: Collective violence-reducing function	−1	The criminal justice system's collective interest in reducing violence by protecting its monopoly on force here favours the hallucinating Andrew because, in the context of a balancing of harms, the system is being asked to sanction deadly force against the morally innocent attacker so that Victor can avoid slight bruising. From a collective perspective, permitting such outcomes in cases like this threatens to, without compelling reason, undermine the state's monopoly on force.
Value #2: Protecting the individual attacker's (presumptive) right to life	+1	Andrew is facing deadly force merely because Victor wants to avoid possible slight bruising. Given this balance of harms, the presumption that Andrew has a right to life is not overcome.

(continued)

[288] See generally Rönnau and Hohn (n 49) side-note 66 (deterrence largely not implicated in innocent attacks).

Table 2 ***(Continued)***

Decision Ground	Weight	Summary of Reasoning
Value #3: Maintaining equal standing (see Chapter 2(IV)(C))	0	Andrew is mentally incompetent and is, therefore, not following a self-willed action plan. As a morally innocent attacker, he thus is only posing a threat of *harm*, and not wrong, to Victor. Maintaining equal standing is, consequently, not implicated.
Value #4: Protecting the defender's autonomy (see Chapter 2(IV)(D))	0	Andrew's attack is threatening Victor's right to non-interference (even though the threatened harm from the slap is both relatively trivial and compensable). Given the nature of the threatened attack, the interest in protecting the defender's autonomy is neutral (though one could reasonably argue that it should be +1 because the compensable and trivial nature of the attack are accounted for elsewhere).
Value #5: Ensuring the primacy of the legal process (see Chapter 2(IV)(E))	−1	Victor, if he were so inclined, could bring a civil suit against Andrew or his guardians to try to receive nominal compensation for the trivial harm. Because this is an acceptable alternative to deadly force, this value favours not authorising deadly force.
Value #6: Maintaining the legitimacy of the legal order (see Chapter 2(IV)(F))	−1	Permitting a defender to use deadly force against an incompetent (and, thus, morally innocent) person in order to avoid receiving a slight bruise will likely be broadly viewed as harsh and unjust, threatening to undermine the public's view of the criminal justice system's moral legitimacy.
Value #7: Deterrence (see Chapter 2(IV)(G))	0	Andrew is incompetent and unable to control his conduct. Allowing self-preferential defensive force in such a circumstance would have no specific or general deterrent impact on Andrew or others similarly situated.
TOTAL	−2	**Deadly force is presumptively (and narrowly) unjustifiable.**[289]

[289] Note that a fully culpable attacker threatening serious harm could have a +6-point total. But the sliding-scale nature of the analysis naturally means that changes in the assumptions change potential outcomes. See generally Rönnau and Hohn (n 49) side-notes 113, 226.

3

The Scholarly Community's Surprising Neglect of Values as Self-Defence Decision-Grounds

The core objective of this undertaking is to determine whether, and why, a more detailed accounting of the underlying values believed to provide the rationale for self-defence will aid in both highlighting and minimising some of the hidden normativity characterising much of the past and present self-defence discourse. Relatedly, we are examining the broader claim that a more value-centric approach will enhance the transparency and quality of the decision-making (regardless of whether – and perhaps precisely *when* – one disagrees with the precise value-array proposed here; for it is in a discussion about what values might have been overlooked, or accorded excessive or insufficient weight, that the benefits of a value-centric approach most clearly come to light). This, in turn, will go far to helping shore up this core defence's legitimacy and creditworthiness. As a foundational matter, then, it is sensible to determine the extent to which, when viewed against the backdrop of the approaches championed by the leading scholars in the field, our proposed value-centric approach adds something 'extra' to the long-standing and ongoing scholarly debate on the subject (or whether, instead, self-defence scholars have already developed fully comprehensive, persuasive theories grounded on the full array of values-as-decision-grounds implicated in self-defence cases).[1] As we shall see, the scholarship to date has, to a surprising extent, glossed over the importance of understanding how and why values provide self-defence's driving rationale.

I. Protecting the State's Monopoly on Force (and the Primacy of the Legal Process)

Ashworth's and Leverick's analyses differ on the topic of the state's interest in protecting its monopoly on force. Leverick more explicitly mentions the justice

[1] Note that the discussion that follows largely focuses on the scholars who have developed the most comprehensive theories of self-defence. That said, none of the discussed (and undiscussed) commentators' treatment considers the full range of values discussed here.

system's collective interest in reducing overall societal violence (and, thus, protecting the state's monopoly on force).[2] But it is among the German scholars that we find the most searching treatment of this topic. Pest,[3] Greco,[4] Nourse,[5] and Roxin[6] are just a few of the scholars who have emphasised that reducing interpersonal violence advances the systemic interest in helping protect the fundamental right to life[7] because self-defence functions as a necessary *alternative* to state power. Specifically, they persuasively explain why justified self-preferential force is (and, in fact, must be) available in those situations where police protection is not reasonably accessible. And so Kühl and Heger have argued that a state's obligation to protect individual rights creates a default priority for state force as a means of thwarting attacks, and, conversely, requires presumptive deference to state action (when available and effective).[8] Similarly, according to Rönnau and Hohn, only when the police are unavailable is self-preferential force 'necessary' as an exception to the state's monopoly on force.[9] Necessity and imminence, then, are generally (though not universally) considered critical limits on self-preferential

[2] F Leverick, *Killing in Self-Defence* (Oxford, Oxford University Press, 2006) 45, citing C Ryan, 'Self-Defense, Pacifism and the Possibility of Killing' (1983) 93:3 *Ethics* 510. See also M Weber, 'Politics as a Vocation' in HH Gerth and CW Mills (eds), *From Max Weber: Essays in Sociology* (London, Taylor and Francis, 1919/1946) 78 (defining the state as 'a human community that (successfully) claims the monopoly of the legitimate use of physical force').

[3] R Pest, 'Die Erforderlichkeit der Notwehrhandlung' in F Stam and A Werkmeister (eds), *Der Allgemeine Teil des Strafrechts in der aktuellen Rechtsprechung* (Baden-Baden, Nomos Verlagsgesellschaft, 2019) 137.

[4] L Greco, 'Notwehr und Proportionalität' [2018] GA 665, 670 (defining self-defence as an exception to the state's monopoly on force ('*Gewaltmonopol*'); the citizen who defends the legal order is thus operating as a surrogate of the state).

[5] See V Nourse, 'Reconceptualizing Criminal Law Defenses' (2003) 151 *University of Pennsylvania Law Review* 1692–1726 (arguing that the criminal law is an instrument of the state, designed to maintain a liberal political order and contending that defences, like offences, accomplish the common task of preserving the state's monopoly on force).

[6] C Roxin, *Strafrecht Allgemeiner Teil. Grundlagen. Der Aufbau der Verbrechenslehre, "Bd. I"*, § 15 (Beck CH, 2006) side-note 4.

[7] See generally GA Res 217 (III) A, Universal Declaration of Human Rights (Dec 10, 1948) [hereinafter UN Declaration] Art 3; Council of Europe, European Convention for the Protection of Human Rights and Fundamental Freedoms [hereinafter ECHR], Nov 4, 1950, ETS No. 005, Art 2. See also K Kühl and M Heger, 'Vorbemerkung' in *Strafgesetzbuch: Kommentar* § 32 (Heymanns Verlag GmbH, 2018) side-note 11a; V Erb, 'Notwehr als Menchenrecht – Zugleich eine Kritik der Entscheiduing des LG Frankfurt am Main im "Fall Daschner"' (2005) 25 *Neue Zeitschrift für Strafrecht* 593, 596–97. But see UNCHR (Sub-Commission), 'Prevention of Human Rights Violations Committed with Small Arms and Light Weapons' (2006) UN Doc. A/HRC/Sub.1/58/27 (prepared by Barbara Frey), www.smallarmssurvey.org/fileadmin/docs/N-Instruments/2006-UNGA-Prevention%20of%20human%20rights%20violations.pdf [hereinafter UNCHR 'Small Arms'] (concluding that the 'principle of self-defence' is not a broadly recognised human right).

[8] See Kühl & Heger (n 7) side-note 11a. See also T Fischer, '§ 32 Vorbemerkungen' in *Strafgesetzbuch* (Heymanns Verlag GmbH, 2019) side-note 35; H Lesch, 'Die Notwehr' in G Widmaier et al (eds), *Festschrift für Hans Dahs* (Schmidt, Dr Otto, 2005) 111–12.

[9] See T Rönnau and K Hohn, '§ 32 Notwehr' in G Cirener et al (eds), *Strafgesetzbuch: Leipziger Kommentar, Band 3* (Berlin, De Gruyter, 2019) side-notes 183–84.

force intended to ensure that self-defence does not become an alternative to, or undermine, the state's collective obligation to protect its citizens.[10]

II. Respect for the Attacker's 'Right to Life'

Efforts to engage in a comprehensive discussion of the values at play in self-defence cases are notably rare. And those (non-German) scholars who do discuss self-defence from a value-centric perspective tend to narrowly focus on the *attacker's* right to life. Schopp, in contrast, champions the more 'libertarian'[11] perspective and would permit deadly force to avert even non-deadly (and, arguably, trivial) threats when such defensive force is 'necessary.'[12] He contends that 'culpable transgressions move aggressors beyond the boundaries of their protected domains.'[13]

While Erb also invokes a *defender's* right to life as an 'imperative human right requirement' requiring protection,[14] the majority of contemporary scholars, including most prominently Ashworth,[15] Ryan,[16] Fletcher,[17] Leverick, Robinson,[18] Darley,[19] Fontaine,[20] and Schulhofer,[21] have endorsed different variants of the 'pacifist' position which in the main focuses on the *attacker's* right to life.

By way of an example of this self-described 'humanitarian' focus, Ashworth, in his influential 1975 *Cambridge Law Journal* article on self-defence against deadly attacks, proposed one of the early value-based approaches to thinking about self-defence.[22] In an effort to find consistency in the law of self-defence, Ashworth

[10] See generally J Isensee, 'Die Friedenspflicht der Bürger und das Gewaltmonopol des Staates' in G Müller and K Eichenberger (eds), *Staatsorganisation und Staatsfunktionen im Wandel: Festschrift für Kurt Eichenberger zum 60 Geburtstag* (Duncker & Humblot, 1982) 23; D Merten and G Arzt, *Rechtsstaat Und Gewaltmonopol (Recht Und Staat in Geschichte Und Gegenwart)* (1975) 33.

[11] See VF Nourse, 'Self-Defense and Subjectivity' (2001) 68 *University of Chicago Law Review* 1271–72 (distinguishing between 'pacifist' and 'libertarian' conceptions of self-defence).

[12] See RF Schopp, *Justification Defenses and Just Convictions* (Cambridge, Cambridge University Press, 1998) 9.

[13] Ibid at 77.

[14] Erb (n 7) 594.

[15] See AJ Ashworth, 'Self-Defence and the Right to Life' (1975) 34 *Cambridge Law Journal* 282, 289.

[16] See Ryan (n 2) 508.

[17] See GP Fletcher, *A Crime of Self-Defense: Bernhard Goetz and the Law on Trial* (New Jersey, Prentice Hall, 1988) [hereinafter Fletcher, *A Crime of Self-Defense*] 34.

[18] See PH Robinson and JM Darley, *Justice, Liability, and Blame: Community Views and the Criminal Law* (Taylor & Francis, 1995) 60, cited in PH Robinson, 'Punishing Dangerousness: Cloaking Preventive Detention as Criminal Justice' (2001) 114 *Harvard Law Review* 1429, 1443.

[19] See ibid.

[20] See RG Fontaine, 'In Self-Defense Regarding Self-Defense: A Rejoinder to Professor Corrado' (2010) 47 *American Criminal Law Review* 97, 101–02.

[21] See S Schulhofer, 'The Gender Question in Criminal Law' (1990) 7 *Social Philosophy & Policy* 105, 129, 132–133.

[22] Ashworth (n 15) 282, discussed in Nourse (n 11) 1272. See also M Raymond, 'Looking for Trouble: Framing and the Dignitary Interest in the Law of Self-Defense' (2010) 71 *Ohio State Law Journal* 287, 326; B Sangero, 'A New Defense for Self-Defense' (2006) 9 *Buffalo Criminal Law Review* 506 [hereinafter Sangero, 'New Defense']; GP Fletcher, 'The Right to Life' (1979) 13 *Georgia Law Review* 1371, 1376–80.

set out to examine the values and interests involved in self-defence cases. Ashworth advances what he terms a 'human rights approach' to self-defence. He, in the course of arguing against justifying deadly force to prevent serious bodily injury short of death (regardless of the attacker's culpability), contends that:

> The harm caused by homicide is absolute and irredeemable, whereas the harm caused by many other crimes is remediable to a degree. Even in crimes of violence which leave some permanent physical disfigurement or psychological effects, the victim [maintains] his or her life and, therefore, the possibility of further pleasures and achievements, whereas death is final.[23]

As this passage illustrates, Ashworth, by according central importance to the proportionality of harms, sets forth what in practice amounts to the rule that even the fully culpable aggressor's right to life must be protected whenever possible. He then uses this point of analytical departure to conclude that, out of 'respect for the attacker's right to life and physical security,'[24] defenders must always avoid conflict, seek to retreat, use an amount of force that is strictly proportionate to the amount of harm threatened, and never use deadly force to defend property. What Ashworth ultimately advances, then, is a largely monistic justification of self-defence anchored on the attacker's right to life; posits that certain principles are important; evaluates the principles independently; and then stipulates that one or the other principle should be considered *prima facie* superior.

While Ashworth imposes a presumptive duty on putative defenders acting outside their homes to avoid and retreat from conflict if reasonably possible, and, like Smith, also assesses the compatibility of self-defence and the right to life,[25] he derives this position from the requirement of necessity.[26] (That said, and even though the same necessity analysis could compel a different outcome, Ashworth also takes the 'pro-defender' position that individuals can remain in, and even go to, places where they know an attack is possible or even likely.[27])

Leverick, on the other hand, devotes less attention than Ashworth to the moral asymmetry between the attacker and the defender.[28] But she, building her approach on Ashworth's (attacker-oriented) human rights focus, is also generally open and honest about the monistic decision-ground she relies on to reach her various conclusions, namely, that the life of the aggressor and the life of the defender are almost always equally worthy of the law's protection.[29] Put another

[23] AJ Ashworth and J Horder, *Principles of Criminal Law*, 5th edn (Oxford, Oxford University Press, 2006) 249. See similarly C Elliott, 'Interpreting the Contours of Self-Defence Within the Boundaries of the Rule of Law, the Common Law and Human Rights' (2015) 79 *Journal of Criminal Law* 339; R Young, 'What Is So Wrong with Killing People?' (1979) 54 *Philosophy* 515, 518.

[24] Ashworth (n 15) 297. See also Sangero, 'New Defense' (n 22) 533.

[25] See JC Smith, 'The Use of Force in Public or Private Defence and Article 2' [2002] *Crim LR* 961, 961–62.

[26] Ashworth (n 15) 293–94.

[27] Ibid at 295–96.

[28] See generally A Grabczynska and KK Ferzan, 'Justifying Killing in Self-Defence' (2009) 99 *Journal of Criminal Law & Criminology* (book review) 235, 254.

[29] Leverick (n 2) 2.

way, because she views 'all human life [as being] of equal value,' and notes that the 'right to life uniquely cannot be remedied once it is lost,'[30] Leverick's perspective is that the right to life must *always* be accorded paramount importance and respected as much as reasonably possible (though, as discussed below, the challenge for her is to identify that dividing line). '[I]n a legal system that holds the equality of life to be a fundamental value, the aggressor has a right to life just as the victim does.'[31]

In fact, a fair reading of Leverick's position is that she views the right to life as so important that, in the final analysis, no true balancing need take place. In this sense, Leverick is, as a practical matter, considerably more protective of culpable attackers than Ashworth. She posits that the right to life is an ultimate touchstone that cannot be outweighed by, and trumps the consideration of, any other values (and therefore, operates to disallow the use of deadly force to fend off even fully culpable attacks threatening significant injury short of death).[32] As Leverick candidly states in the Preface of her book:

> My primary concern is with the right to life of both aggressor and victim and *it is my firm conviction* that the rules governing self-defence should be formulated with this in mind. As such, this is a book about the right to life, as much as it is a book about self-defence.[33]

Leverick does allow that human dignity, civil liberties, and sexual autonomy are values that some argue *may* 'outweigh' the value of the attacker's life. But she ultimately, and with only minimal space dedicated to considering any counter-argument, declares her view that they do not.[34] (Indeed, her repeated references to her personal/'firm' conviction on this point highlight that, in the end, Leverick's personal value-judgements concerning the paramount value of the 'right to life' drive her analysis and dictate its outcomes.) Under Leverick's parity-assuming model, then, only when a defender's right to life is threatened can the defender use deadly force and deprive the attacker of his right to life.[35] Leverick, however, regrettably does not address why other circumstance-dependent values, such as those discussed in Chapter 2(IV), do not also deserve consideration (or, for that matter, even mention).

George Fletcher, like Ashworth and Leverick (though following different reasoning), also pursues a largely monistic, autonomy-focused approach to addressing values in self-defence.[36] Fletcher, however, does not detail what

[30] Ibid at 2, 58–68 (contending that the 'right to life [is the] most fundamental of all human rights').

[31] Ibid at 45, citing Ryan (n 2) 510.

[32] See ibid at viii.

[33] See ibid.

[34] Ibid at 3.

[35] Ibid at 45 (Leverick adopts Uniacke's position – which will be discussed at some length later – by contending that the aggressor 'forfeits' his right to life by becoming an 'unjust immediate threat' to the defender).

[36] See generally GP Fletcher, 'The Right and the Reasonable' (1985) 98 *Harvard Law Review* 949, 971. See also DAJ Richards, 'Rights, Resistance, and the Demands of Self-Respect' (1983) 32 *Emory Law Journal* 405, 424–25.

'autonomy' actually is; he, instead, simply describes it as a 'pre-legal' concept and posits that it is under attack whenever an attacker threatens the defender's legally protected rights and interests.[37] In the end, however, Fletcher, like Ashworth and Leverick, pursues a theory of self-defence heavily invested with pacifism and social responsibility toward the attacker's right to life.[38] And so a defender's deadly self-preferential force would only be justified when strictly necessary, where 'necessity' means that the defender had *no alternative* but to kill her (culpable) attacker.[39]

Further, Fletcher takes Germany's below-described 'right need never yield to the wrong' concept and uses it as the theoretical (and, at first blush, moral absolutist) basis for treating self-defence as a justification.[40] But he then adds the moderating, flexible, German-law-inspired concept of 'abuse of rights.' In the end, then, Fletcher infuses the traditional German approach to self-defence with the personal value-judgement that self-preferential killing is only 'necessary' when it serves to right the wrong of a *deadly* attack.[41] The imminence requirement, moreover, for Fletcher becomes an essential dividing line between retaliatory and defensive behaviour.[42] The requirement that an attacker's use of force be unlawful, in turn, ensures that defensive force is employed as a matter of right.[43] These may all be defensible points. But what, once again, is missing is a recognition that each of these posited 'rules' necessarily implicates important trade-offs between competing value-based interests.

III. Protecting Equal Standing Among People

Self-defence as a method of avoiding the implication of unequal standing between people has received surprisingly little attention. In fact, Erb is among the very few to explicitly endorse equal standing between defender and attacker as an important, independent consideration. He, similar to Schopp, concludes, in the context of advancing the position that protection of the individual defender should be the only objective of any self-defence regime, that individuals must be authorised

[37] GP Fletcher, *Rethinking Criminal Law* (New York, Oxford University Press, 1978) [hereinafter Fletcher, *Rethinking*] 857–60.

[38] See generally GP Fletcher, 'Domination in the Theory of Justification and Excuse' (1996) 57 *University of Pittsburgh Law Review* 553, 560; Fletcher, *A Crime of Self-Defense* (n 17) 33. See also Nourse (n 11) 1271 (discussing Fletcher's theory of self-defence).

[39] See Fletcher (n 38) 559.

[40] See generally GP Fletcher, 'The Nature of Justification' in S Shute et al (eds), *Action and Value in Criminal Law* (Oxford, Oxford University Press, 1993) 181; GP Fletcher, 'Punishment and Self-Defense' (1989) 8 *Law & Philosophy* 201, 210, 213–15 [hereinafter Fletcher, 'Punishment and Self-Defense']; Fletcher, *Rethinking* (n 37) 860–74; Fletcher, *A Crime of Self-Defense* (n 17) 32–33, 35–36; GP Fletcher, 'Proportionality and the Psychotic Aggressor: A Vignette in Comparative Criminal Theory' (1973) 8 *Israel Law Review* 367, 378–87 [hereinafter Fletcher, 'Proportionality']. See also ch 5(II).

[41] See generally Fletcher, 'Punishment and Self-Defense' (n 40) 181; Fletcher, *Rethinking* (n 37) 860–74; Fletcher, 'Proportionality' (n 37) 368, 390.

[42] See Fletcher (n 38) 553.

[43] Ibid at 558–59.

to use whatever force is necessary to ward off imminent threats.[44] In support, he largely stands alone in contending that protecting the right of the individual includes allowing the individual to ensure equal standing (*Gleichordnung*) between herself and her attacker.[45] Ashworth and the vast majority of his scholarly peers, in contrast, omit any consideration of whether protecting peoples' equal standing should play any role in self-defence (though it is fair to assume, based on his focus on the attacker's right to life, that Ashworth would likely reject equal standing as an independent decision-ground).[46]

Leverick, on the other hand, as part of her 'strict proportionality' analysis, implicitly *rejects* the notion that the threatened imposition of unequal standing between attacker and defender should play any outcome-determinative role. Rather, consider Leverick's claim that, even accepting that rape equates to serious bodily injury, deadly force to defend against it is only justified if accompanied by threat of *death*.[47] The 'very serious injury' rape causes to the 'honour' of victims (which can fairly be viewed as a variant of equal standing), moreover, purportedly is also insufficient to justify the use of deadly force.[48] Leverick, thus, rejects the near-universally accepted position[49] that threatened serious bodily injury in the form rape is sufficiently injurious to justify deadly self-preferential force.

This result is not a surprise, given Leverick's view that, after all, unless defensive force is being deployed by the defender to save her *life*, it can never qualify as justified self-defence.[50] Leverick seeks to further buttress her position in the context of the factual claim that cases in which rape results in death are rare. According to Leverick, studies reveal that 'only' one to three per cent of 'rapists kill their victims.'[51] It, therefore, is *prima facie* objectively unreasonable for a defender to, without more, believe that a rapist is always threatening death.[52]

Building on her broader premise that serious bodily injury, regardless of the culpability of the attacker, cannot ever justify deadly defensive force, Leverick, echoing Ashworth, claims that '[a]ttacks on bodily integrity, although painful, are

[44] See V Erb, 'Notwehr und Notstand' in Bernd von Heintschel-Heinegg (ed), *Münchner Kommentar zum Strafgesetzbuch, Band 1* (Beck CH, 2017) side-note 18.

[45] See ibid at side-note 18; S Retzko, *Die Angriffsverursachung bei der Notwehr* (Lit Verlag, 2001) 127; J Renzikowski, *Notstand und Notwehr* (Duncker & Humblot GmbH, 1994) 275.

[46] Ashworth (n 15) 282.

[47] Leverick (n 2) 143–58.

[48] Ibid.

[49] See, eg, *State v Baker*, 441 SE2d 551, 555 (NC 1994), cited in L Hoyson, 'Rape Is Tough Enough Without Having Someone Kick You from the Inside: The Case for Including Pregnancy as Substantial Bodily Injury' (2010) 44 *Valparaiso University Law Review* 565, 580; M Kremnitzer and K Ghanayim, 'Proportionality and the Aggressor's Culpability in Self-Defense' (2004) 39 *Tulsa Law Review* 875, 894; S Kadish, 'Respect for Life and Regard for Rights in the Criminal Law' (1976) 64 *California Law Review* 882.

[50] Leverick (n 2) 151.

[51] Ibid at 151.

[52] Ibid.

generally events from which the victim can recover and go on to lead a fulfilling life. Deprivations of life are not.'[53] She, in the context of rape, asserts:

> Traumatic as the harmful psychological effects of a rape may be, they are psychological effects that are almost certainly remediable over time. Granted, the rape victim's life may never be quite the same again, but the psychological harm of rape does at least leave open the possibility of recovery and readjustment [whereas] the harm of killing does not leave open this possibility.[54]

Leverick next examines the impact of a potential unwanted pregnancy resulting from rape. '[W]hile pregnancy is an extremely unpleasant potential consequence of a rape, the harm caused is not permanent because the rape victim will generally be able to have an abortion.'[55] From Leverick's perspective, then, deadly force to prevent rape (or, for that matter, *any* kind of attack or injury), regardless of the culpability, sadistic motivation, etc. of the attacker may only be authorised if the facts of the case establish that the rape attempt 'approaches the standard of a wrong *equivalent to a deprivation of life itself*.'[56]

It must be noted that Leverick's position that culpably threatened serious bodily injury stopping just short of death cannot ever justify deadly defensive force runs against the bulk of the literature (which is already notably sympathetic to what we have termed the 'pacifist' conception of self-preferential force). More tellingly, it also finds no support in any known jurisdiction.[57] One of the harms rape uniquely inflicts, moreover, is that it objectifies and dehumanises the victim (even in the absence of physical violence or injury), thereby upending the equal standing between attacker and victim (value #3).[58] But this argument does not inform Leverick's analysis.

[53] Ibid at 152. *Cf* J Herring, 'Law and the Relational Self' 23 (MS on file with author) (discussing the various traditional arguments against forfeiture theory). ('The right to bodily integrity is one of the most strongly protected rights that one can have.').

[54] Leverick (n 2) 155.

[55] Ibid at 153.

[56] Ibid at 157 (emphasis added). Note, however, that determining the 'standard of a wrong' inevitably involves the same line-drawing that Leverick finds so objectionable in the context of deadly force in defence of property.

[57] See generally *Commonwealth v Emmons*, 43 A2d 568 (Pa 1945) (ruling that '[a] homicide is justifiable when committed by necessity and in good faith in order to prevent a felony … such as … rape'), cited in CW Watson, 'Justifiable Use of Deadly Force in Law Enforcement' (1973) 78 *Dickinson Law Review* 115, 129; *People v Cebalos*, 526 P2d 241, 245 (Cal 1974) (ruling that rape is among crimes that may be resisted with deadly force). See also Kremnitzer and Ghanayim (n 49) 894 ('[T]he law of self-defense allows deadly force in order to prevent death or rape, but not simple assault or theft.'); DB Kates, Jr. and NJ Engberg, 'Deadly Force Self-Defense Against Rape' (1982) 15 *University of California Davis Law Review* 873, 881 ('Judicial decisions regularly include rape, and sometimes sodomy, in illustrative lists of crimes which may be resisted with deadly force.'); Kadish (n 49) 882 (noting that the common law permitted a victim to take life even when lesser interests were threatened and that, therefore, a woman could use deadly force to prevent rape or kidnapping); MPC § 3.04(2)(b) (authorising deadly force when necessary to prevent 'sexual intercourse compelled by force or threat').

[58] See generally C Ginn, 'Ensuring the Effective Prosecution of Sexually Violent Crimes in the Bosnian War Crimes Chamber: Applying Lessons from the ICTY' (2013) 27 *Emory International Law Review* 565, 580; J Harrelson, 'Genocide and the Rape of Armenia' (2010) 4 *University of St Thomas Journal of Law & Public Policy* 163, 178.

In fact, Leverick throughout remains true to her self-described baseline 'firm conviction' about the equal value of the lives of aggressors and defenders, including in the context of 'battered women.'[59] According to Leverick:

> [S]elf-defence is only permissible where the accused faced a threat of death (or one of near equivalent seriousness) or where such a threat might reasonably be assumed. The level of violence faced by the majority of battered women is unlikely to meet this threshold.[60]

Leverick's position, then, is that equality of lives is presumptive, and that this presumption can *only* be overcome in cases of threatened unlawful *killing*. This position is a rather stark outlier even among the very attacker-friendly contemporary scholarship. What is particularly surprising is that Leverick does not appear to recognise, let alone seek to reconcile, the reality that her 'personal conviction'-based self-defence theory deviates so markedly from the mainstream self-defence scholarship, as well as (and to my thinking even more importantly) from the contemporary morality as embodied by self-defence laws around the world. Put another way, having a firmly-held personal conviction about something is a common human experience. But constructing a comprehensive theory of self-defence around such a particular – and, in fact, demonstrably idiosyncratic – view, without seeking to explain why her theory should be accepted when it finds no support in any of the world's legal systems, is a surprising oversight in Leverick's otherwise very comprehensive and thoughtful model.

Turning to Sangero, he, in contrast to Leverick, places ultimate emphasis on the moral culpability of the attacker. He, however, omits a discussion of the unique 'wrong' threatened by a culpable attack.[61] Ashworth, like Sangero, also recognises that attackers threatening greater concrete harm deserve less protection. Focusing on the respect for the attacker's right to life and physical security, moreover, Ashworth argues that the amount of force used must be strictly proportionate to the amount of harm threatened.[62] Like Sangero, however, Ashworth does not explain what in particular it is that distinguishes innocent attackers threatening a *harm* and culpable attackers threatening a *wrong*.

In additional contrast to Leverick, Kates' and Engberg's discussion of deadly force to protect victims from both mental harm and psychological damage reflects an understanding that protecting the victim's equal standing should play a part in self-defence theory (even though they do not use this term). For Dsouza, on the other hand, self-defence is a justification that 'negate[s] the wrongness of what

[59] For the leading, and controversial, research-based study of the syndrome, see LE Walker, *The Battered Woman Syndrome*, 4th edn (New York, Springer Publishing, 2016). See also A Gruber, 'The Duty to Retreat in Self-Defense Law and Violence Against Women' *Oxford Handbooks Online* (6 July 2017), https://doi.org/10.1093/oxfordhb/9780199935352.013.5 (discussing the complex relationship between the duty to retreat in self-defence law and violence against women).

[60] Leverick (n 2) 91.

[61] See B Sangero, *Self-Defence in Criminal Law* (Oxford, Hart Publishing, 2006) [hereinafter Sangero, *Self-Defence*] 90–106.

[62] Ashworth (n 15) 296–97.

occurred.'[63] In fact, Dsouza views the right to use defensive force to protect life and limb as 'constituently human'; asking the question of whether this conduct is moral, and hence, is akin to asking a person whether it is moral 'for us to have opposable thumbs.'[64] In other words, in circumstances where defensive force is necessary, there is no point of asking whether the defensive force used is right or wrong, blameworthy or blameless, good or bad – it is (or, rather, must be) acceptable because it is inherent in our natures.

As Dsouza puts it, such conduct must 'logically stand outside the realm of moral guidance and assessment.'[65] But Dsouza's argument appears a bit tautological, in that it stakes out the position that self-defence is uniquely incapable of being evaluated by third parties (including judges and legislators). This position also side-steps the foundational question of when a criminal justice system should sanction such self-preferential force (or, rather, what makes self-defence justified as a matter of law).

In contrast to Dsouza, Sangero, Leverick, and Ashworth, Schopp's focus on vindicating the *defender's* individual autonomy when faced with a culpable threat is explicitly grounded in what he views as the normative asymmetry in the form of imputation of lesser standing created by the culpable attack.[66] Erb, reflecting agreement with value-based model value #3, likewise believes that protecting the right of the individual *includes* allowing the individual to ensure the equal standing between herself and her attacker.[67]

IV. Protecting the Defender's Autonomy

Schopp, once again swimming against the current of virtually all contemporary scholars, places near-singular importance on protecting the *defender's* interest in vindicating his individual autonomy when faced with an attacker's culpable threat. Similar to Wallerstein,[68] Schopp contends that self-defence and punishment 'reflect a deeper value for the equal status of persons as autonomous individuals with their own spheres of personal sovereignty.'[69] Accordingly, Schopp endorses the position

[63] M Dsouza, *Rationale-Based Defences in Criminal Law* (Oxford, Hart Publishing, 2017) 3.

[64] Ibid at 50–51.

[65] Ibid at 51.

[66] Schopp (n 12) 83–84.

[67] See Erb (n 44) side-note 18. See also S Wallerstein, 'Justifying the Right to Self-Defense: A Theory of Forced Consequences' (2005) 91 *Virginia Law Review* 1028.

[68] See Wallerstein (n 67) 1028 (self-defence allows a defender to ward off 'an indirect threat to autonomy, a threat that is generated by the fear and instability that the lack of such a right would bring about. It constitutes one of the basic conditions that allow people to live together in society').

[69] Schopp (n 12) 75. See also RF Schopp, 'Justifying Capital Punishment in Principle and in Practice: Empirical Evidence of Distortion in Application' (2002) 81 *Nebraska Law Review* 805, 830–32; RF Schopp, 'Verdicts of Conscience: Nullification and Necessity as Jury Responses to Crimes of Conscience' (1996) 69 *Southern California Law Review* 2075–76; RF Schopp et al, 'Battered Woman Syndrome, Expert Testimony, and the Distinction Between Justification and Excuse' [1994] *University of Illinois Law Review* 45, 69.

that any criminal justice system that refuses to recognise a defender's right to use whatever force is necessary to protect his autonomy and self-determination in the absence of state protection ultimately aids and abets the culpable aggressor's threatened violation of the defender's *non-compensable* sovereignty and the corresponding imputation of lesser standing (thus implicating value #3).[70]

Schopp, echoing Kopel,[71] therefore, justifies the use of deadly force to avert a non-deadly culpable threat so long as such force is 'necessary.' The threat to the 'victim's sovereignty and standing takes priority over the concrete interest in the culpable aggressor's life.'[72] Effectively breaking the linkage between proportionality and the justified exercise of self-defence, Schopp believes the attacker's act of engaging in 'culpable transgressions move aggressors beyond the boundaries of their protected domains.'[73] The defender, as a consequence, is authorised to inflict '*any* necessary injury to the aggressor's concrete interests as the lesser sacrifice of important moral value.'[74]

Erb likewise advocates for an interpretation of self-defence that, in a departure from the majority view of German scholars and the value-based model, focuses narrowly on maximized protection of the individual defender's rights.[75] Erb, in fact, concludes that the state owes it to the individual to permit her to use all available means to ward off a threatened attack when the state is unable to offer protection.[76] To Erb, such a position is consistent with the conception of self-defence as mediating a conflict between right and wrong. And any approach that would limit such a necessary defence threatens to make the justice system an 'accomplice' of the attacker.[77] Sangero does not go as far as Schopp and Erb in according protection of the defender's autonomy such a central role. But he agrees with them that 'the autonomy of the person attacked' is the key interest self-defence law must protect.[78]

Don Kates has written about self-defence from many perspectives, but his most prominent theoretical discussion (in which he was joined by Engberg) focuses on using deadly force to prevent rape.[79] From Kates and Engberg's perspective, such deadly force is justified because of rape's threatened 'intrusion of mind and body.'[80] Their theory is grounded on what they describe as the 'ancient principle' that deadly force necessary to 'avert death or serious bodily harm' is justified.[81]

[70] Schopp (n 12) 75, 79.
[71] DB Kopel, et al 'The Human Right of Self-Defense' (2007) 22 *Brigham Young University Journal of Public Law* 43, 177–78.
[72] Schopp (n 12) 9.
[73] Ibid at 77.
[74] Ibid (emphasis added), discussed in Elliott (n 23) 337–38.
[75] See Erb (n 44) side-note 18. See also Erb (n 7) 601.
[76] See Erb (n 44) side-note 18.
[77] Ibid.
[78] Ibid at side-notes 72–73.
[79] See, eg, Kates and Engberg (n 57).
[80] Ibid at 873.
[81] Ibid at 874–79.

In sharp contrast to Leverick's conception of self-defence, then, Kates and Engberg endorse the near-universal position that deadly force should be justified to ward off death *or* great bodily harm (the latter term, from their perspective, encompassing both physical injury and psychological trauma).[82] And while they posit that rape poses the threat of a unique 'violation,' Kates and Engberg curiously do not specify what exactly that violation is (other than stating that 'the law and common sense recognise [it]').[83]

V. Ensuring the Primacy of the Legal Process

Most theorists agree that the availability of the legal process to resolve conflicts and disputes is a fundamental human right.[84] As Hart and Kantorowicz observe, individuals have collective interests in maintaining a stable society that punishes only after affording the accused due process, and that does not tolerate vigilante law enforcement or acts of revenge.[85] Uniacke agrees that vigilantism and similar 'self-help' crime-control options seek to wrest from the state the authority to punish and condemn threatening, non-democratic lawlessness.[86]

But other commentators, including many of the German scholars discussed below, turn this argument around: The right to self-defence, according to scholars such as Kremnitzer and Ghanayim, 'is intended to preserve the legal order by granting every person the right to fend off unlawful attacks.'[87] This conception of self-defence's rationale, however, can perhaps more accurately be viewed as reflecting fact-specific instances justifying *exceptions* to the state's default collective interest in minimising violence by maintaining its monopoly on force (value #1).[88]

[82] Ibid at 886–88, 894–903.

[83] Ibid at 906.

[84] See generally UN Declaration (n 7) Arts 6, 7, 8, and 11; ECHR (n 7), Nov 4, 1950, ETS No. 005, Arts 1 and 13. See also MJ Perry, 'The Morality of Human Rights' (2013) 50 *San Diego Law Review* 775, 808–09; LA Crippa, 'Multilateral Development Banks and Human Rights Responsibility' (2010) 25 *American University of International Law Review* 531, 572–73.

[85] See generally HL Hart, *The Concept of Law* (Oxford, Oxford University Press, 1994) 1 (providing a comprehensive discussion of the function of the law); L Nader, 'The Anthropological Study of Law' in P Sack and J Aleck (eds), *Law and Anthropology* (New York, New York University Press, 1992) 3 (same, but from an anthropological perspective); H Kantorowicz, *The Definition of Law* (Octagon Press Ltd, 1980) 1 (same, discussing the function of law).

[86] See S Uniacke, 'Self-Defense and Natural Law' (1991) 36 *American Journal of Jurisprudence* 79. See also D Markel, 'Retributive Justice and the Demands of Democratic Citizenship' (2012) 1 *Virginia Journal of Criminal Law* 33; K Bilz, 'The Puzzle of Delegated Revenge' (2007) 87 *Boston University Law Review* 1101 (noting that states in the South and the West allow for broader definitions of self-defence than the laws of the Northern states); W Gossett, 'The Rule of Law or the Defiance of Law' (1969) 55 *American Bar Association Journal* 824.

[87] See Kremnitzer and Ghanayim (n 49) 899, discussed in JD Moore, 'Reasonable Provocation – Distinguishing the Vigilant from the Vigilante in Self-Defense Law' (2013) 78 *Brooklyn Law Review* 1659.

[88] See Moore (n 87) 1659. See also DL Creach, 'Partially Determined Imperfect Self-Defense: The Battered Wife Kills and Tells Why' (1982) 34 *Stanford Law Review* 627.

VI. Maintaining the Legitimacy of the Legal Order

As we already discussed, this value is one that is assuming an even more significant role in an era when large parts of the population in the US and elsewhere view criminal justice systems with great skepticism and distrust. Trust and respect, after all, play an important part in shoring up the legitimacy of the law.[89] Stated differently, the public's 'law-related behavior [is] powerfully influenced by people's subjective judgements' about the system's fairness.'[90] Yet, there does not appear to be any comprehensive commentary on self-defence that treats avoiding self-defence outcomes threatening to erode the moral legitimacy of the legal order as a stand-alone value.

Stepping back a bit, we have already examined the position, championed most prominently in the German scholarship,[91] that self-defence protects the 'socio-legal order.'[92] According to this perspective, 'the person attacked acts as the representative and protector of society, public order and the legal system, since his actions are directed at neutralising a violation of the law.'[93] Sangero's account is generally in accord, providing that protection of the socio-legal order is of 'immense importance' but should play a role subsidiary to 'the autonomy of the person attacked and … the guilt of the aggressor, while also taking the interest of the aggressor into account.'[94] It is worth noting, however, that acts of self-defence may not always serve to 'protect' the socio-legal order. Rather, and as discussed in Chapter 2(IV)(F), 'extreme' self-defence outcomes, whether favouring attackers or defenders, can also operate to *undermine* the legitimacy of the legal order.

VII. Deterrence

Deterrence has long been widely recognised as a primary value providing self-defence's rationale. Robinson, for example, comments that '[f]orce in self-defence may injure the aggressor, but the injury is outweighed by the societal value of the defensive force … in avoiding the threatened harm to the victim and in condemning and deterring unjustified aggression generally.'[95] Sangero agrees with Robinson that, in the context of self-defence law, the 'deterrent function has a dual character: the individual aggressor is effectively deterred by the repelling of his attack, and

[89] See ch 2(IV)(F).

[90] TR Tyler, 'Procedural Justice, Legitimacy, and the Effective Rule of Law' (2003) 30 *Crime & Justice* 284, [hereinafter Tyler, 'Procedural Justice'].

[91] See ch 5(II)(A).

[92] See ch 2(IV)(E)(ii).

[93] Sangero, *Self-Defence* (n 61) 68–69, discussing M Kremnitzer, 'Proportionality and the Psychotic Aggressor: Another View' (1983) 18 *Israel Law Review* 181–91.

[94] Ibid at 72–73.

[95] PH Robinson, 'Competing Theories of Justification: Deeds v. Reasons' in A Simester and A Smith (eds), *Harm and Culpability* (1996) 45, 46.

the potential offenders will be deterred when they know that their plan may be frustrated not only by the police.'[96]

Stell echoes Robinson and Sangero, commenting that imposing limits on defensive force will result in attackers fearing 'violence from the police only.'[97] Kremnitzer and Ghanayim similarly take the position that self-defence is 'intended to deter potential aggressors' and protect the 'legal order.'[98] (Presenting a challenge to this deterrence position, Cheng and Hoekstra have, in the context of a study on 'stand your ground' laws, concluded that, while it would be 'reasonable to expect that strengthening self-defence law would deter crime, we find this is not the case.'[99])

VIII. Self-Defence Scholarship's Treatment of Values as Decision-Grounds

The foregoing thematic literature review demonstrates that, to the extent that values as decision-grounds are discussed in the mainstream scholarship, they are typically framed very generally as a broad 'struggle' or 'clash' between the criminal justice system's (1) obligation to safeguard the (generally undefined) 'autonomy' of the defender, and (2) interest in protecting broader welfarist concerns, typically the attacker's 'right to life.'[100] Scholars such as Ashworth, Fletcher, Schopp, and Leverick, in their comprehensive theories of self-defence, moreover, at least on some level ground their individual analyses on one or two values (such as protecting the attacker's right to life) that they personally believe should carry the most analytical sway.[101]

The prevailing value-dichotomous (defender's autonomy versus attacker's right to life) discussion is, in fact, a natural starting point for a value-centric dialogue about self-defence. But it is not more than that. A genuine understanding of the moral, ethical, and public-policy underpinnings of self-defence theory requires a far more in-depth value-centric discussion. The proposed value-based model, by offering a reasonable accounting of the values that, depending on the

[96] Sangero, *Self-Defence* (n 61) 68.

[97] LK Stell, 'Close Encounters of the Lethal Kind & The Use of Deadly Force in Self-Defense' (1986) 49 *Law & Contemporary Problems* 113, 120.

[98] See Kremnitzer and Ghanayim (n 49) 885–86. See similarly K Ghanayim and MS-A Wattad, 'Reconsidering the Grounds and the Causing Conditions for the Necessity Defense: Between Justification and Excuse – A Comprehensive Study' (2017) 86 *University of Missouri at Kansas City Law Review* 111, 138–39; JQ La Fond, 'The Case for Liberalizing the Use of Deadly Force in Self-Defense' (1983) 6 *University of Puget Sound Law Review* 237, 283.

[99] See C Cheng and M Hoekstra, 'Does Strengthening Self-Defense Law Deter Crime or Escalate Violence? Evidence from Expansions to Castle Doctrine' (2013) 48 *Journal of Human Resources* 821, 849, discussed in D Sweeney, 'Standing Up to Stand Your Ground Laws: How the Modern NRA-Inspired Self-Defense Statutes Destroy the Principle of Necessity, Disrupt the Criminal Justice System and Increase Overall Violence' (2016) 64 *Cleveland State Law Review* 734.

[100] See generally Lesch (n 8) 81, 82.

[101] See generally Rönnau and Hohn (n 9) side-note 226.

circumstances, become self-defence decision-grounds, provides the vehicle for such a discussion concerning self-defence doctrine's deeper rationale.

Consider, by way of example, the relatively short shrift values-as-decision-grounds receive even in some of the most comprehensive scholarly accounts of self-defence, such as Leverick's quickly-abandoned effort to discuss values in the context of 'avoiding trouble.'[102] Leverick in her analysis of when a person might have to stay away from a place where she knows an attack will, or is likely, to occur, mentions: (1) freedom of movement (encompassed in value #4 – protecting the defender's autonomy), and (2) the duty to avoid violent conflict that might result in the loss of life.[103] Leverick, in so doing, refers to violence reduction and protection of the attacker's right to life. But she does not engage in a searching analysis of when and why these values pertain, how they interact with each other, or whether there are other values that should in fairness also be considered.[104]

Fletcher, despite adapting certain aspects of the German law of self-defence to his approach, like Leverick and Ashworth in the end sides with the more pacifist conception of self-defence.[105] While one may expect to see his scholarship take on a value-centric approach, Fletcher's focus instead is on what he considers 'logical consequences' – technical legal questions, such as the applicability of the 'incompatibility thesis' (that there cannot be two mutually justified defenders) and the related requirement that defenders be both internally and externally justified.[106]

The closest Fletcher in his groundbreaking work comes to a value-centric analysis is when he considers the role 'humanitarian grounds' might play in the state's effort to reduce overall societal violence (value #1).[107] That said, Fletcher also concedes that requiring proportionate force may conflict with the 'absolute' right to defend one's individual autonomy.[108] But Fletcher only goes so far with his consideration of values (and the tension between them). What is absent from his exceptionally extensive self-defence scholarship is a deeper discussion of what actually makes his defenders' purportedly justified acts so 'right.' And this is so, even though the normative distinction between justified ('right') and excused ('wrongful but acceptable') conduct anchors most of his work.[109] Fletcher, then, ultimately focuses on 'logical consistency' as the 'overriding legal value.'[110]

[102] See generally Leverick (n 2) 127–28.

[103] See ibid.

[104] See ibid.

[105] See generally ibid at 560 (discussing the 'social point of view' that requires a proportionality rule sensitive to the 'competing interest' in life of the aggressor); Fletcher, *A Crime of Self-Defense* (n 17) 33.

[106] See generally Fletcher (n 36) 971–80; GP Fletcher, 'Should Intolerable Prison Conditions Generate a Justification or an Excuse For Escape?' (1979) 26 *UCLA Law Review* 1355, 1358; GP Fletcher, 'Paradoxes in Legal Thought' (1985) 85 *Columbia Law Review* 1263, 1264 [hereinafter Fletcher, 'Paradoxes']. On the incompatibility thesis, Fletcher appears to have been inspired by Immanuel Kant. See I Kant, 'The Doctrine of Right' in I Kant (ed), *The Metaphysics of Morals* (Cambridge, Mass, Hackett Publishing, 1991) 60 ('It is evident that were there such a right the doctrine of right would have to be in contradiction with itself.').

[107] See Fletcher (n 38) 559–60.

[108] Fletcher, 'Proportionality' (n 37) 371–80. See also Rönnau and Hohn (n 9) side-notes 68, 113.

[109] See Fletcher, *Rethinking* (n 37) 559–60.

[110] See Fletcher, 'Paradoxes' (n 106) 1264–65.

Schopp, like Leverick, anchors his analysis on a near-singular focus on autonomy – but in sharp contrast to Leverick's aggressor-centric approach, Schopp focuses narrowly on the autonomy of the defender.[111] Schopp's all-or-nothing approach, however, places outsized importance on protecting the defender's interest in his individual autonomy (and, relatedly, on the claimed normative asymmetry created by the culpable attack). It, for no stated or good reason, ignores other competing values and legitimate collective or welfarist goals. For example, Schopp does not address the danger that, in according defenders near-unlimited discretion to use defensive force, he might increase overall societal violence by paying insufficient attention to the state's monopoly on force (value #1) and essentially invalidates any right to life the attacker might have (value #2). Similarly, Schopp's detailed writings do not address whether and how his conception of justified self-defence can be squared with the primacy of the legal process (value #5), and leaves similarly unexamined whether the harsh self-defence outcomes flowing from his theory threaten to undermine the moral legitimacy of the legal order (value #6).

In short, scholars like Schopp, Ashworth, and Leverick, on some level at least, recognise that certain values should matter. But they differ markedly on which ones and why – and none engage in a sustained, comprehensive value-centric examination. Nourse, who has become one of the leading commentators on self-defence in the context of the battered intimate partner syndrome, in fact *rejects* the notion that studying the values underlying self-defence is sensible.[112] Instead, she believes that the analysis of self-defence must proceed 'in a different key, not as a set of values or functions or end-states but as a question of the key relationships involved between citizens and between citizens and state.'[113]

Setting aside for now Nourse's debatable differentiation between 'values' and 'key relationships between citizens and between citizens and the state,' she conceptualises the justice system as being designed to serve the 'demands of majorities and the state.'[114] While this perspective, if accurate, could be labelled as descriptive, it explicitly foregoes a discussion over what values and interests might drive such purported majoritarian state interests. In other words, even if Nourse is correct that the justice system is in reality just a means of enforcing certain 'key relationships,' this does not necessarily mean that such relationships are any less value-driven.

Uniacke in her comprehensive work (the only complete pre-2006 book devoted entirely to the theory of self-defence) argues that an individual's rights – including, most fundamentally, the right to life – are limited from the outset: 'Our possession of the right to life is conditional, the condition relevant to the justification of self-defence being that we not be an unjust immediate threat to another person.'[115]

[111] See Schopp (n 12) 83–84.
[112] Nourse (n 11) 1274 n 200. See also Nourse (n 5) 1692–1726.
[113] Nourse (n 11) 1274 n 200.
[114] Nourse (n 5) 1726. See also JY Kim, 'The Rhetoric of Self-Defense' (2008) 13 *Berkeley Journal of Criminal Law* 288 (discussing Nourse's theory).
[115] S Uniacke, *Permissible Killing: The Self-Defence Justification of Homicide* (Cambridge, Cambridge University Press, 1994) 213.

Uniacke's focus on double-effect and the incompatibility thesis (also known as the 'paradox of unknowing justifications'), and her normative theory based on a person not becoming an 'unjust immediate threat' to another, like Fletcher's, advances a juridical conception of criminal defences premised largely on logical expedience and consistency. She does not, however, pursue the additional step of engaging in a more searching analysis of the underlying values that might, for example, support her forfeiture theory.[116] Had she done so, she could have fortified her conception of an 'unjust threat' by injecting it with more analytic content.

Frowe takes a different approach from her peers. She broadly divides self-defence theorists into objectivists (who, following consequentialist approaches, are most concerned with 'how the world really is') and subjectivists (who are most concerned with 'how the world appears').[117] According to Frowe, most accounts of self-defence have an 'objectivist slant' because attention is focused on what a person *should* be permitted to do in light of various possible outcomes.[118] Per Frowe, self-defence doctrine should not be constructed around knowledge that a defender cannot have because, given less-than-perfect knowledge, self-defence cannot be conduct-guiding.[119] While Frowe's account is focused on advancing the broad position that permissible self-defence should be 'practical,' in the sense of action-guiding, she, like Uniacke, does not conduct an analysis of the values that would make certain self-preferential actions more acceptable than others.

Dsouza's interesting conception of the positionality of blame and his reliance on fact-finders assessing morality on a case-by-case basis (in essence building on the concept of jury nullification)[120] does not provide what Frowe is most concerned about.[121] Dsouza, consistent with the approach taken below, broadly cleaves conduct he characterises as 'existentially immune'[122] from the criminal law's moral judgements (basically, excusatory defences) from justificatory defences (including self-defence) that 'society' on a case-by-case basis deems 'moral' (and thus unpunishable).

[116] For more on forfeiture theory – and recommendations on how its shortcomings can be overcome – see ch 2(V)(A).

[117] H Frowe, 'A Practical Account of Self-Defence' (2010) 29 *Law & Philosophy* 245, 245–47 [hereinafter Frowe, 'Practical Account']. See also H Frowe, *Defensive Killing* (Oxford, Oxford University Press, 2014) 1–2.

[118] See Frowe, 'Practical Account' (n 117) 249.

[119] Ibid at 250–51 (noting that self-defence accounts must take into consideration that defensive actions are taken under conditions of particular epistemic limitations and typically must be performed urgently).

[120] See generally CE Royer, 'The Disobedient Jury: Why Lawmakers Should Codify Jury Nullification' (2017) 102 *Cornell Law Review* 1401, 1404–15.

[121] It is important to distinguish the specific 'blame' flowing from systemic conviction and punishment as described in the value-based model (see discussion at ch 2(IV)(F)(v)) from the broader concept of 'societal blame' (including species of blame that may not have resulted in criminal proscription). See generally J von Talge, 'Victimization Dynamics: The Psycho-Social and Legal Implications of Family Violence Directed Toward Women and the Impact on Child Witnesses' (1999–2000) 27 *Western State University Law Review* 111, 131 ('A second dimension of the multiple victimization of women [in the context of rape cases] is societal blame – blaming the domestic violence victim often occurs.').

[122] Dsouza (n 63) 51, 65-63.

Dsouza dedicates a lengthy subchapter to his model's implications on persons contemplating defensive action.[123] But other than distinguishing between two broad categories of rights (inherent 'constituent' rights versus subsidiary/state-granted 'posited' rights),[124] he does not examine the role values play in determining when and why a state ought to permit citizens to resort to self-preferential force.[125] I believe that by not grappling with these challenging questions, Dsouza in his very challenging and in-depth analysis creates dissonance with his book's stated purpose of disentangling the 'moral norms relevant to defensive action.'[126] Additionally, while Dsouza acknowledges that there may be a 'hierarchy of rights,' and that 'the right to possess purposive agency' may be the 'most important right,'[127] his analysis ultimately stops short of sketching out the contours of the right to 'possess purposive agency.' Nor does he specify what rights are included in his 'hierarchy' (a term implying a relative ranking, and thus an array) of rights.

In contrast to his peers, Sangero has taken the step of developing a self-defence theory animated by a balancing between multiple values, namely, the autonomy of the person attacked (his 'crucial factor'), protection of the socio-legal order, and the 'legitimate' interest of the attacker.[128] According to Sangero, these 'abstract interests' must be 'placed on the scales' and evaluated by the fact-finder using a 'lesser evils framework.'[129] From Sangero's perspective, then, unlawful attack not only threatens injury to the defender but, in line with the position advanced by German theorists for generations,[130] also constitutes a harmful and malicious attack on the broader socio-legal order.[131]

According to Sangero, his model's 'main innovation' is that it seeks to integrate '*all the important factors* in justifying private defence ….'[132] And Sangero does, in fact, recognise the importance of protecting the 'social-legal order.' He does so by adopting the German perspective that the defender's conduct must ensure that the 'wrong not triumph over the right.'[133] Self-preferential force helps ensure that, in the absence of police assistance, the person threatening the (culpable) wrong cannot 'get away with it.'[134]

But Sangero does not consider whether transforming citizens into de facto law enforcement officers, animated by the more collective objective of protecting the broader legal order, threatens to devalue the 'self' in self-defence.[135] Even his

[123] Talge (n 121) 138–65.
[124] Ibid at 138.
[125] Dsouza (n 63) 69–72, 139.
[126] Ibid at i.
[127] Ibid at 74–75.
[128] See generally Sangero, *Self-Defence* (n 61) 67–73, 93–106. Sangero also mentions deterrence, but only in the context of describing Kremnitzer's approach. Ibid at 68.
[129] See Sangero, *Self-Defence* (n 61) 73–77.
[130] See the discussion of German law's treatment of this topic at ch 5(IV).
[131] See Sangero, 'New Defense' (n 22) 521–31.
[132] See ibid at 558 (emphasis added).
[133] See ibid at 542–58.
[134] Ibid.
[135] See ch 2(IV)(D).

more value-centric analysis, moreover, leaves unaddressed the collective interest in reducing violence by protecting the state's monopoly of force (value #1), ensuring the primacy of the legal process (value #5), or maintenance of the legitimacy of the legal order (value #6). And while he recognises that an attacker's culpability should play a role in determining when and to what extent to authorise defensive force,[136] Sangero does not treat protecting the defender's equal standing (value #3) or deterrence (value #7) as representing independent potential decision-grounds.

As this survey demonstrates, most of the leading self-defence scholars recognise that values, at some level at least, inform the defence's underlying rationale. By articulating what values they personally consider implicated in different self-defence scenarios, moreover, it can be said that these scholars, implicitly at least, agree that at some level engaging in a value-centric dialogue is important. This fairly broad consensus among scholars can, therefore, be said to support the position that a broader consideration of the values implicated when a person elects to engage in the self-preferential use of force improves the transparency of decision-making and, relatedly, reduces the role of hidden normativity. Nevertheless, only Sangero comes close to developing a truly value-centric analysis. And, in contrast to the value-based model proposed here, even Sangero's effort falls short by not providing the necessary broader accounting of a broader set of key values informing self-defence's true rationale.

[136] See Sangero, 'New Defense' (n 22) 542–58.

4

The Value-Based Model's Answer to Common Theoretical ('Hard Case') Questions

To test the value-centric position introduced in Chapter 1, we thus far have identified an array of values and justified why they deserve to be considered self-defence decision-grounds. Further, we have compared and contrasted those values, described when and how they most frequently will come into conflict with (or, alternatively, reinforce) each other, and proposed a means of ordering them when they are in tension. Finally, we determined that this comprehensive, value-centric approach adds something new and valuable to the extensive scholarship on self-defence surveyed in Chapter 3. The value-based model offers a more transparent and comprehensive means of evaluating self-defence doctrine, generally, and individual scenarios, specifically. Having engaged in this foundational work, we are now in a position to examine how (and, relevant to testing the position we are examining, *how well*) the value-based model answers some of the theoretical questions common to self-defence scholarship and judicial decision-making.

I. Is Self-Defence a Justification or Excuse (or Neither)? … And Why the Answer Matters[1]

We have examined and discussed why justified conduct is best conceived of as creating an exception to the proscription contained in the offence definition (and, therefore, to the fully expressed public morality).[2] The position advanced is that an excused defendant, in contrast, in fact does violate the offence definition; she, however, does so under circumstances that, in retrospect, make punishment

[1] This book does not purport to be a comparative work, and so this section will not undertake a detailed comparison between German and English law's differing approaches to justifications/excuses. See generally A Eser, 'Justification and Excuse: A Key Issue in the Concept of Crime' in A Eser et al (eds), *Justification and Excuse: Comparative Perspectives* vol 1, (1987) 17, 61–66.

[2] See ch 2(IV)(F)(v)(f) & (g).

inappropriate because her conduct cannot be morally attributed to her (that is, she did not pursue a freely chosen action-plan manifesting her moral character).[3] As Fletcher articulated it, '[a] justification speaks to the rightness of an act; an excuse, to whether the actor is accountable for a concededly wrongful act.'[4] The necessity requirement, in turn, distinguishes justified from merely 'tolerated' or 'excused' conduct,[5] with proportionality serving a similar moderating function.[6]

But this bifurcation between justification, excuse, and necessity is not universally accepted. Dsouza's perspective on the 'positionality of blame,' for example, draws on what he terms the 'hypocrisy-based conception of excuses and defences.'[7] At the crux of his account is the belief that excuses are defences granted to defendants because not granting them would be hypocritical; society is not in a moral position to blame a defender for the conduct.[8] Dsouza takes the position that his approach is both intuitively plausible and compatible with 'most familiar accounts of rationale-based excuses.'[9]

The challenge to this interpretation, however, is that it appears to be based almost entirely on an assessment of social morality – and, so, if a particular society has, say, racist tendencies, a person who assaults another based on the colour of his skin would likely be excused because a conviction under these circumstances would, per Dsouza, constitute 'hypocritical blaming.'[10]

As discussed in Chapter 2(IV)(F)(ii), under the value-based model, conviction, and subsequent punishment, condemns the defendant as an accountable agent who by systemic standards has transgressed the 'fully expressed public morality,' and who is therefore morally blameworthy for the wrong he inflicted or intended to inflict.[11] As Packer, consistent with this approach, put it, punishment without reference to the actor's state of mind 'is unjust because the actor is subjected to the stigma of a criminal conviction without being morally blameworthy.'[12] In short, moral blameworthiness must be inherent in criminal punishment for it

[3] See ibid. See also RF Schopp, 'Justification Defenses and Just Convictions' (1993) 24 *Pacific Law Journal* 1233, 1275; J Feinberg, *Doing and Deserving: Essays in the Theory of Responsibility* (New Jersey, Princeton University Press, 1970) 274–75.

[4] GP Fletcher, *Rethinking Criminal Law* (New York, Oxford University Press, 1978) 759. See also K Greenawalt, 'The Perplexing Borders of Justification and Excuse' (1984) 84 *Columbia Law Review* 1897, 1900.

[5] Fletcher (n 4) 559.

[6] Ibid at 559–60.

[7] See M Dsouza, *Rationale-Based Defences in Criminal Law* (Oxford, Hart Publishing, 2017) 111–20.

[8] See ibid.

[9] Ibid at 112–13.

[10] Compare ch 3(I).

[11] See also RF Schopp, *Justification Defenses and Just Convictions* (Cambridge, Cambridge University Press, 1998) 29; S Uniacke, *Permissible Killing: The Self-Defence Justification of Homicide* (Cambridge, Cambridge University Press, 1994) 137–41.

[12] HL Packer, 'Mens Rea and the Supreme Court' [1962] *Supreme Court Review* 107, 109. See also M Boggiani, 'When Is a Trafficking Victim a Trafficking Victim: Anti-Prostitution Statutes and Victim Protection' (2016) 64 *Cleveland State Law Review* 915, 951.

to maintain its stigmatic effect. A defendant who is not morally accountable for his conduct should be excused and remain free from criminal liability.[13]

In addition to being excused on the basis of insanity, a defendant may also be excused as not blameworthy because his volitional and reasonable action-plan did not accord with the result actually achieved (even though, depending on the offence definition, it may have formally met the *mens rea* requirement(s)).[14] Consider the case of Andrew, who reasonably thinks he is being attacked. Because of this subjective and reasonable belief, Andrew may select an action-plan that includes using deadly force in self-defence. This action-plan ultimately proves to be mistaken, however, because there is no actual attack. A defendant in Andrew's position is not morally accountable for his actions, even though he violated the fully expressed public morality, because he did not intend to wrong another by engaging in the act he was charged with (to wit, he did not intentionally and without justification kill another).

As articulated here, then, offence definitions require action-plans, whereas excuses function retrospectively to undermine the required relation between the proscribed conduct and the actor's *pursuit* of his action-plan with regard to the offence.[15] The defences of duress and provocation discussed below reflect this perspective.[16] They undermine the required voluntary selection of an action-plan that reflects a disrespect of the victim's equal standing. The will of the person acting under duress is said to be overborne by the threat to the point where most reasonable people would have acted in the same way, whereas the person who was provoked lost self-control under extreme circumstances.[17] In neither case does the action compel an adverse judgement about the actor, for the actor was not acting in accordance with a freely selected action-plan manifesting his moral character. He, rather, was acting as the result of an external threat, or a loss of self-control, which permits us to say that his conduct was morally involuntary – though, depending on the circumstances, perhaps still subject to a lower level of criminal sanction if he, for example, acted negligently or recklessly.[18]

[13] See generally D Ormerod and K Laird, *Smith, Hogan, and Ormerod's Criminal Law* 15th edn (Oxford, Oxford University Press, 2018) 7–8; RL Christopher, 'Exculpation as Inculpation' (2017) 49 *Arizona State Law Journal* 1141, 1146–48; K Harker and E Wright, 'The HIV Stigma: Duty or Defence' (2015) 4 *University of Columbia Journal of Law and Jurisprudence* 55, 70–71; *Garnett v State*, 632 A2d 797, 801 (Md 1993).

[14] See generally ch 4(I)(B) (discussing mistakes).

[15] See generally DJ Baker, *Textbook of Criminal Law* 4th edn (Oxford, Oxford University Press, 2015) 56; Schopp (n 3) 1320–21.

[16] See ch 4(II)(A).

[17] See generally discussion at ch 4(II)(A). See also J Herring, 'Law and the Relational Self' 643–59 (MS on file with author) (discussing the various traditional arguments against forfeiture theory); E Colvin, 'Ordinary and Reasonable People: The Design of Objective Tests of Criminal Responsibility' (2001) 27 *Monash University Law Review* 197, 210–16.

[18] See generally discussion at ch 2(IV)(F). See also C Fehr, '(Re-)Constitutionalizing Duress and Necessity' (2017) 42 *Queen's Law Journal* 99, 103; AN Enker, 'In Support of the Distinction Between Justification and Excuse' (2009) 42 *Texas Technical Law Review* 273, 283–84; IH Dennis, 'On Necessity

At this point, a hypothetical may be useful. Assume Victor honestly and reasonably believes Andrew is about to kill him because Andrew is pointing an object that looks like a gun in Victor's direction. Because of this belief, Victor selects an action-plan that includes using defensive force against Andrew to fend off the perceived threat. While Victor's belief in Andrew's attack may be reasonable, Andrew is in fact not attacking Victor. Rather, Andrew is merely holding a mobile phone that in the dark vaguely resembles a handgun. An actor such as Victor who acts under a *reasonable*, but ultimately mistaken, action-plan is not properly subject to the sixth category of condemnation (the defendant is not excused) because, though he is competent, his reasonable error resulted in his selection of an action-plan that did not include wronging another.[19] Victor acted as the result of a reasonable mistake, and therefore did not select an action-plan on the basis of all the objectively relevant information. Victor's objectively mistaken action consequently cannot be subjectively attributed to him.[20] To the extent Victor took the action for *no* objectively good reason (such as racism, homophobia, or some other suspect motivation), however, self-defence, as discussed below, could be unavailable.

Under this account, self-defence can only provide a justification. It cannot excuse, for the excused actor, unlike the justified actor, violated the fully expressed public morality.[21] One would not, after all, usually say 'unlawful killing is wrong except when the killer is insane.' Rather, when discussing excused conduct, adherents to the orthodox position followed here would say 'unlawful killing is wrong, but we will not criminally condemn and punish actors who were insane when they killed.'

A. Aggressors v Passive Threats v Innocent Bystanders – The Importance of Accurate Labelling

Not only is the justification of self-defence less susceptible to abuse via false claims concerning the motivation of the action than is an excuse, but fair labelling compels separate treatment.[22] Put another way, citizens are entitled to have the courts label

as a Defence to Crime: Possibilities, Problems and the Limits of Justification and Excuse' (2009) 3 *Criminal Law & Philosophy* 29, 41. *Cf* B Kotecha, 'Necessity as a Defence to Murder: An Anglo-Canadian Perspective' (2014) 78 *Journal of Criminal Law* 341, 357.

[19] See ch 2(IV)(F)(v)(g).

[20] Fletcher distinguishes 'objective attribution' (did the actor cause the violation?) from 'subjective attribution' (is the actor accountable for the violation?). See Fletcher (n 4) 492–504.

[21] See ch 2(IV)(F)(ii). This view is inconsistent with the approach taken in Germany. See generally ch 5(III).

[22] See generally Kotecha (n 18) 352; B Krebs, 'Justification and Excuse in Article 31(1) of the Rome Statute' (2013) 2 *Cambridge Journal of International and Comparative Law* 382, 385; G Williams, 'Convictions and Fair Labelling' (1983) 42 *CLJ* 85.

their defensive conduct as accurately as possible because those labels inherently include a normative (and potentially stigmatising) element.[23] And while, as noted, claims of justification focus primarily on the *act* itself, excuses focus on the *actor* (and, more to the point, on the actor's *motivation* for acting).[24] Society at large, like criminal justice professionals,[25] intuitively judges a person based on how the courts classify that person's conduct.[26] And so it is posited here that saying 'I did it out of self-defence' carries less of a stigma than saying 'I killed him, but I was under duress' or 'my conduct was deemed acceptable because it was ruled to be necessary under the circumstances.'[27]

And in line with this perspective, the commonly (and for good reason) held distinction is that self-defence functions as a justification that considers the conduct to be, all things considered, acceptable.[28] This is so even though the conduct may have met the offence definition (the value-based model's first stage of condemnation)[29] and received condemnation during the three stages that follow (bringing of charges, mental fitness to proceed, and fact-finder's conclusion that the conduct meets the offence definition, respectively).[30] Duress and necessity, in contrast, are considered excuses, in that the conduct, while wrong, was engaged in for a reason rendering the accused blameless (and thus immune from value-based model stage-six condemnation).[31] By stating clearly why a person is being punished, as well as why a person is *not* being punished, the distinction between justifications and excuses provides the type of moral clarity that has long, and for good reason, been the criminal law's objective.[32] As a result, from the value-based

[23] See generally ch 4(I).

[24] Ibid.

[25] See JL Anderson, 'Playing with Fire: Contemporary Fault Issues in the Enigmatic Crime of Arson' (2016) 39 *University of New South Wales Law Journal* 950, 952, citing J Chalmers and F Leverick, 'Fair Labelling in Criminal Law' (2008) 71 *MLR* 217, 234. See also W Chan and A Simester, 'Four Functions of Mens Rea' (2011) 70 *CLJ* 381, 388–93.

[26] See CO Finkelstein, 'Self-Defense as a Rational Excuse' (1996) 57 *University of Pittsburgh Law Review* 621, 621–49. See also J Radice, 'The Reintegrative State' (2017) 66 *Emory Law Journal* 1315, 1329–31.

[27] See generally MP Wilt, 'Civil Disobedience and the Rule of Law: Punishing Good Lawbreaking in a New Era of Protest' (2017) 28 *George Mason University Civil Rights Law Journal* 43, 49–51.

[28] See generally Finkelstein (n 26) 621–49. See also JY Kim, 'The Rhetoric of Self-Defense' (2008) 13 *Berkeley Journal of Criminal Law* 266.

[29] See ch 2(IV)(F)(v)(b).

[30] See ch 2(IV)(F)(v)(c)–(e).

[31] See generally discussion at ch 2(IV)(F)(v)(g). See also ME Gilman, 'The Poverty Defense' (2013) 47 *University of Richmond Law Review* 495, 507; TL Meares et al, 'Updating the Study of Punishment' (2004) 56 *Stanford Law Review* 1171, 1202; HL Hart, *Punishment and Responsibility* (New York, Oxford University Press, 1968) 212–22 (describing justified conduct as 'something the law does not condemn or even welcomes').

[32] See generally GJ Chin, 'Unjustified: The Practical Irrelevance of the Justification/Excuse Distinction' (2009) 43 *University of Michigan Journal of Law Reform* 79, 91; G Mousourakis, 'Distinguishing Between Justifications and Excuses in the Criminal Law' (1998) 9 *Stellenbosch Law Review* 165, 180. *Cf* Greenawalt (n 4) 1924–27.

perspective, there is no compelling reason to deviate from this intuitive and common distinction.

B. Mistakes: External, Internal, and Legal Justification

Although self-defence is, as discussed, best considered a justification, and, therefore, constitutes an exception to the fully expressed public morality discussed in Chapter 2(IV)(F)(v), additional case-specific limitations to the justifiable exercise of self-defensive force deserve discussion. Specifically, and as detailed below, the defender must be both externally *and* internally justified (adopting the 'deeds and reasons' view[33]) before he can claim a positive right to self-defence. That is to say that the facts as they *actually exist* must objectively justify the defendant,[34] and she must also *know* of, and in fact *act because of*, these justificatory circumstances (which, of course, include the facts implicating the seven value-based decision-grounds).

i. *External Justification*

Turning first to the requirement of external justification, the criminal law is best described as providing the public with minimum standards of acceptable conduct.[35] Justified conduct therefore need not be the morally best conduct, but rather is conduct that is legal by the appropriate standard.[36] By way of recap, the value-based model and its eight stages of condemnation uses a transparent approach to endorse the orthodox view that justifications focus on the act, whereas excuses focus on the actor.[37] The value-based model's fully expressed public morality does

[33] See generally Herring (n 17) 688.

[34] Note that, when this book speaks of the 'objective facts' establishing that there was or would be an 'actual attack,' it is nearly always dealing at least partly with supposition based on probabilities or witnesses' potentially mistaken perceptions and recollections. This is not an impediment to the analysis, however, because the fact-finder decides what, based on all the evidence, the actual facts were and whether an actual attack was in fact in progress. The fact-finder's conclusion as to what occurred or would have occurred therefore takes the place of the conclusion that the fictional omniscient observer would have reached.

[35] See generally ch 2(IV)(F)(i) & (ii). See also DL Bazelon, 'The Morality of the Criminal Law' in T Morawetz (ed), *Criminal Law* (New York, New York University Press, 1991) 5 ('[T]he criminal code should define only the minimum conditions of each individual's responsibility to the other members of society in order to maximize personal liberty.').

[36] See generally BB Sendor, 'Mistakes of Fact: A Study in the Structure of Criminal Conduct' (1990) 25 *Wake Forest Law Review* 772.

[37] See generally L Alexander et al, *Crime and Culpability* (Cambridge, Cambridge University Press, 2009) 89, quoted in BM Fissell, 'Federalism and Constitutional Law' (2017) 46 *Hofstra Law Review* 489, 536 n 310; CMV Clarkson and HM Keating, *Criminal Law: Text and Materials* 9th edn (London, Sweet & Maxwell, 2017) 278–80; Uniacke (n 11) 6, 23; Fletcher (n 4) 759; E D'Arcy, *Human Acts* (Oxford, Oxford University Press, 1963) 85; J Feinberg, *Harm to Others* (New York, Oxford University Press, 1984) 108; WO Russell, *A Treatise on Crimes and Indictable Misdemeanours* 2nd edn (Charleston, Gale, 2010/1826) 509–10; 4 Bl Comm 181.

not justify mistaken actors, however reasonable the mistake, because their actions are not considered positively lawful exceptions to offence descriptions (that is, they are still subject to stage-five condemnation).[38] Not only is a putative defender objectively unjustified, but he also harms the 'attacker' by violating her right to life (value #2). That said, the putative defender does not *wrong* the attacker (in the sense of creating an unequal standing between the attacker and the defender, in accordance with value #3) because the defender is acting under a mistaken belief in the rightness of his conduct.[39]

An actor who honestly believes that he is acting in self-defence, but actually acts under a mistaken belief regarding the justificatory circumstances, can therefore at best claim that he was *internally* justified because he subjectively and reasonably believed that his conduct was necessary to prevent an immediate attack.[40] The putative defender is not externally justified, however, because he in reality was not being attacked (and thus value #1 – violence reduction; value #3 – protecting equal standing; and value #4 – protecting the defender's autonomy were not implicated).[41] Because justifications, as defined here, require both internal *and* external justification, an actor acting in putative self-defence is subject to stage-five condemnation, though he may of course be excused from punishment at stage six if his mistake was reasonable, or if he was legally incompetent.[42]

ii. Internal Justification

Turning from external to internal justification, actors may act under circumstances in which reasons exist for exempting their conduct from the fully expressed prohibitory norm, but where they are not aware of these reasons.[43] Because of their lack of awareness, then, they cannot be said to have selected their action-plans because of these reasons. Such actors are considered 'unknowingly justified' because they lack internal (that is, 'subjective') justification.[44]

Assume that, as Andrew is coming out of a movie one afternoon, his old nemesis Victor rushes towards him holding an uplifted sword. Andrew reasonably believes that Victor is about to attack him and therefore pulls out his gun. In reality, however, Victor is merely excited about the sword he just purchased from an antiques store down the road. Victor, realising that Andrew is about to shoot him, stabs Andrew through the heart with his sword because this is the only

[38] See ch 2(IV)(F)(v)(f).
[39] See ch 2(IV)(C).
[40] See generally *People v White*, 409 NE2d 73 (Ill App Ct 1980); *People v Pappas*, 383 NE2d 1190 (Ill App Ct 1978); *People v Kelly*, 322 NE2d 527 (Ill App Ct 1975); *Gunn v State*, 365 NE2d 1234 (Ind Ct App 1977).
[41] See ch 2(IV)(A), (C) & (D).
[42] See ch 2(IV)(F)(v)(f) & (g).
[43] See generally Schopp (n 3) 1284.
[44] See generally T Rönnau and K Hohn, '§ 32 Notwehr' in G Cirener et al (eds), *Strafgesetzbuch: Leipziger Kommentar, Band 3* (Berlin, De Gruyter, 2019) side-note 262; L Alexander, 'Unknowingly Justified Actors and the Attempt/Success Distinction' (2004) 39 *Tulsa Law Review* 851, 854–57.

way Victor can protect himself against the mistaken Andrew. In this unfortunate situation both Victor and Andrew acted in reasonable apprehension of imminent death or serious bodily harm, and both are, therefore, internally justified. Only Victor was externally justified in acting as he did, however, for Andrew's belief, while perhaps entirely reasonable under the circumstances, was mistaken. If internal (subjective) justification alone was sufficient to justify self-defence, then both Andrew and Victor would be justified in killing each other. The 'incompatibility thesis'/'paradox of mutual justifications' precludes such a result.[45]

iii. The Value-Based Model's Requirement of Both External and *Internal Justification*

The value-based model has concluded that justificatory circumstances only provide exceptions to the fully expressed public morality if the actor is (a) aware of them, and (b) acting *because* of them.[46] External justification alone, therefore, cannot exempt the actor's conduct from stage-five condemnation, for an actor must also be internally justified.[47] By requiring external *and* internal justification, the law prevents mutually justified attacks that conflict with the above-mentioned incompatibility thesis.[48] The paradoxical result that the incompatibility thesis seeks to ward against is that, if each of the actor's force is justified, then neither actor's force can be justified, and if neither actor's force can be justified, then both actors' force is justified.[49] Indeed, regardless of how reasonable the mistake may have been, it will not *justify* the conduct because the mistaken actor has no objectively superior social interest or right that would support creating an exception to the general prohibitory norm. As a result, self-defence provisions ought to be drafted in terms of conduct, circumstances, result, and *knowledge*.[50] This approach is coherent, and reflects the above-discussed normative significance of justifications.

[45] See generally H Rosenau, 'Notwehr und Notstand' in H Satzger and W Schluckebier (eds), *Strafgesetzbuch: Kommentar*, vol 4 (Heymanns Verlag GmbH, 2019) side-note 118; LE Chiesa, 'The Rise of Spanish and Latin American Criminal Theory' (2008) 11 *New Criminal Law Review* 363, 380; Eser (n 1) 31–32. See also GP Fletcher, 'The Right and the Reasonable' (1985) 98 *Harvard Law Review* 949, 975; J Dressler, 'New Thoughts About the Concept of Justification in the Criminal Law: A Critique of Fletcher's Thinking and Rethinking' (1984) 32 *UCLA Law Review* 61, 86–88; PH Robinson, 'Punishing Dangerousness: Cloaking Preventive Detention as Criminal Justice' (2001) 114 *Harvard Law Review* 278; C Fried, *Right and Wrong* (Cambridge, Mass, Harvard University Press, 1978) 48; I Kant, *The Metaphysics of Morals* (Cambridge, Mass, Hackett Publishing, 1991) 60. *Cf* M Baron, 'Justifications and Excuses' (2005) 2 *Ohio State Journal of Criminal Law* 387, 404.

[46] See ch 2(IV).

[47] See ch 2(IV)(F)(v)(f).

[48] See generally Rönnau and Hohn (n 44) side-note 113; RG Fontaine, 'An Attack on Self-Defense' (2010) 47 *American Criminal Law Review* 57, 77–79; RL Christopher, 'Mistake of Fact in the Objective Theory of Justification: Do Two Rights Make Two Wrongs Make Two Rights …?' (1994) 85 *Journal of Criminal Law & Criminology* 295, 319–20.

[49] See Rosenau (n 45) side-note 18; RL Christopher, 'Unknowing Justification and the Logical Necessity of the *Dadson* Principle in Self-Defence' (1995) 15 *OJLS* 229, 242; Christopher (n 48) 307.

[50] Schopp (n 11) 37.

The value-based model's decision-grounds providing weight to the principle of protecting the defender are necessarily limited in cases when a defender lacks subjective perception of the nature and seriousness of the attack. Assume Victor thinks he is about to be hit on the head with a harmless toy hammer. In fact, Andrew is about to hit him on the head with a real iron hammer. Because Victor thought that he would be subjected to only very minor discomfort, the value-based model dictates that he would not be justified in using deadly force to deflect what he believes to be a culpable, but minor, threat. The fact that the actual threat was in fact much greater than Victor perceived it to be will not provide him with an after-the-fact justification, as his subjective assessment of the threat is not changed by the objective facts. The value-based model's conception of self-defence as a justification is, therefore, partially agent-centred, and partially target-centred. It requires both a particular mental state on the part of the defender, as well as an actual threat of harming or wronging.[51]

iv. The Value-Based Model's Rejection of the Utilitarian 'Legal Justification'

England's Lord Macaulay was one of the first commentators to expressly examine the issue of unknowing justification. And he reached a conclusion contrary to the one advanced here. Macaulay, like Robinson, adopted a utilitarian approach, arguing that the defender's mental state is unimportant; a defensive act that ultimately benefits society should be encouraged:

> [W]hen an act is really useful to society, an act of a sort which it is desirable to encourage, has been done, it is absurd to inquire into the motives of the doer, for the purpose of punishing him if it shall appear that his motives were bad.[52]

Other commentators, including Simester, have taken an opposing, public-policy based position, contending that unknowingly justified conduct should in fact be discouraged because it results in social *dis*-utility by encouraging the commission of *prima facie* offences in the hope that they might turn out to be fortuitously defensible.[53] Still others have criticised the requirement that defenders must be aware of the justifying circumstances on the ground that the principle weakens the

[51] Russell Christopher refers to this approach as the 'partially agent-centered subjective approach.' See R Christopher, 'Self-Defense and Objectivity: A Reply to Judith Jarvis Thomson' (1998) 1 *Buffalo Criminal Law Review* 537, 565.

[52] HM Trevelyan, *The Works of Lord Macaulay* vol 7 (Hardback Publishing, 2019/1866) 552–53. See also B Sangero, 'A New Defense for Self-Defense' (2006) 9 *Buffalo Criminal Law Review* 499; MS Moore, *Act and Crime: The Philosophy of Action and Its Implications for Criminal Law* (Oxford, Oxford University Press, 1993) 180–81; Robinson (n 45), at 289–90.

[53] A Simester, 'Mistakes in Defence' (1992) 12 *OJLS* 295, 303. See also L Alexander, 'Lesser Evils: A Closer Look at the Paradigmatic Justification' (2005) 24 *Law & Philosophy* 611, 626–36.

legitimacy of the criminal law.[54] As noted above, however, unknowingly justified actors are not, in fact, candidates for the justification of self-defence.[55]

Having ploughed this theoretically dense ground, we turn next to the question of why the presence of justificatory facts does not negate the offence definition's *actus reus* requirement at the value-based model's fourth stage of condemnation (the fact-finder determines that the defendant meets the offence definition).[56] The answer to this question can be found in the distinction between offence and defence definitions, and in the difference between the value-based model's conception of the partially expressed public morality and the fully expressed public morality.[57]

If the offence–defence distinction is applied, the question of whether a defence is available (that is, whether the defendant's conduct is an exception to, or a justified infringement of, the fully expressed public morality) is distinct from the question of whether the defendant violated the partially expressed public morality represented by the offence definition. Contrary to the arguments advanced by Professors Williams[58] and Robinson,[59] the availability of a defence, and the corresponding negation of condemnation at either stage five (if the defendant's defensive conduct is justified) or stage six (if the defendant is excused), is considered independently and has no bearing on whether the defendant satisfied the offence definition's *actus reus* requirement.[60] The defence, then, renders the commission of the *prima facie* offence permissible[61] on the basis of accompanying circumstances not directly contemplated in the definition of the *actus reus*.[62]

If the distinction between offences and defences is disregarded, on the other hand, defences become nothing more than negative definitional elements of the offence.[63] The *actus reus* of an assault, for example, would require both the typical features of an assault, *and* would require that the assault occur in such circumstances that no defence pertains. A defendant's unlawfulness would, therefore, be treated as a circumstance that is part of the *actus reus* necessary for criminal liability.[64]

[54] Robinson (n 45) 266. See also Schopp (n 11) 35–36 (arguing that unknowingly justified actor could still be liable for attempt); AJ Ashworth, 'Belief, Intent and Criminal Liability' in J Eekelaar and J Bell (eds), *Oxford Essays in Jurisprudence* (Oxford, Oxford University Press, 1987) 1, 28.

[55] See generally Rönnau and Hohn (n 44) side-note 262.

[56] See ch 2(IV)(F)(v)(e).

[57] See ch 2(IV)(F)(v).

[58] GL Williams, *Criminal Law: The General Part*, 2nd edn (London, 1961) 24 ('[T]he rule hardly accords with the requirement of an *actus reus*.').

[59] See Robinson (n 45) 266.

[60] See ch 2(IV)(F)(v)(f) & (g).

[61] The conduct is either an exception to (in the case of justified conduct), or an excusable infringement of (in the case of excused defendants), the fully expressed conventional morality embodied in the prohibitory norm. See generally J Gardner, 'Justifications and Reasons' in A Simester and A Smith (eds), *Harm and Culpability* (Oxford, Oxford University Press, 1996) 103, 118–22.

[62] See A Simester (n 53) 296–302. See also D Lanham, 'Larsonneur Revisited' [1976] *Crim LR* 276 ('[A]s a matter of analysis we can think of a crime as being made up of three ingredients, *actus reus*, *mens rea* and (a negative element) absence of a valid defence.').

[63] See generally Rosenau (n 45) side-note 4; Rönnau and Hohn (n 44) side-note 15; G Lamond, 'Core Principles of English Criminal Law' in M Dyson and B Vogel (eds), *The Limits of Criminal Law: Anglo-German Concepts and Principles* (Cambridge, Intersentia, 2018) 26. *Cf* Enker (n 18) 278–79.

[64] See generally Herring (n 17) 684.

Such a conception of utilitarian 'legal justifications' is flawed, however, because viewing unlawfulness as part of the *actus reus* puts the proverbial cart before the horse. 'Unlawful' merely describes conduct that satisfies both the *actus reus* and *mens rea* requirements of the offence definition.[65] Only after the fact-finder determines that the defendant fits the offence definition, and that he therefore is condemnable at stages one through four, does the issue of a possible defence become relevant.[66] This approach, which also finds support among German theorists, appropriately recognises the basic normative distinction between offences and defences that, among other things, allows the public to better understand proscribed conduct.[67]

The result is that self-defence, as discussed, can only be 'legally justified' if the actor was both internally *and* externally justified. Smith argues that any requirement of internal justification is based on public policy rather than on logic.[68] Indeed, requiring both internal and external justification represents a principled, coherent, and logically compelled method of preventing unknowingly justified actors from benefitting from their fortuitous justification, while concurrently avoiding the paradox of unknown justifications. Requiring internal justification is furthermore consistent with the requirement found in stage six providing that excuses can only be claimed by actors to whom the harm cannot be 'subjectively attributed' in the sense that they are not morally accountable for the harm.[69]

C. 'Unreasonable' Mistakes of Fact

Mistakes of fact in the context of self-defence can be made with regard to three distinct issues, namely, whether: (a) the actor is *actually* being attacked; (b) the degree of defensive force is *necessary* to ward off the attack; and (c) the degree of defensive force is grossly *disproportionate* to the harm threatened.[70] The first two questions are matters of fact, whereas the third question is ultimately a value judgement that is answered by reference to the fully expressed public morality (though the facts underlying the assessment concededly could of course also be

[65] See *Albert v Lavin* [1982] AC 546, 561 (HL) (arguing that in setting forth the elements in criminal offences the word 'unlawful' is tautologous).

[66] See ch 2(IV)(F)(v)(b)–(e).

[67] See generally Rosenau (n 45) side-note 4; G Duttge, '§ 16 Irrtum über Tatumstände' in *Gesamtest Strafrecht* (Baden-Baden, Nomos Verlagsgesellschaft, 2017) side-note 14; H-H Jescheck and T Weigend, *Lehrbuch des Strafrechts, Allgemeiner Teil* 5th edn (Duncker & Humblot GmbH, 1996) 250 [hereinafter Jescheck and Weigend, 5th edn]. See also PH Robinson, 'Criminal Law Defenses: A Systematic Analysis' (1982) 82 *Columbia Law Review* 199, 291 n 164 ('The distinction between offenses and defences is perhaps the most basic distinction in criminal law that lawyers … recognize.'), cited in *United States v Ortiz*, 927 F3d 868, 873 (5th Cir 2019).

[68] JC Smith, *Justification and Excuse in the Criminal Law* (London, Sweet & Maxwell, 1989) 31–32.

[69] See ch 2(IV)(F)(v)(g).

[70] See generally KW Simons, 'Self-Defense, Mens Rea, and Bernhard Goetz' (1989) 89 *Columbia Law Review* 1179, 1186.

subject to a mistake of fact). The discussion above has demonstrated that a reasonable mistake of fact as to the extant circumstances will not justify defensive force, but instead may constitute an excusable infringement of the prohibition (because external justification is required for conduct to be justified).[71] Still unresolved, however, remains the important foundational question of what an 'unreasonable' mistake is, and what impact such a mistake should have on the analysis.

People form unreasonable beliefs in the self-defence context for two basic reasons: (a) they fail to take sufficient *care* in evaluating the circumstances that confront them before resorting to defensive force; or (b) their *capacity* to evaluate the relevant circumstances is to some extent impaired.[72] The first scenario presents the least analytical difficulty because an actor who simply does not take the proper care in evaluating whether defensive force is necessary can surely (at some level at least) be morally blamed for his mistake. Because of his carelessness, such an actor culpably infringes on an innocent victim's autonomy, and he, therefore, may not claim self-defence. Such an actor meets the requirements of the value-based model's stage-five condemnation because he was not externally justified, and he passes through stage six because he neither lacked legal competency nor chose a reasonably mistaken action-plan.[73] The defender's relative lack of blameworthiness may, nevertheless, be taken into account by the judge at the sentencing stage as a mitigating circumstance; or it may prevent him from having the necessary *mens rea* required by a particular offence definition; or, if merely negligent, it may make him inappropriate for certain categories of criminal punishment.

The second type of unreasonable mistake is made by an actor whose *capacity* to properly evaluate the situation is impaired due either to a psychological disability or because of some other personal characteristic, such as fearfulness or a bad temper. An unreasonably mistaken person suffering from a psychological disability preventing him from properly evaluating the circumstances will be excused because he was legally incompetent at the time of the act and therefore is not appropriate for the value-based model's stage-six condemnation.[74] While an insane attacker infringes on the private domain of another, and is, therefore, subject to justified defensive force, he cannot be said to be legally accountable for his actions or for the harm he threatens.[75]

On the other hand, actors who are impaired in their ability to evaluate the relevant circumstances because of fear, nervousness, or natural aggressiveness – and

[71] See ch 4(I). See also Fletcher (n 4) 696–97, 762–69, cited in V Bergelson, 'Duress Is No Excuse' (2018) 15 *Ohio State Journal of Criminal Law* 395, 401, n 34.

[72] See generally BB Sendor, 'Crime as Communication: An Interpretive Theory of the Insanity Defense and the Mental Elements of Crime' (1986) 74 *Georgia Law Journal* 1399, n 127.

[73] See ch 2(IV)(F)(v)(f) & (g). See also JJ Johnson, 'Why Mississippi Should Reform Its Penal Code' (2019) 37 *Mississippi Commercial Law Review* 107, 134; JL Diamond, 'The Myth of Morality and Fault in Criminal Law Doctrine' (1996) 34 *American Criminal Law Review* 123–24.

[74] See ch 2(IV)(F)(v)(g). See also Fontaine (n 48) 85–88.

[75] See generally D Yeager, 'Decoding the Impossibility Defense' (2018) 56 *University of Louisville Law Review* 359, 362–64.

therefore unreasonably think that they are acting in self-defence – *do* impermissibly infringe on the 'attacker's' personal domain without justification or excuse (thereby implicating value #2; and, depending on the circumstances, value #3 – equal standing).[76] In contrast to legal insanity, personality traits, such as fearfulness or aggression, are, broadly speaking, within the actor's control.[77] The fictitious 'reasonable person' should not be endowed with traits such as timidity or fearfulness, for the law expects people to control such 'flawed' personal characteristics.[78] The moral norm inherent in the 'reasonable person' test is, thus, that persons who fail to overcome personal characteristics that they can fairly be expected to surmount are blameworthy, and are, therefore, liable for punishment.[79]

While such actors are not what I will term 'strongly culpable,' in the sense that they did not act with an evil purpose, they can be described as 'weakly culpable' because of their failure to control their excessive fearfulness or aggression. Such weakly culpable actors are undeserving of an excuse or justification because their conduct reflects a disregard for the interests of others and therefore inflicts a wrong (implicating value #3 – equal standing; value #4 – protecting the defender's autonomy; and value #7 – deterrence).[80] A contrary result would allow actors who are sane (and, thus, subject to all eight stages of value-based model moral condemnation),[81] but overly aggressive or fearful, to unjustly infringe on the private domains of others. (Note, however, that the actor's fearfulness or aggression may of course be considered as a mitigating circumstance but will provide neither a justification nor a complete excuse.)

II. When Is Defensive Force 'Necessary'?[82]

We can now turn to self-defence's most fundamental (and most litigated) limitation, namely, the requirement of 'necessity.'[83] For defensive force to have been 'necessary,' the force used must have been indispensable or unavoidable if the actor

[76] See ch 2(IV)(B) & (C).

[77] This is in contrast to other factors that are relevant to determining whether a person acted reasonably, such as the actor's physical size, ability, and age.

[78] See generally AC McGinley, 'Reasonable Men?' (2012) 45 *Connecticut Law Review* 1, 26–27; G Mogridge, 'The Reasonable Man: Negligence and Criminal Capacity' (1980) 97 *South African Law Journal* 267, 270–71.

[79] See generally JD Armour, 'Race Ipsa Loquitur: Of Reasonable Racists, Intelligent Bayesians, and Involuntary Negrophobes' (1994) 46 *Stanford Law Review* 781, 789, discussing GP Fletcher, 'The Individualization of Excusing Conditions' (1974) 47 *Southern California Law Review* 1269, 1291.

[80] See ch 2(IV)(C), (D), & (G). See also MN Berman, 'Justification and Excuse, Law and Morality' (2003) 53 *Duke Law Journal* 1, 17.

[81] See ch 2(IV)(F)(v).

[82] The issue of proportionality will be addressed in ch 4(III).

[83] See generally F Allhoff, 'Self-Defense Without Imminence' (2019) 56 *American Criminal Law Review* 1527, 1531–48; R Leider, 'Taming Self-Defense: Using Deadly Force to Prevent Escapes' (2018) 70 *Florida Law Review* 995–1002.

was to successfully block or fend off the threat.[84] The (forced-choice) logic is that the attacker cannot complain that his rights were violated if he puts the defender in a position where the defender faces the Hobson's choice of either tolerating the serious intrusion or using reasonable means available to him that are required to block or fend off the attack.[85]

But necessity also plays a (and, perhaps, *the*) critical part in reinforcing the humanitarian core of self-defence law, as reflected most directly in value #2 (protection of the attacker). As Leider has maintained, the centrality of the necessity requirement not only protects aggressors' rights to due process of law, but it relatedly also prevents situations where the putative defender might otherwise employ self-preferential force too early.[86] Put another way, the limitation is thought to make self-defence unavailable if the aggressors have not yet made up their minds to attack.[87] Necessity, therefore, helps us understand the boundaries of self-defence. In so doing, it defines the role of citizens and the roles of the state and, consistent with value #1, allocates their respective permissions to lawfully deploy violence.[88]

A. Distinguishing Self-Defence from Necessity and Duress

Is self-defence a species of necessity, or perhaps an example of duress? The defence of necessity, after all, is said to apply in cases of emergency when an individual is faced with a choice between two 'evils.'[89] Similar to duress situations,[90] the individual in such a predicament must decide whether to break the literal terms of the criminal law, or whether to instead abide by the law's requirements and thereby permit the even greater harm to occur.[91] The answer proffered here is that self-defence is neither an example of necessity, nor a form of duress.

[84] See Uniacke (n 11) 32.

[85] T Hobbes, *Leviathan* (London, Penguin Classics, 1982/1651) ch XIV, discussed in H Lesch, 'Die Notwehr' in G Widmaier et al (eds), *Festschrift für Hans Dahs* (Schmidt, Dr Otto 2005) 113–14. See also L Greco, 'Notwehr und Proportionalität' [2018] GA 665, 675; V Erb, 'Notwehr und Notstand' in B von Heintschel-Heinegg (ed), *Münchner Kommentar zum Strafgesetzbuch, Band 1* (Beck CH, 2017) § 32, side-note 5; S Wallerstein, 'Justifying the Right to Self-Defense: A Theory of Forced Consequences' (2005) 91 *Virginia Law Review* 1005–15. See also ch 2(V)(A)(ii).

[86] Leider (n 83) 1002. See also V Nourse, 'Reconceptualizing Criminal Law Defenses' (2003) 151 *University of Pennsylvania Law Review* 1725.

[87] See Leider (n 83) 1002.

[88] See KK Ferzan, 'Self-Defense and the State' (2008) 5 *Ohio State Journal of Criminal Law* 460–61.

[89] See generally I Coca-Vila, 'Conflicting Duties in Criminal Law' (2019) 22 *New Criminal Law Review* 34, 37–40; Christopher (n 13) 1153–54; M Cotton, 'The Necessity Defense and the Moral Limits of Law' (2015) 18 *New Criminal Law Review* 35, 40.

[90] See generally FE Chapman and J MacLean, 'Pulling the Patches of the Patchwork Defence of Duress: A Comment on *R v Aravena*' (2015) 62 *Criminal Law Quarterly* 420, 426–27; S Zgaga, 'The Defence of Duress in International Criminal Law' (2013) 68 *Pravnik* 95, 126.

[91] See generally M Bedi, 'Excusing Behavior: Reclassifying the Federal Common Law Defenses of Duress and Necessity Relying on the Victim's Role' (2011) 10 *Journal of Criminal Law & Criminology* 575, 577–78; G Binder, 'The Rhetoric of Motive and Intent' (2002) 6 *Buffalo Criminal Law Review* 1, 48–49; WR LaFave and AW Scott, *Substantive Criminal Law* (Eagan, Cengage Learning, 1986) § 5.4.

Assume Andrew is driving a train with defective breaks. Andrew approaches a 'Y' in the tracks and discovers to his horror that Peter, Michael, and John are tied to the left tracks, whereas Steve is doing repair work on the track to the right. Steve is facing away from the train and from the others and is unable to hear the oncoming train due to his deafness. Andrew is thus faced with a conflict of rights in which either outcome will cause the death of innocent life. Under these circumstances, Andrew decides to divert the train to the right tracks because this saves the lives of Michael, Peter, and John, although it causes the death of Steve. Andrew will be able to claim necessity.

It might therefore be argued that, if Victor is attacked by the insane Thomas, Victor is normatively in the same position as Andrew in the prior hypothetical. After all, both, through impersonal necessity, find themselves in a conflict of rights situation. In the case of the insane Thomas, this impersonal necessity is brought about by the disease working on Thomas' powers of perception and judgement.

While this parity argument has initial appeal, on a deeper level it overlooks the relevance of the *source* of the threatened harm.[92] Instead, it merely relies on necessity's utilitarian/teleological public policy claim that otherwise illegal conduct is permitted because 'higher values' are achieved at the expense of 'lesser values.' In the first scenario, Andrew diverts the train even though this act causes Steve's death. Andrew is immune from punishment because there was a moral imperative for his actions that provided an overriding reason for the otherwise illegal conduct. Although Steve's rights are thus violated, the violation is deemed legal.

Necessity cases, therefore, involve an actor who is said to be morally *compelled* to act in the way that he did.[93] If, for example, Andrew forces Victor at gunpoint to block the road with Victor's car so that the insane Thomas is unable to drive to town with a bomb, Andrew's actions clearly violate Victor's rights. Andrew's conduct furthermore would not qualify as self-defence, since Victor was not the source of the threat.[94] Andrew may, nevertheless, be justified under the doctrine of necessity, because his commandeering of Victor's car avoids a 'greater evil.'[95] Nevertheless, and as discussed in Chapter 4(V)(A)(iv), there certainly are difficult cases involving passive threats where drawing the line is more challenging.

Self-defence cases do not involve violations of the attacker's rights, for the attacker *himself* poses the threat,[96] thereby conditionally creating a gap in his

[92] See generally M Bayles, 'Reconceptualizing Necessity and Duress' (1986) 33 *Wayne Law Review* 1191, 1191–92.

[93] See generally DJ Baker, 'Mutual Combat Complicity, Transferred Intention/Defenses and the Exempt Party Defense' (2016) 37 *University of La Verne Law Review* 205, 260–61; T Keren-Paz, 'Injuries from Unforeseeable Risks Which Advance Medical Knowledge: Restitution-Based Justification for Strict Liability' (2014) 5 *Journal of European Tort Law* 275, 282–83.

[94] See generally A Grabczynska and KK Ferzan, 'Justifying Killing in Self-Defence' (2009) 99 *Journal of Criminal Law & Criminology* (book review) 235.

[95] See generally P Westen, 'Poor Wesley Hohfeld' (2018) 55 *San Diego Law Review* 449, 452; DO Brink, 'Retributivism and Legal Moralism' (2012) 25 *Ratio Juris* 496, 505.

[96] See generally J Horder, 'Self-Defence, Necessity and Duress: Understanding the Relationship' (1998) 11 *Canadian Journal of Law & Jurisprudence* 143.

otherwise inviolable personal domain.[97] The insane Thomas, for example, is the source of the unjust threat (and threatens value #4 – protection of the defender's autonomy); his rights are not violated when Victor uses reasonable force to repel the threat he poses. In short, whether there is a conditional gap, and what the size of it might be, are in turn determined on a sliding scale informed by the balance of the implicated decision-grounds.[98]

Duress cases are even more readily distinguishable. They involve compliance with an illegal *threat*, rather than the avoidance or neutralisation of harm through force.[99] The evil Andrew forces Victor to steal Peter's car and threatens to kill Victor's son if he fails to comply. Peter does not pose an unjustified threat to Victor, and Victor may, therefore, not claim that he was acting in self-defence. Victor may, however, argue that he was acting under duress and should not be punished because he does not pass through the value-based model's stage-six condemnation. But duress of circumstance cases (where the threat emanates from the circumstances, rather than from a verbal command[100]) are more challenging in that they share a great deal in common with the passive threat issues discussed below in Chapter 4(V)(A)(iv).[101]

B. The Relationship between Necessity and Imminence

Assume that Andrew and Victoria both live on an isolated ranch in Colorado. The ranch lacks telephones or other means of communicating with the outside world and is surrounded by a vast and inhospitable high-mountain desert. It would be impossible for anyone to cross the desert to the nearest town of Walden by foot. All of the ranch's water, moreover, is supplied by a single water main that runs from Walden to the ranch. Andrew and Victoria therefore have to drive their car to Walden when they need supplies. One cold night, Andrew is very angry because he believes that Victoria has been unfaithful to him. He verbally and physically abuses Victoria. After severely beating her, Andrew says 'now that that's taken care of, I am going to drive to Walden, turn off the water supply to the house, and let you die a slow death of dehydration.'

Based on Andrew's past behaviour, Victoria has no doubt that Andrew will in fact fulfil his threat and kill her. Andrew gets into the car and starts to drive off. Victoria knows that if she does not stop Andrew he will act on his plan. She, therefore, grabs a rifle out of the closet and fatally shoots Andrew as he drives by the

[97] See ch 2(V)(A).

[98] See ibid.

[99] See generally Baker (n 15) 1119–20; K Levy, 'Does Situationism Excuse – The Implications of Situationism for Moral Responsibility and Criminal Responsibility' (2015) 68 *Arkansas Law Review* 731, 777; O Gan, 'Contractual Duress and Relations of Power' (2013) 36 *Harvard Journal of Law & Gender* 171, 178.

[100] See generally G Williams, 'Necessity: Duress of Circumstances or Moral Involuntariness' (2014) 43 *Common Law World Review* 1, 26–27.

[101] See generally *R v Hasan* [2005] 2 AC 467 (requiring defendant to reasonably believe there was a threat of death or serious injury, and that defendant's reaction was also reasonable).

house on his way to Walden. Andrew of course was not yet in a position where he could turn off the water supply, but if Victoria had not used deadly force to prevent Andrew's 'escape,' her death would have been certain. The question is whether our value-based model will permit this sort of 'pre-emptive' strike.

Self-defence is frequently formulated so that defensive force is authorised only if it is '*necessary* to prevent an *imminent* attack.'[102] Such a formulation treats necessity and imminence as independent requirements; the threatened attack must be imminent, *and* the defensive force must also be necessary to prevent the attack.[103] Under this decoupled standard, Victoria's use of force could be viewed as unjustified because the threatened harm was not technically imminent. Andrew, after all, still had to make the long drive to Walden to turn off the water supply. Although Victoria's defensive force remains her only way of escaping certain death, this common standard would not authorise it (more on this in Chapter 4(V)(A)(vi) discussing the value-based model's treatment of battered intimate partner syndrome).

Recall that the self-defence regime developed here is also concerned with the equal standing of defenders and attackers (value #3) and protecting the defender's private domain (value #4).[104] As such, the value-based model must permit appropriate force to be used whenever it is *immediately necessary* to block or fend off an unjust threat.[105] This formulation thus treats *immediacy* of the threat as a *factor* in determining whether the defensive force was necessary, reflecting an unwillingness to leave defenders without the ability to lawfully protect themselves.[106]

Applied to our hypothetical case, this admittedly broader formulation allows the type of pre-emptive strike Victoria delivered. By clearly threatening Victoria and engaging in physical conduct that demonstrates his intention to act on his threat (beating her and driving off in the car), Andrew became an immediate and culpable threat to Victoria. Victoria is, therefore, both internally and externally justified in killing Andrew in order to save her own life.[107]

Leverick, in contrast, relies on her personal baseline 'firm conviction' about the equal value of the lives of aggressors and defenders to reject such a test in cases involving battered women.[108] According to Leverick:

> [S]elf-defence is only permissible where the accused faced a threat of death (or one of near equivalent seriousness) or where such a threat might reasonably be

[102] See, eg, Allhoff (n 83) 1541–47; *United States v Jennings*, 855 F Supp 1427, 1435–36 (MD Pa 1994), citing *United States v Oakie*, 12 F3d 1436, 1443 (8th Cir 1993), *aff'd*, 61 F3d 894 (3d Cir 1995); *United States v Acosta-Sierra*, 690 F3d 1111, 1126 (9th Cir 2012).

[103] See generally Leider (n 83) 994 n 158; KK Ferzan, 'Defending Imminence: From Battered Women to Iraq' (2004) 46 *Arizona Law Review* 213, 247.

[104] See ch 2(IV)(C) & (D).

[105] This formulation has been accepted in a number of US jurisdictions. See, eg, 18 Pa Cons Stat § 505 (2019); Tex Penal Code §§ 9.31, 9.32 (2019); NJ Stat Ann §§ 2C:3–4(a) (2019).

[106] See Lesch (n 85) 110–11; S Wallace, 'Beyond Imminence: Evolving International Law and Battered Women's Right to Self-Defense' (2004) 71 *University of Chicago Law Review* 1749, 1761–62.

[107] See ch 4(I)(B).

[108] It will be conceded that the term 'battered women' is admittedly dated. 'Battered intimate partner' is more contemporary and appropriately descriptive. That said, because the literature for years has used

> assumed. The level of violence faced by the majority of battered women is unlikely to meet this threshold.[109]

Leverick, therefore, favours a strict temporal interpretation of imminence and disfavours a substitute 'necessity test.' She contends that such 'loosening' of the imminence requirement basis of 'lesser values, such as personal honour or the desire for revenge,' fails to accord maximum protection to the value of protecting the attacker's life.[110] But by not engaging in the more challenging discussion of what other values might be implicated in battered intimate partner cases, and by focusing on motivations such as 'revenge,' Leverick misses the opportunity to anchor her analysis with stouter analytical gear.[111]

The sceptic may of course assert that Andrew could possibly cool down and change his mind during his drive. He in the end may decide not to kill Victoria (or at least not to kill her today). But the same argument can be made in the context of any attack. It is always possible that an aggressor will at the last minute or second stop just short of, say, pulling the trigger of his gun or plunging his knife into the defender's chest.

And so if the fact-finder believes, given the surrounding circumstances and the relationship between the parties, that the threat will in fact be carried out (that is, that the defender is *externally* justified), and that the defender acted in reaction to this threat (that is, that the defender is *internally* justified), then the defender's conduct must be legally justified.[112] The common 'necessary to prevent an imminent threat' language, in contrast, for no good reason forecloses the possibility that a jury could rule Victoria's action as self-defensive. The position taken here is that such an outcome is normatively undesirable and inconsistent with the balance of the decision-grounds.[113]

For illustrative purposes, what follows is intended to graphically illustrate how the value-based model might approach such a challenging fact pattern as set out at the beginning of this subchapter:

'battered woman' or 'battered spouse,' those terms are on occasion repeated here (though not exclusively so). For the leading, albeit controversial, research-based study of the syndrome, see LE Walker, *The Battered Woman Syndrome*, 4th edn (New York, Springer Publishing, 2016). See also A Gruber, 'The Duty to Retreat in Self-Defense Law and Violence Against Women' *Oxford Handbooks Online* (6 July 2017) (discussing the complex relationship between the duty to retreat in self-defence law and violence against women).

[109] F Leverick, *Killing in Self-Defence* (Oxford, Oxford University Press, 2006) 91.

[110] Ibid at 102. Interestingly, however, Leverick momentarily appears to adopt a diluted equality of life position when she advocates in favour of replacing the imminence test with one focused on 'inevitable harm' because that would 'bring at least some battered women within the ambit of the law of self-defence.' Ibid at 108.

[111] Cp Lesch (n 85) 110 (arguing that defenders have the right to defend against the fear of future attack violent intimate partners may create).

[112] See generally S Choudhry and J Herring, 'Righting Domestic Violence' (2006) 20 *International Journal of Law, Policy and the Family* 95, 109 ('[T]he key question should be whether the infringement of the right is necessary to avoid an inevitable attack, rather than whether there is imminence.'). See also ch 4(I)(B).

[113] See generally ch 2(IV) & (V).

Table 3 Culpable Threat

Nature of Threat: Culpable
Seriousness of Threat: Severe (Death)
Defensive Force: Severe (Death)

Decision Ground	Weight	Summary of Reasoning
Value #1: Collective violence-reducing function (see Chapter 2(IV)(A))	+1	Andrew is culpably posing a serious threat. He, therefore, has conditionally waived his right to non-interference. Victoria, moreover, is only using necessary force to ward off the threatened harming *and* wronging. From a systemic perspective, permitting deadly force here does not inappropriately threaten the state's monopoly on violence.
Value #2: The attacker's right to life (see Chapter 2(IV)(B))	0	Andrew's decision to engage in a culpable attack threatening death overcomes the presumption that the attacker's right to life must be safeguarded.
Value #3: Maintaining equal standing (see Chapter 2(IV)(C))	+1	Andrew is aggressively claiming he will kill Victoria, and he, therefore, is threatening to impose his will on her and to elevate his interests above hers. Defensive force is necessary to ward off this threatened imputation of unequal standing.
Value #4: Protecting the defender's autonomy (see Chapter 2(IV)(D))	+1	Andrew's culpable attack threatens a severe injury (namely, death).
Value #5: Ensuring the primacy of the legal process (see Chapter 2(IV)(E))	+1	Victoria is facing a non-compensable injury at the hands of a fully culpable attacker. She, therefore, has no acceptable or practicable legal recourse. As a consequence, the primacy of the legal process is not threatened by her use of defensive force.
Value #6: Maintaining the legitimacy of the legal order (see Chapter 2(IV)(F))	+1	Refusing to permit Victoria to use defensive force under these circumstances could reasonably be perceived as very unjust and, therefore, could cause damage to the legal system's legitimacy (in the sense of moral authority in the eyes of the public).
Value #7: Deterrence (see Chapter 2(IV)(G))	+1	The fully culpable Andrew is threatening Victoria with deadly force. Permitting Victoria to counter this threat with deadly force will, on balance, add to self-defence's specific and general deterrent impact.
TOTAL	**+6**	**Deadly force is presumptively justifiable (and +6 indicates relatively strong justification).**

C. Retreat and Avoiding Conflict

The private domain consists of concrete interests and sovereignty.[114] Some may conclude therefrom that any requirement that the defender retreat from, or avoid going to, a place where he has a legal right to be would impermissibly infringe on his autonomy (value #4), and in fact would strengthen the imputation of lesser standing inherent in the threatened wronging (value #3).[115] Victor, they would say, may, therefore, go to the local pub even though he believes it to be certain that the aggressive Andrew will also be there and will likely pick a fight with Victor. In fact, the argument often advanced is that, in a liberal society, individuals should have the right to go anywhere they are legally permitted to be, regardless of what aggressors they may find there, because freedom of movement is part of individual autonomy (value #4).[116]

Leverick disagrees with this position. She characterises the 'strong retreat rule' (requiring the defender to make an attempt to retreat before using force) as the most 'morally appropriate' because, by requiring retreat whenever it is a safe possibility, it 'promotes maximum respect for the right to life.'[117] She conversely dismisses the 'no-retreat rule' because it does not seek to 'save[] both the life of the aggressor and the life of the victim.'[118] She, similarly, rejects the 'weak retreat rule' because:

> Allowing the accused to make the choice to use violence on any occasion where this could have been avoided implies that the law does not respect the right to life of an aggressor and places some other value, such as honour, dignity, or vengeance, higher than that of the aggressor's life.[119]

Leverick's approach, in short, places paramount, and in effect near-exclusive, emphasis on value #2 (protecting the attacker's right to life). The value-based model, however, considers a broader spectrum of values and, accordingly, rejects any such categorical duty to, under all circumstances, retreat or avoid places where one may become a victim.[120] That said, broader welfarist concerns,[121] as reflected in the balance of the value-based model's decision-grounds,[122] do suggest that the

[114] See generally RF Schopp, 'Verdicts of Conscience: Nullification and Necessity as Jury Responses to Crimes of Conscience' (1996) 69 *Southern California Law Review* 2075. See also A Tsesis, 'Balancing Free Speech' (2016) 96 *Boston University Law Review* 1, 22–23.

[115] See generally V Erb, 'Notwehr als Menchenrecht – Zugleich eine Kritik der Entscheiduing des LG Frankfurt am Main im "Fall Daschner"' (2005) 25 *Neue Zeitschrift für Strafrecht* 593, 597 (in extreme cases a strict duty to retreat could force a person out of the public sphere).

[116] See ibid. See also ch 2(IV)(D).

[117] Leverick (n 109) 76.

[118] Ibid at 78–79.

[119] Ibid at 81.

[120] See discussion in ch 4(II)(C).

[121] See generally M Kremnitzer and K Ghanayim, 'Proportionality and the Aggressor's Culpability in Self-Defense' (2004) 39 *Tulsa Law Review* 875, 894.

[122] Consider, eg, value #1 (reduction in overall societal violence), value #2 (protecting the attacker), and value #5 (ensuring the primacy of the legal process). See ch 2(IV)(A), (B), & (E).

value-based model requires retreat when (1) the attacker is an innocent, and (2) it can be done safely. In fact, Richardson and Goff have argued with some persuasive force that a failure to retreat under these conditions establishes that the defender is 'no longer morally innocent.'[123]

But going back to the value-based model's approach, if the defender knows that he will be set upon by an innocent attacker (a person labouring under a mistake, a child, etc), and retreat can be accomplished without materially increasing a risk of serious harm, then value #1 and value #2 would counsel in favour of requiring retreat.[124] But, as already noted, these determinations occur on a sliding scale and the related value-judgements are heavily fact-dependent. It, therefore, is not possible to provide *post-facto* rules governing every conceivable action.

To further illustrate this point, assume that Victor knows that Andrew will threaten Victor with a beating as soon as Victor appears at the pub, and that Victor in fact sees Andrew through the window of the pub. According to Leverick:

> Where it does not conflict with any other value, the accused should have the freedom to go to any public place she chooses, but [in a situation like this] the value of freedom of movement is outweighed by the weightier value of minimising violence.[125]

The model developed here agrees with Leverick to a point. By entering into the pub with this knowledge, Victor knowingly increases the likelihood that a conflict will arise (thus negatively implicating value #1 and value #2 – collective violence reduction by protecting the state's monopoly on force, and protection of the individual attacker, respectively; and value #5 – ensuring the primacy of the legal process).[126] The criminal justice system's interest in protecting Victor's rights can, therefore, fairly be said to be negatively impacted by the fact that Victor in essence 'assumed' a certain amount of risk when he entered the pub (weakening the impact of value #3 – equal standing; value #4 – protecting the defender's autonomy; and value #7 – deterrence).[127]

It, after all, would not be asking too much for Victor to avoid this particular pub, even if this causes him to have to suffer some minor inconvenience (he could, for example, inform the police of the situation).[128] Similarly, if a defender refuses to retreat from a place when escape is possible, decision-grounds such as protecting the equal standing among people (#3) and protecting the defender's autonomy (#4) become less weighty, particularly if it is reasonably foreseeable that the defensive conduct necessary to thwart the attack will be severe (thus adding weight to

[123] See LS Richardson and PA Goff, 'Self Defense and the Suspicion Heuristic' (2012) 98 *Iowa Law Review* 293, 333.

[124] See ch 2(IV)(A) & (B).

[125] Leverick (n 109) 126.

[126] See ch 2(IV)(A), (B), & (E).

[127] See ch 2(IV)(C), (D), & (G).

[128] But see Erb (n 115) 597 (restricted duty to retreat allows aggressors to limit innocents' personal freedom).

safeguarding the collective violence-reduction function of the criminal law (#1), protecting the attacker (#2), and ensuring the primacy of the legal process (#5)).[129]

While the burden of course always remains on others not to become threats in the first place, the value-based model places a corresponding responsibility on individuals to at least attempt to avoid places where they *know* they are likely to be faced with a situation where they either submit to the attack, or (more likely) must impose serious costs on the attacker. Similarly, individuals facing innocent threats (not implicating value #3 and value #7) should retreat if they can do so safely; and even if the threat is culpable, depending on the nature of the threatened attack and the harm threatened (most directly involving consideration of value #1, value #2, and value #4), retreat may be called for.

III. Proportionality of Defensive Force

A. Rejecting Strict Proportionality and Addressing Excessive Force

Some, like Leverick[130] and Wallerstein,[131] wish to impose exacting proportionality between the harm threatened and the defensive force used.[132] In this view, the systemic demand for precise proportionality between the severity of the punishment and the severity of the committed abstract crime should also apply in the context of actions taken in self-defence.[133]

Leverick, by way of illustration, concedes what is hoped is a self-evident point, namely, that pregnancy is an 'extremely unpleasant potential consequence of a rape;' but, adopting a strict proportionality approach, she also asserts that deadly force to prevent even knowing and intentional (that is, morally culpable) rape should only be permitted if the threatened attack 'approaches the standard of a wrong *equivalent to a deprivation of life itself*.'[134] Given, moreover, that respect

[129] See ch 2(IV)(A), (B), & (E).

[130] See Leverick (n 109) 143–52 (demanding precise proportionality, so that severe injury (such as loss of a limb) is not enough to, without more, justify deadly defensive force).

[131] See Wallerstein (n 85) 1024–25.

[132] See generally RJ Arneson, 'Self-Defense and Culpability: Fault Forfeits First' (2018) 55 *San Diego Law Review* 231, 261–62; M Lim, 'A New Approach to the Ethics of Life: The Will to Live in Lieu of Inherent Dignity or Autonomy-Based Approaches' (2014) 24 *Southern California Interdisciplinary Law Journal* 27; B Porat, 'Lethal Self-Defense against a Rapist and the Challenge of Proportionality: Jewish Law Perspective' (2013) 26 *Columbia Journal of Gender & Law* 128; Kremnitzer and Ghanayim (n 121) 894–99. *Cf* CB Ramsey, 'Provoking Change: Comparative Insights on Feminist Homicide Law Reform' (2010) 100 *Journal of Criminal Law & Criminology* 33, 74; RL Lerner, 'The Worldwide Popular Revolt Against Proportionality in Self-Defense Law' (2006) 2 *Journal of Law, Economics & Policy* 331, 361.

[133] See Leverick (n 109) 143–52.

[134] Ibid at 157 (emphasis added). See also discussion at ch 3(III). Note, however, that determining the 'standard of a wrong' inevitably involves the same 'line-drawing' that Leverick finds objectionable in the context of deadly force in defence of property.

for autonomy requires the wrongdoer to in some sense 'will' his own coercion (by threatening a *wrong*, rather than a mere *harm*),[135] the argument advanced by commentators like Leverick is that the same principle could be said to also require that the wrongdoer will the *measure* of his coercion.

This argument, however, overlooks that punishment is an institutionalised legal response to wrongdoing that is constrained by systemic factors in the way it is distributed.[136] Stated another way, while consistency may require a uniform system of sentencing that incorporates strict proportionality, the value-based model recognises that the same cannot reasonably be said to be true for unpredictable, heat-of-the-moment actions taken in self-defence. Self-defence, after all, is *anticipatory* in the sense that its aim is the avoidance of harm.[137] Punishment (through sentencing), in contrast, is largely *retrospective* in that it responds to harm with retaliatory harm that is meted out for a variety of reasons, including general and specific deterrence, incapacitation, and prevention.[138] Punishment, in short, occurs under different circumstances and for different reasons than self-defensive conduct. Attempts to analogise the two on the basis of 'willed coercion' thus lack persuasive force.

Under the approach developed here, the argument for cabining a defender's ability to exercise force is stronger when the attacker is morally innocent (and, therefore, does not fully implicate value #3 – equal standing; value #4 – protecting the defender's autonomy; value #5 – primacy of the legal process; and value #7 – deterrence).[139] As discussed previously in the context of the decision-grounds' concern with ensuring equal standing among people and deterring crime,[140] beyond 'willed coercion,' there are sound normative (and utilitarian) reasons for imposing additional limitations on the amount of force that can be used against an innocent attacker.

It is of course true that the innocent attacker also threatens concrete harm to the defender. But it is important to consider that the innocent attacker, as the value-based model recognises, does not deny the intersubjective foundation of the defender's rights (value #3) in the way that a culpable attacker does.[141]

[135] See generally ch 2(IV)(C).

[136] See generally MR Secula, 'Particularities of Contraventions Against Other Forms of Legal Liability' [2010] *Law Annals from Titu Maiorescu University* 159, 161–62; V Tadros, 'The Scope and the Grounds of Responsibility' (2008) 11 *New Criminal Law Review* 91, 113–17; F Haldemann, 'Another King of Justice: Transitional Justice as Recognition' (2008) 41 *Cornell International Law Journal* 675, 705–06.

[137] See generally M Angel, 'Why Judy Norman Acted in Reasonable Self-Defense: An Abused Woman and Sleeping Man' (2008) 16 *Buffalo Women's Law Journal* 65, 65–88.

[138] See generally RL Rausch, 'Reframing Roe: Property over Privacy' (2012) 27 *Berkeley Journal of Gender, Law & Justice* 28, 50–51; V Behr, 'Punitive Damages in American and German Law – Tendencies Towards Approximation of Apparently Irreconcilable Concepts' (2003) 78 *Chicago-Kent Law Review* 105, 113.

[139] See ch 2(IV)(C)–(E) & (G). See also Rönnau and Hohn (n 44) side-notes 6, 13, and 74; Erb (n 85) side-notes 60, 209.

[140] See ch 2(IV)(C) & (G).

[141] See ch 2(IV)(C). See also Erb (n 85) side-note 18; S Retzko, *Die Angriffsverursachung bei der Notwehr* (Lit Verlag, 2001) 127; J Renzikowski, *Notstand und Notwehr* (Duncker & Humblot GmbH, 1994) 275.

And, as already noted, the law cannot expect a defender to absorb an attacker's seriously harmful and unjustified, though innocent, attack. Such a requirement would compel the defender to subordinate his autonomy and concrete interests to the welfare of the attacker.[142] A defender may, therefore, under the value-based method use force even against an innocent attacker. But the amount of harm threatened by the attacker will be more carefully weighed against the amount of defensive force that may be used, whether safe retreat is required, and what amount of harm the defender can be expected to absorb.

Whenever a defender uses force, moreover, he may err and use more force than is actually necessary to ward off the culpable threat. Pace Grotius,[143] an unreasonable error that results in the defender using excessive force to ward off the threat, intrudes on the violence-reducing function of the criminal law by threatening the state's monopoly on force (value #1). It also impermissibly harms the individual attacker (value #2) because such force lies outside the conditional gap created by the person purportedly posing the threat. Consistent with the value-based model's treatment of mistake,[144] then, a reasonable mistake as to the amount of force necessary to thwart the attack will excuse the defender (that is, exempt the defendant from value-based model stage-six condemnation).[145] An unreasonable mistake of fact, on the other hand, renders self-defence unavailable.

B. Deadly Force in Defence of Property

Controversially in some circles,[146] the value-based model is in accord with the US and English courts holding that deadly force in defence of property should, as a general rule, be rejected. While certainly susceptible to different normative appraisals, and recognising the power of the argument that property can in fact be a genuine extension of the 'self,'[147] the value-based model nevertheless

[142] See ch 2(IV)(D).

[143] See generally R Feenstra, 'Dutch Kantharos Case and the History of Error in Substantia' (1973–1974) 48 *Tulsa Law Review* 846, 856.

[144] See ch 2(IV)(A) & (B).

[145] See ch 2(IV)(F)(v)(g).

[146] The majority position among German scholars, eg, holds that deadly force may be used to defend property. See, eg, C Roxin, *Strafrecht, Allgemeiner Teil* 3rd edn (Beck CH, 1997) 590. See also Jescheck and Weigend, 5th edn (n 67) 348 n 49. But see Greco (n 85) 671 (discussing a minority position that even the threatened loss of €5,000 is insufficient to justify deadly defensive force); K Bernsmann, 'Überlegungen zur tödlichen Notwehr bei nicht lebensbedrohlichen Angriffen' (1992) 104 *ZStW* 290, 326 (contending that deadly force in defence of property is never justified). See also Tex Penal Code Ann § 9.42(3)(A) (2019) (stating that the use of deadly force in defence of property is justified when 'the land or property cannot be protected or recovered by any other means'); R Schopp, 'Self-Defense', in J Coleman (ed), *In Harm's Way* (Cambridge, Cambridge University Press, 1994), discussed in W Kaufman, 'Is There a Right to Self-Defense?' (2004) 23 *Criminal Justice Ethics* 20, 28.

[147] See generally DA Green, 'Indigenous Intellect: Problems of Calling Knowledge Property and Assigning It Rights' (2009) 15 *Texas Wesleyan Law Review* 335, 344–45; M Dan-Cohen, 'The Value of Ownership' (2001) 1 *Global Jurist* 1, 25; J Waldron, *The Right to Private Property* (Oxford, Oxford University Press, 1989) 343; RL Abel, 'Should Tort Law Protect Property Against Accidental Loss' (1986) 23 *San Diego Law Review* 79, 91.

agrees that, on balance, while most (though not necessarily all) property interests are generally compensable, a human life is not.[148]

Of course, it is difficult to *ex ante* determine whether law enforcement will be able to recover the property or arrest the thieves so that alternative compensation can be sought. As articulated here, however, the criminal law's objectives include violence reduction and protection of the state's monopoly on force (value #1), protection of the attacker's presumptive right to life (value #2), ensuring the primacy of the legal process (value #5), and avoiding results that could threaten the legitimacy of the criminal law (value #6).[149] Consequently, the law, on balance, would be challenged to permit a defender to extinguish another's life solely because the defender at that time believes this to be the only way for him to ensure that his property is not damaged or permanently taken away (impacting value #3 – equal standing; and value #4 – protecting the defender's autonomy) or to send a deterrent message to would-be criminals (value #7).[150]

That said, and on a more practical note, 'pure' threats to property, such as occurred in the case of the German apple thief, will in the real world occur relatively infrequently. Any indication by the attacker that he also poses a physical threat – for example, if the defender attempts to stop the theft of, or damage to, the property – will take the case outside of the realm of defence of property, shifting the value-based model's balance of concerns.

As a slight aside, I will note that my thinking on this topic has shifted over the years (and that having children, candidly, has materially contributed to the 'softening' of my views on deadly force in defence of property – and, for that matter, also in other contexts). I, therefore, today find myself challenged to fully agree with either of the standard hard-edged 'yes' (Schopp) or 'no' (Leverick, Ashworth, etc) answers when it comes to whether deadly force should *ever be* authorised in defence of *any* property. But the distinct advantage of the value-based model is that it provides the analytical flexibility to consider different circumstances and normative assumptions – not everyone will reach the same conclusions when it comes to what values matter, and why, in a particular fact scenario. The analysis, however, can still follow the same common framework so that the differences in perspective can be more accurately teased out and discussed.

C. Responding to 'Trivial' Threats

We have shown that both innocent and culpable threats infringe on the defender's autonomy (value #4).[151] We have also discussed how and why the value-based

[148] See generally Kaufman (n 146) 28.

[149] See ch 2(IV)(A), (B), (E), & (F).

[150] See R Pest, 'Die Erforderlichkeit der Notwehrhandlung' in F Stam and A Werkmeister (eds), *Der Allgemeine Teil des Strafrechts in der aktuellen Rechtsprechung* (Baden-Baden, Nomos Verlagsgesellschaft, 2019) 165; SP Green, 'Castles and Carjackers: Proportionality and the Use of Deadly Force in Defense of Dwellings and Vehicles' [1999] *University of Illinois Law Review* 1, 38. See also ch 2(IV)(C), (D), & (G).

[151] See ch 2(IV)(D).

model devalues threats to property when compared with threats of physical harming.[152] So, does this mean that a person can use deadly force to, say, prevent another from stepping on one's toes if that is the only way to avoid the threatened physical 'harm' (or, rather, discomfort)?

i. A Comparison with Schopp's Approach

Schopp, as noted, argues that a liberal society must treat *any* culpable infringement of an individual's autonomy as extremely serious.[153] At the very heart of this argument lies the strict separation between public and private spheres of action. Relying heavily on the work of Feinberg[154] and Rawls,[155] Schopp argues that 'substantive liberals' (like him) consider sovereignty a categorical, underivative, non-instrumental, and, most significantly, non-compensable fundamental value.[156] The right to self-determination in the public sphere, the right to unfettered choice in those matters falling into the private domain, and equality of citizenship are, thus, central to Schopp's thesis. He concludes that only a system allowing largely *unlimited* discretionary authority in the private sphere can be described as 'liberal' in this sense. The private sphere should, therefore, largely be beyond the reach of political interference.[157]

Schopp uses the example of an elderly farmer who is working at her market stall (this example may ring familiar, as it is a variation on the German fruit thief case introduced in Chapter 1). A local bully approaches the stall and takes one of the farmer's apples. When she asks the bully to return the apple, he replies '[t]ough, old lady, what are you going to do about it?' The farmer in response takes a handgun from under her apron and kills the bully. According to Schopp, the shooting was necessary to prevent the theft of the apple. It, therefore, 'does not seem counterintuitive to say that [the victim] was justified [in shooting the bully dead].'[158] This outcome certainly is harsh by pretty much any standard, but it is predictable in light of Schopp's stipulations.

When subjected to closer examination, however, it becomes apparent that it is in these very stipulations that the weakness of this argument becomes manifest. Schopp provides that 'gratuitous' defensive force is not to be permitted.[159] This, however, is not saying very much more than that necessity is required. Moreover,

[152] See ch 4(III)(B).
[153] See Schopp (n 11) 83–88. See generally ch 3(IV). *Cf* ch 2(IV)(D).
[154] See generally J Feinberg, *Harm to Self* (New York, Oxford University Press, 1986) 28–31.
[155] See generally J Rawls, *Political Liberalism* Lect. I (New York, Columbia University Press, 2011/1993) §§ 1–3.
[156] Schopp (n 11) 67.
[157] Ibid at 77. See also *Thornburgh v American College of Obstetricians & Gynecologists*, 106 S Ct 2169, 2184–85 (1986).
[158] Schopp (n 11) 84.
[159] Ibid at 78.

to simply assert, as Schopp does, that the 'private sphere' is outside the reach of the criminal law's influence or that an individual's sovereignty can never be infringed because it is non-compensable are conclusory assertions of belief demanding principled (and, it is argued, value-based) support. Schopp, however, provides no such arguments.

The fundamental difficulty with Schopp's categorical conception of individual autonomy (much like with the old German law's treatment of the fruit thief), in short, is that it is challenging to square it with life in modern society. Whether called 'welfarist' or 'humanitarian' concerns, or 'value #1, #2, and #5 issues,' life routinely, predictably, and justifiably imposes on citizens demands that they must at times restrict their otherwise autonomous spheres of activity in order to promote other legitimate interests.[160] As discussed above, restricting certain purely autonomous action can in fact be said to be the very function of the criminal law.[161]

In sum, the position taken here diverges from Schopp's theory in part because the value-based model views trivial harms as adding little (or, indeed negative) weight to competing decision-grounds such as violence reduction and protection of the state's monopoly on force (value #1), protection of the attacker (value #2), and ensuring primacy of the legal process (value #5).[162] While Schopp's position may add additional protection to the defender's autonomy (value #4) and increase deterrence (value #7),[163] it does so at such a great cost in the sense of the exercise of disproportionate force, implicating value #1 and value #2. Indeed, it can be said to potentially undermine the moral legitimacy of the legal order (value #6).[164]

In cases involving trivial threats, defensive force must be limited by more than simple necessity. Contrary to Schopp's claim, then, and providing further support for the value-based model's assumptions about the importance of transparency to sound decision-making, the *nature* and *amount* of harm threatened very directly impact the implicated values. The interplay with the facts and the values, in turn, provide a reasonable (and reasoned) argument for whether the conduct should qualify as justified self-defence.[165]

ii. Subjective or Objective Evaluation of Triviality?

Assume Andrew is about to dispossess Victor of a stamp that, viewed objectively, is of little financial value. To Victor, however, the stamp holds immense value

[160] See generally J Desautels-Stein, 'The Market as a Legal Concept' (2012) 60 *Buffalo Law Review* 387, 466–67; GR Stone, 'Autonomy and Distrust' (1993) 64 *University of Colorado Law Review* 1171, 1174–75.

[161] See generally ch 2(IV)(A)–(D). See also A Simester and A von Hirsch, 'On the Legitimate Objectives of Criminalisation' (2016) 10 *Criminal Law & Philosophy* 367, 376–78.

[162] See ch 2(IV)(A), (B), & (E).

[163] See ch 2(IV)(D) & (G).

[164] See ch 2(IV)(A), (B), & (F).

[165] See generally ch 2(IV)(C).

because it was a special gift from his grandfather who spent years trying to locate and purchase it. To remain consistent with the logic underlying the requirement that mistakes of fact must be objectively reasonable,[166] the position taken here is that triviality ought likewise be determined objectively, based on a 'reasonable person' standard.[167]

An exception to this rule, however, is carved out for situations in which the attacker in fact *knows* that the object he is threatening has a particular subjective value to the defender (that is, Andrew is aware that the stamp's theft constitutes a subjectively serious intrusion on Victor's personal autonomy (value #4) and, relatedly, realises that such a theft reflects significant disrespect to Victor's equal standing (value #3)).[168] In contrast, an individual who, due to some personal idiosyncrasy, *unreasonably* places a non-trivial value on an objectively worthless item such as, say, a napkin, will not qualify for this possible exception to the general rule.

If, then, the attacker knows that the (objectively) trivial interest threatened has a special (subjective) value for the defender, and if this attribution of subjective value is reasonable under the circumstances, the otherwise trivial threat is weighted based on the subjective non-trivial value due to the parties' shared understanding of the object's value. The attacker's knowledge of the sentimentality magnifies the imputation of lesser standing (value #3) such a threat implies.[169]

IV. Necessity, Proportionality, Mistakes, and the European Convention on Human Rights

For starters, we recognise that: (1) Germany and England are subject to the jurisdiction of the European Court of Human Rights ('ECtHR'),[170] (2) this is an evaluative (and, at some level, comparative) undertaking, and (3) the value-based model analyses the seven posited rights in the context of whether and how they reflect fundamental human rights. It, therefore, is appropriate to include a short

[166] See ch 4(I)(B).

[167] See generally *Caleshu v SC Merrill Lynch*, 737 F Supp 1070, 1083–87 (ED Mo 1990) (using reasonable person standard to determine triviality of alleged misconduct in employment context). *Cf* T Hörnle, 'Social Expectation in the Criminal Law: The Reasonable Person in a Comparative Perspective' (2008) 11 *New Criminal Law Review* 1, 32 ('A reference to the "prudent and reliable person in the specific situation and social role of the actor," which is the standard phrase in German criminal law, is better suited.').

[168] See ch 2(IV)(C) & (D).

[169] See ch 2(IV)(C).

[170] See generally Rönnau and Hohn (n 44) side-notes 54–55; Rosenau (n 45) side-note 37; B Vogel, 'The Core Legal Concepts and Principles Defining Criminal Law in Germany' in M Dyson and B Vogel (eds), *The Limits of Criminal Law: Anglo-German Concepts and Principles* (Cambridge, Intersentia, 2018) 41; R Macmillan Moon, 'An Examination of UK Law as It Pertains to the Unmarried Father: Current Legal Thinking in an International Context' (2010) 6 *Cambridge Student Law Review* 259, 262.

discussion of the European Convention on Human Rights ('ECHR'). Article 2 of the ECHR aims to protect the 'right to life,' providing, in part, that:

> 1. Everyone's right to life shall be protected by law. No one shall be deprived of his life intentionally save in the execution of a sentence of a court following his conviction of a crime for which this penalty is provided by law.
> 2. Deprivation of life shall not be regarded as inflicted in contravention of this article when it results from the use of force which is no more than absolutely necessary:
>   a. in defence of any person from unlawful violence ....[171]

A. The Current Status of Positive Obligations Imposed by Article 2

Today, modern liberal states are expected not only to refrain from the intentional and unlawful taking of life directly through their agents (police, army, etc), but should also take appropriate steps to safeguard the lives of those within their jurisdiction (in particular by putting in place effective criminal-law provisions backed up by law-enforcement machinery).[172] That said, positive obligations flowing from Article 2 should 'be interpreted in a way which does not impose an impossible or disproportionate burden on the authorities.'[173]

B. Article 2 in the Self-Defence Context: Defensive Force Must Be 'Absolutely Necessary'

The *McCann* Court, in line with the text of Article 2(2)(a), ruled that Article 2 allows for exceptions to the right to life only when 'absolutely necessary,' a term indicating

> that a stricter and more compelling test of necessity must be employed than that normally applicable when determining whether state action is 'necessary in a democratic society' under paragraph 2 of Articles 8 and 11 of the Convention.[174]

[171] Council of Europe, European Convention for the Protection of Human Rights and Fundamental Freedoms [hereinafter ECHR], Nov 4, 1950, ETS No. 005, Art 2. See generally WA Qureshi, 'Legal Exceptions to the Inalienable Right to Life' (2019) 53 *University of San Francisco Law Review* 263, 273.

[172] See *LCB v United Kingdom* [1998] ECtHR 108 (judgment of 9 June 1998); *Osman v United Kingdom* [1998] ECtHR 101 (judgment of 28 Oct 1998); *HLR v France* [1998] 26 EHRR 29; *Stubbings v United Kingdom* [1997] 23 EHRR 213. See also *Oneryildiz v Turkey* [2005] 41 EHRR 20 (ruling that Art 2 'entails above all a primary duty on the state to put in place a legislative and administrative framework designed to provide effective deterrence against threats to the right of life'). That said, some have argued that Art 2 only applies to the state, and not to relationships between citizens. See generally T Fischer, '§ 32 Vorbemerkungen' in *Strafgesetzbuch* (Heymanns Verlag GmbH, 2019) side-note 39; Rosenau (n 45) side-note 37; J Wessels and H Satzger, *Wessels/Beulke: Strafrecht – Allgemeiner Teil* (Müller Jur Vlg CF, 2018) § 32 side-note 526. But see Rönnau and Hohn (n 44) side-notes 235–37.

[173] *Osman v United Kingdom* [1998] ECtHR 101, 116.

[174] *McCann and Others v United Kingdom* [2016] 21 ECtHR 97, 146–49 GC. The *McCann* case concerned the death of three members of the IRA suspected of having on them a remote-controlled

C. Article 2 in the Self-Defence Context: 'Strict Proportionality' Required

Note first that the proportionality principle does not appear in the text of Article 2. But, as it turns out, it is clearly established in the Court's caselaw. In most ECtHR cases, proportionality is in fact simply viewed as part and parcel of the 'absolute necessity' requirement. Indeed, the Article itself provides that '[d]eprivation of life shall not be regarded as inflicted in contravention of this article when it results from the use of *force* which is *no more* than *absolutely necessary*.'[175] Put another way, the requirement of 'absolute necessity' in Article 2 means that any force used for any of the purposes mentioned in Article 2 must be 'strictly proportionate' to the achievement of any of the aims set out in subparagraphs 2(a), (b), and (c) of that article.[176]

D. Article 2 and Deadly Force in Defence of Property

The ECtHR has not yet ruled explicitly on whether state actors (or individuals) violate Article 2 if and when they use deadly force in defence of property.[177] Nonetheless, given that Article 2(2)(a) provides that the use of force must be 'no more than absolutely necessary … in defence of any *person* from unlawful *violence*,' it is difficult to see how the Court could permit deadly force in defence of property (since a threat to belongings is not a threat of 'violence').[178] Only if the threat of violence happened to accompany a threat to property, then, would deadly force likely be authorised by the Court. Some German commentators, however, have pointed to Article 2's limitation of state power (rather than citizens' use of force) to argue that the German law's permission of deadly force against property is not implicated by the Article.[179]

device intended to be used to explode a bomb. The men were shot dead on the street by Special Air Service soldiers in Gibraltar. The Court concluded that there had been a violation of Article 2 because the operation could have been planned and controlled without the need to kill the suspects. See also *Putintseva v Russia* [2012] ECtHR 820.

[175] See ECHR (n 171) Nov 4, 1950, ETS No. 005, Art 2(2). See also S Trechsel, 'Comparative Observations on Human Rights Law and Criminal Law' [2000] *St Louis-Warsaw Transatlantic Law Journal* 1, 22.

[176] *McCann* GC judgment, § 149.

[177] See JA Hessbruegge, *Human Rights and Personal Self-Defense in International Law* (New York, Oxford University Press, 2016) 266 (noting that '[i]n academic literature the question remains in dispute'). *Cf* D Rietiker, 'Police Violence and How to Fight It, in Particular When Racially Motivated: The Example of the European Court of Human Rights' (2019) 52 *Suffolk University Law Review* 417, 419–25.

[178] See generally Fischer (n 172) side-note 40; Rönnau and Hohn (n 44) side-note 55.

[179] See, eg, Fischer (n 172) side-note 39; Rosenau (n 45) side-note 37; Wessels and Satzger (n 172) side-note 526. But see Rönnau and Hohn (n 44) side-notes 235–37; *Oneryildiz v Turkey* [2005] 41 EHRR 20.

E. Article 2 and Mistakes

As noted, it is now well-settled that Article 2 requires lethal force to have been 'absolutely necessary' to defend a person from unlawful violence.[180] And, read strictly, this seemingly would require that the force was, as a matter of objective fact, indeed 'absolutely necessary.' Article 2, after all, does not provide that the person must 'believe' or 'reasonably believe' the force to be 'absolutely necessary.' But that, rather inexplicably, is not the position the Court has adopted.

In *Kelly v United Kingdom*, the Court was confronted with the case of a 17-year-old joy rider whom soldiers in Northern Ireland shot and killed because they mistakenly believed that he and the other three occupants of the vehicle were escaping terrorists.[181] The Court ruled that the soldiers in that case 'reasonably believed' that the occupants of the vehicle were, in fact, escaping terrorists. Whether mistaken or not, the soldiers' conduct, therefore, apparently met the Court's absolute necessity test.[182] Whether this counter-textual holding stands the test of time remains to be seen.

V. Application of the Value-Based Model to Other Challenging Cases[183]

A. Innocent Attackers – The 'Standard' Case

Andrew is playing with his younger cousin's air gun in his back yard. Andrew thinks that it is a harmless toy, but, in reality, the gun is loaded, the safety mechanism is disengaged, and the gun is fully pressurised. Andrew playfully points the gun at his friendly neighbour Victor, who happens to be walking by on his way

[180] See generally *Da Silva v UK* [2016] 63 EHRR 12 (addressing England's law of self-defence in the context of Art 2), discussed in L Lazarus and J Blackbourn, 'Intelligence and the Criminal Law in England and Wales' in Dyson and Vogel (n 170) 501; *Bubbins v UK* [2005] 41 EHRR 24 (same).

[181] [1993] 16 EHRR 20, 21.

[182] Ibid at 22. See also *Makaratzis v Greece* [2005] 41 EHRR 49; *Bubbins v United Kingdom* [2005] 41 EHRR 24; *Gul v Turkey* [2002] 34 EHRR 28; *McCann and Others v United Kingdom* [1996] 21 EHRR 97. *Cf* C Wang, 'The Police Are Innocent as Long as They Honestly Believe: The Human Rights Problems with English Self-Defense Law' (2017) 49 *Columbia Human Rights Law Review* 373, 375 (describing England's subjective approach as resulting in 'unfair verdicts' and being in 'blatant violation' of Art 2 of the ECHR); AJ Ashworth, *Positive Obligations in Criminal Law* (Oxford, Hart Publishing, 2013) 196.

[183] The cases that follow are described as theoretically challenging because they have become regularly debated features of scholarly discussions on the subject. Other issues, such as provocation, battered intimate partner cases, defence of home, retreat, and mistake, have already been discussed (or in the case of battered intimate partner cases, will be discussed later). See ch 4(V)(A)(vi). As Russell puts it, the challenge inherent in an undertaking such as this is to 'devise a theory which yields the same conclusions as our nearly undisputed intuitions' and that explains why 'the initial application of force is not impermissible aggression but rather permissible self-defense.' See Christopher (n 51) 571–72.

home from work. Victor immediately recognises that Andrew is in fact pointing an armed and loaded air gun at him, and he also realises that Andrew is about to discharge it. Victor believes Andrew does not understand that the gun is loaded. The only way for Victor to avoid being injured by the pellet is to throw his heavy briefcase at Andrew a split-second before Andrew pulls the trigger, thereby knocking Andrew off balance and causing him to sustain a concussion.

Andrew's conduct clearly constitutes a threat of harm to Victor's autonomy and concrete interests (value #4), for Victor will be injured by the pellet if he does not throw his briefcase at Andrew.[184] Setting aside, for now, the possibility that Andrew's conduct is subjectively reckless because Andrew knows that he should never point even a toy firearm at a person, it can be said that Andrew is morally innocent in the sense that he does not *intend* to inflict any injury on Victor, nor does he seek to place his own interests or desires over those of Victor (that is, his conduct does not implicate value #3).[185]

The following simplified table, in a general sense at least, again confirms the position we are testing by demonstrating how the value-based model facilitates a more transparent discussion about how the values operate on a sliding scale (as well as whether some values might be missing). This approach, moreover, illustrates how a more value-centric dialogue helps root out the hidden normativity that has characterised much of the self-defence debate and has resulted in questionable and unpredictable decision-making.

Table 4 Innocent Threat

Nature of Threat: Innocent
Seriousness of Threat: Moderate to Serious (pellet injury; potential eye injury)
Seriousness of Defensive Force: Moderate (concussion)

Decision Ground	Weight	Summary of Reasoning
Value #1: Collective violence-reducing function (see Chapter 2(IV)(A))	+1	Both Victor and Andrew are facing similar levels of force, and Andrew is not acting culpably. That said, the law cannot compel someone in Victor's position to absorb Andrew's harmful and unjustified force, for this would require Victor to subordinate his non-compensable interests. The collective violence reduction function, therefore, *narrowly* leans towards authorising defensive force (narrowly because value #1 serves to protect all individuals from harm and, therefore, in part serves 'humanitarian' objectives; if the injury to Andrew were greater, this value would begin to disfavour authorising self-preferential force).

(continued)

[184] See ch 2(IV)(D).
[185] See ibid.

Table 4 ***(Continued)***

Decision Ground	Weight	Summary of Reasoning
Value #2: Protecting the individual attacker's (presumptive) right to life (see Chapter 2(IV)(B))	−1	Andrew is facing moderately serious physical injury and is not engaging in morally culpable conduct. Under these circumstances it is not appropriate to treat as overcome the presumption that Andrew's right to life continues on.
Value #3: Safeguarding equal standing (see Chapter 2(IV)(C))	0	Victor realises that Andrew is about to accidentally cause him harm, and he also knows that Andrew is not pursuing an action plan that includes wronging Victor. Victor, therefore, is being threatened with harm (pellet injury) but is not about to be wronged. Maintaining the equal standing is not implicated.
Value #4: Protecting the defender's autonomy (see Chapter 2(IV)(D))	+1	Andrew's attack, though non-culpable, still threatens a non-trivial (and potentially non-compensable) injury.
Value #5: Ensuring the primacy of the legal process (see Chapter 2(IV)(E))	0	Although one could argue that Victor could simply sustain the pellet injury and then proceed against Andrew through the civil court system, the competing harms here are not trivial. Victor cannot be morally blamed for being unwilling to absorb the potentially serious injury. Because of the potentially non-compensable nature of the injury (damage to Victor's eyes), the primacy of the legal process is not being challenged by authorising defensive force.
Value #6: Maintaining the legitimacy of the legal order (see Chapter 2(IV)(F))	+1	While this is a relatively close decision, there is more potential for broad criticism if the legal system forced Victor to absorb the potentially serious injury. Therefore, this decision-ground leans slightly in favour of authorising defensive force. That said (and once again highlighting the model's adaptability and ability to help avoid hidden normativity), an argument can also be made that in a case like this the public does not have a strong reaction and the value, therefore, should be zero.
Value #7: Deterrence (see Chapter 2(IV)(G))	0	Andrew is not purposefully posing a threat to Victor. The deterrent impact of permitting self-defence is, therefore, negligible. It can be argued that Andrew is being reckless, and that authorising defensive force here will deter Andrew and others like him from acting similarly carelessly in the future; the known facts fall short of establishing such recklessness.
TOTAL	+2	**Deadly force is presumptively justifiable (+3 indicates moderate justification).**

i. Nozick's 'Well Hypothetical'

Consider next a version of Nozick's famous hypothetical in which Brutus throws the faultless Andrew down a deep and narrow well. The hapless Victor is at the bottom of the well. If Victor does not first vaporise him with his ray gun, Andrew is certain to crush Victor to death (or, at a minimum, cause him great bodily injury).[186] While Andrew cannot be described as an 'attacker' in the ordinary sense of the word because cruel Brutus threw him down the well against his will (that is, value #3 – safeguarding equal standing is not implicated),[187] Andrew does, in fact, pose an actual and immediate threat of serious harm to Victor. Whether he likes it or not, he is about to seriously injure or crush Victor to death (thus placing great weight on value #4 – protecting a defender's autonomy – while arguably not implicating value #1 – collective violence-reduction, value #2 – protecting the individual attacker, value #5 – primacy of the legal process, and value #7 – deterrence).[188]

While Andrew, as an innocent threat, would generally be entitled to heightened protection because of his lack of moral culpability, the overwhelming balance of scholars who have examined this hypothetical are in accord that the gravity of the threatened harm (namely, death) justifies Victor vaporising Andrew with his ray gun (a result that, moreover, will likely not so offend widely held moral standards of right and wrong as to implicate value #6[189]). Victor will not be punished because he is not subject to the value-based model's stage-five condemnation (because his action was justified).[190] If Victor were to merely suffer slight bruising as a result of Andrew's fall, however, then the comparatively minor threatened harm (lessening the pro-defence impact of values #1, #2, #3, #4, and #5) would shift the balance in favour of the innocent Andrew and would, therefore, likely require Victor to absorb the slight injury.[191]

ii. The Foetus as an Innocent Threat

A difficult, unpleasant, and surely controversial (though necessarily addressed) application of the value-based model's self-defence regime under circumstances similar to those invoked by Nozick's 'well hypothetical' discussed immediately above may be implicated when a woman seeks an abortion. For the sake of argument, we will assume that a foetus is, in fact, an individual vested with human rights. Even given this assumption, however, one could reasonably conclude that self-defence law may, under specific circumstances, have an unexamined role to play in the abortion debate.

[186] R Nozick, *Anarchy, State, and Utopia* (New York, Ingram Publisher Services, 1974) 34–35. See also P Westen, 'Reflections on Joshua Dressler's Understanding Criminal Law' (2018) 15 *Ohio State Journal of Criminal Law* 311, 326–27.

[187] See ch 2(IV)(C).

[188] See ch 2(IV)(A), (B), (D), (E), & (G).

[189] See ch 2(IV)(F).

[190] See ch 2(IV)(F)(v)(f).

[191] See ch 2(IV)(A)–(F).

Turning to some baseline assumptions, it is stipulated that the foetus, like the person thrown down Nozick's well, is morally innocent. It will be assumed further that the mother contemplating the abortion, like the person at the bottom of the well, has only one means of stopping the 'injury' the foetus threatens (namely, through an abortion). Through no personal fault, moreover, the foetus is in a position where he threatens the mother with the arguable equivalent of 'serious bodily injury' resulting from the pregnancy and delivery.[192]

As we will discuss, the self-defence laws of Germany, England, and the US, like the value-based model, would authorise the innocent person in Nozick's well to use deadly force to ward off the morally innocent threat. And so, it is up for discussion whether a meaningful distinction can be drawn between the innocent person in those cases and a situation in which an innocent foetus threatens similar *harm* (though, of course, not a *wrong*).[193] This analogy, moreover, arguably is even closer in cases of rape, where any argument that the mother somehow played a knowing role in becoming pregnant is foreclosed. While there undoubtedly can be persuasive arguments made for and against the competing argumets sketched out here, and while coming up with a dispositive answer to such a morally and legally complicated matter is well outside of the scope of this endeavour, the near-universal acceptance of defensive force in the well hypothetical invites it to at least be similarly considered in other contexts.

iii. Contingent Threats and Innocent Shields

Contingent threats are only perceived as threats because of the direct danger coming from someone or something else. Consider, for example, a case in which an arrow is shot at the innocent Victor by crazed assassin Andrew. Ida happens to be standing directly behind Victor. If Victor were to jump out of the way of the arrow, Ida would certainly be killed. Ida would nevertheless be *un*justified in grabbing Victor and holding him in place as a sort of shield because Victor is merely a contingent threat (not implicating the previously discussed values); Andrew's arrow is the identifiable immediate threat.[194]

[192] See generally L Hoyson, 'Rape Is Tough Enough Without Having Someone Kick You from the Inside: The Case for Including Pregnancy as Substantial Bodily Injury' (2010) 44 *Valparaiso University Law Review* 565, 597 ('[T]he physical effects of pregnancy exceed the requirements set forth by the common definition of substantial bodily injury …'). See also BA Manninen, 'Rethinking *Roe v. Wade*: Defending the Abortion Right in the Face of Contemporary Opposition' (2010) 10 *American Journal of Bioethics* 33–46; NH Rev Stat § 625:11 (2019) (defining serious bodily injury as 'any harm to the body which causes severe, permanent or protracted loss of or impairment to the health or of the function of any part of the body'); *Commonwealth v Caterino*, 678 A2d 389 (Pa Sup Ct 1996) (broken nose qualifies as 'serious bodily injury').

[193] For more on the related issue of passive threats, see ch 4(V)(A)(iv), below.

[194] And this result would not change even if it were certain that the arrow would only hit Victor in the hand, whereas it would go straight through Ida's heart. While some other defence such as lesser evils may apply, the right to freedom of Victor's discretionary control over his personal domain would make Ida's intrusion offensive, rather than defensive, thus eliminating the possibility that he would be able to claim self-defence.

Innocent shields, while used as a *means* to ward off a threat, are themselves not threats. Their 'use,' therefore, once again amounts to impermissible self-preference.[195] (Of course, if Victor somehow colluded with the assassin Andrew and purposefully placed himself in front of Ida to prevent her from seeing the incoming arrow, Victor himself would become part of the immediate threat and Ida could use self-preferential force against him.)

iv. Passive Threats

The value-based model provides that a passive immediate threat can be blocked or fended off using justified defensive force. Consider a case in which the shipwrecked Andrew is on a ship's rescue ladder paralysed by fear and unable to move.[196] His inability to either go up or down the ladder prevents the shipwrecked Victor from escaping the pounding seas. Andrew under these circumstances poses a serious, though innocent, direct threat of harm to Victor. Because the threatened harm is very great, Victor is subject to self-defensive force.

The reader, however, may recall our discussion immediately above and understandably wonder why Andrew under these circumstances is not considered a mere contingent threat who may not be met with defensive force? While the distinction between a direct and a contingent threat may not always be readily drawn, perhaps the most sensible means of distinguishing the two is to consider whether there is an objectively good reason for the paralysed Andrew's threatening conduct. Consider also the herein-discussed case of shipwrecked Andrew and Victor clinging to the same piece of driftwood that will support the weight of only one of them.[197] Any force to shove off the other would constitute improper self-preferential killing because there is an objectively good reason for why both men are hanging on to the driftwood – they, after all, are trying to save their own lives from a roiling sea.

While it is true that each is exacerbating the threat to the other, neither is directly causing the threat (and thus implicating value #3 – equal standing).[198] If Andrew is paralysed by fear and unable to climb up the rescue ladder, on the other hand, he is preventing Victor from escaping certain death for no objectively good reason (that is, he is unjustifiably threatening Victor's autonomy – value #4),[199] and this shifts the sliding-scale balance in favour of protecting the defender. Although Andrew's reason – fear – may be understandable and non-culpable, it is not objectively speaking a good reason, for Andrew is directly preventing Victor from saving himself by blocking the only escape route.

[195] For the related discussion on necessity, see ch 4(II). See also JA Cohan, 'Homicide by Necessity' (2006) 10 *Chapman Law Review* 119, 177–79; J Waldron, 'Self-Defense: Agent-Neutral and Agent-Relative Accounts' (2000) 88 *California Law Review* 711, 715–16.

[196] This hypothetical is drawn from the Zeebrugge disaster, discussed below in ch 7(III)(D).

[197] See ch 4(V)(A)(iv).

[198] See ch 2(IV)(C).

[199] See ch 2(IV)(D).

So, while Andrew is not morally culpable for staying in place, he without objectively good reason is threatening Victor's autonomy and right to life (value #4; the other values are largely left neutral in this scenario).[200] This outcome can be contrasted with the situation in which Victor is clinging to a plank following a ship-sinking. If Andrew tries to push Victor off of the plank, Victor is uniquely entitled to use self-defence to resist because Victor is not a direct threat to Andrew (though the converse is true).[201]

v. The Case of the Plank and the Two Shipwreck Survivors

Imagine next a case similar to the one discussed by Carneades of Cyrene, Sanford Kadish, and others, and already noted above,[202] in which Andrew and Victor are shipwrecked and have been clinging to the same piece of driftwood.[203] Assume that the driftwood slowly begins to sink because it cannot take the weight of both men. Under our analysis, if either shoved off the other to save himself, his action would not be justified as self-defence because neither's equal standing (value #3) nor autonomy (value #4) is being threatened by the other's actions or inactions.[204] Such a use of force would instead constitute an impermissible self-preferential act of aggression that would justify the other in using defensive force to thwart the attack. If, in contrast, Victor held on to the driftwood first, and Andrew subsequently tried to also cling to it, causing it to sink, Victor would be justified in using defensive force against Andrew because Andrew's actions would implicate value #3 (equal standing), value #4 (protecting the defender's autonomy), and (arguably) value #6 (legitimacy of the criminal law), and would, thus, amount to impermissible self-selection.[205]

vi. Battered Intimate Partner Cases

The analysis turns next to the particularly challenging cases posed when the person claiming self-defence is a battered intimate partner. Such cases can generally be divided into two categories. In the first, the battered partner exercises force during an episode of physical abuse by the batterer. In the other category of cases, the partner uses deadly force against her batterer in the absence of any occurrent abuse, but in *fear* or *anticipation* of future renewed attacks. In the most controversial cases fitting into this latter (and more challenging) group, there is no overt evidence of a temporally 'immediate' threat because the batterer was, for example, sleeping.

[200] Ibid.
[201] See discussion at ch 4(V)(A). See also Dsouza (n 7) 52.
[202] See ch 4(V)(A).
[203] See SH Kadish, 'Excusing Crime' (1987) 75 *California Law Review* 274. This thought experiment was first proposed by Carneades of Cyrene and is referred to as the 'plank of Carneades.' See S von Pufendorf, *Of the Law of Nature and Nations*, vol 2 (Wentworth Press, 2016/1710) 95.
[204] See ch 2(IV)(C) & (D).
[205] See ch 2(IV)(C), (D), & (F).

I will term these two contrasting fact patterns, respectively, as 'confrontation' and 'non-confrontation' cases. Theorists generally agree that the latter group of cases presents the greatest challenge under traditional legal doctrine. While some commentators concentrated on the substantive law of self-defence and on the admissibility of expert testimony regarding the battered intimate partner syndrome as relevant to self-defence, others have criticised substantive self-defence law as biased against the battered partner (or against women generally) and advocated either modifications of the self-defence standards or a separate defence.[206] Proponents of both perspectives will largely agree, however, that expert testimony regarding the battered intimate partner syndrome is necessary to dispel stereotypes of battered partners and to establish various components of the traditional (or modified) defences.[207] (There is, in fact, a lively and ongoing debate over the long-term psychological effects of prolonged battery.)[208]

Some, like Dressler, have suggested that a battered woman acts under duress when she kills her sleeping violent partner in order to forestall future violence. That is, the woman avoids harm by complying with the 'demands' made by a person threatening the accused.[209] This argument is flawed, however, because the battered partner at bottom is still making a self-preferential decision to kill her battering partner. It is unconvincing to argue that the batterer is 'demanding' that his victim kill him. That is, she is not simply complying with any demand he has issued (which, after all, is the definition of duress – though the concept of 'duress of circumstances,' which is sometimes treated as a species of necessity,[210] may, as discussed herein, also apply).

The particular difficulty with battered intimate partner cases is not analytical. Rather, their *facts* are typically unique and challenging. Indeed, if the matter were a simple deadly-force-in-defence-of-life situation, then there would be no need to create a separate category of self-defence cases dealing with the particularities of intimate partners who are battered and, therefore, react differently than a 'reasonable person' would under like circumstances.

[206] Cp PL Crocker, 'The Meaning of Equality for Battered Women Who Kill Men in Self-Defense' (1985) 8 *Harvard Women's Law Journal* 121, 152 (calling for a reconsideration of substantive self-defence doctrine), with K Kinports, 'Defending Battered Women's Self-Defense Claims' (1988) 67 *Oregon Law Review* 393, 415–22 (advocating for a 'reasonable battered woman standard').

[207] See generally K Altantulkhuur, 'A Second Rape: Testing Victim Credibility Through Prior False Accusations' [2018] *University of Illinois Law Review* 1091, 1108; EM Schneider, 'Describing and Changing: Women's Self-Defense Work and the Problem of Expert Testimony on Battering' (1986) 9 *Women's Rights Law Reporter* 195, 205–20. See also *United States v Lopez*, 913 F3d 807, 820–22 (9th Cir 2019); *State v Pisciotta*, 968 SW2d 185, 186 (Mo Ct App 1998).

[208] See generally M Blinder, 'The Battered Woman's Syndrome' in *Psychiatry in the Everyday Practice of Law*, 5th edn (West Group Publishing, 2019) § 8:15.

[209] J Dressler, 'Battered Women Who Kill Their Sleeping Tormenters: Reflections on Maintaining Respect for Human Life While Killing Moral Monsters' in S Shute and A Simester (eds), *Criminal Law Theory: Doctrines of the General Part* (Oxford, Oxford University Press, 2002) 259–82.

[210] See *Hasan* [2005] 2 AC 467; *R v Conway* [1989] QB 290, 297. While some may argue that these circumstances involve an implied threat of harm, such a fact-specific argument cannot be given blanket acceptance.

England, in an effort to protect victims of domestic violence, enacted legislation criminalising controlling or coercive behaviour[211] in the context of intimate and family relationships.[212] In particular, section 76 of the Serious Crime Act of 2015 created the new offence, which seeks to capture abusive conduct that may not formally fit the definitions of assault, threatening to kill or seriously injure, or stalking, but that has a serious impact on the victim even in the absence of physical violence (or the fear thereof).[213] This law, following Evan Stark's model of coercive control, reflects an evolution in the thinking about domestic abuse in that it helps explain why a purported defender (1) stayed in the abusive relationship and (2) felt trapped, without any viable option other than the use of deadly force. Such information (supported by numerous studies[214]), in turn, relates to a defender's good-faith, subjective fear of imminent injury or death. It, moreover, appreciates the objective reality of domestic violence (in terms of patterns of violence, degree, triggers, etc) and the related reasonableness of the response.[215]

As relevant here, and as detailed above, the value-based model's concern is with protecting the equal standing (value #3) and private domain (value #4) of both defenders and attackers. It, therefore, permits force to be used to the extent that it is *immediately necessary* to block or fend off an unjust threat.[216] By endorsing such a relatively broad formulation of what otherwise is the 'imminence' requirement, the value-based model leaves battered intimate partners with a comparatively flexible ability to lawfully protect themselves (and, more to the point, with the *opportunity* to persuade courts and juries that their conduct was, under the circumstances, justified self-defence).

[211] See generally E Stark, *Coercive Control: How Men Entrap Women in Personal Life* (New York, Oxford University Press, 2007) 83–170.

[212] Serious Crime Act 2015, § 76(1). See generally EE Gorbes, 'The Domestic Abuse (Scotland) Act 2018: The Whole Story' (2018) 22 *Edinburgh Law Review* 406, 406–09; M McMahon and P McGorrery, 'Criminalising Controlling and Coercive Behaviour: The Next Step in the Prosecution of Family Violence' (2016) 41 *Alternative Law Journal* 98, 98–100.

[213] See generally McMahon and McGorrery (n 212) 98–100.

[214] See generally R Aitken and VE Munro, 'Domestic Abuse and Suicide Report 2018' *Refuge Publications* (2018), www.refuge.org.uk/wp-content/uploads/2018/07/domestic-abuse-suicide-refuge-warwick-july2018.pdf; T Pitman, 'Living with Coercive Control: Trapped Within a Complex Web of Double Standards, Double Binds and Boundary Violations' (2016) 47 *British Journal of Social Work* 143; LE Watkins et al, 'The Longitudinal Impact of Intimate Partner Aggression and Relationship Status on Women's Physical Health and Depression Symptoms' (2014) 28 *Journal of Family Psychology* 655; M Johnson, *A Typology of Domestic Violence: Intimate Terrorism, Violent Resistance, and Situational Couple Violence* (Boston, Mass, Northeastern University Press, 2008), www.researchgate.net/publication/320809177_A_Typology_of_Domestic_Violence; Stark (n 211) 83–170; D Loxton et al, 'Psychological Health in Midlife Among Women Who Have Ever Lived with a Violent Partner or Spouse' (2006) 21 *Journal of Interpersonal Violence* 1092; MA Dutton and LA Goodman, 'Coercion in Intimate Partner Violence: Toward a New Conceptualization' (2005) 52 *Sex Roles* 743, 747. See also A Pichhadze, 'Proposals for Reforming the Law of Self-Defence' (2008) 72 *Journal of Criminal Law* 409, 428–29. *Cf* JS Meier, 'Dangerous Liaisons: A Domestic Violence Typology in Custody Litigation' (2017) 70 *Rutgers University Law Review* 115, 159.

[215] See generally J von Talge, 'Victimization Dynamics: The Psycho-Social and Legal Implications of Family Violence Directed Toward Women and the Impact on Child Witnesses' (1999–2000) 27 *Western State University Law Review* 163–64; E Stark, 'Re-Presenting Woman Battering: From Battered Woman Syndrome to Coercive Control' (1995) 58 *Albany Law Review* 973, 996–1026. See also Blinder (n 208) § 8:15; J Herring, 'The Severity of Domestic Abuse' (2018) 30 *National Law School of India Review* 37, 40–43.

[216] See ch 4(II).

B. Special Rules for 'Attacks' on the Police?

Few topics have in recent years generated as much passionate debate as the use of force by (and against) the police. Police officers the world over are by dint of their vocation frequently compelled to use force to subdue and arrest individuals with whom they come into contact. They, accordingly, tend to receive special training in dealing with unruly and violent individuals who pose a threat against them (though the quality and extent of that training – and the relative lack of emphasis placed on de-escalation techniques – is very much a subject of ongoing debate).[217] Yet, despite this training, instances of alleged (and, in contemporary times, recorded) excessive force have become a regular fixture of the evening news in the US, England, Germany, and elsewhere.[218] Determining the legitimate extent of police violence in self-defence against attackers, is, therefore, a very topical issue.[219]

Because the value-based model, as discussed in Chapter 4(I)(B), recognises the paradox of mutual justification, if an officer's exercise of defensive force is justified, then a citizen will not receive the justification of self-defence if she counters the officer with force.[220] On the issue of retreat, for policy-based reasons there is broad agreement that officers as a general rule are not legally obligated to retreat when facing potential aggression.[221] That said, basic prudence and common de-escalation methodologies teach that strategic retreat from a volatile or otherwise escalating decision is frequently the officer's best and most professional response.

Turning to the reasonableness of the officer's belief, the problem with the 'reasonable belief' standard in the police context is that the term is open-ended (or, as Baker puts it, a 'woolly word'[222]) and is often equated with typicality (that is, it is measured against the beliefs of the typical officer). Article 2(2) of the ECHR, for its part, rather reasonably dictates that self-defence is unavailable in cases where the officer was labouring under an objectively unreasonably mistaken belief because such force is not 'absolutely necessary.'[223]

[217] See generally Erb (n 85) side-note 187.

[218] See generally CKY Lee, 'Reforming the Law on Police Use of Deadly Force: De-Escalation, Preseizure Conduct, and Imperfect Self-Defense' [2018] *University of Illinois Law Review* 629, 629–35.

[219] See Dsouza (n 7) 169–72.

[220] Because external justification is not required in England, citizens are in fact able to act in self-defence if they honestly believe they are being attacked. See ch 7(II). See also Rönnau and Hohn (n 44) side-notes 129–30; Erb (n 85) side-note 192; Baker (n 15) 917, 926–31. Because an officer's use of deadly force to apprehend a fleeing felon or to effectuate an arrest does not, without more, implicate self-defence, those situations will not be discussed here.

[221] See NY Penal Law § 35.15(2)(a)(ii) (2019); *Boykin v People*, 45 P 419, 421 (Colo 1896); K Levine, 'Police Suspects' (2016) 116 *Columbia Law Review* 1197, 1234; B Sangero, *Self-Defence in Criminal Law* (Oxford, Hart Publishing, 2006) 90–106 [hereinafter Sangero, *Self-Defence*] 202–03; G Rodwan, 'Criminal Law' (1993) 39 *Wayne Law Review* 503, 538.

[222] Baker (n 15) 919.

[223] See generally *Bubbins v United Kingdom* [2005] 41 EHRR 24; *McCann v United Kingdom* [1996] 21 EHRR 97; *Stewart v United Kingdom* [1984] 7 EHRR 453; Council of Europe & European Court of Human Rights, *Guide on Article 2 of the European Convention on Human Rights* (2019) 22–23; I Park, *The Right to Life in Armed Conflict* (Oxford, Oxford University Press, 2018) 36–41. As discussed in

Consistent with the value-based model's emphasis on value #1 – collective violence-reduction, value #2 – protection of the individual attacker, and value #6 – maintenance of the legitimacy of the legal order,[224] and in line with the articulated policy reasons, law enforcement officers operating reasonably (that is, within their roles) should be considered *prima facie* justified when using reasonable force to effectuate arrests when the circumstances dictate that such arrests are necessary. Any use of force to 'defend' against officers operating reasonably cannot, therefore, qualify as self-defence lest the situation fall under the paradox of mutual justifications.[225] Any other outcome would make it exceedingly difficult for the police to, as a practical matter, effectively fulfil their professional obligations.

Consistent with Lee's position,[226] traditional self-defence doctrine applying to civilians, and the value-based model's emphasis on the right to life, we conclude that the officer exercising defensive force must: have reasonable beliefs *and* reasonable actions, must be subjectively motivated by those reasonable beliefs and actions, and her conduct must be immediately necessary and proportional to the threat she is facing. While retreat should not be required[227] as part of the reasonableness evaluation, the fact-finder should be directed to consider whether the officer engaged in any available de-escalation measures[228] prior to deploying deadly self-preferential force. This more balanced approach reasonably recognises the attacker's individual right to life (value #2) without inappropriately infringing on the officer's rights (value #4 and possibly value #3) or the state's collective interest in preserving law and order (value #1). The value-based model, moreover, does not elevate the officer over the citizen by according him unique protections when he is acting objectively unreasonable or lacks the requisite subjective defensive will (as we will discuss, some US jurisdictions still offer such difficult-to-justify protections to their law enforcement officers).

ch 7(II), this objective test appears to conflict with the subjective 'genuine belief' standard adopted in England. H Russell, *The Use of Force and Article 2 of the ECHR in Light of European Conflicts* (Oxford, Hart Publishing, 2017) 27; Leverick (n 109) 190. But see *R (Bennett) v Coroner* [2007] EWCA Civ 617 (contending Art 2 and England's reasonableness test not incompatible; presuming objective reasonableness of state agents).

[224] See ch 2(IV)(A), (B), & (F).

[225] Also referred to as the 'incompatibility thesis.' See ch 4(I). See also Rosenau (n 45) side-note 18; Fontaine (n 48) 78–79.

[226] See Lee (n 218) 661–75. See also CKY Lee, 'The Act-Belief Distinction in Self-Defense Doctrine: A New Dual Requirement Theory of Justification' (1998) 2 *Buffalo Criminal Law Review* 191, 236–37.

[227] See ch 4(II)(C).

[228] See generally R Abanonu, 'De-Escalating Police-Citizen Encounters' (2018) 27 *Southern California Review of Law and Social Justice* 239, 268–69; R Geisser, 'A Just War Inquiry of Police, Prosecutors & Deadly Force' (2017) 10 *Washington University of Jurisprudence Review* 59, 63. *Cf* JP Blair et al, 'Reasonableness and Reaction Time' (2011) 14 *Police Quarterly* 323, 336 (noting that officer reaction time is very limited).

5

Examining German Law's Treatment of Self-Defence from a Value-Centric Perspective

England, Germany, and the US are three jurisdictions with broadly similar political and cultural backgrounds but with notably different self-defence laws. In the next three chapters, we will deploy the value-based framework to test the value-centric position by evaluating how these jurisdictions grapple with the difficult issues analysed above – and how their approaches differ from, or mirror, the model's value-explicit approach. More specifically, in these chapters we will examine whether, within a broadly liberal paradigm, these jurisdictions explicitly (or, in the context of hidden normativity, implicitly) treat values as decision-grounds that influence the authorisation of self-preferential force.

True, one can as a normative matter disagree with the subject jurisdictions' outcomes (and thus conclude that the ultimate 'quality' of the decisions is flawed in terms of its social effects, even though the values animating the thinking about self-defence are commonly understood). But, as discussed, the hypothesis' assessment of 'quality' does in the main focus on individual normative evaluations of end-states, nor on some sort of purity test when it comes to the precise value-array proposed by the value-based model. Rather, the inquiry concerns the application of self-defence rules in terms of whether being at some level value-explicit facilitates more nuanced, incremental, transparent, and focused decision-making.

We turn first to Germany's explicitly value-informed approach. Because the values driving German self-defence law largely anchor, and have historically anchored, the debate, scholars, judges, legislators, and laymen alike share a common analytical language through which to approach their disagreements. As we shall see, the precise hierarchy, cataloguing, and weighting of these values continues to be a matter of heated debate; but the reality that there is, in fact, *some* hierarchy of values has enjoyed near-universal acceptance.

It will be contended that German courts and commentators, therefore, are better-positioned to evaluate whether and why reforms to, or adjustments of, self-defence doctrine are appropriate, and the extent to which, at the level of specific application, particular self-defence decisions are acceptable. This, in turn, permits the German justice system to reach self-defence decisions in a more democratic, logical, and policy-based manner, and to, relatedly, identify and narrow areas of dispute (even though one, as observed, can still disagree, as a normative matter, with the outcomes reached). By in this manner encouraging a procedurally more democratic discussion around jurisprudential matters of value, moral principles, and fundamental human rights, and by leaving less room for hidden normativity, the 'quality' of the German justice system's decision-making process (and outcomes) is, comparatively speaking, enhanced.

While we could have expanded the focus to other countries, going beyond the chosen subject jurisdictions would, given space-limitations, necessarily prevent the required thorough examination of the subject jurisdictions' positive laws and the theories and analyses buttressing them. The development of Germany's codified and heavily theory-driven self-defence law,[1] from a values-as-decision-grounds perspective, also presents a useful contrast to the common-law development of self-defence in England and the US.

I. Putting Germany's Self-Defence Law in Context

Germany's self-defence regime is exceptionally value-driven. That said, its traditional conception of the implicated values has in the past been so narrow as to, from a normative perspective, produce results that are challenging by contemporary standards. In fact, even Germany's current self-defence law, allowing deadly force in defence of property, not requiring retreat or avoidance of conflict except under certain circumstances, and generally rejecting strict proportionality, has been fairly described as uniquely permissive.[2]

It is also important to recognise at the outset that the value-based model encompasses certain *functional* reasoning (principally, value #1 – reducing overall societal violence by protecting the state's monopoly on force, value #5 – ensuring the primacy of the legal process, value #6 – maintaining the legitimacy of the legal order, and value #7 – deterring crime). The below-discussed German rulings and literature, in contrast, largely do not support the view that deterrence

[1] See generally B Vogel, 'The Core Legal Concepts and Principles Defining Criminal Law in Germany' in M Dyson and B Vogel (eds), *The Limits of Criminal Law: Anglo-German Concepts and Principles* (Cambridge, Intersentia, 2018) 41–42.

[2] See T Rönnau and K Hohn, '§ 32 Notwehr' in G Cirener et al (eds), *Strafgesetzbuch: Leipziger Kommentar, Band 3* (Berlin, De Gruyter, 2019) side-notes 72, 181–82. See also H Rosenau, 'Notwehr und Notstand' in H Satzger and W Schluckebier (eds), *Strafgesetzbuch: Kommentar*, vol 4 (Heymanns Verlag GmbH, 2019) side-note 1.

(*Abschreckung*)[3] and social cohesion are recognised rationales for determining the scope of self-defence.[4]

II. An Introduction to Self-Defence in Germany

Self-defence is a justification that section 32 of the German criminal code (*Strafgesetzbuch*[5] or '*StGB*') defines as follows:

> (1) Whoever commits an act that is appropriate as self-defence does not act unlawfully.
> (2) Self-defence is that defence which is necessary in order to prevent a present unlawful attack on oneself or another.

Only under the exigencies of a case meeting these criteria can a defender ignore the state's monopoly on force (*Gewaltmonopol*).[6] If a defender's self-defensive conduct is justified (*gerechtfertigt*),[7] the defender need not absorb harm (*Duldungspflicht*) because he is acting lawfully.[8] The attacker, on the other hand, must absorb

[3] For support of this minority view, see C Roxin, 'Die "Sozialethische Einschränkungen" des Notwehrrechts' (1981) 93 *ZStW* 68; G Geilen, 'Notwehr und Notwehrexzess' [1981] *Jura* 200, 200–10. Opponents of this position, however, argue that this perspective ignores that the only question is whether, in a particular case, self-defence is *necessary* and could result in each citizen becoming a 'quasi-policeman' and 'punishment' of an individual for impermissible utilitarian reasons – questions of deterrence, then are, in the majority view, not relevant. See, eg, B Vogel, 'The Core Legal Concepts and Principles Defining Criminal Law in Germany' in M Dyson and B Vogel (eds), *The Limits of Criminal Law: Anglo-German Concepts and Principles* (Cambridge, Intersentia, 2018) 43–44; H Lesch, 'Die Notwehr' in G Widmaier et al (eds), *Festschrift für Hans Dahs* (Schmidt, Dr Otto 2005) 86–87, 106.

[4] See, eg, T Fischer, '§ 32 Vorbemerkungen' in *Strafgesetzbuch* (Heymanns Verlag GmbH, 2019) side-note 2; R Pest, 'Die Erforderlichkeit der Notwehrhandlung' in F Stam and A Werkmeister (eds), *Der Allgemeine Teil des Strafrechts in der aktuellen Rechtsprechung* (Baden-Baden, Nomos Verlagsgesellschaft, 2019) 139; Rosenau (n 2) side-note 2; K Kühl and M Heger, 'Vorbemerkung' in *Strafgesetzbuch: Kommentar* § 32 (Heymanns Verlag GmbH, 2018) side-notes 1–2; B Heinrich, *Strafrecht Allgemeiner Teil* (Stuttgart, Kohlhammer, 2016) § 32, side-note 337; C Roxin, *Strafrecht Allgemeiner Teil. Grundlagen. Der Aufbau der Verbrechenslehre, "Bd. I"*, § 15 (Beck CH, 2006) 650–57; Lesch (n 3) 82, 88–89. But see Rönnau and Hohn (n 2) side-notes 66–67.

[5] This and all other translations in this chapter are the author's.

[6] See generally Fischer (n 4) side-note 35; Pest (n 4) 137; V Erb, 'Notwehr und Notstand' in B von Heintschel-Heinegg (ed), *Münchner Kommentar zum Strafgesetzbuch, "Band 1"* (Beck CH, 2017) side-notes 3, 31–33, 147–48; M Pawlik, 'Die Notwehr nach Kant und Hegel' (2002) 114 *Zeitschrift Für Die Gesamte Strafrechtswissenschaft* 259, 278. See also [2018] BGH NStZ 69, 70; Rönnau and Hohn (n 2) side-notes 67, 73, 106, 120, 221.

[7] See generally Rosenau (n 2) *Vorbemerkung* § 32, side-notes 1–3; Pest (n 4) 139–40; Rönnau and Hohn (n 2) side-notes 114, 154; Vogel (n 1) 51–52; K Kühl, *Strafrecht Allgemeiner Teil* 8th edn (Vahlen Franz GmbH, 2017) § 32, side-note 1; Kühl and Heger (n 4) side-note 2; M Deiters et al *SK-StGB – Systematischer Kommentar zum Strafgesetzbuch, "Band 1"* (Luchterhand (Hermann), 2017) § 32, side-note 1.

[8] See generally [2018] BGH 1 StR 208/18; [2015] BGH 1 StR 606/14; [2003] BGH 4 StR 267/02; [2000] BGH 3 StR 331/00. See also Rosenau (n 2) side-note 18; Fischer (n 4) side-note 22; Rönnau and Hohn (n 2) side-notes 154, 285; L Greco, 'Notwehr und Proportionalität' [2018] GA 665, 670, 676; Erb (n 6) side-note 192; V Erb, 'Notwehr als Menchenrecht – Zugleich eine Kritik der Entscheidung des LG Frankfurt am Main im "Fall Daschner"' (2005) 25 *Neue Zeitschrift für Strafrecht* 593, 595; Lesch (n 3) 91.

the damage without a right to exercise his own defensive force.[9] Procedurally, moreover, if the court determines that the elements of the defence are reasonably in place, then the defendant is entitled to the defence.[10]

Section 33, addressing the excuse of excessive force, caveats excessive force:

> The perpetrator will not be punished if he exceeds the bounds of self-defence because of confusion, fear, or fright.[11]

German law, citing to this rather laconic text, historically justified the use of defensive force under a very wide range of circumstances, and with little reference to proportionality between the harm inflicted and the harm threatened (*Güterproportionalität*).[12] It, moreover, treats an attack on one person's rights as an attack on the entire legal order (*Rechtsordung*).[13]

The German metaphysics of rights, thus, crafted a link between an attack on the rights of a defender and an attack on the broader legal order.[14] This linkage, as discussed below, was used to argue that the German defender must be permitted to use whatever force is necessary to thwart or repel the attack, irrespective of the damage to the defender resulting therefrom or the amount of harm threatened.

A. The Theoretical Foundations of Self-Defence in Germany

In contrast to the self-defence laws of England and the US, the German law is based on an articulated and value-explicit moral framework that determines when, why, and to what extent self-defence is authorised. As we will discuss,[15] the undulating development of self-defence in England and the US can in the main be traced to oft-undiscussed public-policy considerations and hidden normativity. German cases and commentators, in contrast, continue to be guided by the law's text and the overarching commitment to the values driving the idea that the 'right need not yield to the wrong' (though, as will be discussed, commentators and the courts have disagreed on how this commitment is to be construed and justified, both in terms of legal theory as well as in application to particular cases[16]).

[9] See generally Rönnau and Hohn (n 2) side-notes 154, 285; Lesch (n 3) 91, 101.

[10] See Rönnau and Hohn (n 2) side-note 289.

[11] See generally [2017] BGH 3 StR 622/17; [2017] BGH 2 Str 188/17. See also Fischer (n 4) § 33, side-notes 1–8; Rosenau (n 2) § 33 at side-note 1.

[12] See Rönnau and Hohn (n 2) side-note 225; Erb (n 6) side-note 2; Roxin (n 4) side-note 47. See also H Mayer, *Das Strafrecht des Deutschen Volkes* (tredition GmbH, 2018/1936) 258; M Mayer, *Der Allgemeine Teil des Deutschen Strafrechts* (Forgotten Books, 2018/1923) 280 (contending that, in the context of proportionality, 'the wise may be able to suggest to the weak that he should cowardly yield to the wrong, but the state cannot reasonably demand this of the citizen, or else cowardice would be a legal requirement'); [1969] BGH GA 23, 24; [1968] BGH GA 182, 183; [1938] 72 RGSt 57, 58; [1935] 69 RGSt 308, 309–10; [1920] 55 RGSt 82, 85.

[13] See generally Rönnau and Hohn (n 2) side-note 66; Greco (n 8) 667; Erb (n 6) side-note 12.

[14] See generally Lesch (n 3) 86. See also ch 2(IV)(F).

[15] See chs 6 & 7.

[16] See generally Kühl and Heger (n 4) side-note 15; Erb (n 6) side-note 12.

i. Self-Defence Justification #1: Protecting the 'Legal Order'

One view of the historical foundations of German self-defence holds that self-defence is justified solely because it defends the empirical inviolability of the legal order (the *Rechtsbewährungsprinzip*, which translates into 'protection of the legal order justification').[17] On this view, every exercise of legitimate defensive force ensures that the collective legal order is protected and preserved and that the 'right need not yield to the wrong' (*das Recht muss dem Unrecht nicht weichen*).[18] In fact, the contemporary majority/consensus view is that German self-defence law's 'harshness' (*Schneidigkeit* or *Schärfe*) is derived from this traditional collective legal order justification.[19]

In situations of conflict, then, the collective importance of in this manner protecting the legal order was given primacy over the attacker's right to life (value #2).[20] The traditional view was that defenders may exercise all force necessary to protect their autonomy (value #4) without regard for proportion. After all, their actions, unlike with the value-based model, need not be justified on the basis of a 'balancing of harms.' Correspondingly, defenders (except under certain circumstances) have no duty to retreat or to request the help of third parties.[21]

Because the German criminal law's traditional focus was not on welfarist interests and did not consider a weighing of harms, then, it historically rejected the concept of 'trading off' autonomy by measuring it on a balance of utilities. This explains why the defender was justified not only in defending against the attack (*Schutzwehr* or *Gegenwehr*),[22] but also at times in using offensive force to neutralise or limit an attack (*Trutzwehr*).[23]

[17] See generally Pest (n 4) 140; Greco (n 8) 667; Erb (n 6) side-note 18; [2016] BGH 2 StR 523/15; E Schmidhäuser, 'Die Begründung der Notwehr' [1991] GA 97, 101; H Mayer (n 12) 254.

[18] See ch 5(II). This grounding principle of German self-defence, which provides the foundation for the *Rechtsbewährungsprinzip*, is explicitly discussed in A Berner, 'Die Notwehrtheorie' in *Archiv des Criminalrechts* (1884) 547, 557, 562. See also [2016] BGH 2 StR 523/15 (holding that the possibility of retreat does not vitiate the right to self-defence); [1920] 55 RGSt 82, 85; [1890] 21 RGSt 168, 170; Rönnau and Hohn (n 2) side-notes 4, 65–66; Pest (n 4) 141; Kühl and Heger (n 4) side-notes 15–16; Lesch (n 3) 82; T Lenckner, '§32 Notwehr', in A Schönke and H Schröder, *Strafgesetzbuch* 25th edn (Beck CH, 2018/1997) 527; H-Heinrich Jescheck and T Weigend, *Lehrbuch des Strafrechts, Allgemeiner Teil* 5th edn (Duncker & Humblot GmbH, 1996) 336–40 [hereinafter Jescheck and Weigend, 5th edn]; A Berner, *Lehrbuch des deutschen Strafrechtes* (Wentworth Press, 2018/1989) 107. *Cf* Rönnau and Hohn (n 2) side-note 66 n 174, 225.

[19] See generally Rönnau and Hohn (n 2) side-note 66; Kühl and Heger (n 4) side-notes 15–16; Erb (n 6) side-notes 12–13; Vogel (n 1) 43–44; Lesch (n 3) 83; R Haas, *Notwehr und Nothilfe: Zum Prinzip der Abwehr Rechtwidriger Angriffe* (1978) 144.

[20] See generally Pest (n 4) 140; H Matt and J Renzikowski, *Strafgesetzbuch* (Vahlen Franz GmbH, 2013) § 32 n 2.

[21] See [2019] LG Dortmund 39Ks 8/14 (requiring retreat because putative defender's right to self-defence was limited because the defender armed himself and knowingly entered into a group fight prior to stabbing the unarmed putative attacker); Rosenau (n 2) side-notes 1 & 25; Fischer (n 4) side-note 232; Rönnau and Hohn (n 2) side-notes 66, 157, 181–82 (no retreat or avoidance of conflict required); Erb (n 8) 593 (no retreat requirement).

[22] See generally Rönnau and Hohn (n 2) side-note 176; Erb (n 6) side-note 120; Erb (n 8) 593.

[23] See generally [2018] BGH 4 StR 107/18; Pest (n 4) 141–42; Fischer (n 4) side-note 23; Rönnau and Hohn (n 2) side-note 158; M Bohlander, 'When the Bough Breaks – Defences and Sentencing Options

ii. Self-Defence Justification #2: Protecting the Individual

While those championing the protection of the legal order justification of self-defence are chiefly concerned with collectively safeguarding the respect for the legal system,[24] an increasingly vocal segment of German scholars now argues that self-defence can only be justified as a means of protecting the individual who is being attacked from harm (*Individualrechtliche begründung*, which translates into 'personal protection justification').[25] This personal protection justification broadly aligns with value #3 – equal standing; and value #4 – protection of the defender's autonomy.

iii. Self-Defence Justification #3: Protecting Both the Legal Order and *the Individual*

While both of the above-described monistic views have received their fair share of scholarly support, contemporary commentators in the main endorse a dualistic position (*dualistische Begründung*). This approach finds the law's basis *both* in the protection of the (1) individual (*Individualinteresse*, also referred to as the *Schutzprinzip*) and (2) broader legal order (*Rechtsbewährungsprinzip*).[26] In the words of the *Bundesgerichtshof* (the Federal Court of Justice, which is the highest court in the system of ordinary jurisdiction), self-defence 'does not only serve to protect the person being attacked, but also *concurrently* protects the legal order.'[27]

Available to Battered Women and Similar Scenarios Under German Law' in A Reed and M Bohlander (eds), *Loss of Control and Diminished Responsibility* (Ashgate Publishing, 2011) 250; Roxin (n 4) side-note 70.

[24] See generally ch 2(IV)(E).

[25] See generally Erb (n 6) side-note 18; Erb (n 8) 601. See also Rosenau (n 2) side-note 2; J Hruschka, *Strafrecht Nach Logisch-Analytischer Methode* (Berlin, De Gruyter, 1988) 142. Others view protection of the broader legal order at the heart of self-defence. See, eg, E Schmidhäuser, 'Über die Wertstruktur der Notwehr' in *Festschrift für Richard M Honig* (1970) 193. See also Jescheck and Weigend, 5th edn (n 18) 336–37; P Klose, 'Notrecht des Staates aus staatlicher Rechtsnot' (1977) 89 *ZStW* 61, 86.

[26] See generally Fischer (n 4) side-note 2; Pest (n 4) 139; Rosenau (n 2) side-note 2; Rönnau and Hohn (n 2) side-notes 64–68; Kühl and Heger (n 4) side-notes 1–2; A Montenbruck, *Deutsche Straftheorie* (Freie Universität Berlin, 2018) 233; Heinrich (n 4) 337; Roxin (n 4) 650–57; Lesch (n 3) 82, 88–89. See also [1972] BGH 2 StR 679/71; Lenckner (n 18); C Roxin, *Strafrecht, Allgemeiner Teil* 3rd edn (Beck CH, 1997) 551–52, 527; R von Maurach and H Zipf, *Strafrecht, Allgemeiner Teil* (Heidelberg, CF Müller, 1992) 354; K Bernsmann, 'Überlegungen zur tödlichen Notwehr bei nicht lebensbedrohlichen Angriffen' (1992) 104 *ZStW* 290, 291; G Spendel, '§ 32 Notwehr' in B Jähnke, et al (eds), *Strafgessetzbuch: Leipziger Kommentar* 11th edn (Berlin, De Gruyter, 1992) 15–16. But this view has its critics. See, eg, Erb (n 6) side-note 202; Matt and Renzikowski (n 20) § 32 n 3; Lesch (n 3) 88–89; Pawlik (n 6) 261. In fact, some contend that the individual's 'subjective' act to defend herself is simply part and parcel of protecting the legal order (which, after all, is focused on protecting individual rights); viewed this way, the individual and collective justifications collapse into one. See Rönnau and Hohn (n 2) side-notes 66–69; Lesch (n 3) 85.

[27] [1972] BGH 2 StR 679/71 (emphasis added). See also W Kargl, 'Die Intersubjektive Begründung und Begrenzung der Notwehr' (1998) 110 *Zeitung der Allgemeinen Deutschen Strafrechtswissenschaft* 38, 38–39; G Warda, 'Die Geeignetheit der Verteidigungshandlung bei der Notwehr Strittiges in der aktuellen Diskussion' [1996] GA 405, 406; Schmidhäuser (n 17) 101.

But this view is not universally endorsed. Erb, for example, argues that the current focus on collective/societal/welfarist interests in protecting even culpable attackers ignores the concrete interests of the individual defender, and, in so doing, violates the defender's human rights.[28] Some German scholars, moreover, have begun to also consider the role of the unique violation of equal standing (*Störung des Gegenseitigkeitsverhältnises* – roughly in accord with value #3) that, as maintained in Chapter 2(IV)(C), accompanies culpable attacks.[29] They, generally consistent with the position articulated in Chapter 2, maintain that self-defence at its core is a right grounded in the attacker's (knowing and intentional) refusal to respect the equality of his victims and to follow legal norms.[30]

When an individual claims self-defence today, then, the court will consider not only whether the act served to protect the *individual* defender from a threat (value #3 and value #4),[31] but also whether it served to protect the wider *legal order*. (As discussed in Chapter 2(IV)(C)(ii), however, this protection of the legal order is a broader concept than value #6's maintenance of the legitimacy of the law[32]).

What is, therefore, particularly remarkable about German self-defence law, and in particular bears on the value-centric position we are testing, is that it engages in a unique type of (generally) explicit value-ordering. As will be discussed, this is largely absent when US and English courts consider self-defence doctrine or render self-defence rulings.[33] Instead of simply announcing ad hoc changes in the rules of self-defence, the German courts, and the scholars that influence them, pay a great deal of attention to competing values that may be impacted by any reform proposals (though, as will be discussed, the range of values may still be too narrow when compared to the array in the value-based model).

In this sense, then, the German law comes closest to pursuing a value-explicit approach along the lines of the value-centric position examined here. Indeed, considering the belief that a common value-centric analytical language will foster greater transparency, thereby improving the quality (as defined above) of decision-making, the herein-described depth of German scholarly analysis of self-defence law is distinct from what is seen in the US and England. This, in turn, leads to a more nuanced, incremental, and all-things-considered dialogue.

[28] Erb (n 8) 600 (rejecting claim that focus on the individual/victim is part of a fundamentalist ideology). See also Rönnau and Hohn (n 2) side-note 64 (noting increasing popularity of view according more weight to the individualistic justification); Greco (n 8) 677–78 (self-defence at bottom is grounded on protection of the individual).

[29] See, eg, Rönnau and Hohn (n 2) side-notes 64, 68–73, 226 (also conceding that a determination of 'relative weights' is not testable).

[30] Ibid.

[31] See ch 2(IV)(C) & (D).

[32] See ch 2(IV)(F).

[33] See generally ch 5(II). See also M Dyson and B Vogel, 'Reflections on Criminal Law in England and Germany' in M Dyson and B Vogel (eds), *The Limits of Criminal Law: Anglo-German Concepts and Principles* (Cambridge, Intersentia, 2018) 567–70 (noting that the purpose of German criminal law doctrine is to 'provide a coherent set of reasons for why specific conduct is criminalized and punished …. [T]he need to give reasons for criminalization and punishment is rarely questioned by German constitutional law or academics.')

B. Understanding the Arrival and Impact of 'Socio-Ethical' Limitations on Defensive Force

After World War II, and in particular during the past half century or so, so-called 'socio-ethical limits' (*sozialethische Einschränkungen)* on self-defence have gained prominence within the legal framework.[34] The appearance of these 'humane' bounds reflected a growing scepticism about individual self-help. It represented an emerging sense that the aforementioned *Schneidigkeit* or *Schärfe* ('severity' or 'harshness') of Germany's self-defence law went too far and ignored, or at least undervalued, the 'minimal solidarity' (*Mindestsolidarität*) between people and the related expectation that citizens exhibit some level of tolerance toward each other (*Pflicht zur Rücksichtsnahme* or *Nachsicht gegenüber Rechtsgenossen*).[35] Such restrictions, moreover, are said to accord with the high regard for human life reflected in Articles 1 and 2 of the German Constitution.[36] Finally, these limits have also been characterised as being consistent with the 'relatively tolerant approach of [German] society with regard to slight deviations [from the law].'[37]

In fact, a survey of public attitudes in Germany toward self-defence law revealed that the broader public as a statistical matter neither knew of, nor agreed with,

[34] See, eg, [2018] OLG Zweibrücken 42; [2016] BGH 2 StR 523/15; [1995] BGH 4 StR 294/95. See also Rönnau and Hohn (n 2) side-notes 226, 242–44; Greco (n 8) 667; Erb (n 6) side-notes 201–28; D Bock, *Strafrecht, Allgemeiner Teil* (Berlin, Springer-Verlag Berlin and Heidelberg GmbH & Co KG, 2018) 289–90; B Jähnke et al, *Strafgesetzbuch (Leipziger Kommentar)* (De Gruyter, 2018) 147; C-F von Scherenberg, *Die Sozialethischen Einschränkungen der Notwehr* (Bern, Peter Lang AG, 2009) 76 (noting that the term is not provided for in the statute and is a largely contentless term in that it only becomes relevant in the most extreme situation that for other reasons would likely not be deemed self-defence); M Koller, *Not Kennt Kein Gebot* (Lit Verlag, 2006) 196 (contending that the necessity of the defensive force must also be viewed in the context of protecting the legitimacy of the criminal justice system); Lesch (n 3) 82, 106. This concept of lenity has also variously been described as arising out of 'socio-ethics considerations,' the 'humane nature of criminal law,' and the 'duty of social solidarity.' See, eg, M Kremnitzer and K Ghanayim, 'Proportionality and the Aggressor's Culpability in Self-Defense' (2004) 39 *Tulsa Law Review* 875, 893–94. But consider that even in the late 1800s, German scholars noted how the distinction between innocent and knowing attackers impacted the 'gap' between the state-sanctioned, 'energetic' right of self-defence, on the one hand, and the 'barriers to its exercise required by custom.' H Tobler, *Die Grenzgebiete Zwischen Notstand und Notwehr* (Whitefish, Kessinger Publishing, 1894) 62.

[35] See generally Rönnau and Hohn (n 2) side-notes 70, 226–27; Erb (n 6) side-note 214; Lesch (n 3) 92–93, 106–09; Kargl (n 27) 39; Lenckner (n 18) 540–45; K Kühl, 'Die gebotene Verteidigung gegen provozierte Angriffe. Überlegungen aus Anlass der neusten Rechtsprechung des Bundesgerichtshofs zur Notwehrprovokation' in J Schulz and G Bemmann (eds), *Festschrift für Günter Bemmann* (Nomos Verlagsgesellschaft, 1997) 194; Roxin (n 26) 575–77; Jescheck and Weigend, 5th edn (n 18) 344–49; Burkhard Koch, 'Prinzipientheorie der Notwehreinschränkungen' (1992) 104 *ZStW* 785, 785–820; Spendel (n 26) 15–16; Schmidhäuser (n 17) 123–24 (arguing that the state monopoly on force is not challenged by self-defence because the right to self-defence is not delegated by the state); Roxin (n 3) 68. See also Koller (n 34) 196.

[36] See generally Rönnau and Hohn (n 2) side-note 226; Kühl & Heger (n 4) side-note 16.

[37] Kargl (n 27) 38. Article 1 of the German Constitution speaks of the dignity of man and human rights, whereas Article 2 addresses the citizens' right to life and bodily integrity. See generally HD Jarass and B Pieroth, *Grundgesetz für die Bundesrepublik Deutschland* 4th edn (Beck CH, 1997) 36, 49.

the 'harsh' traditional aspects of German self-defence.[38] As Rönnau and Hohn put it, the public's sense of justice shows that Germany's permissive, pro-defender self-defence law is, by international comparisons, an outlier that is neither 'desired nor justified' by the public.[39] For even with these added socio-ethical restrictions in place, in the 'typical' case (*Normalfall*), German self-defence still grants defenders remarkably wide latitude.[40] (But note that the ability to identify and with nuance discuss these perceived shortcomings is, again, aided by German self-defence law's value-explicit approach.)

Ever since the introduction of these socio-ethical limitations, German scholars, in line with their tradition, have debated over the textual foundation justifying such limits on the historically rigid and unforgiving section 32.[41] A persuasive textual argument may in fact be compelled.[42] For by limiting the scope of the self-defence justification, the German justice system necessarily was criminalising otherwise justified conduct (that is, it was narrowing the carve-out for what under the value-based model is 'stage five' condemnation[43]).[44] Considering that Article 103(2) of the German Constitution forbids any expansion in the scope of criminal activity without prior legal enactment (under the '*Legalitätsprinzip*' principle of *nulla poena sine lege*), in this manner limiting a defence through interpretation, rather than statutory revision, has been characterised as problematic.[45]

The ongoing debate has specifically focused on whether these humanitarian or empathy-based limits are authorised by the 'appropriate' (*geboten*) language in section 32(1),[46] whether they instead derive from the 'necessary' (*erforderlich*) language in section 32(2),[47] or whether both terms actually mean the same thing.[48] The majority opinion is that the *erforderlich* language asks whether the defender has a normative right to self-defence at all,[49] whereas *geboten* is descriptive in

[38] See Rönnau and Hohn (n 2) side-notes 72–73.

[39] Ibid.

[40] See Pest (n 4) 665–83; Rönnau and Hohn (n 2) side-notes 226–27.

[41] See generally Rönnau and Hohn (n 2) side-note 76.

[42] See Erb (n 8) 596.

[43] See ch 2(IV)(F)(v)(f).

[44] See Erb (n 8) 596.

[45] See ibid; D Kratzsch, *Grenzen der Strafbarkeit im Notwehrrecht* (Berlin, De Gruyter, 1968) 29. For the argument that Art 103 is not infringed by § 32, see Rosenau (n 2) side-note 30; J Wessels and H Satzger, *Wessels/Beulke: Strafrecht – Allgemeiner Teil* (Müller Jur Vlg CF, 2018) side-note 520; Roxin (n 26) 576; Jescheck and Weigend, 5th edn (n 18) 344. See also Rosenau (n 2) *Vorbemerkung* at side-notes 11–12.

[46] See, eg, Rönnau and Hohn (n 2) side-note 228; Rosenau (n 2) side-notes 30, 32; Wessels and Satzger (n 45) side-note 522; Kühl and Heger (n 4) side-note 13; Roxin (n 4) side-note 47.

[47] See J Renzikowski, *Notstand und Notwehr* (Duncker & Humblot GmbH, 1994) 303.

[48] See generally [2017] BGH 3 StR 622/17 (finding that a knife attack to ward off insults 'exceeded the limits of what is appropriate [for self-defense]'). See also Rönnau and Hohn (n 2) side-notes 76, 166–67, 180, 228; Erb (n 6) side-note 205; D Dölling et al, *Gesamtes Strafrecht* (Baden-Baden, Nomos Verlagsgesellschaft, 2017) 375–99; Pest (n 4) 137, 142–43.

[49] See Kühl and Heger (n 4) side-note 9.

that it refers to the type and manner of appropriate defensive conduct. The argument, therefore, is that the *geboten* language is the source for most limitations (*Schranken*) on defensive conduct (for example, distinguishing attacks by fully culpable individuals from attacks by moral innocents such as young children and those labouring under a reasonable mistake) and for denying self-defence in cases of gross disproportion (*krasses Missverhältnis*).[50]

The introduction of socio-ethical limitations on the right to self-defence, and the emerging focus on the principle of protecting the attacker (a principle that broadly aligns with value #1 – reducing overall societal violence and maintaining the state's monopoly on force; value #2 – protecting the attacker's right to life; value #5 – ensuring the primacy of the legal process; and value #6 – avoiding harsh outcomes that could undermine the law's legitimacy),[51] has certainly received its share of criticism. Lenckner, for example, maintains that the limitations threaten to 'devalue' self-defence.[52] Schmidhäuser has commented that the limitations may be a result of a 'contemporary German vanity' whereby the professors who urge these new limitations enjoy thinking of themselves as being in solidarity with the attacker, whom they view as a victim of society.[53] And Erb more recently contended, with some persuasive force, that the text of section 32 is at odds with contemporary efforts to further expand 'humanitarian' restrictions on self-preferential force.[54]

Whatever the merits of these critiques, the socio-ethical limitations are now part of Germany's self-defence law. The German law, by introducing an element of concern for the welfare of the attacker, is now also more in line with the value-based model and the attention it pays to according appropriate value to all lives, including to those who become the lawful object of defensive force.[55]

[50] See generally [2018] BGH 4 StR 242/18; [2018] BGH 4 StR 214/18; [2017] BGH 2 St 252/17; [2016] BGH 2 StR 523/15; [1966] AG Bensberg NJW 733, 735; Fischer (n 4) side-note 39; Pest (n 4) 137; Rönnau and Hohn (n 2) side-notes 76, 225–26, 228, 230; Rosenau (n 2) side-notes 34–35; Kühl and Heger (n 4) side-notes 13–14; Wessels and Satzger (n 45) side-note 524; Erb (n 6) side note 212; C Rückert, *Effektive Selbstverteidigung und Notwehrrecht* (Tübingen, Mohr Siebeck, 2017) 5, 13; Roxin (n 4) side-notes 83–85; Erb (n 8) 593; Lenckner (n 18) 544; Roxin (n 26) 575–77; Kühl (n 35) 197; Jescheck & Weigend, 5th edn (n 18) 344–45; Spendel (n 26) 124–25; Schmidhäuser (n 17) 133–34; U Schroth, 'Notwehr bei Auseinandersetzungen in engen persönlichen Beziehungen' [1984] NJW 2562, 2562–63; V Krey, 'Zur Einschränkung des Notwehrrechts bei der Verteidigung von Sachgütern' (1979) 34 JZ 702, 710; T Lenckner, '"Gebotensein" und "Erforderlichkeit" der Notwehr' [1968] GA 1, 7; K Himmelreich, 'Erforderlichkeit der Abwehrhandlung, Gebotensein der Notwehrhandlung; Provokation und Rechtsmissbrauch; Notwehrexzeß' [1966] GA 129.

[51] See ch 2(IV)(A), (B), (E), & (F).

[52] See Lenckner (n 18) 545.

[53] Schmidhäuser (n 17) 137. See also Spendel (n 26) 147–55.

[54] Erb (n 8) 596.

[55] See generally ch 2(IV)(B). But see Erb (n 8) 596 (contending that the BGH 'corrected' the 'questionable tendency' toward an overbroad expansion of the limitation).

III. Subjective or Objective Standard as to Justificatory Circumstances?

Both the text of section 32, the overwhelming German scholarly consensus, and the relevant case-law support the interpretation that the relevant justificatory circumstances must objectively exist before a defender can claim self-defence.[56] This formulation, which is consistent with the incompatibility thesis, also prevents situations in which self-defence can be used against self-defence.[57] And so defensive action is evaluated based on the facts as they actually are, which is consistent with the value-based model's approach.[58]

Indeed, and as discussed more fully below,[59] the only subjective justificatory requirement in German self-defence law is that the defender possess the necessary 'defensive will' (*Verteidigungswillen*).[60] So, the defender must be aware of the justificatory circumstances, *and* act, in part at least,[61] with defensive intention.[62] That said, while the consensus view is that the defender must act with the subjective intention of defending herself, a considerable (and growing) minority view is that the defender's mere knowledge or awareness of the justificatory circumstances should suffice.[63]

A small minority of commentators have also argued that self-defence should be available to persons who honestly (though perhaps inaccurately) believe defensive force is necessary.[64] The overwhelming scholarly consensus, however, as

[56] See, eg, [2017] BGH 4 StR 35/17; [2016] BGH 4 StR 235/16; [1985] BayObLG NJW 2600, 2601; [1963] BayObLG NJW 824, 825; [1930] 64 RGSt 101, 102; [1890] 21 RGSt 189, 190; Rosenau (n 2) side-note 26; Fischer (n 4) side-note 4; Rönnau and Hohn (n 2) side-notes 94, 154; Pest (n 4) 143–44, 166–67; Kühl and Heger (n 4) side-notes 6, 10; Lenckner (n 18) 537; Roxin (n 26) 557–58; Jescheck and Weigend, 5th edn (n 18) 338 n 7; Spendel (n 26) 109; Maurach and Zipf (n 26) 373; H Welzel, *Das Deutsche Strafrecht* 11th edn (Berlin, De Gruyter, 1969) 86.

[57] See generally Rosenau (n 2) side-note 18; Rönnau and Hohn (n 2) side-note 113. That said, earlier commentators would allow self-defence against self-defence. See, eg, W Frisch, *Vorsatz und Risiko* (Heymanns, 1983) 424; A Kaufmann, 'Zum Stande der Lehre vom personalen Unrecht' in *Festschrift für Hans Welzel zum 70 Geburtstag am 25 März 1974* (Berlin, De Gruyter, 1974) 393, 400.

[58] See ch 4(I)(B).

[59] See ch 5(III)(B).

[60] See generally [2019] BGH 1 StR 363/18; Fischer (n 4) side-note 25; Erb (n 6) side-notes 239–43.

[61] The defensive intention need not be the only motivator (*Motivbündel*); others may also be present. See Fischer (n 4) side-note 26; Rönnau and Hohn (n 2) side-note 267; Kühl and Heger (n 4) side-note 3.

[62] See [2015] BGH 3 StR 199/15; [2013] BGH 4 StR 551/12. See also [2019] LG Muenster 123; [2018] OLG Zweibrücken 42; [1953] BGH 3 StR 151/53; [1919] 54 RGSt 196, 199; Fischer (n 4) side-notes 25–27; Rosenau (n 2) side-note 49; Kühl and Heger (n 4) side-note 7; Roxin (n 4) side-note 129; Lenckner (n 18) 551; Maurach and Zipf (n 26) 362; Welzel (n 56) 86. But see Spendel (n 26) 72–73 (arguing that the consensus view is incorrect). Note, however, that the text of § 32 does not necessarily compel this subjective element. *Cf* Rönnau and Hohn (n 2) side-notes 262–63, 266 (disagreeing with the consensus view and denying the necessity of a defensive will).

[63] See, eg, Fischer (n 4) side-note 25; Rosenau (n 2) side-note 49; Kühl and Heger (n 4) side-note 7; Erb (n 6) side-notes 41, 241.

[64] See, eg, Warda (n 27) 419 n 29 (discussing the 'new direction in the literature' toward a subjective standard).

noted above, continues to reject this contemporary English[65] position. Opponents note that such a subjective approach would (1) be incompatible with the text of section 32 and (2) unduly disadvantage the person incorrectly identified as an attacker.[66]

A. Mistakes of Fact

While German scholars have advanced various competing theoretical approaches for addressing mistakes concerning the justificatory circumstances, the one that has received the preponderance of scholarly and judicial support is the 'theory of limited guilt' (*eingeschränkte Schuldtheorie*).[67] Section 16, which addresses mistakes of fact relating to the elements of the offence (*Tatbestandsirrtümer*), provides:

> (1) Whoever in committing an act is mistaken about the existence of facts which are part of the statutorily defined constituent elements of a crime does not act intentionally. The possibility of imposing criminal punishment for negligent conduct remains unaffected.
> (2) Whoever in committing an act mistakenly assumes the existence of circumstances which would form part of the statutorily defined constituent elements of a lesser offence can only be punished for intentional conduct in accordance with the statute defining the lesser offence.[68]

Although section 16 strictly speaking only addresses mistakes relating to the *elements* of the offence, the theory of limited guilt has been applied by analogy to section 16 cases involving mistakes regarding justificatory facts (*Erlaubnistatbestandsirrtümer*).[69] In one example, the *Bundesgerichtshof* reasoned:

> The defender acting under a mistake concerning the true facts is basically law-abiding; he wants to follow the law but fails to do so simply because of a mistake concerning the factual circumstances upon which he based his behavior. This is why [§ 16] applies to him, in that it does not attribute to him the objective factual circumstances, but rather those circumstances that he believed existed.[70]

[65] See ch 7(II). See also ch 5(III)(B).

[66] See, eg, Erb (n 6) side-note 246. See similarly [2017] BGH 4 StR 35/17; [2016] BGH 4 StR 235/16; Rosenau (n 2) side-note 26; Fischer (n 4) side-note 4; Rönnau and Hohn (n 2) side-notes 94, 154; Pest (n 4) 143–44, 166–67; Kühl and Heger (n 4) side-notes 6, 10; Lenckner (n 18) 537; Roxin (n 26) 557–58; Jescheck and Weigend, 5th edn (n 18) 338 n 7; Spendel (n 26) 109; Maurach and Zipf (n 26) 373.

[67] See generally Erb (n 6) side-note 246; J Hruschka, 'Der Gegenstand des Rechtswidrigkeitsurteils nach heutigem Strafrecht' [1980] GA 1, 20 n 48; F Schaffstein, 'Putative Rechtfertigungsgründe und finale Handlungslehre' (1951) 5 MDR 196, 200. *Cf* JA Dieckmann, 'Plädoyer für die eingeschränkte Schuldtheorie beim Irrtum über Rechtfertigungsgründe' (1994) 4 *Jura* 178, 179.

[68] See also Kühl and Heger (n 4) § 16 at side-note 3; Bohlander (n 23) 249.

[69] See Rönnau and Hohn (n 2) side-note 281; Fischer (n 4) side-note 51.

[70] [1952] BGH 2 StR 105/51. See also [1969] BGH GA 117, 118; [1952] BGH 2 StR 8/50; [1926] 60 RGSt 261, 262; [1994] OLG Düsseldorf NJW 1971, 1972; P Cramer, '§ 16 Irrtum über Tatumstände' in A Schönke and H Schröder, *Strafgesetzbuch* 25th edn (Beck CH, 2018/1997) 282, 285–86; Warda (n 27) 418–19.

Putative excessive force, in turn, applies to cases in which the defender objectively errs both about the existence of an attack, *and* about the amount of force necessary to repel the attack.[71] Section 33, which deals with cases of excessive force during self-defence, and is discussed in greater detail below,[72] notably does not apply to cases of *putative* excessive force.[73] In putative excessive force cases, the prevailing view is that there in fact was no section 32 'attack' that was reacted to in an excessively forceful manner.[74] Such a putative defender will instead be treated under the general rules relating to mistakes of fact dealt with in section 16.[75]

B. Unknowingly Justified Defenders

The once-dominant German scholarly view was that, in contrast to the principle announced in the English *Dadson* case discussed below,[76] an actor was always justified if the objective facts (even if unknown to her) provided her with a justification.[77] Today, German scholars and the courts take the position that the defensive will forms the basis of self-defence, that there is no 'present and unlawful' attack if the attacker is justified by self-defence, and that self-defence accordingly cannot be exercised against self-defence (*Notwehr gegen Notwehr*).[78] Self-defence is, by its very nature, said to require that the defender be aware of, and in fact believe in, the justificatory circumstances.[79]

That said, 'defensive will' need not be the only, or even the primary, motivator for the use of force.[80] Motives such as hate and revenge may all play a role in a defender's conduct,[81] provided that there is sufficient evidence to establish the

[71] See generally [2015] BGH 3 StR 199/15.

[72] See the discussion in ch 5(V)(B).

[73] See generally Fischer (n 4) § 33 at side-note 5.

[74] See generally [2017] BGH 1 StR 588/16.

[75] See [1988] LG München NJW 1860, 1861; [1968] BGH NJW 1885; [1962] BGH NJW 308, 309. See also Rönnau and Hohn (n 2) side-note 281; Lenckner (n 18) 555; Spendel (n 26) 181–82. Section 16, rather than § 33, applies in such a case. See generally Fischer (n 4) §16.

[76] See ch 7(II)(B)(i).

[77] Spendel was among the few who in the recent past supported this position. See Spendel (n 26) 72–73 (citing to sources supporting his view).

[78] See [2019] BGH 4 StR 456/18; Fischer (n 4) *Vorbemerk* side-note 22; Erb (n 6) side-note 49.

[79] See, eg, [2019] BGH 4 StR 456/18, citing [1983] BGH 4 StR 703/82; [2012] BGH 4 StR 197/12; [2003] BGH 1 StR 403/02; [2000] BGH StR 331/00; [1980] BGH NJW 1806; [1972] BGH MDR 16; [1926] 60 RGSt 261, 262; [1921] 56 RGSt 259, 268; [1919] 54 RGSt 196, 199; Roxin (n 26) 539; Jescheck and Weigend, 5th edn (n 18) 342–43; B Schünemann, 'Die deutschsprachige Strafrechtwissenshcaft nach der Strafrechtsreform im Spiegel des Leipziger Kommentars und des Wiener Kommentars' [1985] GA 341, 371; C Prittwitz, 'Zum Verteidigungswillen bei der Notwehr' [1980] GA 381 (arguing that issue has been settled since 1963).

[80] See [2018] OLG Zweibrücken 42; [2013] BGH 4 StR 551/12; [1953] BGH 3 StR 151/53 [1926] 60 RGSt 261, 261–62; [1919] 54 RGSt 196, 199.

[81] See, eg, [1926] 60 RGSt 261, 262 (holding that wife's motive for exercising her right to self-defence is irrelevant). See also Erb (n 6) side-note 240.

concurrent presence of defensive intention.[82] Today, however, an unknowingly justified actor could be convicted of no greater crime than an impossible attempt.[83]

IV. The Attack

A. What Interests Can Be Defended?

German self-defence law at one time provided protection only against physical attacks. But by 1870, the law stipulated that defensive force could be used to protect against *all* threats to a defender's legally protected interests.[84] Today, section 32 continues to permit self-defence to protect against attacks on any legally protected interests a defender may have.[85] So self-defence can be used to defend interests such as one's freedom and honour,[86] life,[87] non-deadly assaults,[88] property,[89] the right to hunt,[90] the right to engage in religious services,[91] home ownership rights,[92] a person's right to privacy,[93] and the right to be free from excessive noise.[94]

Section 32 does not, however, allow for the protection of relative rights such as contract rights, because a contrary outcome would lead to a situation where every creditor, for example, could use force to extract the money owed him by debtors.[95] Likewise, attacks on the 'public order' or the law in general do not

[82] See generally [1980] BGH GA 67, 68; Rosenau (n 2) side-notes 43–49; Erb (n 6) side-note 240.

[83] Which is essentially the same line of reasoning employed by Robinson. See generally Rönnau and Hohn (n 2) side-note 270; PH Robinson, *Structure and Function in Criminal Law* (Oxford, Oxford University Press, 1997) 111, discussed in L Crocker, 'Justification and Bad Motives' (2008) 6 *Ohio State Journal of Criminal Law* 277, 278.

[84] See F Schwarze, *Das Strafgesetzbuch für den Norddeutschen Bund* (Berlin, De Gruyter, 1870) 88. See also Vogel (n 1) 46–47; F Liszt, *Lehrbuch des Deutschen Strafrechts* 9th edn (Berlin, De Gruyter, 1899) 137–38 (stating that, during the Middle Ages, self-defence was limited to defence of a person from physical attack).

[85] See Rosenau (n 2) side-note 7; Fischer (n 4) side-note 8; Rönnau and Hohn (n 2) side-notes 78–79; Erb (n 6) side-notes 83–99; Roxin (n 4) side-note 30. See also [2019] BGH 1 StR 363/18.

[86] See, eg, [2017] BGH 3 StR 622/17 (noting that, because a person's honour is a legally protected interest, defensive force can be used to protect it); [1935] 69 RGSt 265, 268 (attack on soldier's honour); [1890] 21 RGSt 168, 168–70 (attack on defender's honour by priest during religious sermon). See also Kühl and Heger (n 4) side-note 3.

[87] See, eg, [2014] BGH 5 StR 134/14; Rosenau (n 2) side-note 7.

[88] See, eg, [2019] BGH 1 StR 363/18.

[89] See, eg, [1926] 60 RGSt 273, 277; Roxin (n 4) side-note 87.

[90] See, eg, [1906] 35 RGSt 403, 407, discussed in Rönnau and Hohn (n 2) side-note 86. See also Erb (n 6) side-notes 83–99. See, eg, [1920] 55 RGSt 167.

[91] See generally Rosenau (n 2) side-note 7; Lenckner (n 18) 529; Jescheck and Weigend, 5th edn (n 18) 339; G Erdsiek, 'Umwelt und Recht' [1962] NJW 2240; Liszt (n 84) 140; Schwarze (n 84) 88.

[92] See Lenckner (n 18) 529.

[93] [1994] OLG Düsseldorf NJW 1971. See also [1962] BayObLG NJW 1782, 1782–83; Kühl and Heger (n 4) side-note 3.

[94] See, eg, [1992] OLG Karlsruhe NJW 1329.

[95] See generally Rosenau (n 2) side-note 8; Kühl and Heger (n 4) side-note 3; Lesch (n 3) 93.

constitute 'attacks' under section 32 because only the state (generally consistent with collective value #1) is thought to be authorised to defend against attacks that do not harm any individually recognisable interest of the defender.[96] A different result, it is said, would turn each citizen into a 'quasi-policeman.'[97] No individual can thus, for example, remove pornographic material from a newsstand because the individual believes the material offends the 'public morality.'[98]

B. Need the Attacker's Conduct Be Criminal?

The 'unlawful attack' (*Rechtswidriger Angriff*) that section 32 allows defensive force against does not refer to the legal guilt of the defender. Rather, it simply describes the objective nature of the act.[99] This explains why one may lawfully defend against the attack of a child,[100] a drunk,[101] a madman,[102] or a person acting under a mistake who may be legally excused from criminal liability.[103] The traditional definition of an 'unlawful attack' under section 32, therefore, refers to an attack on a person's legally protected interests that she is not obligated to tolerate.[104]

Contemporary scholarship, however, consistent with the value-based model has increasingly – though for markedly different reasons[105] – distinguished between the traditional 'sharp' or 'robust' self-defence available to ward off attacks by culpable attackers, and the 'small' or 'limited' self-defence available against young children, the mentally incompetent, innocently mistaken attackers, and other moral innocents where defensive force does not 'protect the legal order' in the same degree as with (morally) culpable attacks.[106] And a minority

[96] See Fischer (n 4) side-note 10; Rönnau and Hohn (n 2) side-note 79; Erb (n 6) side-note 100; [1975] BGH NJW 1161, 1162–63; [1966] OLG Stuttgart NJW 745, 748; [1953] BGH 3 StR 151/53.

[97] See [1975] BGH NJW 1161, 1162.

[98] [1953] BGH 3 StR 151/53.

[99] See generally Fischer (n 4) side-notes 5 & 21; Kühl and Heger (n 4) side-note 5; Roxin (n 4) side-note 14; Erb (n 8) 595; Lesch (n 3) 94–96; Lenckner (n 18) 528; Jescheck and Weigend, 5th edn (n 18) 341; Spendel (n 26) 19; R Frank, *Das Strafgesetzbuch für das Deutsche Reich* (Whitefish, Kessinger Publishing, 2010/1931) 159–61.

[100] See, eg, [1991] BayObLG NJW 2031, 2031–32.

[101] See, eg, [1952] BGH 3 StR 217/52.

[102] See, eg, [1895] 27 RGSt 44, 45–47.

[103] See generally [1991] BayObLG NJW 2031; Kühl and Heger (n 4) side-note 5; Lesch (n 3) 101–04.

[104] See [1895] 27 RGSt 44, 45–46; [1890] 21 RGSt 168, 171. See also Fischer (n 4) side-note 21; Rönnau and Hohn (n 2) side-note 109 (describing change in predominant view); Kühl and Heger (n 4) side-note 5 (same).

[105] Proffered reasons include absent/limited deterrent value and interest in protecting the legal order or reduction in the relative interest in protecting the defender. Lesch (n 3) 103–04. Because the value-based model's respect for the equal standing of the defender is not considered in German law, that interest is not discussed. The prevailing position is that the socio-ethical limitations on self-defence take into consideration that a defender has (or should have) greater human solidarity with an innocent attacker. See generally Kühl and Heger (n 4) side-note 5; Lesch (n 3) 103.

[106] See, eg, Fischer (n 4) side-note 37; Rosenau (n 2) side-note 32; Rönnau and Hohn (n 2) side-notes 66–67, 225; Kühl and Heger (n 4) side-note 14; Erb (n 6) side-note 212; Roxin (n 4) side-note 61; Lesch (n 3) 102–04. See also H Kudlich, 'Praxiskommentar' (2019) 39 *NStZ* 599, 599–600

of commentators would go so far as to permit the use of self-defence only against culpable (criminal) attackers.[107] An emerging opinion, moreover, is moving in the direction of at least limiting the 'attack' to situations where the attacker at a minimum is subjectively negligent (even if not fully culpable) in creating the need for the defensive force; the prior focus, in contrast, was only on the objective threat (regardless of whether culpable, blameworthy, or innocent).[108]

The subject jurisdictions, as well as the value-based model, are, therefore, in broad agreement that attacks need not be criminal or culpable (that means, they do not need to threaten a wrong or implicate corresponding value #3 – equal standing)[109] to justify defensive force. That said, the trend in contemporary German self-defence scholarship is to increasingly add the normative responsibility of the attacker for the attack to the conversation.[110]

This trend can be said to, as noted, add value #3 (protection of the defender's equal standing and its related focus on harming versus wronging) to the analysis, while also placing greater emphasis on value #2 (safeguarding the attacker's presumptive right to life). The German justice system has thus demonstrated adaptability in terms of considering additional values, changing the weight given to already-considered values, and employing a common value-centric language to perform the analysis. This supports the position that a broad and systematic consideration of values improves transparency, reduces hidden normativity, and in so doing facilitates better decision-making.

C. Special Rules for 'Attacks' on the Police?

Self-defence is typically unavailable against the exercise of force by German state agents, such as the police or prison guards acting in the line of duty.[111] In contrast to the US position, which in these circumstances (and, therefore, on balance) provides the police greater latitude to exercise defensive force, regulations on the police (collectively *Hoheitsträger*) in Germany impose strict restrictions so that the police officer's ability to deploy deadly defensive force can be subject to disciplinary

(contending that the BGH is more likely to reach 'self-defense friendly' decisions than the lower courts because the BGH judges reach their rulings 'on the papers' and never meet those against whom potentially deadly defensive force has been used).

[107] See, eg, G Jakobs, *Strafrecht: Allgemeiner Teil* (Berlin, De Gruyter, 2011) 14–20. See also Rosenau (n 2) side-note 19.

[108] See Rönnau and Hohn (n 2) side-note 109; Kühl and Heger (n 4) side-note 5; Erb (n 6) side-notes 35–41; Lesch (n 3) 94–98.

[109] See ch 2(IV)(C).

[110] See Lesch (n 3) 94–98. For the minority view, see G Jakobs, *Rechtfertigung und Entschuldigung IV* (Carlsen Verlag GmbH, 1993) 148 (seeking to limit self-defence to cases of 'blameworthy' attacks).

[111] This is because their actions, even if wrongful, were generally not considered as a matter of law to be unlawful. But if a police officer does not follow the basic requirements set out by the law (*wesentliche Förmlichkeiten*), her actions can constitute an 'attack' and provide a basis for self-defence. See generally [1928] 72 RGSt 305, 311; Fischer (n 4) side-notes 12 & 12a; Liszt (n 84) 138.

sanction even when it is formally deemed lawful. The prevailing view among scholars, however, is that a police officer acting in the course of her duties can rely on self-defence if the objective facts support such a claim.[112] A minority considers self-defence a 'private right' of the citizens that, generally consistent with value #1,[113] limits the state's monopoly on force (and is, therefore, not something police officers can claim when acting in an official capacity). The argument is that when the authorities intrude in citizens' activities (*hoheitlicher Eingriff*),[114] they are doing so under the colour of law.

The officers are acting pursuant to the public law's (*öffentliches Recht*) legal permissions as reflected in the state-specific laws governing the police and policing (*Polizeirecht*), thus rendering the 'attack' justified.[115] Under the *Spaltungslösung*, an officer could face discipline and requests for compensation when she exceeds the authority provided by police regulations.[116] That said, some German commentators have objected to such limitations, arguing that they could lead to the public losing faith in the state's ability to effectively exercise its monopoly on force (implicating value #1 and value #6).[117] But, as noted above, while the officer using excessive force may not be subject to criminal penalties, under the *Spaltungslösung*, she could still face discipline and demands for compensation if she exceeds the authority provided by police regulations.[118]

D. Can Passive Conduct Constitute an 'Attack'?

Though some scholars disagree,[119] the prevailing view is that physical action is not the prerequisite of an attack under German self-defence law.[120] The trespassing Andrew passively sitting without permission on Victor's couch in Victor's house is, therefore, deemed to be attacking Victor's legally protected interests in his property for purposes of section 32.[121] Courts have similarly ruled that, if an individual standing in a parking spot refuses to move because she is unlawfully trying to hold the spot for a friend, the driver of a car may use 'defensive force' to defend his right to the parking spot.[122]

[112] Kühl (n 7) § 7, side-note 153 ff. See also [1958] BGH NJW 1405; [1991] BayObLG JZ 936; Peter Kasiske, 'Begründung und Grenzen der Nothilfe' [2004] *Jura* 832, 832–39.

[113] See Chapter 2(IV)(A).

[114] See Rönnau and Hohn (n 2) side-notes 216–24.

[115] See generally Rönnau and Hohn (n 2) side-note 117; Kurt Seelmann, 'Grenzen privater nothilfe' (1977) 89 *ZStW* 36, 49 ff; Jakobs (n 107) § 12, side-note 41 ff.

[116] See generally Rönnau and Hohn (n 2) side-notes 216–220.

[117] See generally von Scherenberg (n 34) 248–49.

[118] See generally Rönnau and Hohn (n 2) side-notes 216–220.

[119] See, eg, Walter Perron, '§ 32' in A Eser et al (eds), *Schönke/Schröder: Strafgesetzbuch* 30th edn (Beck CH, 2019) side-note 10 (requiring active conduct).

[120] See generally Rosenau (n 2) side-notes 4–6; Fischer (n 4) side-note 5a; Roxin (n 4) side-note 11.

[121] See [1938] 72 RGSt 57. See also Fischer (n 4) side-note 5a.

[122] See [1963] BayObLG NJW 824, 824–25, discussed in Rönnau and Hohn (n 2) side-note 90.

Andrew, in contrast (and in deviation from the value-based model), would not be justified in pushing Victor out of his way in order to escape from a burning house unless Victor was purposefully blocking Andrew's escape, for Victor cannot be considered an 'attacker' under such circumstances. But Andrew would likely be able to claim necessity pursuant to section 34.[123] These examples illustrate the consensus view that a passive actor can only be considered a section 32 'attacker' when the *law requires* him to behave in a certain way (and this outcome is at odds with the value-based model's approach discussed at Chapter 4(V)(A)(iv), which would permit self-defence against a passive actor who *without objectively good reason* is threatening the defender's right to life).[124]

E. Imminence

i. The General Rule

German self-defence law has always required that the attack be imminent or present (*gegenwärtig*).[125] The common definition of imminence (again on all fours with the value-based model's approach)[126] is in turn pegged to the question of whether a later use of defensive force will, objectively speaking, be futile or more problematic (invoking the *Effizienzlösung*).[127] Moreover, it is not the bare *harm* stemming from the attack that must be imminent under German law, but, rather (and consistent with the value-based model's approach), it is the *danger* of harm that must be close at hand.[128]

[123] See Erb (n 8) 595; O Lagodny, 'Notwehr gegen Unterlassen' [1991] GA 300. In such a case, the accused would have to claim that, under § 34, there was a justifying necessity (*rechtfertigender Notstand*), however.

[124] See Rönnau and Hohn (n 2) side-notes 100–01; Lenckner (n 18) 534; Jescheck and Weigend, 5th edn (n 18) 339; Maurach and Zipf (n 26) 356. But see R Felber, *Die Rechtswidrigkeit des Angriffs in den Notwehrbestimmungen* (1979) 195 (attack requires action, not *in*action).

[125] See generally [2017] BGH 2 StR 188/17 ('An attack is imminent when the conduct of the attacker can immediately turn into a rights-violation, so that a delay in engaging in defensive force can reduce the chances of it being successful or risks significant injury to the defender.'), citing [2007] BGH 5 StR 404/06. See also [2017] BGH 1 StR 588/16; Fischer (n 4) side-notes 16–18; Rönnau and Hohn (n 2) side-note 140; Rosenau (n 2) side-note 12; Kühl and Heger (n 4) side-note 4; Erb (n 6) side-note 103; Roxin (n 4) side-note 21; Erb (n 8) 601.

[126] See ch 4(II)(B).

[127] See [2017] BGH 4 StR 635/16; [2017] BGH 1 StR 486/16; [2017] BGH 2 StR 188/17; [2016] BGH 4 StR 235/16; [1933] 67 RGSt 337, 339–40; [1918] 53 RGSt 132, 133. See also Rönnau and Hohn (n 2) side-notes 145–46 (attack is imminent when it is in the 'narrow final phase of the preparation').

[128] Cp [2017] BGH 4 StR 635/16; [2017] BGH 1 StR 486/16; [2017] BGH 4 StR 35/17; [2016] BGH 4 StR 235/16; [1991] BGH 2 StR 535/91; [1973] BGH NJW 255; [1927] 61 RGSt 216, 217; [1918] 53 RGSt 132, 133; and [1995] BGH NJW 973, with [1931] 65 RGSt 159, 160; [1979] BGH NJW 2053 (holding that defender's use of deadly force against the fleeing intruder failed to satisfy imminence requirement). See also Rönnau and Hohn (n 2) side-note 140; Fischer (n 4) side-note 5. But see H Frister, 'Die Notwehr im System der Notrechte' [1988] GA 291, 302 (the attack, rather than the danger flowing from it, must be temporally imminent).

So when three men in the course of ejecting a belligerent and previously insult-hurling New Year's party-goer cause him injury, they were not justified by self-defence because the party-goer was not insulting anyone *at the time* of the physical attack.[129] The attack would, however, be considered imminent/present as long as it is objectively reasonable for the defender to fear a renewed attack (or, in the context of the partygoer, impending additional insults).[130] Put another way, the focus is on an objective evaluation of the attacker's intention and the danger he presents.[131]

By way of additional illustration, in one 2017 case, the defender, who was physically weaker than the putative neighbour-attacker, armed himself with a handgun loaded with plastic bullets prior to knocking on the neighbour's apartment door and asking the neighbour to turn his music down.[132] The neighbour opened the door and in an intimidating fashion walked towards the defender, causing him to walk backwards to the top of a flight of stairs. With the neighbour less than six feet away, the defender shot the victim in the abdomen; the defender was later charged with attempted murder.

The Court ruled that 'imminent,' as used in section 32, includes situations where there has not yet been a violation of the defender's rights, but where delaying the use of defensive force could limit its effectiveness or result in additional risk to the defender.[133] The Court, moreover, emphasised that the question of whether the attack was imminent was to be determined objectively, rather than being based on the subjective perception of the defender.[134] And so an attack is considered imminent or ongoing until the objectively unlawful threatened action is abandoned or has failed, or until the damage has been done.[135]

ii. *Subjective or Objective Evaluation of Imminence?*

As discussed above, although some German commentators have asserted that it is unclear whether German law requires an actor's beliefs about the elements of

[129] [2019] BGH 1 StR 585/18.

[130] See [2017] BGH 1 StR 588/16; [2005] BGH 1 StR 99/05.

[131] [2016] BGH 5 StR 138/16 (finding that uncertainty about the facts cannot adversely impact the defendant).

[132] [2017] BGH 4 StR 635/16. See also [1933] 67 RGSt 337, 339–40.

[133] [2017] BGH 4 StR 635/16. See also [2017] BGH 1 StR 588/16; [2017] BGH 1 StR 486/16; [2005] BGH 1 StR 99/05; Pest (n 4) 144. In this context, commentators have discussed how effective particular defensive measures (knife versus gun, eg) are to stop/immobilise the attacker (*Mannstoppwirkung*). See Pest (n 4) 159.

[134] [2017] BGH 4 StR 635/16, citing [2002] BGH 3 StR 503/01 and [2015] BGH 5 StR 397/15. See also [2017] BGH 1 StR 588/16; [2017] BGH 1 StR 486/16; [2016] BGH 4 StR 235/16; [2005] BGH 1 StR 99; [2002] BGH 3 StR 503/01.

[135] See [2018] BGH 5 StR 421/18 (holding that the defender may use whatever defensive means are available to immediately stop the threat and need not deploy less-certain, but also less-damaging, defensive means). See also [1998] BGH 4 StR 114/98; [1920] 55 RGSt 82, 83–84; Erb (n 8) 598–99.

self-defence to be both honest and reasonable,[136] German law in the main treats the imminence requirement as part of 'justifying necessity.'[137] As such, and given that both the text of section 32 and the scholarly consensus are in agreement that the relevant justificatory circumstances must objectively exist before a defender can claim self-defence,[138] it follows, consistent with the value-based model's approach,[139] that imminence is also evaluated objectively (that is, based on the facts as they actually were).[140]

iii. German Law's Treatment of Battered Intimate Partner Syndrome

The German caselaw addressing battered intimate partner cases is relatively sparse. That said, the seminal 2003 *Bundesgerichtshof* 'family tyrant/house tyrant' case (*Haustyrannenfall*) has not been abrogated.[141] In that case, Germany's highest court ruled on a case involving a woman who killed her sleeping, abusive husband.[142]

The facts of the case were largely undisputed. The husband (an 'outlaw' biker gang member) for over a decade regularly exposed the defendant and her two minor daughters to considerable physical violence and psychological torture.[143] On the day of the homicide in September of 2001, the deceased came home from a bar and proceeded to once again assault his wife and threaten the children. Around noon that day, the defendant (who it was revealed had for some months contemplated killing her husband) fired six shots from her sleeping husband's .22 calibre handgun, hitting him twice and killing him.[144]

The Court, noting the defendant's three failed suicide attempts, agreed that the defendant at the time of the shooting in fact subjectively felt she had 'no way out.'

[136] See KW Simons, 'Self-Defense: Reasonable Beliefs or Reasonable Self-Control' (2008) 2 *New Criminal Law Review* 51, 53, citing GP Fletcher, *Basic Concepts of Criminal Law* (New York, Oxford University Press, 1998) 159.

[137] See generally MD Dubber and T Hörnle, *Criminal Law: A Comparative Approach* (Oxford, Oxford University Press, 2014) 444.

[138] See, eg, [2017] BGH 1 StR 486/16; [2001] BGH 1 StR 48/01; [1930] 64 RGSt 101, 102; [1890] 21 RGSt 189, 190; [1985] BayObLG NJW 2600, 2601; [1963] BayObLG NJW 824, 825; Lenckner (n 18) 537; Roxin (n 26) 557–58; Jescheck and Weigend, 5th edn (n 18) 338 n 7; Spendel (n 26) 109; Maurach and Zipf (n 26) 373; Welzel (n 56) 86.

[139] See ch 4(I)(B) & (II)(B).

[140] See generally [2016] BGH 5 StR 564/15; [2013] BGH 1 StR 449/13; [2012] BGH 2 StR 311/12; [2012] BGH 4 StR 197/12; [1989] BGH 1 StR 741/88. See also Erb (n 6) side-note 104; K Bernsmann, 'Private Self-Defence and Necessity in German Penal Law and in the Penal Law Proposal – Some Remarks' (1996) 30 *Israel Law Review* 171, 179 ('Justification of self-defence requires the presence of a subjective element in addition to the presence of an objective element. An actor must know that he is acting in a situation giving rise to a right to self-defence; he must, eg, be aware of the imminent attack.').

[141] [2003] BGH 3 StR 483/02.

[142] Ibid, discussed in Rosenau (n 2) side-note 17, and Rönnau and Hohn (n 2) side-note 146.

[143] Ibid.

[144] Ibid.

The Court further observed more specifically that the defendant honestly believed leaving her victimiser and moving to a women's shelter was not a viable option. The Court reached this decision because, during a prior visit to the women's shelter, the deceased reportedly told her he would harm her and their children if she ever left him again (and claimed he could do so through his confederates if incarcerated).[145]

The Federal Court of Justice in its ruling noted the trial court's conclusion that the defendant killed her husband 'by stealth' (*mit Heimtücke*) because he was sleeping at the time of the attack, and that she 'exploited' the defendant's defencelessness.[146] As a consequence, the defendant in the lower court was convicted of aggravated murder as dictated by section 211 of the StGB. Germany's highest court, however, interestingly left open the possibility of section 35(1) 'excusable necessity' (*entschuldigenden Notstand*) because the purportedly defensive act was motivated by the defendant's belief that shooting her husband was the only way to avoid future violence.[147] The Court noted that, while self-defence requires an immediate *attack* (*Angriff*), excusable necessity only requires an immediate *danger* (*Gefahr*). The Court went on to observe that the defendant and her children were in a perpetual state of ongoing fear of danger (including fear of being killed by defendant's husband).[148]

Despite evincing sympathy for the defendant's position, the Court ultimately concluded that the defendant did, in fact, have 'other options' for avoiding the danger. The Court, among other things, found that the defendant could have moved to a shelter with her children or called the police.[149] Indeed, the Court *prospectively* noted that

> the ongoing danger caused by the reoccurring and significant violence on the part of a 'Family Tyrant' is always avoidable by means other than killing the 'Tyrant,' including by seeking the help of third parties, and, specifically, the state authorities.[150]

It is, however, difficult to distinguish the battered partner's situation from that of a bar-owner who late one night overhears two patrons discussing their plan to break into the bar after closing time and, therefore, mixes sedatives into their beer. Historically, both cases would have qualified as anticipatory self-defence (*Präventiv-Notwehr*). Today, however, it appears a defendant at best will have her *non*-lethal defensive conduct against a sleeping or incapacitated intimate partner

[145] Ibid at 7–8.

[146] Ibid at 9–10 (commenting that the defendant had claimed she only shot her husband after he woke up, but that the forensic evidence and testimony from a cellmate proved he was sleeping at the time he was shot).

[147] Ibid at 13–14.

[148] Ibid at 13.

[149] Ibid at 15–16.

[150] Ibid at 17.

classified as an instance of justifying necessity (*rechtfertigender Notstand*) under section 34,[151] or as excusable necessity under section 35(1),[152] because other options, such as calling the police or retreating have, as noted, been judicially determined to be available.[153]

F. A New Definition of 'Attack'?

At the outset of this chapter, it was noted that an emerging line of scholarly thought would disallow section 32 force against the attacker who is behaving with care (to wit, non-negligently/non-culpably).[154] To, under this emerging modern trend, qualify as an 'unlawful attack' justifying self-defence, the behaviour at issue must, therefore, not only result in an unjust outcome (*Erfolgsunrecht*), but it also must result from *wrongful behaviour* (*Handlungsunrecht*). The argument advanced in support of this modern trend is that there is no need to use defensive force to vindicate the legal order when the attacker is blameless and is trying to conform his behaviour to the strictures of the law (this argument finds support in the value-based model's analysis of value #2 (protection of the attacker's presumptive right to life) and value #3 (safeguarding of equal standing)). In such a case, then, the defender's behaviour is to be judged by the requirements corresponding to 'justifying necessity' under section 34.[155]

Recall, however, that German self-defence law is not punitive. And so justified section 32 defensive force can still be exercised against morally innocent 'attackers,' such as children and madmen (though it is not unreasonable to predict that, consistent with the value-based model and the overall trend in German self-defence law away from 'harshness,' this position will, supported by considerable value-centric dialogue, shift in the next decade or so).[156]

[151] See generally Rosenau (n 2) 1–43.

[152] See generally ibid at 1–24.

[153] See generally [2003] BGH 3 StR 483/02, at 17. Although § 34 also provides the defender with a justification that indicates the legal order's acceptance of the conduct, § 34, unlike § 32, offers less protection to the defender in that it, inter alia, requires that the harm cannot be averted by any other means, and that the potential harm defended against must be greater than the harm inflicted (*Prinzip des überwiegenden Interesses*).

[154] See Rönnau and Hohn (n 2) side-note 109; Kühl and Heger (n 4) side-note 5; Erb (n 6) side-notes 35–41; Lesch (n 3) 94–98. But see Erb (n 6) side-notes 244–51.

[155] See, eg, C Bertel, 'Notwehr Gegen Verschuldete Angriffe' (1972) 84 *ZStW* 1, 11 n 41. See also Roxin (n 26) 558; Roxin (n 3) 82–83. But see Erb (n 6) side-notes 209–38, 244–51. See also the discussion at chs 2(III) & 4(V)(A).

[156] See ch 5(IV)(B). See also [2017] BGH 2 StR 118/16; [2012] BGH 2 StR 311/12; [1952] BGH 3 StR 217/52; Erb (n 6) side-note 209. Cp Roxin (n 26) 559 (arguing that 'unlawful' § 32 behaviour must at a minimum evidence an objective lack of care) and Roxin (n 3) 82–83, with Spendel (n 26) 19–20, 32–36.

V. Defensive Conduct

A. Necessity

The term 'necessary' (*erforderlich*) in section 32 refers solely to the defensive *means* selected.[157] Section 32's necessity requirement, moreover, follows the 'principle of the most gentle available treatment of the attacker' (*Grundsatz der möglichsten Schonung des Angreifers*).[158] The defender, therefore, must select the *least harmful* defensive means (*mildeste Mittel* or *mildeste Abwehrmittel*) available to him, so long as opting for such means does not, all things considered, increase the risk of harm to him or his property.[159] Such an evaluation, moreover, is to be conducted from an objective, ex ante perspective.[160] In situations where it will not reduce the defensive effectiveness, the armed defender prior to using his deadly weapon should thus first threaten its use, then fire a warning shot, and only if that fails or is not available, resort to a potentially lethal shot (particularly when the attacker is unarmed).[161]

The experienced boxer, moreover, should not throw punches at the attacker's head when a simple punch to the stomach would be equally effective.[162] And a counter-attack (*Trutzwehr*) is impermissible where purely defensive force (*Schutzwehr*) would suffice.[163] These limitations are consistent with the logic of the rule discussed above, pursuant to which a defender, armed with a gun or knife, should draw the attacker's attention to them prior to using such defensive means,

[157] See generally [2019] LG Muenster 123; [1995] BGH NJW 973; [1938] 72 RGSt 57, 58; Fischer (n 4) side-note 28; Jescheck and Weigend, 5th edn (n 18) 343. Although the literature and the caselaw in the US and England often confuse the respective definition(s) of necessity, this approach is consistent with those US jurisdictions that define self-defensive force as being that force which is 'necessary to prevent an imminent harm.' In these jurisdictions, imminence is treated as an independent requirement, in that the means of force selected must be necessary given the circumstances, and the unlawful harm must be immediately forthcoming. In the jurisdictions that require force to be 'immediately necessary,' in contrast, imminence is treated as a factor regarding necessity.

[158] See generally Pest (n 4) 142.

[159] See [2019] BGH 1 StR 363/18; [2019] LG Muenster 123; [2018] BGH 5 StR 421/18; [2017] BGH 2 StR 219/16; [2017] BGH 2 StR 188/17; [2017] BGH 2 StR 118/16; [2016] BGH 5 StR 564/15; [2016] BGH 5 StR 138/16; [2014] BGH 5 StR 134/14; [2013] BGH 4 StR 347/13; [1998] BGH 4 StR 114/98; [1996] BGH 5 StR 432/95; [1989] BGH NJW 3027; [1972] BGH 2 StR 679/71; [1969] BGH GA 23, 24; [1965] BGH GA 147, 148–49; [1938] 72 RGSt 57, 58–59; [1920] 55 RGSt 82, 85. See also Rosenau (n 2) side-note 21; Pest (n 4) 145; Fischer (n 4) side-note 30; Rönnau and Hohn (n 2) side-notes 75, 172; Erb (n 6) side-notes 129, 185; Roxin (n 4) side-note 42; Erb (n 8) 593, 599.

[160] See [2019] BGH 1 StR 363/18; [2017] BGH 2 StR 188/17; [2017] BGH 2 StR 118/16; Erb (n 6) side-note 208.

[161] See [2019] BGH 1 StR 363/18; [2012] BGH 4 StR 197/12; Pest (n 4) 146–47, 149–52; Fischer (n 4) side-notes 33–35.

[162] See [2002] BGH 3 StR 490/01; [2000] BGH 3 StR 331/00.

[163] See [2002] BGH 3 StR 490/01; [2000] BGH 3 StR 331/00; [1972] BGH 2 StR 679/71. See also Rönnau and Hohn (n 2) side-note 158.

provided that such a 'warning' does not objectively increase the risk to the defender and the defender has sufficient time to appropriately evaluate the situation.[164]

Whether defensive force is necessary in a particular case will, in short, be evaluated based on the objective circumstances. Considerations include how the conflict came to be, the strength and dangerousness of the participants, and the defensive options open to the defender.[165] In this, the German law is in accord with the value-based model and the laws of the US and England.

In one illustrative case, the defender called the police. But prior to their arrival, he was repeatedly beaten by the belligerent attacker living in the same homeless shelter. The court ruled that the defender, who had his head pressed against a window while armed with a kitchen knife, was not required to first stab his attacker in the arms or legs.[166] As the court put it, '[c]onsidering the difficulty in calculating the risk of making a bad self-defence decision, expecting the defendant to, in a moment of stress (*zugespitzte Situation*), first threaten the use of the knife or use the knife in a less deadly way is asking too much.'[167] Under the German law, moreover, the selected means of defence must, viewed from an ex ante perspective, also have the possibility of preventing, weakening, postponing, or otherwise interfering with the attack.[168]

B. Proportionality and Excessive Force

i. *The Traditional Rule*

As noted, Germany's self-defence law traditionally rejected all attempts to require that the defensive force employed be proportional to the harm threatened by the attacker(*Güterproportionalität* or *Abwägung der betroffenen Rechtsgüter*).[169] A 1923

[164] See [2017] BGH 4 StR 635/16; [2017] BGH 2 StR 219/16; [2016] BGH 5 StR 564/15; [2016] BGH 5 StR 138/16; [2014] BGH 1 StR 630/13; [2014] BGH 5 StR 134/14; [2013] BGH 1 StR 449/13; [2013] BGH 4 StR 347/13; [2012] BGH 2 StR 311/12; [2012] BGH 4 StR 197/17; [2010] BGH 1 StR 351/10; [2003] BGH 3 StR 458/02; [2001] BGH 1 StR 48/01.

[165] See [2017] BGH 4 StR 197/17; [2017] BGH 4 StR 35/17; [2003] BGH 2 StR 529/02; [1992] BGH 4 StR 464/92; [1982] BGH 3 StR 375/82. See also [2017] BGH 2 StR 188/17, citing [2015] BGH 3 StR 84/15; Rönnau and Hohn (n 2) side-note 177; Rosenau (n 2) side-note 27; Kühl and Heger (n 4) side-note 9. In the context of the use of firearms, this expectation of, when possible, using escalating force is called '*Stufenlehre*.' See Pest (n 4) 163–64.

[166] [2016] BGH 5 StR 564/15. See also [2017] BGH 2 StR 188/17, citing [2011] BGH 2 StR 375/11.

[167] [2016] BGH 5 StR 564/15. See also [2016] BGH 5 StR 138/16.

[168] See [1994] OLG Düsseldorf NJW 1971 (holding that defender's otherwise legitimate use of force against an intruding photographer was not necessary under § 32 because the photographer did not have any film in his camera). See also [1988] LG München NJW 1860, 1861; [1985] BayObLG NJW 2600, 2601; Kühl and Heger (n 4) side-note 10; Erb (n 6) side-note 208.

[169] See generally Pest (n 4) 138–39, 141; Fischer (n 4) side-note 31; Kühl and Heger (n 4) side-note 11; Roxin (n 4) side-note 4; Erb (n 8) 593. See also Matt and Renzikowski (n 20) § 32, side-note 10; [1935] 69 RGSt 308, 310.

textbook, for example, informed that '[o]ne can shoot down an attacker to defend one's ownership of a match ....'[170] Mayer, in 1936 criticising the suggestion that there be proportionality between the harm done and the threat averted (and in so doing invoking value #3 – equal standing; and value #4 – defender's autonomy),[171] similarly opined:

> It is understandable that an era which only half-heartedly fights criminality would want to rid itself of the severity of the law of self-defence. But it is obvious that, if proportionality were required, the struggle between the attacked and the criminal would then be destined to be a losing one [for the attacked].[172]

Necessity was, therefore, historically the *only* requirement that limited the use of defensive force.

ii. The 'Grossly Disproportionate Force' Exception

The overwhelming consensus view continues to reject a general requirement of strict proportionality between the competing goods (*Abwägung der betroffenen Rechtsgüter*).[173] As part of the socio-ethical limitations, however, an exception to this rule was developed in cases of 'gross disproportion' (*grobes* or *krasses* or *unerträgliches Missverhältnis*) between the harm threatened and the defensive force used.[174] In cases of relatively trivial threats, for example, it is said that neither the interest in protecting the individual nor the interest in protecting the legal order are implicated.[175]

Today, then, German law limits make self-defence unavailable when the interests being defended are grossly disproportionate to the defensive force used (and so deadly force would be unavailable to, for example, protect against the theft of a bag of fruit).[176] Viewed from the value-based model's vantage point, because the defender's personal protection justification (from the value-based model's perspective, roughly value #3 and value #4)[177] are said to carry diminished weight

[170] Mayer (n 12) 280. See also Entwurf Eines Strafgesetzbuchs [Draft Criminal Code] E 1962, BT-Drucks IV/650 (1962) 16, 156–57 [hereinafter 1962 Draft Code]; [1935] 69 RGSt 308, 310; Kühl (n 35) 195–96; Liszt (n 84) 140–41.

[171] See ch 2(IV)(C) & (D).

[172] Mayer (n 12) 258.

[173] See generally [2019] LG Muenster 123; [2010] BGH 2 StR 454/09; [1972] BGH 2 StR 679/71; [1963] BayObLG NJW 824, 825; Greco (n 8) 667; Erb (n 8) 593; Lesch (n 3) 84; Lenckner (n 18) 539; Roxin (n 26) 572–73; Jescheck and Weigend, 5th edn (n 18) 343; Spendel (n 26) 111; Maurach and Zipf (n 26) 363.

[174] See [2018] OLG Zweibrücken 42, citing [2003] BGH 1 StR 403/02; Fischer (n 4) side-note 39; Rosenau (n 2) side-note 34; Greco (n 8) 667.

[175] See generally Rosenau (n 2) side-note 34. See also Fischer (n 4) side-note 39; Greco (n 8) 667.

[176] See generally Rosenau (n 2) side-note 34.

[177] See ch 2(IV)(C) & (D).

in cases of trivial or relatively minor harm, self-defence will be unavailable if the force used is grossly disproportionate to the harm sought to be averted.[178]

Turning to what happens when an individual who is justified in using self-defence *exceeds* the boundaries of self-defence, section 33 provides that a defender will not be criminally liable 'if [he] goes beyond the limits of self-defence because of confusion, fear, or fright.'[179] What these 'limits' are is not defined in section 32 or section 33, and must, therefore, be determined on the facts of the specific case.[180]

C. Duty to Retreat and Avoid Conflict

i. The General Rule

As far back as the Middle Ages, the defender was, consistent with the value-based model's approach,[181] required to, if possible, retreat before he could use defensive force.[182] Today, in contrast, defenders are not bound to retreat before using defensive force.[183] That said, some fairly narrow exceptions to the no-duty-to-retreat rule have emerged.[184]

ii. Socio-Ethical Limitations and the Duty to Retreat and Avoid Conflict

As detailed in the subsections immediately below, a view is developing that retreat – like avoiding conflict[185] – should be required in some cases of attacks by innocents, such as madmen, children, and those labouring under a known mistake. Retreat, and avoiding conflict by not going to places where the defender knows the attacker

[178] See [1995] OLG Stuttgart NJW 2646 (threatening to drive into pedestrian who was holding parking space for friend excessive); [1965] BayObLG MDR 65; [1963] BayObLG NJW 824, 825 (holding that physical harm to woman who refused to move from parking space was abuse of right to self-defence); Kühl and Heger (n 4) § 33 at side-note 14; Jescheck and Weigend, 5th edn (n 18) 348; Spendel (n 26) 151; Koch (n 35) 785; Krey (n 50) 711.

[179] See generally [2017] BGH 3 StR 622/17 (the Court ruled that the putative defender's reaction was excessive when he inflicted multiple stab wounds on person who insulted him). See also Pest (n 4) 137–38; Rückert (n 50) 1.

[180] See Pest (n 4) 137–38.

[181] See ch 4(II)(C).

[182] R His, *Das Strafrecht des deutschen Mittelalters* (Wentworth Press, 2018/1964) 36.

[183] See Rönnau and Hohn (n 2) side-note 66 (noting that, pursuant to the prevailing opinion, the interest in protecting the legal order is 'immeasurably high').

[184] See generally Erb (n 6) side-notes 119–21.

[185] See generally M D'Angelo, 'Merkmal Der Gegenwärtigkeit' in *Notwehrrech Bei Neuen Konfliktmustern Aus Rechtsvergleichender Sicht* (2016) 187 (unpublished PhD dissertation, University of Freiburg), https://freidok.uni-freiburg.de/data/11175.

is, is also increasingly required before fending off attacks by close relatives, such as a spouse, and in cases where the defender provoked (*provoziert*) the attack.[186] Some, in fact, have taken the more novel position that section 32 should be *entirely* unavailable in cases where the defender is set upon by an innocent such as a child, a madman, or a person labouring under a mistake because these moral innocents are not threatening an 'attack' as defined by section 32.[187] Whatever the merit of this position, it appears that, at a minimum, retreat and avoiding conflict are now required in many situations where 50 years ago they were not.[188]

iii. Retreat When Attacked by 'Innocents'

As just noted, in cases involving morally innocent attackers, the defender is now likely required to retreat if practicable. The motivation for this position is the lack of the attacker's moral responsibility (adding weight to value #2, and de-emphasising value #3 and value #7, as well as arguably value #4).[189] Where retreat is not a viable option, moreover, the defender may even have to accept slight injury or damage before resorting to defensive force.[190] This requirement of 'risky care' (*riskante Schonung*) is narrowly limited, however.[191] Under German law, then, as under the value-based model, a person cannot be legally compelled to take a serious beating from, say, a legally innocent juvenile or madman.[192]

iv. Attacks by Close Family Members

As in the case of attacks by innocents, it has been argued that there is less interest in protecting the legal order when close family members, such as husband and wife, are attacking each other. In those cases, the defender is to some extent said to be the guarantor of the attacker (this is, depending on the context, known as the *Garantenpflicht* or *Garantenstellung*), obligating the defender to exercise special

[186] See generally [2019] LG Dortmund 39Ks 8/14 (retreat required when defender is armed with a deadly weapon and intentionally engages in fight – engages in 'disapproved prefatory activity' (*misbillingendes Vorverhalten*) with drunk, unarmed attacker). But see Rosenau (n 2) side-note 40; Kühl and Heger (n 4) side-note 14 (retreat only required when provoking behaviour is unlawful); G Freund, *Strafrecht: Allgemeiner Teil* (Berlin, Springer-Verlag Berlin and Heidelberg GmbH & Co KG, 2008) § 3, side-note 117 (same).

[187] See, eg, FW Krause, 'Zur Einschränkung der Notwehrbefugnis' [1979] GA 329, 335–36; Bertel (n 155) 11 n 41; [1962] BGH JR 186, 187. But see [1962] BGH NJW 308, 332. This contention lacks merit, however, because § 32 allows defensive force to be used against 'unlawful attacks,' rather than just against 'criminal attacks.'

[188] See generally Erb (n 6) side-notes 116–21; Erb (n 8) 593.

[189] See generally Erb (n 6) side-notes 212, 247; [1952] BGH 3 StR 217/52. See also E Schlüchter, 'Kein Recht zur Beweisvernichtung nach einem potentiellen Selbstbedienungsladendiebstahl' [1987] JR 309, 310; [1975] BGH MDR 194, 195.

[190] See Lenckner (n 18) 546; Roxin (n 3) 81. See also Krause (n 187).

[191] See generally Erb (n 6) side-note 211.

[192] See ibid.

care/consideration (*Rücksichtsnahmeverpflichtung*).[193] A defender consequently may not use potentially lethal force to prevent slight discomfort or a minor physical injury resulting from a spousal or child's attack, regardless of whether such force may be authorised if the culpable attack was by a stranger.[194]

Particularly relevant to battered intimate partner cases, however, the consensus view is that this limitation is abandoned in cases where the defender runs the risk of serious physical injury requiring medical care if she does not defend herself. Similarly, there is no requirement of 'heightened care' where, for example, the spouse is subjected to ongoing, though not necessarily always very violent, mistreatment that takes away her dignity and makes her the object of her husband's will.[195]

D. Intentionally Provoked Attacks and Other Blameworthy Conduct on the Part of Defenders

Absichtsprovokation refers to intentional, calculated provocation by the defender solely for the purpose of later being able to claim self-defence after the attacker 'rises to the bait.' (*Vorsatzprovokation*, in contrast, describes situations, such as those involving recklessness, that have not yet crossed over to the level of *Absichtsprovokation*, but where a person considers it to be possible that a situation of self-defence may follow from his actions, and accepts that.)[196] Some German commentators argue that self-defence should be entirely unavailable in cases of *Absichtsprovokation* (and in some cases *Vorsatzprovokation*) because there is no, or at least a far more limited, interest in protecting the legal order.[197] Others have

[193] See generally [2016] BGH 2 StR 523/15; [2003] BGH 3 StR 153/03; [1984] BGH NJW 986; [1975] BGH NJW 62; [1969] BGH NJW 802; Fischer (n 4) side-note 5a; Rönnau and Hohn (n 2) side-notes 238–41; Kühl and Heger (n 4) side-note 14; Erb (n 6) side-note 71; Roxin (n 4) side-note 93; Lesch (n 3) 82–93, 104–05; Bernsmann (n 26) 298–99; Schroth (n 50) 2563; Roxin (n 3) 81. See also [1976] BGH JR 335, 335–36; [1969] BGH GA 117, 117–18; G Geilen, 'Eingeschränkte Notwehr unter Ehegatten?' [1976] JR 314, 315–16.

[194] [1985] BGH JR 113, 115; [1984] BGH JZ 507; [1984] BGH NJW 986, 986–87; [1975] BGH NJW 62, 62–63. See also Rönnau and Hohn (n 2) side-notes 238–41; Erb (n 6) side-note 71. See also ch 4(V)(A).

[195] Cp [1969] BGH NJW 802 (holding that wife should not have used deadly force against her husband, even though less-harmful force may not have repelled the attack, because he was unarmed and they had engaged in similar physical arguments before), with [1975] BGH NJW 62 (no self-defence in husband-wife conflict) and [1984] BGH JZ 529, 529–30 (distancing itself from previous holdings). See also Erb (n 8) 597 (noting the difficulty of 'retreating' from an aggressive partner); Lesch (n 3) 104–05; Roxin (n 3) 101–03 (arguing that limitation on the right to self-defence does not apply to situations where partner routinely mistreats the other).

[196] See [2019] BGH 4 StR 456/18 (denying self-defence to attacker who intentionally provoked defendant in order to claim the justification and noting the absence of 'defensive will'); [2019] LG Muenster 123. See also [2015] BGH 2 StR 473/14; [2014] BGH 1 StR 630/13; [2010] BGH 2 StR 118/16; [2005] BGH 2 StR 237/05; Fischer (n 4) side-note 42; Rosenau (n 2) side-notes 43–44; Kühl and Heger (n 4) side-note 14; Erb (n 6) side-note 226.

[197] See, eg, Wessels & Satzger (n 45) side-note 534; Roxin (n 3) 85–86.

taken the position that, unless the intentional provoker is engaging in a positively *unlawful* attack, his defensive options should remain entirely unchanged.[198] Others, still, contend that such purposeful provokers lack the genuine 'defensive will' the German law requires.[199]

The contemporary majority view preserves the self-defence option for the provoking defender, provided that he first retreat and accept the risk of slight injury.[200] If retreat is not possible, the provoking defender who is facing serious harm is permitted to act in self-defence because it is thought that putting an individual in a situation where he has to choose between giving up his physical safety to the attacker or being exposed to criminal liability is untenable.[201]

In 2019, for example, the court was faced with a situation in which a drunk defender acted as a watch-out while his girlfriend urinated in a train station waiting area.[202] A man walking by pointed out that the waiting area was not a bathroom, which resulted in a verbal altercation between the drunk boyfriend and the man. The boyfriend, after verbally challenging the man, pulled out a hunting knife. When the man approached the boyfriend to hit him, the boyfriend stabbed the man in his left side to ward off the attack. The court remanded the matter for additional fact-finding concerning to what extent the boyfriend provoked the attack, and, therefore, should be restricted in terms of his defensive options.[203]

Although it is, therefore, clear that provocation under some circumstances limits one's ability to use self-defence, disagreements persist over what behaviour amounts to 'provocation' and how self-defence can as a matter of legal theory be restricted.[204] Must the provoking activity be positively unlawful, or is it sufficient for the activity to be rude, annoying, or otherwise socially unacceptable (*sozialethisch zu missbilligen*)? And should such asocial conduct be measured on the basis of intent, recklessness, negligence, or some other basis?[205]

Though subject to vigorous ongoing debate,[206] today's majority view requires the behaviour to be positively unlawful before the defender's ability to use

[198] See, eg, Rönnau and Hohn (n 2) side-notes 190, 245–60 (unless unlawful, intentional provocation no limit to defensive force).

[199] See [2015] BGH 2 StR 473/14; [2014] BGH 1 StR 630/13; [2010] BGH 2 StR 118/16; [2005] BGH 2 StR 237/05; Wessels and Satzger (n 45) side-note 534. For a discussion of self-defensive will, see ch 5(III)(B). See also Rönnau and Hohn (n 2) side-note 251.

[200] See [2012] BGH 4 StR 197/12; [1994] BGH NJW 871, 872; [1991] BGH NJW 503, 505; [1972] BGH 2 StR 679/71; Erb (n 6) side-note 227; Lenckner (n 18) 547–48; Kühl (n 35) 200–01; Jescheck and Weigend, 5th edn (n 18) 346–47. See also W Mitsch, 'Nothilfe gegen provozierte Angriffe' [1986] GA 533, 544 (arguing that provoking attacker should retain full right to self-defence).

[201] See [1994] BGH NJW 871, 872; Jescheck and Weigend, 5th edn (n 18) 346–47; Rosenau (n 2) side-notes 39–45.

[202] [2019] BGH 4 StR 456/18.

[203] Ibid. See also [2015] BGH 2 StR 473/14; [2014] BGH 1 StR 630/13; [2010] BGH 2 StR 118/16; [2005] BGH 2 StR 237/05.

[204] See generally Kühl and Heger (n 4) side-notes 14–15 (surveying the breadth of the disagreements).

[205] See generally Rönnau and Hohn (n 2) side-notes 190, 245–60; Fischer (n 4) side-note 44.

[206] See generally Kühl and Heger (n 4) side-note 14.

self-defence is curtailed – that is, provided the defender is not engaging in unlawful conduct, he is able to resort to defensive force even if he knows or must have known that his provoking conduct is likely to result in an attack.[207] As Kühl and Heger put it, self-defence does not apply to cases of attacks that merely resulted from conduct that can be '*disapproved* of for legal or socio-ethical reasons ….'[208] This approach is also consistent with the 'three-level-progression theory' (*Dreistufenlehre* or *Dreistufentheorie*) when it comes to provoked attacks (first seek to flee; then seek to deflect the attack (*Schutzwehr*); then deploy affirmative force to neutralise the attack (*Trutzwehr*)).[209]

VI. Evaluating Germany's Self-Defence Law from a Value-Centric Perspective

The position tested here is that a broader consideration of the values implicated when a person elects to engage in the self-preferential use of force will improve the transparency of decision-making and, relatedly, reduces the role of hidden normativity. The foregoing analysis of the German self-defence law squarely supports this position. The German approach to self-defence law distinguishes itself from the to-be-discussed laws of England and the US in that it employs an explicit and transparent system of value-ordering, both when discussing self-defence doctrine and at the level of specific application. In fact, the primacy of values is carefully analysed in any debate concerning proposed changes in the law.

For example, today, German self-defence is thought to be legally permissible because it both (1) protects the autonomy of the individual and (2) vindicates the legal order.[210] Each act of self-defence and any reform proposals are thus analysed on the basis of how well they protect the individual defender and how well they protect the legal order. And as scholars debate the merits of whether it is appropriate to provide full weight to either or both of these values (or to, as discussed, other values, such as equal standing), their value-explicit conclusions, if accepted, will have a very direct impact on the amount of force legally available, and on the circumstances in which the force can be used.

One of the value-centric areas that deserves particular attention in light of this book's focus on transparency are the post–World War II efforts to

[207] See [2019] BGH 4 StR 456/18; [2018] BGH 1 StR 208/18; [2012] BGH 4 StR 197/12; [2010] BGH 2 StR 483/10; [1993] BGH 3 StR 354/93; [1989] BGH 4 StR 2/89; [1972] BGH 2 StR 679/71; Kühl and Heger (n 4) side-note 14; Roxin (n 26) 584; Jescheck and Weigend, 5th edn (n 18) 347 (arguing that one must tolerate lawful, but provoking, behaviour without resorting to physical violence).

[208] Kühl and Heger (n 4) side-note 14. But see [1996] BGH NJW 2315, discussed in Erb (n 6) side-note 234.

[209] See generally Fischer (n 4) side-note 45; Rönnau and Hohn (n 2) side-note 256; Wessels and Satzger (n 45) side-note 530; Kühl and Heger (n 4) side-note 14.

[210] See ch 5(II)(A).

introduce 'socio-ethical limits' (*sozialethische Einschränkungen*), discussed above in Chapter 5(II)(B).[211] Here, the driving principle ('the right need never yield to the wrong') was augmented by more humanitarian values because of the evolving belief among scholars that the German law was too 'harsh.' Put another way, permitting essentially unlimited defensive force, if necessary to protect *any* legally recognised interest, was considered unreasonable. It was broadly thought that the grossly disproportionate outcomes this rule allowed for created an unacceptable imbalance between the thing protected and the damage inflicted, thereby threatening the state's monopoly on force,[212] as well as undermining the legitimacy of, and respect for, the legal order more generally.[213]

German self-defence doctrine in many respects provides answers similar to the value-based model. Indeed, the biggest deviation (and it, of course, is a significant one) is in the area of what in particular can be defended.[214] In that regard, German law is much more permissive, providing for deadly force in defence of property and under circumstances where US and English law would find the amount of force used to be disproportionate to the harm threatened. Also, while the value-based model would make defensive force available when 'immediately necessary,'[215] German law treats imminence as part of 'justifying necessity.'[216] And as discussed, every proposed change in Germany's self-defence law was accompanied by significant and transparent debate over how that change comports with the statute's text and the values sought to be protected.

While German self-defence law is still significantly 'pro-defender,' it, in a gradual and very transparent manner, has witnessed significant changes that have opened the door for possible future restrictions on the right to self-defence. And these changes, thanks to the more value-centric style of the German debate, have largely come about in a logically incremental, predictable, and justifiable way. What once were minority positions concerning proposed law reform, for example, have over time, and through extensive analysis and debate, become part of the positive law of Germany. All sides of the debate(s) are generally aware of why this

[211] See generally [2016] BGH 1 StR 597/15, citing [1996] BGH 5 StR 432/95; [2014] BGH 1 StR 630/13; [1995] BGH 4 StR 294/95. See also Kühl and Heger (n 4) side-note 13; Bock (n 34) 289–90; Jähnke et al (n 34) 147; von Scherenberg (n 34) 76 (noting that the term is not provided for in the statute and is a largely contentless term in that it only becomes relevant in the most extreme situation that for other reasons would likely not be deemed self-defence); Koller (n 34) 196 (contending that the necessity of the defensive force must also be viewed in the context of protecting the legitimacy of the criminal justice system).

[212] See generally Kargl (n 27) 39; Lenckner (n 18) 540–45; Kühl (n 35) 194; Roxin (n 26) 575–77; Jescheck and Weigend, 5th edn (n 18) 344–49; Koch (n 35) 785–820; Spendel (n 26) 15–16; Roxin (n 3). But see Schmidhäuser (n 17) 123–24 (arguing that the state monopoly on force is not challenged by self-defence because the right to self-defence is not delegated by the state).

[213] See Koller (n 34) 196.

[214] Cp ch 4(III)(B) with 5(IV)(A).

[215] See ch 4(II).

[216] See ch 5(IV)(E).

is so, what values are at issue, how these values are said to have been impacted by this law reform, and what future reform proposals may logically follow.

From the perspective of the position we are examining, then, while there continues to, as a normative matter, be disagreement over the morality/appropriateness of certain German self-defence outcomes, the foregoing survey demonstrates that the application of self-defence rules and the common analytical language promote nuanced, incremental, and focused decision-making. Specifically, the discussion reveals that German scholars and jurists use this common value-centric language to evaluate whether and why reforms to, or adjustments of, German self-defence doctrine are appropriate. This value-aware approach, moreover, yields outcomes reached in a more democratic, logical, and policy-based manner. By in this manner encouraging more thoughtful choices among the various available perspectives and narrowing the areas of dispute, the German value-centric approach leaves limited room for hidden normativity. In short, the examination of Germany's value-based approach, particularly once contrasted with the US and English approaches, provides considerable support for the position we are evaluating here.

6

Examining the US Law's Treatment of Self-Defence from a Value-Centric Perspective

I. Putting US Self-Defence Law in Context

When studying the self-defence law of the US, one must bear in mind that there is no such unitary entity, such as the 'US criminal law.'[1] Rather, each state has its own unique mix of criminal code and common law decisions. In addition to the laws of the individual states, an expansive system of federal courts interprets both their own and state criminal statutes and cases.[2]

While this jurisdictional complexity may tempt one to limit the examination to, say, three 'representative' state jurisdictions, the substantial national diversity of opinion and approach renders this alternative inadequate. This chapter will, therefore, identify select cases representative of more widely held – or emerging – positions.

A few words on the chronological range of cases examined are also in order. The US caselaw naturally encompasses self-defence cases that were decided well before the late 1800s. These earlier discussions, however, unsurprisingly focused largely on the common law of England, as put forward by commentators such as East, Hale, Blackstone, Russell, and Foster.[3] Because the law of self-defence in the US was, therefore, substantially similar to England's law,[4] and because before the

[1] See generally W Partlett, 'Criminal Law and Cooperative Federalism' (2019) 56 *American Criminal Law Review* 1663, 1685–86.

[2] See generally JL Larsen, 'State Courts in a Federal System' (2019) 69 *Case Western Reserve Law Review* 525, 530. See also *Frisby v Schultz*, 487 US 474, 482 (1988).

[3] See generally T Rönnau and K Hohn, '§ 32 Notwehr' in G Cirener et al (eds), *Strafgesetzbuch: Leipziger Kommentar, Band 3* (Berlin, De Gruyter, 2019) side-note 14. On a historical/linguistic note, the first time that self-defence was spelled with an 's' (to wit, 'self-defense') in the US caselaw was apparently in *United States v Travers*, 28 F Cas 204, 206 (CCD Ma 1814).

[4] See, eg, F Wharton, *A Treatise on the Criminal Law of the United States* 7th edn (Arkose Press, 2015/1874) 85–112; JP Bishop, *Commentaries on the Criminal Law* (Arkose Press, 2015/1858) 349–75; F Wharton, *A Treatise on the Criminal Law of the United States* 3rd edn (Arkose Press, 2015/1855) 456–69. See also *United States v Herbert*, 26 F Cas 287 (DC Crim Ct 1856).

mid-1800s the domestic caselaw on self-defence did not develop its independent existence, this section will largely confine itself to examining cases and commentary decided and written after the middle of the nineteenth century.

Some readers, moreover, may expect to see a heavy emphasis on the American Law Institute's influential 1962 Model Penal Code ('MPC'). The reason that the thesis will not discuss the MPC at great length is that most states have not, in fact, aligned their codes with the MPC's self-defence provisions. While the MPC's section 3.04 and accompanying sections have surely influenced the thinking of some judges and commentators,[5] it can be said that the MPC in the self-defence context has a tendency to seek to innovate the law, rather than restate it.[6] For example, it treats self-defence as an instance of 'lesser evils' justification, makes the issues of necessity and proportionality turn on the subjective beliefs of the defender, provides that a failure to retreat results in a complete loss of the right to self-defence, and seeks to replace the traditional imminence requirement with a broad requirement that the defensive force be 'immediately necessary … on the present occasion.'[7] These directives do not fully comport with the actual state of the law, and a detailed review of the MPC's self-defence provisions is, therefore, not particularly helpful.

Having discussed the scope and approach of this section, the book now turns to how the defence of self-defence is actually raised in American courts. If evidence in a trial permits a 'reasonable inference' that the accused may have acted in self-defence, the court in most states must allow the defence to go to the jury.[8] Unlike in England,[9] however, in the US, the defendant has the burden of raising the affirmative defence of self-defence.[10]

In the years around the turn of the twentieth century, this American concept of self-defence was often referred to as the 'right to self-preservation' because it was seen as an underivative right founded on the laws of nature. A number of US jurisdictions, moreover, continue to divide these cases into two general

[5] See, eg, H Dyan and E Gross, 'Between the Hammer and the Anvil: Battered Women Claiming Self-Defense and a Legislative Proposal to Amend Section 3.04(2)(b) of the US Model Penal Code' (2015) 52 *Harvard Journal on Legislation* 17, 32–34.

[6] See generally CKY Lee, 'Reforming the Law on Police Use of Deadly Force: De-Escalation, Preseizure Conduct, and Imperfect Self-Defense' [2018] *University of Illinois Law Review* 663; GP Fletcher, 'Dogmas of the Model Penal Code' (2018) 2 *Buffalo Criminal Law Review* 3, 15–16.

[7] See MPC § 3.04 (Proposed Official Draft 1962). This approach is in accord with the value-based model. See ch 4(II)(B).

[8] See generally *People v Tyson*, 2019 WL 3852432, at *11–12 (Cal Ct App Aug 16, 2019); *Jenkins v State*, 942 So 2d 910, 914 (Fla 2d DCA 2006); *State v Gagnon*, 567 NW2d 807, 808 (ND 1997); *Commonwealth v Mayfield*, 585 A2d 1069, 1071 (Pa Super Ct 1991); *State v Herriges*, 455 NW2d 635, 639 (Wis Ct App 1990). See also *Foreman v State*, 257 NW 237, 240 (Neb 1934); *State v Walker*, 59 SE 878, 878–79 (NC 1907).

[9] See ch 7(I).

[10] See *Rosemond v United States*, 134 S Ct 1240, 1256–57 (2014).

classes: *perfect* and *imperfect* self-defence.[11] Perfect self-defence describes those cases in which the defender was entirely free from blame in making his defensive force necessary.[12] A defender, for example, is justified as acting in perfect self-defence if he kills an attacker who makes an unprovoked murderous assault, or attempts any other forcible felony. Imperfect self-defence, in contrast, refers to a class of cases in which the defender's blameworthy conduct contributed to the defensive necessity arising, such as when the defender and the attacker get into a fight with each other, and the defender attempts to resist the non-felonious attack with force instead of seeking redress from the law.[13] Today, imperfect self-defence, which in contrast to perfect self-defence merely justifies a reduction in the *degree* of the offence of which the defender may be found guilty,[14] is typically used to describe situations in which the defender was subjectively justified, though a reasonable person would have found the defensive action unnecessary.[15]

Judicial pronouncements and scholarly commentary, generally consistent with the German approach,[16] previously took the position that it was not only a person's right, but in fact a person's *duty*, to the broader legal order, to prevent a felony; any killing necessary to achieve this end was, therefore, justified rather than merely excused.[17] Today, killing to prevent a felony is justifiable only when the felony is attempted by force or surprise, such as in cases of murder, robbery, burglary, arson, rape, or sodomy.[18] A US defender today, therefore, can claim two distinct, but overlapping, defences:[19] if his conduct is carried out both to prevent a felony *and* to protect himself from injury, then both defences will be available.[20]

[11] See, eg, *State v Harvey*, 828 SE2d 481, 484 (NC 2019); *State v Lee*, 811 SE2d 562, 568 (NC 2018); *Porter v State*, 166 A3d 1044, 1053 (Md Ct App 2017). See also *Wallace v United States*, 162 US 466, 472 (1896); *State v Kindred*, 49 SW 845, 849 (Mo 1899); *Hardin v State*, 49 SW 607, 611–12 (Tex Crim App 1899).

[12] See, eg, *State v Flory*, 276 P 458, 462–63 (Wyo 1929); *State v Zorn*, 100 SW 591, 599 (Mo 1907).

[13] See, eg, *Nelson v State*, 2019 WL 3955049, at *4–5 (Miss Aug 22, 2019); *State v Silva*, 2019 WL 3311168, at *5–6 (Utah Jul 23, 2019) See also *Dodson v Commonwealth*, 167 SE 260 (Va 1933).

[14] See, eg, *Harvey*, 828 SE2d at 484 (NC 2019); *State v Barrett*, 442 P3d 492, 499–500 (Kan 2019); *In re Christian S*, 872 P2d 574, 588 (Cal 1994); *Paz v State*, 852 P2d 1355, 1363 (Idaho 1993); *State v Bowens*, 501 A2d 577 (NJ Super Ct 1985), *aff'd*, 532 A2d 215 (NJ 1987).

[15] See, eg, *Mobley v State*, 2019 WL 290063, at *4 (Md Ct App, Jan 15, 2019); *Neevel v Herns*, 2018 WL 6441071, at *2 (WD Wis Dec 7, 2018); *Burch v State*, 696 A2d 443, 458 (Md Ct App 1997); *In re Christian S*, 872 P2d at 575. See also CKY Lee, 'Race and Self-Defense: Toward a Normative Conception of Reasonableness' (1996) 81 *Minnesota Law Review* 367, 377.

[16] See ch 5(II).

[17] See, eg, *Bond v Baltimore & OR Co*, 96 SE 932, 934 (W Va 1918). See also WL Clark, *Handbook of Criminal Law* 3rd edn (Charleston, Nabu Press, 2020/1915) 178; Bishop (n 4) 604–07.

[18] See, eg, *State v Copley*, 828 SE2d 35, 48–49 (NC Ct App 2019); *State v Cardenas*, 380 P3d 866, 870–71 (NM Ct App 2016); *State v Havican*, 569 A2d 1089, 1092 (Conn 1990); *Laney v State*, 361 SE2d 841 (Ga Ct App 1987). See also JM Whiteman, 'Recent Decisions: The Court of Appeals of Maryland' (2002) 61 *Maryland Law Review* 795, 897.

[19] See generally *State v Pollard*, 900 NW2d 175, 178–79 (Minn Ct App 2017).

[20] See generally *People v Wafer*, 907 NW2d 584, 592–92 (Mich 2018); *Laney*, 361 SE2d at 844; *State v Harris*, 222 NW2d 462, 467 (Iowa 1974).

II. Subjective or Objective Standard as to the Justificatory Circumstances

A. Mistakes of Fact

US courts, in keeping with the traditional English rule,[21] but at odds with both the German approach[22] and value-based model,[23] historically required mistakes of fact as to the justificatory circumstances to be objectively reasonable before self-defence could apply.[24] The right to self-defence in the US, thus, has always hinged neither on the actual existence of facts making the self-defensive conduct necessary nor on the actor's purely subjective belief. Self-defence, rather, was sanctioned if it appeared to the jury that such defence was necessary and reasonable under the circumstances the defender at the time knew about.[25] The *Shorter* court, for example, noted that a rule requiring the actual justificatory facts to be present before self-defence could apply (in the parlance of the value-based model, a requirement of 'external justification'[26]) 'would lay too heavy a burden on poor humanity.'[27] The jury, thus, evaluated the defendant's conduct on the basis of how a reasonable person would have acted in such circumstances, and had to place itself into the shoes of the defendant at the time of the act.[28]

Today, jurors are still asked to place themselves in the defender's shoes when evaluating the *reasonableness* of the defender's actions.[29] But they are also generally instructed to, in their 'reasonable person' analysis, ignore the defendant's particular characteristics, such as cowardice, nervous temperament, immaturity,

[21] See ch 7(II)(A).

[22] See ch 5(III).

[23] See ch 4(I)(B) & (C).

[24] See, eg, *Rowe v United States*, 164 US 546, 557 (1896); *Acers v United States*, 164 US 388, 392–93 (1896); *Addington v United States*, 165 US 184, 186–87 (1897); *Beard v United States*, 158 US 550 (1895); *State v Gray*, 77 SE 833 (NC 1913); *People v Williams*, 88 NE 1053, 1056 (Ill 1909); *Young v State*, 104 NW 867 (Neb 1905); *State v Sadler*, 26 So 390, 399 (La 1899); *Nabors v State*, 25 So 529 (Ala 1899); *Redd v State*, 25 SE 268 (Ga 1896); *State v Berkley*, 19 SW 192 (Mo 1892); *State v Harrod*, 15 SW 373, 377 (Mo 1891); *State v Jones*, 7 SE 296, 305–06 (SC 1888); *State v Clifford*, 17 NW 304, 307–08 (Wis 1883). See also Clark (n 17) 178; JH Beale, Jr., 'Homicide in Self-Defense' (1903) 3 *Columbia Law Review* 526, 526–27.

[25] See, eg, *People v McGraw*, 2019 WL 1922855, at *5 (Cal Ct App Apr 30, 2019). See also SF Mandiberg, 'Reasonable Officers vs. Reasonable Lay Persons in the Supreme Court's Miranda and Fourth Amendment Cases' (2010) 14 *Lewis & Clark Law Review* 1481, 1486.

[26] See ch 4(I)(B).

[27] 2 NY 193, 197–98 (NY Ct App 1849).

[28] See *State v George*, 249 P3d 202, 205–06 (Wash App 2011); *State v Cadotte*, 42 P 857, 860 (Mont 1895); *McDonald v State*, 14 SW 487, 487–88 (Tenn 1890); *State v Sterrett*, 25 NW 936, 938–39 (Iowa 1885). But see *Coleman v State*, 320 A2d 740, 742–43 (Del 1974) (subjective standard as to necessity and objective standard as to excessiveness), discussed in *Lloyd v Jefferson*, 53 F Supp 2d 643, 687–88 (D Del 1999).

[29] See, eg, *State v Johnson*, 2019 WL 1125924, at *2 (Wash Ct App March 12, 2019); *People v Wilburn*, 2019 WL 1746844, at *2 (Mich Ct App Apr 18, 2019); *Stillwagon v City of Delaware*, 175 F Supp 874, 895 (SD Ohio 2016).

or weak physical condition.[30] That said, a minority of US courts continue to 'personalise' the objective approach by attributing to the hypothetical 'reasonable person of ordinary firmness' some physical characteristics, such as the defendant's actual height and weight.[31] Outlier cases aside, however, contemporary US courts in the main continue to instruct that the reasonableness of defensive force is to be determined *objectively*, and that the jury should not attempt to graft a particular defender's personal attributes and traits onto the proverbial reasonable man.[32] A reasonably or ordinarily prudent person in the defendant's shoes must consequently have believed both that the danger was imminent and that the defensive conduct was necessary.[33]

B. Unknowingly Justified Defenders

Defenders unaware of the presence of justificatory circumstances found no refuge in the US law of self-defence in the late 1800s and early 1900s. On the contrary, it was remarkably well-settled that, consistent with the value-based method,[34] an actor always had to persuade the jury that he was internally justified by his bona fide belief in the justificatory circumstances, and that he *acted* upon that belief.[35]

Today, defenders still can find no shelter in justificatory circumstances of which they were not aware.[36] To be justified, then: (1) a defender must subjectively believe that the force is necessary to prevent an imminent attack, and (2) the facts must be such that a reasonable person would objectively agree with

[30] See generally *JDB v North Carolina*, 564 US 261, 286-87 (2011), citing *Stansbury v California*, 511 US 318, 323 (1994); L Cohen, 'The "Reasonable Black Child" – Youth, Race, and the Fourth Amendment' (2018) 33 *American Bar Association Criminal Justice* 37, 38. See also *Fisk v State*, 71 P2d 499 (Okla Crim App 1937); *Calloway v State*, 262 P 696 (Okla Crim App 1928); *Ammons v State*, 102 So 642, 645 (Fla 1924); *Bosler v Modern Woodmen of Am*, 160 NW 966, 968–69 (Neb 1916); *State v Usher*, 111 NW 811, 812 (Iowa 1907); *State v Smith*, 71 P 973, 975–76 (Or 1903); *People v Button*, 39 P 1073, 1075 (Cal 1895); *Gallery v State*, 17 SE 863, 864 (Ga 1893); *Sterrett*, 25 NW at 938–39.

[31] See, eg, *People v Matthews*, 30 Cal Rptr 2d 330, 335 (Cal Ct App 1994); *Rodriguez v State*, 641 SW2d 669, 672 (Tex Ct App 1982), *aff'd*, 710 SW2d 60 (Tex Crim App 1986).

[32] See, eg, *People v Khachaturyan*, 2019 WL 4296870, at *3 (Cal Ct App Sept 11, 2019); *Nelson*, 2019 WL 3955049 at *4; *People v Brady*, 232 Cal Rptr 3d 220, 225 (Cal Ct App 2018).

[33] See, eg, *State v Isbell*, 524 SW3d 90, 94 (Mo Ct App 2017); *Castro v State*, 2014 WL 5020052, at *4–5 (Tex Ct App Oct 8, 2014).

[34] See ch 4(I)(B).

[35] See, eg, *State v Keeter*, 174 SE 298 (NC 1934); *Forrester v State*, 4 SW2d 966, 971 (Tex Crim App 1927); *State v Bethune*, 99 SE 753, 754 (SC 1919); *State v Parks*, 183 P 433, 434 (NM 1919); *Williams*, 88 NE at 1056; *People v Emerson*, 62 P 1069, 1071 (Cal 1900); *People v Bennett*, 80 NW 9, 11 (Mich 1899); *Lovett v State*, 11 So 550, 555 (Fla 1892); *Trogdon v State*, 32 NE 725, 727 (Ind 1892); *People v Donguli*, 28 P 782, 783 (Cal 1891); *May v People*, 6 P 816, 824–25 (Colo 1885). See also PH Robinson, *Criminal Law Defenses* (West Publishing Company, 2019) § 122.

[36] See, eg, *Priser v State*, 2019 WL 3216805, at *2 (Alaska July 17, 2019); *Stillwagon*, 175 F Supp at 895; *Humphrey v State*, 966 SW2d 213, 218 (Ark 1998); *State v Carter*, 713 A2d 255, 263 (Conn App Ct 1998); *State v Marshall*, 573 NW2d 406, 410 (Neb 1998).

the defender's conclusion.[37] This is, and has always been, the rule in US jurisprudence, and it is in line with the position taken by the value-based model of self-defence.[38] This rule, however, was the product of hidden normativity in that it was simply brought forward from early judicial pronouncements. It did not have the benefit of being exposed to a substantive debate over the values that justified this outcome, even though such a rule, as discussed above in Chapter 4(I)(B), inherently involves an accommodation between competing values.

III. The Attack

A. What Interests Can Be Defended?

Though the precise formulations sometimes differ, in the US, deadly force can be used to ward off death or serious bodily injury.[39] Serious (sometimes called 'great') bodily injury is generally defined as '[b]odily injury which creates a substantial risk of death or which causes serious, permanent disfigurement, or protracted loss or impairment of the function of any bodily member or organ.'[40] While the courts and legislatures have not expressed a unified view on what 'serious bodily injury' encompasses, there is caselaw support for the position that deadly force can be used to prevent broken noses and severed arteries,[41] bone fractures, and burns of the second or third degree,[42] and broken or fractured cartilage in the

[37] See, eg, *Priser*, 2019 WL 3216805 at *2; *Stillwagon v City of Delaware*, 274 F Supp 3d 714, 748 (SD Ohio 2017); *Washington v State*, 997 NE2d 342, 349 (Ind 2013).

[38] See ch 4(I)(B).

[39] See generally Tex Code Ann § 39-11-611 (2019), quoted in F Allhoff, 'Self-Defense Without Imminence' (2019) 56 *American Criminal Law Review* 1533 n 29; *State v Cook*, 802 SE2d 575, 578 (NC Ct App 2017); *Porter*, 166 A3d at 1067. Note that in some states kidnapping, rape, and forcible sodomy justify deadly defensive force. See, eg, Ala Code § 13A-3-23 (2019); Haw Rev Stat § 703-304 (2019); Tex Penal Code Ann § 9.32(a)(2)(B) (2019); *State v Matuu*, 2017 WL 4339427, at *2 (Haw Ct App Sept 29, 2017).

[40] See, eg, Colo Rev Stat § 18-1-901(3)(p); Haw Rev Stat § 707-700 (2019); Me Crim Code § 2(23) (2019); NJ Rev Stat § 2C:11-1(b) (2019); Pa Cons Stat § 2301 (2019). See also *Fleming v State*, 604 So 2d 280, 292 (Miss 1992).

[41] See, eg, *Camarillo v State*, 82 SW3d 529 (Tex Ct App 2002); *Caterino*, 451 Pa Super Ct at 42, 678 A2d at 389. But see *Truelove v State*, 2010 WL 8231393, at *12 (Miss Dec 20, 2010) (broken nose qualifies as 'bodily injury,' but not 'serious bodily injury'); *State v Kane*, 335 NJ Super 391, 398 (App Div 2000) (broken nose not 'serious bodily injury'); *State v Green*, 318 NJ Super 361, 371 (App Div 1999) (lacerations on hands and bruised leg not sufficient to qualify as serious bodily injury); *Webb v State*, 801 SW2d 529, 531 (Tex Crim App 1990) (holding that an injury that results in surgery to repair a broken bone did not amount to serious bodily injury); *Commonwealth v Alexander*, 383 A2d 887, 889 (Pa 1978) (broken nose, two black eyes and facial lacerations not considered serious bodily injury).

[42] See generally Colo Rev Stat § 18-1-901(3)(p) (2019) (bone breaks or factures and burns of the second or third degree); *Camarillo*, 82 SW3d at 537–38 (broken nose and 'nose trauma' as 'serious bodily injury'); *People v Culton*, 92 Cal App 3d 113, 117 (Cal Ct App 1979) (evidence of bruises, abrasions, and broken bones to support a conviction of substantial bodily injury). See also *People v Williams*, 115 Cal App 3d 446, 454 (1981) (evidence of a torn hymen and accumulation of blood was

nose or elsewhere.[43] Deadly force, in turn, is force that the actor uses with the intent of causing, or which the actor knows to create a substantial risk of causing, death or serious bodily harm.[44]

Early US jurisprudence provided that, while reasonable force could be used to defend both personal property and dwellings,[45] a defender was never authorised to intentionally kill an attacker or use a dangerous weapon against him solely for purposes of protecting his property.[46] This rule, which conflicts with certain popular (and, as will be shown, erroneous) perceptions of US self-defence law's comparative 'harshness,'[47] was typically justified as follows:

> The preservation of human life, and of limb and member from grievous harm, is of more importance to society than the protection of property. Compensation may be made for injuries to, or the destruction of, property; but for the deprivation of life there is no recompense; and for grievous bodily harm, at most, but a poor equivalent.[48]

Applying such limitations on deadly force to instances where it protected 'life and limb' was thought to prevent the 'cheapening' of human life, and was said to 'comport[] with the public tranquillity and the peace of society.'[49] Deadly force to thwart the wrongful taking or detention of personal property, without more, thus was never considered justifiable by the US law;[50] the defender with no option but deadly force, therefore, always had to suffer the wrong and seek redress at law (consistent chiefly with value #1 and value #2 – collective violence reduction and

sufficient to support a finding of substantial bodily injury); L Hoyson, 'Rape Is Tough Enough Without Having Someone Kick You from the Inside: The Case for Including Pregnancy as Substantial Bodily Injury' (2010) 44 *Valparaiso University Law Review* 565, 597 (arguing, in the rape context, that 'the physical effects of pregnancy exceed the requirements set forth by the common definition of substantial bodily injury ….').

[43] See, eg, *People v Jaramillo*, 183 P3d 665, 671 (Colo Ct App 2008).

[44] See generally Haw Rev Stat § 703-300 (2019); *Matuu*, 2017 WL 4339427, at *3.

[45] See, eg, *State v Howell*, 53 P 314, 315 (Mont 1898); *Goshen v People*, 44 P 503, 503–04 (Colo 1896); *State v Dooley*, 26 SW 558, 560–61 (Mo 1894); *Townsend v Briggs*, 34 P 116, 117 (Cal 1893); *Commonwealth v Donahue*, 20 NE 171, 172 (Mass 1889); *Rauck v State*, 11 NE 450, 451 (Ind 1887); *Fosbinder v Svitak*, 20 NW 866, 868–69 (Neb 1884); *Phillips v Jamieson*, 16 NW 318 (Mich 1883).

[46] See, eg, *Wallace*, 162 US at 473–74; *Dryer v State*, 53 P2d 700 (Okla Crim App 1936); *State v Metcalfe*, 212 NW 382, 387 (Iowa 1927); *State v Ciaccio*, 112 So 486, 489 (La 1927); *State v Green*, 110 SE 145, 147–48 (SC 1921); *Bozeman v State*, 104 SE 640 (Ga 1920); *Barkley v State*, 213 SW 642, 644 (Tex Crim App 1919); *Montgomery v Commonwealth*, 36 SE 371, 373 (Va 1900); *Fertig v State*, 75 NW 960, 963–64 (Wis 1898); *Storey v State*, 71 Ala 329 (Ala 1882).

[47] See, eg, M Dyckman, 'Bringing the Wild West to Florida' *St Petersburg Times* (St Petersburg, Fla, 27 Mar 2005) 3P. Setting aside the availability of weapons, the actual US law is, in fact, the most *restrictive* of those reviewed here.

[48] *Russell v State*, 122 So 683, 685–86 (Ala 1929).

[49] *Storey*, 71 Ala at 340–41.

[50] See, eg, *Darling v State*, 225 SW 328 (Ark 1920); *State v Holbrook*, 188 P 947 (Or 1920); *Oldacre v State*, 72 So 303, 304 (Ala 1916); *State v Blane*, 116 P 660, 662 (Wash 1911); *Bloom v State*, 58 NE 81 (Ind 1900); *State v Edgerton*, 69 NW 280 (Iowa 1896); *People v Hecker*, 42 P 307, 312 (Cal 1895); *Crawford v State*, 17 SE 628 (Ga 1893), *overruled in part by Moyers v State*, 197 SE 846 (Ga 1938); *Chapman v Commonwealth*, 15 SW 50 (Ky Ct App 1891).

protection of the attacker, respectively, as well as value #5 – ensuring the primacy of the legal process[51]).[52]

Some courts, however, carved out an exception which authorised deadly force if a non-violent theft occurred at *night-time*. In the Alabama case of *Storey v State*, for example, the Court held that 'a strong case might be presented of one's shooting a felon to prevent the asportation of a stolen horse in the night-time, where no opportunity is afforded to recognise the thief, or obtain speedy redress at law.'[53] A Texas statute went even further with the following unequivocal language:

> [I]n cases of burglary and theft by night, the homicide is justifiable at any time while the offender is in the building, or at the place where the theft was committed, or is within reach of gunshot from such place or building.[54]

These cases, therefore, evidence a narrow exception recognised in only a few states to the general rule prohibiting deadly force in defence of mere property (and they usually do so by following the implicit logic that a night-time intrusion is a particularly grievous attack on a person's autonomy (value #4).[55] The exception imputes to the attacker a greater disrespect for the defender's equal standing (value #3)[56] and also reflects a belief that such conduct must be generally and specifically deterred (consistent with value #7)).[57]

Turning to defence of dwellings, the law in the US used to be that deadly force could only be used if the defender was under a reasonable apprehension that the intruder intended to commit a felony therein or intended to inflict a personal injury that may have resulted in the loss of life or in the infliction of great bodily harm.[58] The earlier treatises and cases were, however, not in agreement as to whether deadly force could be used to prevent the commission of a felony of any kind within the home, or whether it instead was merely limited to preventing 'atrocious' felonies or felonies committed by 'force or surprise,' such as murder,

[51] See ch 2(IV)(A), (B), & (E).

[52] See, eg, *State v Baxendale*, 370 P3d 813, 817 (NM Ct App 2016); *State v McCracken*, 166 P 1174, 1176 (NM 1917); *Driggers v United States*, 95 P 612, 620 (Okla 1908); *Carpenter v State*, 36 SW 900 (Ark 1896); *State v Smith*, 30 P 679, 682 (Mont 1892).

[53] 71 Ala at 340.

[54] Tex Penal Code art 1105, subd 8. See also *Whitten v State*, 16 SW 296, 298 (Tex Ct App 1891); *Gray*, 77 SE at 833.

[55] See ch 2(IV)(D).

[56] See ibid at 2(IV)(C).

[57] See ibid at 2(IV)(G).

[58] See, eg, *Bray v State*, 78 So 463, 464 (Ala Ct App 1918); *State v Perkins*, 91 A 265 (Conn 1914); *Armstrong v State*, 143 P 870, 873 (Okla Crim App 1914); *Gray*, 77 SE at 834; *State v Mills*, 69 A 841 (Del 1908); *Thompson v State*, 85 NW 62 (Neb 1901); *State v Manns*, 37 SE 613, 615 (W Va 1900); *State v Taylor*, 44 SW 785, 788 (Mo 1898); *Wilson v State*, 11 So 556 (Fla 1892); *People v Coughlin*, 35 NW 72, 76 (Mich 1887); *Sparks v Commonwealth*, 20 SW 167, 169 (Ky Ct App 1885).

arson, robbery, burglary, rape, and kidnapping.[59] While some cases went as far as to permit the use of deadly force against persons seeking to forcibly enter after being warned to desist,[60] such decisions were little more than aberrations.

The law has changed surprisingly little since these early decisions. Judges and juries still hand down verdicts that consider it unreasonable to use deadly force to prevent a mere trespass or theft of personal property, regardless of whether the harm could not otherwise be prevented (which is consistent with the value-based model's conclusion[61]).[62] Contradicting certain domestic and international popular assumptions about the harshness of US self-defence law, the broad (but generally only implicit) reasoning supplied by the US courts is, again, that the preservation of human life is assumed to be more important to society than the protection of property.[63]

With regard to defence of dwellings, the law generally continues to provide that a lawful occupant may use deadly force to prevent the attempted unlawful entry to his habitation, provided that: (1) the defender has reasonable cause to believe that there is immediate danger that an entry will occur; (2) the intruder is attempting to enter with the purpose of killing or inflicting serious bodily injury upon one of the occupants, in order to commit a forcible felony therein; and (3) the force is necessary to prevent the entry.[64] The logic is that the house protects the individual, and forcing a person to retreat from it would inevitably leave her open to attack and increase the likelihood of injury.[65] The primary difference between the cases

[59] Cp *Emmons*, 43 A2d at 569 (permitting deadly force against felonies that constituted 'either an atrocious crime or one attempted to be committed by force (or surprise)'), with *Viliborghi v State*, 43 P2d 210, 212 (Ariz 1935) (justifying homicide in prevention of any felony). See also *Harold v State*, 67 So 761, 762 (Ala Ct App 1915); *Foster v Shepherd*, 101 NE 411, 416 (Ill 1913), *overruled in part by Spiegel's House Furnishing Co v Indus Comm'n*, 123 NE 606 (Ill 1919); *State v Marfaudille*, 92 P 939, 940–41 (Wash 1907); *Hecker*, 42 P at 311; *Bostic v State*, 10 So 602, 603 (Ala 1892); Clark (n 17) 179. But see Bishop (n 4) 607–08.

[60] See, eg, *Young v State*, 104 NW 867 (Neb 1905); *State v Peacock*, 40 Ohio St 333 (Ohio 1883); *State v Conally*, 3 Or 69 (Or Cir Ct 1869). Other states put defence of habitation on statutory footing. See *Bailey v People*, 130 P 832, 835 (Colo 1913); *Wells v State*, 141 SW 96, 98 (Tex Crim App 1911); *Freeney v State*, 59 SE 788, 791 (Ga 1907); *Hayner v People*, 72 NE 792, 795 (Ill 1904); *Brown v State*, 18 SW 1051, 1053 (Ark 1892).

[61] See ch 4(III).

[62] See generally *People v Surber*, 2017 WL 281760, at *8 (Cal Ct App Jan 23, 2017); *People v Camacho*, 2015 WL 8551831, at *6 (Cal Ct App Dec 11, 2015); F Stockdale, 'Withdrawing a License to Kill: Why American Law Should Jettison Stand Your Ground and Adopt the English Approach to Retreat' (2016) 39 *Boston College International and Comparative Law Review* 453, 456–60.

[63] See, eg, *Alexander v Commonwealth*, 508 SE2d 912, 914–15 (Va Ct App 1999), *rev'd*, 531 SE2d 567 (Va 2000); *State v Pellegrino*, 577 NW2d 590, 595 (SD 1998); *Washington v State*, 263 SE2d 152, 154 (Ga 1980); *Geralds v State*, 647 NE2d 369, 373 (Ind Ct App 1995). See also *Dearborn v State*, 420 SW3d 366 (Tex Ct App 2014).

[64] See generally *Mornes v State*, 2018 WL 3751351, at *6 (Tex Ct App Aug 8, 2018); *Shipp v Landry*, 147 So 3d 721, 726 (La Ct App 2014); *Alexander*, 508 SE at 915–16; *Commonwealth v Haddock*, 704 NE2d 537, 540 (Mass App Ct 1999); *State v Pendleton*, 567 NW2d 265, 268 (Minn 1997); *State v Ivicsics*, 604 SW2d 773 (Mo Ct App 1980).

[65] See generally *People v Tomlins*, 107 NE 496, 497–98 (NY 1914), citing *Beard*, 158 US at 550; *Willis v State*, 61 NW 254 (Neb 1894); *Estep v Commonwealth*, 4 SW 820, 821 (Ky Ct App 1887); *State v Middleham*, 17 NW 446, 448 (Iowa 1883).

involving defending oneself and defending one's dwelling, then, is that the defender has no duty to retreat in cases of defence of dwelling (more on this later), and one therefore may engage in protective acts earlier than otherwise authorised.[66]

B. Need the Attacker's Conduct Be Criminal?

US law, like the English law[67] and the value-based model,[68] never required that the attacker's threatening conduct be criminal. 'Unlawful' attacks by children, innocents, female spouses, and drunks could and can, therefore, all be met with defensive force.[69]

C. Special Rules for Attacks on the Police?

The use of purportedly defensive force by the police in the US has been hotly debated since Atlanta Police Department officer Garrett Rolfe on June 12, 2020, shot and killed 27-year old Rayshard Brooks near a Wendy's restaurant as Brooks half-turned and attempted to fire officer Devin Brosnan's taser at Rolfe. Much of the controversy has focused on Rolfe's claim that he was justified in using deadly force against Brooks even though the latter was running away and was using what Rolfe knew, or should have known, was an inoperable taser (because it had already been fired twice). Whether the use of a full functioning taser, moreover, could ever constitute a threat of death or serious bodily injury, and the extent to which de-escalation techniques might have helped avoid the deadly confrontation altogether, have also been the subject of much commentary.

In the US, no federal statute governs police use of deadly force.[70] Instead, police use of force is governed by a patchwork of US Supreme Court rulings, state statutes, and state caselaw.[71] Most states require police officers to hold a reasonable belief that force was necessary under the circumstances.[72] The standard view is

[66] See *Hill v State*, 143 So 3d 981, 984 (Fla Ct App 2014).

[67] See ch 7(III)(B).

[68] See ch 4(V)(A).

[69] See generally C Graff, 'The Religious Right to Therapeutic Abortions' (2017) 85 *George Washington Law Review* 954, 989. See also *State v Maney*, 138 SE 441, 442 (NC 1927); *Kelton v State*, 160 SW 342, 343 (Tex Crim App 1913); *Jordan v State*, 146 SW 881, 883 (Tex Crim App 1912); *Lawson v State*, 41 SE 993 (Ga 1902); *Latham v State*, 46 SW 638, 638–39 (Tex Crim App 1898).

[70] See Amnesty International, *Deadly Force: Police Use of Legal Force in the United States* (2015) 17, cited in Lee (n 6) 640 n 37.

[71] See Lee (n 6) 640. See also Amnesty International (n 70) 4 (listing Maryland, Massachusetts, Michigan, Ohio, South Carolina, Virginia, West Virginia, Wisconsin, Wyoming, and the District of Columbia as jurisdictions that lack laws on the use of lethal force by law enforcement officers).

[72] See, eg, Ala Code § 13A-3-27(b) (2019); Ariz Rev Stat Ann § 13-410(C) (2019); Colo Rev Stat § 18-1-707(2) (2019); NY Penal Law § 35.30(1); Tex Penal Code Ann § 9.51 (2019). See also Lee (n 6) 654.

that, like in self-defence cases more generally, the objective reasonableness of the officer's belief as to the appropriate level of force is to be judged from the officer's 'on-scene' perspective.[73]

The Court set out a test that cautioned against the '20/20 vision of hindsight' in favour of deference to the judgement of reasonable officers on the scene.[74] As a result, if an officer reasonably, but mistakenly, believes that a suspect was likely to fight back or otherwise assault the officer, for instance, the officer is justified in using more force than was in fact objectively needed. So, what the officer must show is that he had a 'reasonable belief' that such force was necessary under the circumstances, and that he acted on the basis of that belief.[75] In this regard, then, the law treats officers and civilians the same.[76]

One of the chief problems with this standard, however, is that 'reasonableness' in this context (and particularly when considered by a jury) tends to equate to 'typicality.' That is, in the jurors' minds, the question becomes what would a *reasonable police officer* do, rather than what would a *reasonable person* do. In fact, some state courts explicitly use the heightened 'reasonable police officer' standard; in those jurisdictions, evidence of special training may, therefore, work against officers advancing self-defence claims.[77]

A small minority of states, however, come close to adopting the subjective English approach for officers, so that the officer's subjective belief, rather than objective reasonableness, controls.[78] (This approach is, for the reasons discussed in Chapter 4(I)(B), at odds with the value-based model.) The focus in these states is on the officer's subjective belief.[79] Stated differently, despite a reasonable

[73] See, eg, *State v Ellis*, 186 P3d 245, 260–61 (2008); *State v Smith*, 807 A2d 500, 518 (Conn App Ct Oct 22, 2002); *Graham v Connor*, 490 US 386, 396 (1989). See also R Geisser, 'A Just War Inquiry of Police, Prosecutors & Deadly Force' (2017) 10 *Washington University Jurisprudence Review* 59, 86.

[74] *Graham*, 490 US at 393, 396, quoted in *Costello v Town of Warwick*, 2008 WL 1752486, at *1 (2nd Cir Apr 17, 2008).

[75] See, eg, Ala Code § 13A-3-27(b) (2019); Alaska Stat § 11.81.370(a) (2019); Ariz Rev Stat Ann § 13-410(C) (2019); Ark Code Ann § 5-2-610(b) (2019); Colo Rev Stat § 18-1-707(2) (2019); Conn Gen Stat § 53a-22(c) (2019); Fla Stat § 776.05(3) (2019); 720 Ill Comp Stat 5/7-5 (2019); Kan Stat Ann § 21-5227(a) (2019); La Stat Ann § 14:20(A) (2019); Me Rev Stat tit 17-A, § 107(2) (2019); Mo Rev Stat § 563.046(3) (2019); Mont Code Ann § 45-3-102 (2019); NC Gen Stat § 15A-401(d)(2)(a–b) (2019); NH Rev Stat Ann § 627:5(11) (2019); NJ Stat Ann § 2C:3-7(b)(2) (2019); NY Penal Law § 35.30(1) (2019); Or Rev Stat § 161.239 (2019); RI Gen Laws §§ 12-7-8, 12-7-9 (2019); Tex Penal Code Ann § 9.51 (2019); Utah Code Ann § 76-2-404 (2019).

[76] See *Stillwagon*, 175 F Supp at 895.

[77] See, eg, *Collado v City of New York*, 2019 WL 3996735, at *7 (SDNY Aug 23, 2019); *Kopf v Skyrm*, 993 F2d 374, 379 (4th Cir 1993); *Smith*, 807 A2d at 516–19; *Bell v City of Albany*, 436 SE2d 87, 91 (Ga Ct App 1993). See also SMI Kunen, 'Superhuman in the Octagon, Imperfect in the Courtroom: Assessing the Culpability of Martial Artists Who Kill During Street Fights' (2011) 60 *Emory Law Journal* 1389, 1408.

[78] See, eg, Neb Rev Stat § 28-1412(3) (2019); Wash Rev Code § 9A.16.040(3) (2019). See also M Alcorn, 'Setting the Standard: Changing the Use of Force Standard Used by California Police' (2018) 50 *University of Pacific Law Review* 251, 260–61; MPC § 3.09 (mistakes of law as to unlawfulness of force and legality of arrest).

[79] See, eg, 18 Pa Cons Stat § 508(a) (2019); Haw Rev Stat § 703-307(3) (2019); Neb Rev Stat § 28-1412(3) (2019).

argument that appropriate officer training will make conflict-fueled mistakes less likely, this officer-friendly subjective-belief-standard is a much more lenient and forgiving standard than the one by which civilians in Georgia and elsewhere in the US are judged (and the one the value-based model proposes). Cases like the tragic March 13, 2020, police shooting of 26-year-old emergency room technician Breonna Taylor in Louisville, Kentucky, illustrate the impact of these differing legal standards. If Kentucky adopted the subjective belief standard, then now-fired officer Brett Hankison who following a (it has been argued avoidable) shootout with Taylor's boyfriend Kenneth Walker riddled Taylor's house with eight allegedly indiscriminately-fired bullets (the unarmed Taylor was ultimately hit eight times during the firefight) could mount a successful defence if he could convince the fact-finder that he honestly, though entirely unreasonably, believed the self-preferential force he deployed was needed to save his life. For reasons discussed in Chapter 4(I)(B) & (C) and VII(B), this subjective standard of self-defence must be rejected.

Turning to the use of force *against* the police, in the tradition of the Anglo-American common law, a police officer acting outside of their legal authority was little more than a common trespasser who could be resisted as such.[80] That said, courts and commentators have advanced various process and law-and-order-based justifications to abrogate the common law right to resist what is perceived by the potential arrestee to be an unlawful arrest.[81]

D. Can Passive Conduct Constitute an 'Attack'?

Research has, somewhat surprisingly, not revealed cases that explicitly deal with passive attackers. Passive attacks are most likely not specifically discussed by the US courts because, although a favourite subject of academic debate, such cases in actuality occur rarely. It is worth noting, however, that passive threats can trigger lawful defensive force in Germany and England (as well, per the value-based model);[82] there is nothing unique to US self-defence law that would prevent US courts from reaching the same conclusion.

[80] See generally PG Chevigny, 'The Right to Resist an Unlawful Arrest' (1969) 78 *Yale Law Journal* 1128, 1129, cited in DAH Miller, 'Retail Rebellion and the Second Amendment' (2011) 86 *Indiana Law Journal* 939, 948. See also C Hemmens and D Levin, '"Not a Law at All": A Call for a Return to the Common Law Right to Resist Unlawful Arrest' (1999) 29 *Southwestern University Law Review* 1; AP Wright, 'Resisting Unlawful Arrests: Inviting Anarchy or Protecting Individual Freedom?' (1997) 46 *Drake Law Review* 383.

[81] See, eg, *Hicks v State*, 984 A2d 246, 253 (Md Ct Spec App 2009); *People v Villarreal*, 604 NE2d 923, 929 (Ill 1992); *People v Hess*, 687 P2d 443, 446–47 (Colo 1984); *Ellison v State*, 410 A2d 519, 525 (Del Super Ct 1979); *State v Richardson*, 511 P2d 263, 267 (Idaho 1973); *People v Curtis*, 450 P2d 33, 36 (Cal 1969).

[82] See chs 4(V)(A)(iv), 5(IV)(D), & 6(III)(D).

E. Imminence

i. The General Rule

The law in the 1800s was that mere fear of *future* death or violence could not ground self-defence. What was required was a *present* threat by the attacker.[83] Today, the majority of US jurisdictions still permit self-defence only when 'imminent' harm is threatened.[84] The most common definition of 'imminence' is temporal, in that the attack is 'about to occur,' rather than potentially occurring sometime in the future.[85] Put another way, the threatened injury is likely to happen within minutes or, more likely, seconds.[86]

As detailed in Chapter 4(II)(B), some argue that 'imminent' must be sharply distinguished from the term 'immediate,' on the grounds that the latter implies a far more urgent, pressing, and present threat than does the former.[87] Whether this distinction is linguistically required is, as noted, questionable. But, in any event, neither formulation has ever meant that a defender had to, say, wait until the attacker was within striking distance[88] or had his finger on the trigger of his gun.[89] In this respect the US law has not changed.

ii. Subjective or Objective Evaluation of Imminence?

While a minority of jurisdictions follow England's[90] subjective approach, which requires only an honest belief that the assailant intended unlawful harm,[91] the

[83] See, eg, *Acers*, 164 US at 391–92; *State v Sullivan*, 50 NW 572, 573 (Iowa 1879). See also *Treadway v State*, 144 SW 655, 674–75 (Tex Crim App 1912).

[84] See WR LaFave and AW Scott, *Substantive Criminal Law* 2nd edn (West Group Publishing, 2003) § 10.4(d) n 42 (collecting statutes). See also *People v Nguyen*, 61 Cal 4th 1015, 1045 (Cal 2015); *People v Stevens*, 858 NW 2d 98, 104 (Mich Ct App 2014).

[85] See generally WRP Kaufman, 'Self-Defense, Imminence, and the Battered Woman' (2007) 10 *New Criminal Law Review* 342, 345; S von Pufendorf, *On The Duty of Man and Citizen* (Cambridge, Cambridge University Press, 2007/1991).

[86] See, eg, *United States v Haynes*, 143 F3d 1089, 1090 (7th Cir 1998) (ruling that 'later' and 'imminent' are opposites). See also LaFave and Scott (n 84) § 10.4(d) (describing 'imminent' as 'almost immediately forthcoming').

[87] See generally *Porter*, 166 A3d at 1056–57; *People v Aris*, 215 Cal App 3d 1178, 1187 (Cal Ct App 1989), *overruled in part by People v Humphrey*, 921 P2d 1 (Cal 1996); *State v Hundley*, 693 P2d 475 (Kan 1985).

[88] See *Fortenberry v State*, 55 Miss 403, 409 (Miss 1877). See also *People v Bigford*, 2016 WL 10736071, at *3 (Mich Cir Ct May 16, 2006); *Hundley*, 693 P2d at 469.

[89] See *Goodall v State*, 1 Or 333, 337–38 (Or 1861). See also *Hundley*, 693 P2d at 469.

[90] See ch 7(II).

[91] See, eg, *State v Winters*, 2004 WL 899732, at *4 (Wash Ct App Apr 27, 2004); *State v Hodges*, 716 P2d 563, 569 (Kan 1986); *Leidholm*, 334 NW2d at 817–18; *State v Thomas*, 423 NE2d 137, 139 n 2 (Ohio 1981), *overruled by State v Koss*, 551 NE2d 970 (Ohio 1990); *Fielder v State*, 683 SW2d 565, 592 (Tex Ct App 1985), *rev'd*, 756 SW2d 309 (Tex Crim App 1988); *State v Allery*, 682 P2d 312, 314 (Wash 1984) (en banc).

majority of US states (and the value-based model[92]) disagree. In those states, a defender's belief as to the imminence of an attack – like the value-based model, but unlike the English law – is evaluated objectively.[93]

iii. US Law's Treatment of Battered Intimate Partner Syndrome

In the US and elsewhere, the debate surrounding the battered intimate partner syndrome and self-defence has ultimately turned on the above-described imminence rule (and, specifically, on what a 'reasonable' person would do).[94] While some have called for its elimination,[95] others have argued that it should be interpreted in such a manner that it takes into account the specific circumstances involved in battered intimate partner situations.[96] The fundamental challenge for the syndrome under US law is that the imminence requirement is based on the premise, familiar from the law of premeditated murder, that individuals acting under stressful conditions inconsistent with thoughtful reflection are less culpable than those facing less emotionally compulsive circumstances.[97]

At a deeper level, the imminence requirement is based on moral differences between *reactive* killers defending themselves in the heat of the moment and

[92] See ch 4(I)(B) & (C).

[93] See, eg, *People v Wilkins*, 2018 WL 4091012, at *6 (Cal Ct App Aug 28, 2018); *State v Parnoff*, 186 A3d 640, 650–51 (Conn 2018); *Porter v State*, 148 A3d 1, 15 (Md Ct Spec App 2016); *State v Salary*, 343 P3d 1165, 1173–74 (Kan 2015). For examples of the application of this standard in cases involving battered women who killed their husbands, see *People v Battle*, 129 Cal Rptr 3d 828, 846–47 (Cal App 2011); *State v Gallegos*, 719 P2d 1268, 1270 (NM Ct App 1986), *abrogated by State v Alberico*, 861 P2d 192 (NM 1993); *People v Emick*, 103 AD2d 643, 658 (NY App Div 1984); *People v Reed*, 695 P2d 806, 807 (Colo Ct App 1984); *May v State*, 460 So 2d 778, 784 (Miss 1984); *State v Martin*, 666 SW2d 895, 899 (Mo Ct App 1984); *State v Kelly*, 478 A2d 364, 373 (NJ 1984); *State v Nunn*, 356 NW2d 601, 604 (Iowa Ct App 1984), *overruled by State v Reeves*, 636 NW2d 22 (Iowa 2001); *State v Lynch*, 436 So 2d 567, 569 (La 1983); *Nygren v State*, 616 P2d 20, 22 (Alaska 1980); *Commonwealth v Helm*, 402 A2d 500, 504 (Pa 1979); *Langley v State*, 373 So 2d 1267, 1271 (Ala Crim App 1979); *People v Dillon*, 180 NE2d 503, 504 (Ill 1962); *Easterling v State*, 267 P2d 185, 187 (Okla Crim App 1954). See also AS Burke, 'Rational Actors, Self-Defense, and Duress: Making Sense, Not Syndromes, Out of the Battered Woman' (2002) 81 *North Carolina Law Review* 211, 229.

[94] See, eg, M Skopets, 'Battered Nation Syndrome: Relaxing the Imminence Requirement of Self-Defense in International Law' (2006) 55 *American University Law Review* 753; JC Moriarty, 'While Dangers Gather: The Bush Preemption Doctrine, Battered Women, Imminence and Anticipatory Self-Defense' (2005) 30 *NYU Review of Law & Social Change* (2005) 1; KK Ferzan, 'Defending Imminence: From Battered Women to Iraq' (2004) 46 *Arizona Law Review* 213; S Wallace, 'Beyond Imminence: Evolving International Law and Battered Women's Right to Self-Defense' (2004) 71 *University of Chicago Law Review* 1749.

[95] See, eg, Rosenfeld M and Arato A (eds), *Habermas on Law and Democracy: Critical Exchanges* (Berkeley, University of California Press, 1998) 405–06 (proposing a burden-shifting approach that would eliminate imminence whenever a defendant meets a 'substantial' evidentiary threshold regarding necessity).

[96] See, eg, Kaufman (n 85) 345.

[97] See A Gruber, 'The Duty to Retreat in Self-Defense Law and Violence Against Women' *Oxford Handbooks Online* (6 July 2017).

pre-emptive killers that may go so far as to plan their attacks. Viewed this way, then, the imminence requirement is the equivalent of an 'anti-self-help rule,' requiring the defender to seek the aid of others (thus invoking value #5 – primacy of the legal process)[98] or to leave the area (invoking value #1 – collective violence reduction and value #2 – protecting the individual attacker's presumptive life),[99] rather than engaging in a pre-emptive strike. In contrast, a small number of jurisdictions and the Model Penal Code (as well as the value-based model[100]) require that force be 'immediately necessary,' rather than necessary to respond to 'imminent harm' (thus opening the door for a pre-emptive strike, if necessary, on the present occasion).[101]

While many commentators have argued that in such cases the *necessity* of self-preferential violence should be paramount,[102] rather than the imminence of the threat, that is not the law in the US. When an intimate partner attacks her abuser who is not posing a temporally current threat – for example, when that person is sleeping or unconscious[103] – the US courts have largely held that, as a matter of law, the imminence requirement prevents an acquittal on self-defence grounds.[104]

That said, in the 2017 case of *Porter v State* (one of only a half-dozen or so reported cases discussing the imminence requirement in the context of self-defence since 2014), the Maryland Court of Appeals ruled that a woman who produced evidence showing that she suffered from battered woman syndrome was entitled to an imperfect self-defence[105] jury instruction (even though the woman hired a hitman to kill her husband – the hitman ultimately refused and contacted the police).[106]

[98] See ch 2(IV)(E).
[99] See ch 2(IV)(A) & (B).
[100] See ch 4(II)(B).
[101] See, eg, MPC § 3.04(1); Ariz Rev Stat Ann § 13-404 (2019); Del Code Ann tit 11, § 464 (2019). See LaFave and Scott (n 84) § 10.4(d) n 43 (citing statutes). The MPC, however, does contain a temporal ceiling because it requires the attack to come on 'the present occasion.'
[102] See, eg, Kaufman (n 85); JB Murdoch, 'Is Imminence Really Necessity? Reconciling Traditional Self-Defense Doctrine with the Battered Woman Syndrome' (2002) 20 *Northern Illinois University Law Review* 191, 212; Robinson (n 35) vol. 2 § 131(B)(3); D Rodin, *War and Self-Defense* (Oxford, Oxford University Press, 2003) 41; MPC § 3.04(1).
[103] For examples of such cases, see *State v Guido*, 191 A2d 45, 48 (NJ 1963); *Emick*, 103 AD2d at 644; *Leidholm*, 334 NW2d at 814; *State v Felton*, 329 NW2d 161, 162 (Wis 1983). See also K Kinports, 'Defending Battered Women's Self-Defense Claims' (1988) 67 *Oregon Law Review* 466.
[104] See, eg, *Porter*, 166 A3d at 1051; *Battle*, 129 Cal Rptr 3d at 846–47 (Cal App 2011); *State v Norman*, 378 SE2d 8 (NC 1989). See also Murdoch (n 102) 200; Burke (n 93) 229. But see *Wallace-Bey v State*, 172 A3d 1006, 1025 (Md Ct App 2017).
[105] The elements of imperfect self-defence are similar to those of perfect self-defence, except where those elements require 'an objectively reasonable belief that [the defender] was in apparent imminent danger of death or serious bodily harm from the assailant, requiring the use of deadly force.' *State v Peterson*, 857 A2d 1132, 1148 (Md Ct Spec App 2004), citing *State v Marr*, 765 A2d 645, 648 (Md Ct App 2001).
[106] *Porter*, 166 A3d at 1044. See also J Dodge, '*Porter v. State*: Appropriately Pushing the Limits of the Battered Spouse Syndrome Statute' (2018) 18 *University of Maryland Law Journal of Race Religion Gender & Class* 235–54.

F. Necessity

Under US law, the necessity element in self-defence requires that force, including deadly force, only be used to the extent that it is 'necessary.'[107] The underlying principle behind necessity as it relates to deadly force is that all human life, even the life of a violent criminal, is valuable and worthy of protection (thus drawing not only on value #1 – violence reduction and value #2 – protection of the attacker, but also on value #5 – ensuring the primacy of the legal process).[108] The necessity element likewise precludes the use of deadly force against a potentially deadly imminent assault if a non-deadly response would be sufficient to repel the attack.[109] Generalised fear alone, moreover, never justifies one person to take the life of another. Rather, the attacker must, through some overt act, gesture, or word spoken, induce in the defender a reasonable ground for believing the attacker threatens imminent death or great bodily harm.[110]

G. Proportionality and Excessive Force

As discussed above in Chapter 6(III)(A), under prevailing US law, the use of deadly force is generally restricted to cases where the attacker threatens death or serious bodily harm. In such cases, a defender need not first resort to less forceful means, such as shooting to wound.[111]

The Supreme Court of Georgia in the 1867 case of *Floyd v State* held that, '[a]s a general rule it may safely be asserted that the law will not excuse or justify a man who repels a blow given him with the fist by stabbing the assailant.'[112] A defender who was merely threatened with a non-deadly assault could, therefore, not kill his attacker, nor was he permitted to use a dangerous weapon in his defence. If deadly force was the only available defence, the defender had to submit to being punched and could later seek redress in the courts (implicating value #5).[113]

The law as it relates to proportionality and excessive force has not changed appreciably since these earlier decisions. A defender who kills another in an

[107] See generally *Stillwagon*, 175 F Supp at 895.

[108] J Dressler, *Understanding Criminal Law* 6th edn (London, LexisNexis, 2012) 228.

[109] See generally *Stillwagon*, 175 F Supp at 895; *State v Gheen*, 41 SW3d 598, 606 (Mo Ct App 2001); *United States v Peterson*, 483 F2d 1222, 1229–30 (DC Cir 1973).

[110] See generally *Watkins v State*, 613 A2d 379, 384 (Md 1992); *West v State*, 617 P2d 1362, 1366 (Okla Crim App 1980); *McKee v State*, 372 P2d 243 (Okla Crim App 1962). See also B Ching, 'Mirandizing Terrorism Suspects? The Public Safety Exception, the Rescue Doctrine, and Implicit Analogies to Self-Defense, Defense of Others, and Battered Woman Syndrome' 64 *Catholic University Law Review* 613, 622.

[111] See, eg, *Harbour v State*, 37 So 330, 331–32 (Ala 1904); *People v Newcomer*, 50 P 405, 409 (Cal 1897); *Babcock v People*, 22 P 817 (Colo 1889).

[112] 36 Ga 91, 93 (Ga 1867). See also *Smith v State*, 41 NE 595, 597 (Ind 1895); *Scales v State*, 11 So 121, 124 (Ala 1892); *Stewart v State*, 1 Ohio St 66 (Ohio 1852).

[113] See *State v Doherty*, 98 P 152, 154 (Or 1908); RM Perkins, *Criminal Law And Procedure: Cases And Materials* 3rd edn Minnesota, West Academic, 2017/1966) 600.

honest, but ultimately unreasonable, belief that such amount of force is necessary loses the benefit of perfect self-defence and is guilty of manslaughter.[114]

H. Duty to Retreat

US law provides that, for cases occurring outside of the defender's home, a failure to take advantage of an available safe retreat option renders self-defence unavailable.[115] By 'retreating to the wall,' moreover, even an initially guilty attacker can regain his right to self-defence against a defender, for through this 'break' in the action the initial attacker then no longer is the cause of the conflict.[116]

In 'stand-your-ground jurisdictions,' the person who is attacked does not have a duty to first retreat, and, instead, may stand his ground and defend himself *even if* safe retreat is easily obtainable. Florida law, by way of example, provides that a defender justifiably using or threatening deadly defensive force 'does not have a duty to [first] retreat and has the right to stand his or her ground if the [defender] is not engaged in a criminal activity and is in a place where he or she has a right to be.'[117]

Under widely accepted US state law, an innocent defender is also not required to retreat when he is attacked in his dwelling,[118] whereas a defender who was the initial provoker must retreat as far as possible before using any defensive force.[119] While a defender still need not retreat in cases involving non-deadly defensive force, a narrow majority of courts require innocent defenders to retreat if they can do so safely (regardless of where they are) prior to resorting to deadly force (this, of course, is consistent with value #1 – violence reduction, as well as value #5 – primacy of the legal process[120]).[121] In short, while many commentators continue

[114] See, eg, *State v Sims*, 431 P3d 288 (Kan 2018), cited in *Barrett*, 442 P3d at 499; *People v Vargas*, 2018 WL 6188255, at *5 (Cal Ct App Nov 28, 2018); *State v Reece*, 349 P3d 712, 723 (Utah 2015); *Commonwealth v Niemic*, 696 NE2d 117, 121 (Mass 1998); *People v Mayfield*, 928 P2d 485, 550 (Cal 1997), *abrogated by People v Scott*, 349 P3d 1028 (Cal 2015); *State v Lea*, 485 SE2d 874, 878–79 (NC Ct App 1997); *State v Collins*, 893 P2d 217, 222–23 (Kan 1995); *Bolyard v Commonwealth*, 397 SE2d 894, 899 (Va Ct App 1990). Note that there is a debate whether excessive force can result in a conviction for involuntary manslaughter. See generally *State v Abeyta*, 901 P2d 164, 172–73 (NC 1995), *abrogated by State v Campos*, 921 P2d 1266 (NC 1996); *Reid v State*, 425 SE2d 315, 316 (Ga Ct App 1992); *United States v Skinner*, 667 F2d 1306, 1309–10 (9th Cir 1982).

[115] See LaFave and Scott (n 84) § 10.4(f) n 72 (citing cases and statutes). See also *Haire v State*, 393 P3d 1304, 1311 (Wyo 2017); *State v Beltz*, 388 P3d 93, 99–100 (Kan 2017); *Corn v Rivera*, 108 A3d 779, 787 (Pa 2014).

[116] See, eg, *Allen v United States*, 164 US 492, 497–98 (1896); *Rowe*, 164 US at 549–50; *Hecker*, 42 P at 312; *Hunt v State*, 16 So 753, 755 (Miss 1895); *State v Cable*, 22 SW 953, 954 (Mo 1893); *State v Thompson*, 13 So 392 (La 1893); *Johnson v State*, 23 SW 7, 9 (Ark 1893); *Duncan v State*, 6 SW 164, 167 (Ark 1887).

[117] Fla Stat Ann § 776.012(2) (2019). See also *Dooley v State*, 268 So3d 880, 886–87 (Fla Ct App Apr 3, 2019); *State v Irabor*, 822 SE2d 421, 424 (NC App 2018).

[118] See, eg, *State v Gartland*, 694 A2d 564, 569 (NJ 1997); *People v Lenkevich*, 229 NW2d 298, 300 (Mich 1975).

[119] See, eg, *Lynn v Commonwealth*, 499 SE2d 1, 9 (Va Ct App 1998).

[120] See ch 2(IV)(A) & (E).

[121] See generally *State v Jacobson*, 2018 WL 4395018, at *2 (Minn Ct App 2018), citing *State v Carothers*, 594 NW2d 897, 899 (Minn 1999); *Commonwealth v Schulze*, 2017 WL 665633, at *7 (Penn Ct CP

to claim that safe retreat is never required by US law,[122] it appears that the most recent caselaw contradicts this position.[123]

I. Duty to Avoid Conflict

US law has never supported a requirement that defenders avoid potential conflict. So long as the defender did not provoke his adversary, he could go about his daily business and even arm himself without forfeiting any defensive rights.[124]

The US Supreme Court in its 1896 case of *Rowe v United States* found that the defendant could claim self-defence because he was 'where he had a right to be' when he justifiably killed his attacker.[125] The US law continues to be in line with English law[126] (and, in a general sense, the value-based model's position[127]) that, all other things being equal, a person is not required to avoid a place that he has a legal right to be.[128] That said, the US caselaw here, as well as more generally, like the English law (but unlike the German law), generally does not discuss, for example, whether its rulings consider any competing values (such as value #1 – protecting the state's monopoly on force, value #2 – protecting the individual attacker, or value #5 – ensuring the primacy of the legal process). Rather than engaging in a value-centric discussion, the individual US courts simply make broad pronouncements based on their interpretation of legal precedent and their own interpretation of the facts.

J. Intentionally Provoked Attacks and Other Blameworthy Conduct on the Part of the Defender

If a defendant started a conflict as a pretext to killing his adversary, the law used to provide that he was unable to claim self-defence.[129] This was true regardless

Feb 17, 2017); *State v Friesz*, 898 NW2d 688, 698 (ND 2017); *State v Terry*, 128 A3d 958, 967 (Conn App Ct 2015); *Miller v Comm'r of Corr*, 105 A3d 294 (Conn App Ct 2014). See also NY Penal Law § 35.15(2) (2019).

[122] See, eg, CKY Lee, 'The Act-Belief Distinction in Self-Defense Doctrine: A New Dual Requirement Theory of Justification' (1998) 2 *Buffalo Criminal Law Review* 201–02.

[123] See, eg, Allhoff (n 39) 1533.

[124] See, eg, *Nash v State*, 84 SW 497, 499 (Ark 1904); *Thompson v United States*, 155 US 271, 278–80 (1894); *Gourko v United States*, 153 US 183, 191 (1894); *Wilson v State*, 36 SW 587 (Tex Crim App 1896). See also *People v Gonzales*, 71 Cal 569, 578 (1887); *State v Evans*, 28 SW 8, 11 (Mo 1894); Clark (n 17) 178. *Cf State v Glowacki*, 630 NW2d 392, 402 (Minn 2001).

[125] 164 US 546, 557 (1896). See also *State v Bristol*, 84 P2d 757 (Wyo 1938).

[126] See ch 7(IV)(C).

[127] See ch 4(II)(C).

[128] See, eg, *Wade v State*, 724 So 2d 1007, 1010 (Miss Ct App 1998), *aff'd*, 748 So 2d 771 (Miss 1999). That said, one court has ruled that 'self-defense is not available to a defendant who deliberately puts himself in a position where he has reason to believe that his presence will provoke trouble …' *Sams v United States*, 721 A2d 945, 953 (DC 1998).

[129] See, eg, *Commonwealth v Hammond*, 953 A2d 544, 599–560 (Pa Super Ct 2008); *Matthews v State*, 58 SW 86, 90 (Tex Crim App 1900); *Kennard v State*, 28 So 858, 859–60 (Fla 1900); *Wallace*, 162 US at

of whether he struck the first physical blow, or whether the defendant merely insulted the attacker and thereby started the fight.[130] That said, a reasonable person would have had to anticipate that, taking into account any prior relations between the parties, the provocation would have been sufficiently severe to result in the attack.[131] For example, if a man was committing adultery, he could not claim self-defence if the woman's husband attacked him shortly after finding out about the affair; this even applied if defensive force was the only means of saving his life.[132]

In fact, the conduct did not have to even amount to such intentional provocation before the courts would limit a defender's right to self-defence. The fundamental rule was that a defender could not take advantage of a necessity that was in part caused by his own wrongful conduct.[133] In keeping with these holdings concerning imperfect self-defence, most states provided that if two men engage in a fight by mutual consent, then neither can claim to have acted in self-defence in killing the other if the fight escalated, unless the person completely retreated from the conflict.[134]

The state of the law was a bit hazier on the question of whether provocative or insulting *words* alone generate limits on a defender's right to self-defence. Some cases held that mere words could never limit the defender's right to self-defence.[135]

The law has not changed significantly in this area. The generally accepted view continues to be that a defender who, through his intentional acts or words reasonably calculated to lead to an 'affray' or deadly conflict, displays a willingness to enter into the conflict may not thereafter seek to cloak himself in the justification of self-defence.[136] If the provoker in good faith withdraws from or abandons the conflict and communicates this to the adversary, however, he may use self-defence

474–75; *State v Hawkins*, 23 P 475 (Or 1890), *overruled in part by State v Marsh*, 490 P2d 491 (Or 1971); *Gibson v State*, 8 So 98 (Ala 1890); *State v Cross*, 26 NW 62, 71 (Iowa 1885).

[130] See *State v Scott*, 43 NW 62 (Minn 1889); *State v Rider*, 1 SW 825 (Mo 1886).

[131] See generally *Hunter v State*, 128 SW2d 1176, 1180 (Tex Crim App 1939); *State v Dephenbaugh*, 145 SE 634, 637 (W Va 1928).

[132] See, eg, *Dabney v State*, 21 So 211, 212 (Ala 1897). See also *Drysdale v State*, 10 SE 358 (Ga 1889).

[133] See, eg, *Kennard*, 28 So at 859–60; *State v Ballou*, 40 A 861, 863 (RI 1898); *Frank v State*, 68 NW 657, 659–60 (Wis 1896); *Gaines v Commonwealth*, 14 SE 375, 377 (Va 1892); *Commonwealth v Hourigan*, 12 SW 550, 552 (Ky Ct App 1889).

[134] See, eg, *State v Kennedy*, 85 SE 42, 44 (NC 1915); *Swanner v State*, 58 SW 72, 73–74 (Tex Crim App 1900); *Jackson v Commonwealth*, 36 SE 487 (Va 1900).

[135] See, eg, *State v Doris*, 94 P 44, 53 (Or 1908). See also *Petty v State*, 216 SW 867, 868 (Tex Crim App 1919); *State v Gordon*, 89 SW 1025, 1028 (Mo 1905) (citations omitted). But see *State v Lee*, 67 SE 141 (SC 1910).

[136] See generally *State v Grott*, 2019 WL 1040681, at *3–4 (Wash Ct App March 5, 2019); *State v Sullivan*, 383 P3d 574 (2016); *Elizondo v State*, 487 SW3d 185, 196 (Tex Crim App 2016); *Smith v State*, 965 SW2d 509, 512–13 (Tex Crim App 1998); *State v Jackson*, 936 P2d 761, 767 (Kan 1997); *Commonwealth v O'Neil*, 641 NE2d 702, 705 (Mass 1997); *State v Mize*, 340 SE2d 439, 442 (NC 1986); *State v Bougneit*, 294 NW2d 675, 680 (Wis 1980); *State v Potter*, 244 SE2d 397 (NC 1978); *State v Craig*, 514 P2d 151, 156 (Wash 1973) (en banc). *Cf Lynn*, 499 SE2d at 7–8. See also PH Robinson, 'Causing the Conditions of One's Own Defense: A Study in the Limits of Theory in Criminal Law Doctrine' (1985) 71 *Virginia Law Review* 1, 9–13.

if the adversary nevertheless continues to pursue or attack him.[137] The same holds true in cases of mutual combat.[138] And if the at-fault provoker is unable to inform his adversary of his intention to withdraw, he must bear the consequences without being able to invoke self-defence.[139]

Putting this standard in a contemporary framework, US newspaper headlines drew the Nation's attention to the plight of Ahmaud Arbery, a 25-year-old black man who was being chased by white armed residents of a South Georgia neighbourhood. Gregory McMichael and his son Travis can be seen on a video confronting the unarmed Arbery. Arbery, after seeing Travis McMichael exit his white pickup truck with a shotgun, ducks to the right. McMichael, who later claims he was trying to effect a 'citizens' arrest' because he believed Arbery had trespassed on a neighbour's unoccupied construction site, is on tape wheeling around to find Arbery charging him from around the front of the truck. Arbery is moving towards McMichael when McMichael discharges his shotgun twice into Arbery at short range, killing him. Though the case as of this writing is still in the early phases of adjudication, it is not unreasonable to predict that the prosecution will contend that Georgia self-defence law authorized Arbery to try to disarm Travis McMichael because it was McMichael (not Arbery) who was the initial, unjustified aggressor.

IV. Evaluating US Self-Defence Law from a Value-Centric Perspective

US self-defence law has remained fairly static when compared to the self-defence laws of Germany[140] or England.[141] While the drafters of the MPC and various commentators have, as discussed above, argued for reforms in different areas, the caselaw has shown limited change. What is more, contrary to the perception that US self-defence law is particularly 'harsh' or intolerant of welfarist concerns, it is,

[137] See, eg, Colo Rev Stat § 18-1-704(3)(b) (2019); Tex Penal Code § 9.31(b)(4)(A) & (B) (2019). See also *Commonwealth v Fowlin*, 710 A2d 1130, 1133 (Pa 1998); *State v Lewis*, 717 A2d 1140, 1158 (Conn 1998); *Jackson*, 936 P2d at 767; *State v Stone*, 880 P2d 1296, 1298 (Mont 1994); *State v Williams*, 815 SW2d 43, 48 (Mo Ct App 1991); *Commonwealth v Samuel*, 590 A2d 1245, 1248 (Pa 1991); *Commonwealth v Naylor*, 553 NE2d 542, 543–44 (Mass 1990); *People v Beasley*, 778 P2d 304, 307 (Colo Ct App 1989); *McDonald v State*, 346 NE2d 569, 572 (Ind 1976), *overruled by Watts v State*, 885 NE2d 1228 (Ind 2008); *State v Graham*, 195 NW2d 442, 444 (Minn 1972); *Gann v State*, 383 SW2d 32, 36 (Tenn 1964).

[138] See, eg, *State v Bowers*, 2019 WL 3679665, at *7–8 (SC Ct App Aug 7, 2019); *Johnson v State*, 829 SE2d 652, 655 (Ga Ct App 2019); *State v Meyers*, 781 P2d 700, 705–06 (Kan 1989); *State v Bingman*, 745 P2d 342, 348 (Mont 1987).

[139] See, eg, *State v Williams*, 815 SW2d 43, 48 (Mo Ct App 1991); *Bellcourt v State*, 390 NW2d 269 (Minn 1986), cited in *State v Peou*, 579 NW2d 471, 477 (Minn 1998). See also *Gilbert v Commonwealth*, 506 SE2d 543, 546 (Va Ct App 1998); *People v Armstrong*, 653 NE2d 17, 18–19 (Ill App Ct 1995).

[140] See ch 5.

[141] See ch 7.

in fact, more restrictive than the laws of the other subject jurisdictions (though the means of deploying deadly force – namely, firearms – are of course more widely available).[142]

Turning to how the value-based model's approach differs from US law, the primary material difference is that the value-based model treats a reasonable mistake of fact as an excuse, rather than as justified self-defence.[143] Moreover, in contrast to US law, under the value-based model, individuals must at least attempt to avoid places where they know an attack is likely and must avoid places where they *know* an attack is likely.[144] Finally, the value-based model would make defensive force available when 'immediately necessary,' whereas US law defines imminence temporally to mean 'about to occur' (that is, US law treats imminence and necessity as separate concepts).[145] Notably, while not all US states agree with these majority positions, the research conducted here has demonstrated that changes within and among the states were not accompanied by the type of deeper discussion concerning competing values that the value-based model urges.

More central to the position we are testing, however, the review has revealed that US courts and legislators, like their English counterparts, engage only in a limited value-centric dialogue (focusing largely on protection of the defender and deterrence). And even the US scholarship on these cases in the main leaves undiscussed the value trade-offs and conflicts that are inherent in self-defence rulings, bringing to the fore concerns about hidden normativity.[146] And so while states like Florida, without any deeper discussion of the values implicated (other than passing reference to protecting defenders – value #4, deterrence – value #7, and 'punishing' attackers – which the value-based model does not recognise as a legitimate purpose of self-defence), pass 'stand your ground' laws that do not require retreat or avoidance of conflict, others treat as unlawful instances during which deadly defensive force is used even though safe retreat or avoidance are viable options.

US cases and scholarship rarely discuss what values animate US self-defence doctrine, or how shifting perspectives concerning values impact self-defence outcomes. Instead, and in the absence of a common analytical language of values, courts (presumably deploying the judge's own value system) simply hand down proclamations based, more or less, on precedent that itself devoted little or no time

[142] See generally A Punzo, 'Microstamping: Hot Lead or Dud Round' (2019) 49 *Seton Hall Law Review* 375, 406–07; L White, 'God, Guns & Money: A Global Perspective on Intentional Homicide' (2016) 44 *Western State University Law Review* 47, 51. See also K Behne, 'Packing Heat: Judicial Review of Concealed Carry Laws Under the Second Amendment' (2016) 89 *Southern California Law Review* 1343, 1346 (2016).

[143] See ch 4(I)(B).

[144] See ch 4(II)(C).

[145] Cp ch 4(II) and ch 6(III)(E) & (F).

[146] See generally CKY Lee, *Murder and the Reasonable Man: Passion and Fear in the Criminal Courtroom* (New York, New York University Press, 2003) 33–43, 65–66; AG LeFrancois, 'The Act of Judging and the Performance of Being Earnest: Responding to Professor Chemerinsky's Informalism' (2001) 54 *Oklahoma Law Review* 32.

to examining any values beyond occasionally commenting on the need to protect the autonomy of the defender (value #4). What is lost, then, is the chance to engage in open debate about which values matters when. Such a discussion, in turn, would help replace the hidden normativity characterising US court rulings and legislative enactments and causing members of the public to lose faith in the fundamental integrity, fairness, and creditworthiness of the US justice system (directly implicating value #7).[147]

It is true that many of the US outcomes in fact align with how challenging self-defence issues are resolved in Germany and England, as well as by the value-based model. But the non-transparent way in which those outcomes are achieved, the suddenness in which changes in the law can appear, and the associated hidden normativity inherently fostered by this lack of transparency provide further support for the value-centric position we are testing.

[147] See generally E Chemerinsky, 'Getting Beyond Formalism in Constitutional Law: Constitutional Theory Matters' (2001) 54 *Oklahoma Law Review* 1–7.

7

Examining the English Law's Treatment of Self-Defence from a Value-Centric Perspective

I. Putting England's Law of Self-Defence in Context

Often referred to as 'private defence' or 'necessary defence,' the right to self-defence in England is the right to defend oneself against an unjustifiable attack. The law of self-defence, moreover, is one of the general defences that can be raised by 'a person charged with [an] offence.'[1]

Turning to the burden of proof and persuasion, unlike in the US, a defendant in England need not explicitly rely on self-defence during his trial for the question to go to the jury, so long as sufficient evidence was adduced to raise a *prima facie* case of self-defence.[2] Once the defendant has adduced such sufficient evidence, the prosecution has the burden of disproving self-defence beyond a reasonable doubt.[3]

The law of self-defence in England is now clarified in section 76 of the Criminal Justice and Immigration Act of 2008 ('2008 Act').[4] Specifically, the

[1] See Criminal Justice and Immigration Act 2008, § 76(1)(A). See also *R v Renouf* [1986] 1 WLR 522 (CA); J Herring, *Criminal Law* (Palgrave, 2018) 616.

[2] See *R v Robinson* [2017] EWCA Crim 923; *R v O'Brien* [2004] EWCA Crim 2900; *DPP v Bailey* [1995] 16 Cr App R 257. See also D Ormerod and K Laird, *Smith, Hogan, and Ormerod's Criminal Law* 15th edn (Oxford, Oxford University Press, 2018) 380.

[3] See *R v Robinson* [2017] EWCA Crim 923; *R v Martin* [2001] EWCA Crim 2245; *Beckford v The Queen* [1988] AC 130, at 144 (PC); *R v Wheeler* [1968] 52 Cr App R 28, 30 (CA); *R v Lobell* [1957] 1 QB 547. See also J Richardson, *Archbold: Criminal Pleading Evidence & Practice* 67th edn (London, Sweet & Maxwell, 2019) 1568; A Reed, 'Self-Defence – Applying the Objective Approach to Reasonable Force' (1996) 60 *Journal of Criminal Law* 94, 98; WO Russell, *A Treatise on Crimes and Indictable Misdemeanours* 2nd edn (Charleston, Gale, 2010/1826) 684.

[4] See generally *R v Cheeseman* [2019] EWCA Crim 149; *R v Keane* [2010] EWCA Crim 2514; *R v McGrath* [2010] EWCA Crim 2514 (CA); Ormerod and Laird (n 2) 380; Herring (n 1) 616; T Rönnau and K Hohn, '§ 32 Notwehr' in G Cirener et al (eds), *Strafgesetzbuch: Leipziger Kommentar, Band 3* (Berlin, De Gruyter, 2019) side-note 14. Note that *defence of property* is covered in the Criminal Damage Act of 1971 and arrest and the *prevention of crime* is discussed in § 3 of the Criminal Law Act of 1967, to be read in light of § 76. While similar – and apt to be overlapping, depending on the facts of the case – these are technically different defences. See generally *R v Hitchens* [2011] EWCA Crim 1626 (ruling that self-defence and the defence of using reasonable force in the prevention of crime under the Criminal Law Act 1967, § 3 were capable of extending to the use of force against an innocent third party

Legal Aid, Sentencing and Punishment of Offenders Act of 2012 inserted the new section 76(6)(A) into the 2008 Act to explain, for example, that there is no duty to retreat (though, as discussed below, an opportunity to retreat may still be taken into account in determining whether defensive force was justified).[5]

Controversially, the Crime and Courts Act 2013 further amended section 76 to allow homeowners to use disproportionate force up to, but not including, that which is 'grossly disproportionate.'[6] The amended section 76 also confirmed the common law's contentious subjective standard as to justificatory circumstances, which provides that reasonable force can be justified on the basis of an honest, but mistaken and potentially unreasonable, belief.[7]

Turning back to the 'mechanics' of England's self-defence law, *justifiable* homicides were historically distinguished from *excusable* homicides. The former pertained strictly to cases in which the homicide was necessary, and the defender was faultless. Excusable homicides, in contrast, were divided into two categories: Homicide *per infortunium*, (where the defender did a lawful act without intention to hurt anyone, but through unfortunate chance killed another), and homicide *se defendendo* upon a 'chance medley' or sudden quarrel (where the defender was not 'altogether faultless').[8] Because of this bifurcation, eighteenth- and nineteenth-century textbooks tended to classify 'self-defence' during a sudden affray as an excuse, and described as 'justifiable homicides' situations that now would be considered permissible uses of defensive force.[9] Today, in contrast, the term 'self defence' in England encompasses *both* homicide *se defendendo* and justifiable homicide. Finally, the contemporary English approach tracks that of the value-based model[10] (and Germany and the US), in that self-defence is grounded on the notion that a justified forceful response is to be considered right and proper (not merely excused).[11]

to prevent a crime being committed by someone else); *R v Hayes* [2011] EWCA Crim 2680 (describing this area as 'notoriously difficult').

[5] See Criminal Justice and Immigration Act 2008, § 76(8). See also Ormerod and Laird (n 2) 384. Note, however, that § 76 of the Criminal Justice and Immigration Act of 2008, while not common law, functions to 'clarify the operation of the existing defences.' See generally DJ Baker, *Textbook of Criminal Law* 4th edn (Oxford, Oxford University Press, 2015) 906; *R v Cheeseman* [2019] EWCA Crim 149.

[6] See Criminal Justice and Immigration Act 2008, §§ 76(5)(A) & (6). See also *R v Ray* [2017] EWCA Crim 1391; *R (Collins) v Secretary of State for Justice* [2016] EWHC 33 (Admin), discussed in M Thomas, 'Defenceless Castles: The Use of Grossly Disproportionate Force by Householders in Light of *R (Collins) v. Secretary of State for Justice*' (2016) 80 *Journal of Criminal Law* 407, 407–27; C Wang, 'The Police Are Innocent as Long as They Honestly Believe: The Human Rights Problems with English Self-Defense Law' (2017) 49 *Columbia Human Rights Law Review* 373.

[7] Criminal Justice and Immigration Act 2008, § 76(3). See also *R v Cheeseman* [2019] EWCA Crim 149; *R v Ray* [2017] EWCA Crim 1391.

[8] See Russell (n 3) 511–15; AM Wilshere, *Principles and Practice of the Criminal Law* (Hardpress Publishing, 1936) 205; SF Harris, *Principles of the Criminal Law* (1877) 147–53; EH East, *A Treatise of the Pleas of the Crown* (Charleston, Nabu Press, 2011/1803) 219–22; Hawk PC 108–15.

[9] See, eg, Russell (n 3) 543–52.

[10] See ch 4(I).

[11] See generally J Slater, 'Making Sense of Self-Defence' (1996) 5 *Nottingham Law Journal* 140, 154–57.

With regard to the position we are testing, and as observed in the prior chapter's discussion concerning US law, the examination that will follow reveals that England's law of self-defence developed with little discussion of the values providing its rationale. Because explicit debate concerning the spectrum of values acting as decision-grounds very rarely helped anchor the debate, English scholars, judges, and legislators, unlike their German counterparts, as a general matter lack a common analytical language to help them resolve important jurisprudential matters of value, moral principles, and fundamental human rights. This, in turn, impedes their ability to reach self-defence decisions in a fully democratic, incremental, and policy-based manner. It, moreover, makes it more challenging for them to identify and narrow areas of dispute.

The survey that follows helps illustrate why and how the law of self-defence in England has tended to follow a more haphazard and unpredictable path. This is perhaps most prominently true when it comes to the important topic of subjective, but mistaken, beliefs justifying the exercise of self-preferential force. Because the position taken here is that much of the unpredictability and related hidden normativity characterising England's self-defence law can be traced to the absence of a value-centric approach, the analysis that follows lends further support to the position we are testing.

II. Subjective or Objective Standard as to the Justificatory Circumstances?

A. Mistakes of Fact

A central, vexing question confronting any self-defence regime is whether the necessity of the conduct should be evaluated based on the defender's *subjective* perception of the facts, or whether it, instead, should be left to the fact-finder to evaluate the lawfulness of the putatively defensive conduct on the basis of how the hypothetical 'reasonable person' would have (*objectively*) perceived the situation. This book addresses this issue at the outset because England's answer to this question is, as noted immediately above, unique, diverging markedly from the value-based model,[12] as well as the German[13] and US[14] approaches. The English approach to necessity, indeed, stands as perhaps the most dramatic and controversial departure from what can be considered the 'mainstream' of contemporary self-defence law.[15] It also illustrates some of the pitfalls encountered when

[12] See ch 4(I).
[13] See ch 5(III).
[14] See ch 6(II).
[15] See generally Wang (n 6) 375 (characterising England's subjective approach as resulting in 'unfair verdicts' and 'blatant violation[s]' of Art 2 of the ECHR).

self-defence regimes are not explicitly grounded on guiding values or principles that inform the law's development.

Defendants not infrequently are mistaken in their belief that they are being threatened. The court in *R v Weston* in 1879 held that justifiable self-defence applied if the defendant used deadly force 'against serious violence or in the *reasonable* dread of it.'[16] In the 1884 case of *R v Rose*, moreover, the defendant shot and killed his violent father after concluding that his father was about to slash his mother's throat with a knife.[17] In fact, there was no evidence that his father had a knife in his hand. The defendant was nevertheless acquitted because 'at the time he fired that shot he honestly believed, and had *reasonable grounds* for the belief, that his mother's life was in imminent peril, and that the fatal shot which he fired was absolutely necessary for the preservation of her life.'[18]

The view that a mistake as to the justifying circumstances had to be reasonable was therefore well-established in the English law by the late nineteenth century. And, indeed, there was little reason to believe this position would not continue to be the law of the land throughout the twentieth century.

In 1984, however, the Court of Appeal made what can only be described as a remarkable about-turn in the landmark case of *Williams (Gladstone)*[19] by rejecting both the holdings in *Albert v Lavin*[20] and the prior string of like decisions. The Court held that the common law is, *and has always been*, that a defendant relying on private defence is to be judged solely on his honest belief as to the necessity of the force, whether or not his belief was reasonable.

In light of our preceding historical discussion, it is not unfair to say that *Williams* represents law reform from the bench. The Court was either unaware of, or ignored, the English common law's earlier pronouncements that the reasonableness of defensive force was to be judged objectively. The Court's approach also treats unreasonable mistakes as positively lawful exceptions to the offence description, thereby ignoring the distinction between offences and defences noted by Lord Simon in *Morgan*[21] and discussed in Chapter 4(I). This position, furthermore,

[16] *R v Weston* [1879] 14 Cox CC 346, 351 (emphasis added). See also *Dakin's Case* [1828] 168 ER 999, 999–1000 (instructing the jury to acquit if the defendant 'used no more violence than was necessary to defend himself from the attack made upon him').

[17] [1884] 15 Cox CC 540.

[18] Ibid at 541 (emphasis added).

[19] *R v Williams (Gladstone)* [1987] 3 All ER 411 (CA).

[20] [1981] 1 All ER 628, 637 (QB).

[21] Although a defendant's subjective beliefs as to the circumstances making the defensive force necessary were therefore historically of little moment, the House of Lords in *DPP v Morgan*, [1975] 2 All ER 347 (HL), nevertheless held that a mistaken belief as to a victim's consent to intercourse shielded the defendant from criminal liability because the belief, however unreasonable, made the defendant unable to possess the *mens rea* required for him to be found guilty of the offence. *Morgan's ratio decidendi* seemingly applied to all forms of criminal liability. But the case ultimately had less impact than expected. What is more, in the context of self-defence, *Morgan* is by its own terms entirely inapplicable, because the Lords drew a distinction between the *mens rea* required for the basic elements of an offence, and that required for a defence. See ibid at 366 ('[I]t is clear law that, in order to establish a defence [of self-defence], [the actor's] belief must be based on reasonable grounds.') The *Morgan*

does not take into account the incompatibility thesis (also known as the 'paradox of unknown justifications') discussed in Chapter 4(I)(B), which permits mutually justified attacks.

In short, while the English law for many decades rejected the notion that a defender's actions should be evaluated based on her subjective (rather than objectively reasonable) beliefs, on the basis of *R v Williams (Gladstone)*,[22] *Beckford v The Queen*,[23] *R v Wilson*,[24] and *R v Morris*,[25] such defendants would today be entitled to be judged on the facts as they honestly believed them to be.[26] This common law approach was clarified in sections 76(3) and (4) of the 2008 Act, both as to (1) the threat and (2) the appropriateness of the amount of defensive force. Under consistent English caselaw, however, the type of mistake of fact that negates the requisite *mens rea* as to an element of the charged crime is governed by the law of mistakes, rather than by the law of self-defence.[27]

A defender's *personal* characteristics, moreover, are admissible only insofar as they bear on her ability to be aware of, or to perceive, the circumstances.[28] Similarly, a defender's *physical* characteristics may also be admissible; for example, what might appear threatening to a frail elderly man may not appear threatening to a young athlete.[29] The only relatively minor caveat to this modern subjective

decision, like the principle-based model, therefore emphasised the distinction between offences and defences. The defendant in *Morgan* consequently could rely on his subjective belief in the lawfulness of his conduct as a means to avoid being found guilty of rape because he did not possess the requisite *mens rea* for a conviction (ie, he did not intend to use force against the victim without her consent, which is part of the offence definition of rape). Ibid at 361. Whether a person acted in self-defence however, was, as the Lords quite properly pointed out, always an objective question (though, as we shall discuss, this view was soon to be abandoned).

[22] [1984] 78 Cr App R 276, discussed in *R v Faraj* [2007] EWCA Crim 1033.

[23] [1988] AC 130 (PC). See also *R v Martin* [2001] EWCA Crim 2245.

[24] [2006] EWCA Crim 1880.

[25] [2014] 1 WLR 16.

[26] See generally *R v Robinson* [2017] EWCA Crim 923; *R v Faraj* [2007] EWCA Crim 1033; *R v Ibrahim* [2014] EWCA Crim 121; *R (Bennett) v Coroner* [2007] EWCA Civ 617. See also Ormerod and Laird (n 2) 383; Herring (n 1) 716; G Lamond, 'Core Principles of English Criminal Law' in M Dyson and B Vogel (eds), *The Limits of Criminal Law: Anglo-German Concepts and Principles* (Cambridge, Intersentia, 2018) 26–28. This subjectivism can be criticised because (1) it puts the public at greater risk (since it provides for a full acquittal of an individual who may be predisposed to unreasonably assume that he needs to use force), and (2) allowing for an acquittal on the basis of an unreasonable belief violates Art 2 of the ECHR (the latter issue is discussed in ch 4(IV)(B)–(E)). Note also that a defendant is not entitled to rely on a mistaken belief induced by the effects of self-induced inebriation. See generally *R v Goode* [2014] EWCA Crim 90. Insane delusions, likewise, cannot set the standards of reasonableness as to the degree of force used. See *R v Oye* [2013] EWCA Crim 1725 (ruling that it makes 'little sense to talk of the reasonable lunatic'); *R v Canns* [2005] EWCA Crim 2264 (rejecting argument that jury should have been directed to consider the defendant's delusional state).

[27] See generally *R v Faraj* [2007] EWCA 1033; *Beckford v The Queen* [1988] AC 130, 144 (PC). See also *DPP v Morgan* [1975] 2 All ER 347 (HL); Ormerod and Laird (n 2) 332–40; Herring (n 1) 678–84; Lamond (n 26) 26–28. For a discussion of how such a reasonable mistake of fact is treated under the value-based model, see ch 2(IV)(F)(v)(e) (discussing the fourth state of condemnation, namely, when the fact-finder finds the defendant to have violated the offence definition).

[28] See Ormerod and Laird (n 2) 384.

[29] See *R v Martin (Anthony)* [2001] EWCA Crim 2245; Ormerod and Laird (n 2) 385.

rule is that an honest mistake resulting from voluntary intoxication will not excuse the objectively unnecessary use of force in self-defence.[30] Today, section 76 of the 2008 Act has also clarified this subjective common law trend.[31]

B. Unknowingly Justified Defenders

Another fundamental question concerning the scope of England's self-defence law is whether an actor should be able to rely on unknown facts to convert an otherwise illegal act into an act of self-defence.

i. *The* 'Dadson *Principle*'

Under the value-based model, an actor unaware of the justificatory circumstances would not be able to claim self-defence because he lacked internal justification.[32] To determine whether Andrew is able to avail himself of self-defence to avoid a conviction under English law, one must first turn to the much-debated 1850 case of *R v Dadson*.[33] In *Dadson*, the defendant was a constable assigned to watch a copse from which wood had previously been repeatedly stolen. While performing this task one night, the constable saw a person coming from the copse carrying wood in his arms. The constable called out, but the fleeing thief refused to stop. Because the constable had no other way of apprehending the thief, he shot him in the leg. While the shooting of a fleeing felon was legally permissible at the time of the incident, stealing wood, without more, did not constitute a felony. The prosecution argued that the constable was not justified in discharging his weapon at the thief because he did not know whether or not the fleeing thief was committing a felony.[34]

The thief had in fact previously been convicted of stealing wood, however, therefore making this particular instance of wood theft a felony. While shooting a fleeing felon was not a criminal offence, the constable was unaware of the thief's previous convictions at the time he shot him, and thus did not have any reason to think he was shooting a felon. The question before the Court of Appeal, therefore, was whether the constable could claim his conduct justified even though the underlying facts giving rise to the defence were unknown to him at the time.[35]

In affirming the constable's conviction, the Court held tersely that '[t]he [fleeing thief] not having committed a felony known to the [constable] at the

[30] See Criminal Justice and Immigration Act 2008, § 76(5). See also *R v Taj* [2018] EWCA Crim 1743; *R v Coley* [2013] EWCA Crim 223; *R v O'Grady* [1987] QB 995; J Horder, *Ashworth's Principles of Criminal Law* 8th edn (Oxford, Oxford University Press, 2016) 142.

[31] See generally Ormerod and Laird (n 2) 380.

[32] See ch 4(I)(B).

[33] [1850] 4 Cox CC 358.

[34] Ibid.

[35] Ibid.

time when he fired, the latter was not justified in firing at the [thief]; and having no justifiable cause, he was guilty of shooting at the [thief] with intent to do him grievous bodily harm, and the conviction is right.'[36] The English law has, therefore, required defensive intention (that is, the defendant must be aware of,[37] and in fact act because of,[38] the justificatory circumstances) before a successful plea of self-defence or justifiable homicide could be made out. In this regard, the English law is in agreement with the value-based model's requirement of both external and internal justification before a claim of legal justification can be successful.[39]

ii. Defending the Logic of Dadson

Dadson distinguished between the offence charged and the defendant's defence, ruling that knowledge of the justificatory circumstances was required before the constable's shooting of the thief could be found to be justified. Treating defences as distinct from offences is indeed the rule, rather than the exception, in the English law.[40] If the *Dadson* Court had not applied this distinction, then the defendant's unlawfulness would have been a circumstance that was part of the *actus reus* necessary for liability to exist, and he would have been acquitted. The *Dadson* holding, however, supports the position that the term 'unlawful' describes conduct that satisfies both the *actus reus* and *mens rea* requirements of a particular offence under circumstances where the defendant has no defence. This requirement that, for a defendant to successfully claim self-defence, the defendant must be aware of, and in fact act because of, the justificatory circumstances,[41] is in keeping with the

[36] Ibid. See also Lamond (n 26) 26; A Brudner, 'Constitutionalizing Self-Defense' (2011) 61 *University of Toronto Law Journal* 867, 876.

[37] See B Hogan, 'The *Dadson* Principle' [1989] *Crim LR* 679. See also East (n 8) 273 (contending that a defendant claiming self-defence must show that he either honestly, or honestly and reasonably, believed his use of force to be necessary to avert an imminent attack); *R v Rose* [1884] 15 Cox CC 540, 541–42.

[38] A Brudner, 'Agency and Welfare in the Penal Law' in S Shute et al (eds), *Action and Value in Criminal Law* (Oxford, Oxford University Press, 1996) 12 ('[A]ny defendant who is to benefit from a justification must act for the reason that the justificatory facts obtain, but need not act for the reason that they count as justificatory, which is an ex post matter for the judge.'); Baker (n 5) 914–15.

[39] See ch 4(I)(B).

[40] See generally *R v Knock* [1877] 14 Cox CC 1 (discussing *prima facie* case of unlawful killing and then going on to discuss whether self-defence applies); G Williams, 'The Logic of "Exceptions"' (1988) 47 *CLJ* 261, 269.

[41] See *R v Cheeseman* [2019] EWCR Crim 149 (finding that the defendant, at the point he used purportedly defensive force, lacked a genuine belief that the victim was, in fact, a trespasser); *R v Taj* [2018] EWCA Crim 1743 (ruling that self-defence is 'available even if the defendant is mistaken as to the circumstances as he genuinely believed them to be whether or not the mistake was a reasonable one for him to have made'); *R v Riddell* [2017] EWCA Crim 413 (ruling that self-defence requires an honestly perceived risk of immediate harm); *R v Yaman* [2012] EWCA Crim 1075. See also *Beckford v R* [1987] 3 All ER 425 (PC); *R v Williams (Gladstone)* [1987] 3 All ER 411 (CA); Criminal Justice and Immigration Act 2008, §§ 76(3) & (4) (focusing on the defendant's subjective belief as to the facts); Ormerod and Laird (n 2) 403, citing TM Funk, 'Justifying Justifications' (1999) 19 *OJLS* 631.

value-based model's resolution of this issue.[42] Moreover, it (1) does not create a rule under which unknowingly justified actors could benefit from their fortuitous justification, and (2) avoids the paradox of unknown justifications.[43]

III. The Attack

A. What Can Be Defended?

i. The General Rule

English law has always authorised the use of deadly force in defence of one's life and to prevent serious bodily harm.[44] The English law, however, has, with the narrow caveat discussed immediately below, traditionally rejected deadly force in defence of property. In so doing, it has (implicitly) favoured the principle of protecting the attacker (that is, value #1 – reducing overall societal violence, value #2 – protecting the individual attacker, and value #5 – primacy of the legal process).[45]

ii. The Exception to the General Rule

Homeowners are permitted the use of deadly force in self-defence if they can show that they were in fear of death at the hands of the burglar. But deadly force *purely* in defence of property is not, and has not been, part of the law of England.[46]

B. Need the Attacker's Conduct Be Criminal?

As noted above, section 3(1) of the Criminal Law Act 1967 provides that 'a person may use such force as is reasonable in the circumstances in the prevention of crime ….' Section 3 by its express terms, however, only applies to cases of crime prevention. It is, therefore, necessary to turn to the common law to discover whether attacks had to be criminal before defensive force may be used. The case of *R v Hitchens* is one of many examples demonstrating that, under the common law, self-defence can be deployed against innocent individuals, such as sleepwalkers or a child, not threatening a crime, provided that the threat they pose is 'unjust' (in the sense of not legally justified).[47]

[42] See ch 4(I)(B).
[43] See ibid.
[44] See, eg, *R v Smith* [1837] 171 ER 441, 442–43.
[45] See ch 2(IV)(A), (B), & (E).
[46] See generally Horder (n 30) 134–35, 139–40.
[47] [2011] EWCA Crim 1626, discussed in Herring (n 1) 622–32.

C. Special Rules for 'Attacks' by the Police?

Under English law – like the value-based model[48] – there exists a right of private defence against the police when, for example, an officer performs an illegal arrest.[49] This is so because, under these circumstances, the officer is not objectively acting in the execution of his duty.[50]

In the 2018 *Oraki* case, the defendant was convicted of obstructing a police officer in the execution of his duty.[51] The defendant believed the officer was assaulting his mother and, therefore, intervened. As relevant here, the court ruled that the defence of self-defence (or defence of another) is, as a matter of law, available to the charge of obstructing a constable in the execution of her duty under section 89(2) of the Police Act 1996 – that is, a defender may resist a police officer's unlawful restraint.[52] This holding was reaffirmed in the subsequent *Wheeldon* case, which similarly noted that there was no rule establishing that the defence of self-defence was unavailable to a person who assaulted a police officer.[53]

On the other hand, police officers seeking to use self-defence are, like English citizens more generally, permitted to use deadly force if they honestly believe it is necessary (even if that honest belief turns out to be entirely mistaken).[54] In *Sharman*, for example, the police received a tip that a man was carrying a sawed-off shotgun wrapped in a plastic bag.[55] In fact, however, the man was carrying a table leg. The two officers who confronted him shot and killed him even though he 'was entitled to be where he was and was doing absolutely nothing wrong.' Nevertheless, because the jury concluded that the officers honestly believed the force was necessary, they were acquitted.[56]

D. Can Passive Conduct Constitute an 'Attack'?

English law has relatively consistently provided that passive conduct can in fact constitute an 'attack.' And so in the case of the shipwrecked defendant who finds himself holding onto the same plank as another shipwreck survivor, if the defendant reasonably determines that the plank will not support them both, then the law

[48] See ch 4(V)(B).
[49] See generally Baker (n 5) 926. See also The Police and Criminal Evidence Act of 1984 ('PACE'), § 24A.
[50] B Sangero, *Self-Defence in Criminal Law* (Oxford, Hart Publishing, 2006) 134.
[51] *Oraki v DPP* [2018] EWHC 115 (Admin).
[52] Ibid.
[53] *Wheeldon v CPS* [2018] EWHC 249 (Admin).
[54] See generally Wang (n 6) 393–94.
[55] *Sharman v Coroner* [2005] EWHC 857 (Admin).
[56] Ibid, discussed in Wang (n 6) 393–94.

should permit the defendant to thrust the other person off the plank leading to his certain death.[57]

In the famous 1884 case of *Dudley and Stephens*, however, the three defendants were neither justified nor excused for killing and consuming a cabin boy who was stranded with them in a lifeboat for 18 days after their ship sank.[58] There is, however, a distinction between *Dudley and Stephens* and the plank case. In the plank case, and assuming the first survivor sees the other survivor swimming over, the other survivor's presence on the plank will cause a direct threat to the defender (that is, the other shipwreck survivor is most directly threatening to adversely impact the plank-holder's autonomy (value #4)).[59] The cabin boy, in contrast, did not pose such a threat but rather was 'sacrificed' in order to feed his fellow crewmen.

Today the English law on passive threats is more nuanced, although its precise contours are still somewhat uncertain. The inquest into the deaths caused by the sinking of the ill-fated ferry, The Herald of Free Enterprise, near Zeebrugge, Belgium, serves to illustrate the probable present state of the law as it relates to innocent passive attacks.[60] In that case, a number of individuals were in danger of drowning in the freezing water. Although there was a rope ladder that led to safety, the passage up the ladder was blocked by a young man who, either because of the cold or because of fear, was unable to move. Even after being shouted at for 10 minutes by a corporal the man did not budge. The corporal finally instructed another to push the man off of the ladder and into the water, and the man was never seen again.[61]

As noted in *Dudley and Stephens*, the three defendants killed the cabin boy solely to save their own lives; he did not pose any direct threat to them, and his killing instead merely served an instrumental purpose. The unfortunate man on the escape ladder, in contrast, by his own immobility put himself in a position where he posed a direct threat to those who were trying to escape from the freezing water. While he may not have intended to harm anyone, his continued presence on the ladder did in fact pose a direct threat of death or serious bodily harm to those in the water. Under the value-based model, the man's conduct (or, rather, lack thereof) resulted in a *forfeiture* (as opposed to *waiver*) of his right to non-interference. For it created a gap in his otherwise inviolable personal domain when he, for no objectively good reason, became a direct (though passive) threat to the others; that gap remained open as long as he remained a threat.[62] Pushing him off the ladder was therefore justified, whereas the killing of the cabin boy was not. Defensive force likely continues to be justified against a passive (and perhaps entirely innocent) 'attacker' posing a threat.

[57] See 4 Bl Comm 185. See also M Bacon, *A New Abridgement of the Law* (1832) 776.

[58] [1884] 14 QB 273. See also *R v Howe and Bannister* [1987] AC 417, 453 (HL).

[59] See ch 2(IV)(D).

[60] See generally *R v HM Coroner for East Kent ex p Spooner* [1987] 88 Cr App R 10; *R v P&O European Ferries (Dover) Ltd.* [1990] 93 Cr App R 72, discussed in JC Smith, *Justification and Excuse in the Criminal Law* (London, Sweet & Maxwell, 1989) 73.

[61] See *HM Coroner*, 88 Cr App R 10.

[62] See ch 2(V)(B).

In 2001, the Court of Appeals grappled with the difficult case of conjoined twins who both would have died within months if not separated at the abdomen.[63] The Court ruled that the medically determined weaker twin was still capable of independent breathing and thus was a human being vested with rights. As a result, she fell within the protection of the law of homicide and the operation to separate the twins (which would kill the weaker one) constituted the conduct element of murder with regard to the weaker twin, barring some legal justification for the homicide. The Court, however, held that, under these circumstances, the operation was in fact justified.[64]

Notably, however, the ruling was based on three entirely different lines of reasoning. Lord Justice Alan Ward based his ruling on self-defence and said that the case at bottom was about self-defence (or, rather, defence of others) because the doctors would come

> to Jodie's defence and remov[e] the threat of fatal harm to her presented by [conjoined sister] Mary's draining her life-blood. The availability of such a plea of quasi self-defence, modified to meet the quite exceptional circumstances nature has inflicted on the twins, makes intervention by the doctors lawful.[65]

In contrast, Lord Justice Brooke relied upon *R v Dudley and Stephens* and invoked necessity as a defence.[66] Finally, Lord Justice Robert Walker focused upon the intention of the surgeons – and lack of *mens rea* – in concluding that surgery could proceed.[67]

E. Imminence

Courts and commentators in England have traditionally required self-defensive force to be in response to an 'imminent' threat. The imminence requirement has received little attention in the English common law, however, and most cases and commentary do little more than simply make a passing reference to it. Further, those discussions about imminence that have occurred make no reference to the interplay between the multiple values that, as contended above at Chapter 4(II)(B), are implicated.

i. *The General Rule*

Imminence (or 'immediacy') of the threatened attack, as well as the imminence of the necessity to use force to avoid a future attack, are part of the calculation of whether defensive force was necessary, rather than constituting an

[63] *Re A (Conjoined Twins: Surgical Separation)* [2001] 2 WLR 480.
[64] Ibid.
[65] Ibid.
[66] Ibid.
[67] Ibid.

independent rule.[68] That said, while a defender arguing self-defence can only rely on a threat of (or believed) imminent attack, if she seeks to invoke the defence of loss of control she need only establish that she relied on fear of future non-imminent attack and believed herself at risk of serious violence (including sexual violence).[69] And while self-defence is a defence against all charges, loss of control is available only on a charge of murder and can at best result in a verdict of manslaughter.

ii. Subjective or Objective Evaluation of Imminence

As already discussed, under English law the defender customarily had to have an honest belief that the attack was imminent, and his belief, furthermore, had to be based on objectively reasonable grounds.[70] The question of whether a given threat is imminent, however, is part of the larger question of whether the defensive force is 'necessary' or 'reasonable under the circumstances.'[71] Therefore, it follows that the English law surely must judge imminence on the basis of the same subjective standard. This supposition was confirmed by the Privy Council's decision in *Beckford v The Queen*, where the court held:

> There are two separate matters: (i) the defendant's belief as to the circumstances; and (ii) the degree of force which the defendant is entitled to use. Reasonableness plays no part as to (i) but only as to (ii). If a defendant took steps for his own protection *genuinely believing* that he was in imminent danger, that belief does not have to be reasonable for him to have been acting in self-defence. A genuine belief, however unreasonable, entitles a defendant to be acquitted on the ground of self-defence.[72]

iii. English Law's Treatment of Battered Intimate Partner Syndrome

Those seeking to rely on the battered intimate partner syndrome have in the past received little assistance from England's common law. Under English law, battered partners have, as noted, typically fallen short in their self-defence claims because they were found to have failed to meet the 'immediacy' requirement or the

[68] See generally Baker (n 5) 895. See also Criminal Justice and Immigration Act 2008, § 76(7) (fact-finders in self-defence cases are to consider that 'evidence of a person's having only done what the person honestly and instinctively thought was *necessary* for a legitimate purpose constitutes strong evidence that only reasonable action was taken by that person for that purpose') (emphasis added).

[69] See generally Criminal Law Policy Unit, Ministry of Justice, *Partial Defences to Murder: Loss of Control and Diminished Responsibility; and Infanticide: Implementation of Sections 52, and 54 to 57 of the Coroners and Justice Act 2009*, 2010, Circular 2010/13 (UK), www.justice.gov.uk/downloads/legislation/bills-acts/circulars/moj/2010/circular-12-2010-coroners-justice-act-homicide-provisions.pdf, para 25.

[70] See *Albert v Lavin* [1981] 1 All ER 628, 633 (QB); *R v Fennell* [1971] 1 QB 428, 431; *Owens v HM Advocate* [1946] SC(J) 119, 125; *R v Rose* [1884] 15 Cox CC 540.

[71] See generally *R v Whyte* [1987] 3 All ER 416 (CCA).

[72] [1988] AC 130, 133 (PC) (emphasis added). See also Criminal Justice and Immigration Act 2008, § 76(7).

objective 'reasonable man' standard of self-defences.[73] The standard objection is that women who kill a sleeping or otherwise temporarily defenceless man were not employing force necessary to resist actual or imminent violence, given a 'reasonable person' would have left the house, sought police protection, or taken other steps short of using lethal force (such logic, as discussed at Chapter 4(V)(A)(vi), implicitly places significant weight on value #1 – reducing violence and maintaining the state's collective monopoly on force, value #2 – protecting the attacker, and value #5 – ensuring the primacy of the legal process).[74]

In England, then, the focus has been on the battered woman's purported 'mental abnormality' or 'impairment,' rather than on treating the battered woman syndrome as a normal state of thinking, given the underlying mistreatment.[75] As a consequence, England has not joined the growing number of jurisdictions that allow expert testimony of battered woman syndrome to support establishing the state of mind of battered women accused of killing their abusers.[76] Instead, cases in which the evidence establishes that the husbands engaged in extreme and/or prolonged mistreatment, and the women felt that killing their tormentor was the only 'way out,' typically result in the female defendants successfully claiming provocation or diminished responsibility.[77]

In *R v Ahluwalia*,[78] for example, the battered wife created napalm and set fire to the bed of her husband after he had gone to sleep (the man on the night of the attack allegedly burned her with a hot iron and attempted to break her ankles). The man suffered severe burns over 40% of his body and died 10 days later in the hospital.

Accusing him of domestic violence and marital rape, she claimed provocation. The judge directed the jury to consider whether, if she did lose her self-control, a reasonable person having the characteristics of a well-educated married

[73] See generally Law Commission, *Partial Defences to Murder Final Report*, Law Com No 290 (UK), paras 4.20–21 [hereinafter Law Commission, *Final Report*]; H Kennedy, *Eve Was Framed: Women and British Justice* (London, Vintage Publishing, 1992) 199–200, 211–12 (discussing difficulty battered women have in meeting 'immediacy' requirement of provocation and 'reasonable' standard of self-defence). See also *R v Ahluwalia* [1992] 4 All ER 889, 893–94 (CA) (illustrating failure of defence of provocation at trial court level); *R v Thornton* [1992] 1 All ER 306, 315–16 (CA 1991) (rejecting defence of provocation where stabbing not result of sudden loss of self-control); *R v Duffy* [1949] 1 All ER 932, 932–33 (CA) (denying battered woman use of provocation defence).

[74] Law Commission, *Final Report* (n 73) para 4.21. See also ch 2(IV)(A), (B), & (E).

[75] See S Yeo, 'Battered Woman Syndrome in Australia' (1993) 143 *New Law Journal* 13. Whether the provocative acts or words and the defendant's response met the 'ordinary person' standard prescribed by the statute is the question the jury must consider, not the more open-textured questions of whether, having regard to all the circumstances, the jury considers the loss of self-control sufficiently excusable. The statute, after all, does not leave each jury free to set whatever standard it considers appropriate in the circumstances by which to judge whether the defendant's conduct is 'excusable.'

[76] See generally *R v Ahluwalia* [1992] 4 All ER 889 (CA) (recognising the syndrome in 1992). See also AL Wannop, 'Battered Woman Syndrome and the Defense of Battered Women in Canada and England' (1995) 19 *Suffolk Transnational Law Review* 251.

[77] *R v Ahluwalia* [1992] 4 All ER 889 (CA) (the Court of Appeal ordered a retrial on the basis that the new evidence showed an arguable case of diminished responsibility in English law).

[78] Ibid.

Asian woman living in England (the judge omitted suffering from battered woman syndrome) would have likewise lost her self-control given her husband's provocation.[79] The jury found in favour of the government.[80]

In the 2003 case of *R v Charlton*,[81] following threats of sexual and violent abuse against herself and her daughter, the battered spouse killed her obsessive and controlling partner while he was restrained by handcuffs, blindfolded and gagged as part of what was described as their regular sexual activity. The term of five years' imprisonment was reduced to three and a half years because of the threats made by a man determined to dominate and control the defendant's life. The Court found that the threats created a genuine fear for the safety of herself and her daughter, and this caused the defendant to lose control and commit the murder.[82]

As detailed below, by passing section 54 of the Coroners and Justice Act 2009, Parliament abolished the common law defence of provocation and replaced it with the partial defence to murder – 'loss of control.'[83] This partial defence (reducing the conviction from murder to manslaughter) eases the burden on spouses seeking to argue they suffered from battered spouse syndrome. It is available if the defender commits the killing after losing self-control as the result of a 'qualifying trigger,' provided a person of the same sex, age, and with a normal amount of tolerance and self-restraint operating under like circumstances 'might have reacted in the same or in a similar way ....'[84] The loss of control, moreover, need not be 'sudden.'[85] On the other hand, the force used must not be the result of a 'considered desire for revenge.'[86]

The burden is on the prosecution to prove beyond a reasonable doubt that the defence is not satisfied once the defendant adduces sufficient evidence to reasonably raise the issue.[87] A battered spouse will, as a practical matter, therefore be in a much-improved position to successfully raise this partial 'loss of control' defence.

In addition, using coercive or controlling behaviour towards an intimate partner or family member became a criminal offence under section 76(1) of the Serious Crime Act 2015.[88] While in the past the imminence requirement prevented an

[79] Note that, since the passage of the Coroners and Justice Act 2009, the defence of provocation – used in a number of the aforementioned cases – has been replaced with 'loss of control.'

[80] *R v Ahluwalia* [1992] 4 All ER 889 (CA).

[81] [2003] EWCA Crim 415.

[82] Ibid.

[83] Coroners and Justice Act 2009, § 54.

[84] Ibid at § 54(1).

[85] Ibid at § 54(2).

[86] Ibid at § 54(4).

[87] Ibid at §§ 54(5) & (6). *Cf R v Goodwin (Anthony)*, [2018] EWCA Crim 2287 ('It was by no means the case that a defence of self-defence in a homicide case necessarily of itself would carry with it a sufficient evidential basis in the alternative for a defence of loss of control.').

[88] See Serious Crime Act 2015, § 76(1). See generally EE Gorbes, 'The Domestic Abuse (Scotland) Act 2018: The Whole Story' (2018) 22 *Edinburgh Law Review* 406–09; M McMahon and P McGorrery, 'Criminalising Controlling and Coercive Behaviour: The Next Step in the Prosecution of Family Violence' (2016) 41 *Alternative Law Journal* 98–100.

intimate partner not facing an immediate attack from claiming self-defence, after the introduction of section 76(1), the defender can take the position that she was in imminent danger of being the victim of coercive control.[89]

These changes to the law reflect a significant advance in society's understanding of domestic abuse. Continuous subjugation in intimate partnership relationships makes targeted victims vulnerable.[90] Understanding domestic abuse helps one recognise why a purported defender (1) stayed in the abusive relationship and (2) felt trapped, without any viable option other than the use of deadly force. This information (supported by numerous studies[91]), in turn, relates to a defendant's good-faith, subjective fear of imminent injury or death. It also appreciates the objective reality of domestic violence (in terms of patterns of violence, degree, triggers, etc) and the related reasonableness of the response.[92]

IV. Defensive Conduct

A. Necessity

As discussed above, under the common law and its recent clarification, it is well-settled that force may only be used in self-defence when the use of such force is 'necessary.'[93] A person threatened need not wait until struck before being permitted to strike in self-defence, moreover, and a pre-emptive strike may be lawful, provided that the fact-finder concludes that the strike was reasonably

[89] See V Bettinson, 'Aligning Partial Defences to Murder with the Offence of Coercive or Controlling Behaviour' (2019) 83 *Journal of Criminal Law* 71, 72–78 (reflecting on the adoption of § 76, which criminalizes coercive or controlling behaviour in an intimate or family relationship, and considering an argument for aligning partial defences to murder with it). See also J Herring, 'The Serious Wrong of Domestic Abuse and the Loss of Control Defence' in A Reed and M Bohlander (eds), *Loss of Control and Diminished Responsibility* (Ashgate Publishing, 2011) 68.

[90] See generally R Aitken and VE Munro, 'Domestic Abuse and Suicide Report 2018' *Refuge Publications* (2018), www.refuge.org.uk/wp-content/uploads/2018/07/domestic-abuse-suicide-refuge-warwick-july2018.pdf.

[91] See, eg, LE Watkins et al, 'The Longitudinal Impact of Intimate Partner Aggression and Relationship Status on Women's Physical Health and Depression Symptoms' (2014) 28 *Journal of Family Psychology* 655; D Loxton et al, 'Psychological Health in Midlife Among Women Who Have Ever Lived with a Violent Partner or Spouse' (2006) 21 *Journal of Interpersonal Violence* 1092; MA Dutton and LA Goodman, 'Coercion in Intimate Partner Violence: Toward a New Conceptualization' (2005) 52 *Sex Roles* 743, 747. See also A Pichhadze, 'Proposals for Reforming the Law of Self-Defence' (2008) 72 *Journal of Criminal Law* 408, 428–29. *Cf* JS Meier, 'Dangerous Liaisons: A Domestic Violence Typology in Custody Litigation' (2017) 70 *Rutgers University Law Review* 115, 159.

[92] See generally J von Talge, 'Victimization Dynamics: The Psycho-Social and Legal Implications of Family Violence Directed Toward Women and the Impact on Child Witnesses' (1999–2000) 27 *Western State University Law Review* 111, 163–64; E Stark, 'Re-Presenting Woman Battering: From Battered Woman Syndrome to Coercive Control' (1995) 58 *Albany Law Review* 973, 996–1026. See also J Herring, 'The Severity of Domestic Abuse' (2018), 30 *National Law School of India Review* 37, 40–43.

[93] See generally *Blackburn v Bowering* [1994] 1 WLR 1324, 1329 (CA); *Palmer v R* [1971] AC 814 (PC). See also Criminal Justice and Immigration Act 2008, § 76(7).

necessary under the circumstances to thwart the attack (that is, that no other avenues, such as availing oneself of police protection, were available).[94] And, as the Court of Appeal ruled in the landmark case of *Williams (Gladstone)*, and consistent with section 76(7) of the Criminal Justice and Immigration Act 2008, a defender is judged *solely* on his honest belief as to the necessity of the force, whether or not his belief was reasonable.[95]

B. Proportionality and Excessive Force

i. *The Standard*

In Chapter 7(II) this book discussed that, contrary to earlier English precedent, and in conflict with the value-based model's approach (discussed at Chapter 4(I)), when evaluating whether force was legally justified, today's English law requires judges and juries to limit their inquiry to the defender's honest (subjective) beliefs as to the circumstances under which defensive force was used. It does not necessarily follow, however, that a defender's belief concerning *how much* force is required to repel an attack should likewise be governed by this subjective standard. And so in *R v Bowen*, the Court of Appeal ruled that, in cases of self-defence, the 'law permits the use of no more force than is reasonable in the circumstances.'[96]

While proportionality was given scant consideration in older texts and opinions, a review of the sources that did address the issue reveals that the amount of defensive force was in fact historically judged on the basis of objective reasonableness.[97] The Court in *R v Rose*, for example, held that the defendant would be liable for murder if he did not have a reasonable belief that the amount of force he used was necessary to preserve his mother's life.[98] The law, as set forth in *Williams*[99] and *Palmer*,[100] and as reaffirmed by the 1994 Court of Appeal case

[94] See *R v Deana* [1909] 2 Cr App R 75 (CA). See also *Beckford v The Queen* [1988] AC 130, 144 (PC); Baker (n 5) 894.

[95] [1984] 78 Cr App R 276. See also Ormerod and Laird (n 2) 382–87.

[96] [1996] 4 All ER 837, 841 (CA), quoting *R v Graham* [1982] 1 All ER 801, 806 (CA). See also *R v Wilson*, [2019] EWCA Crim 1882.

[97] See, eg, *R v Rose* [1884] 15 Cox CC 540, 541–42; *R v Huntley* [1852] 175 ER 497; Russell (n 3) 512–13. See also *R v Hinchcliffe* [1823] 168 ER 998 (holding that a person may use such force in defence of his property as is reasonably necessary).

[98] [1884] 15 Cox CC 540, 541–42. See also *R v Owino*, [1995] *Crim LR* 743; *Beckford v The Queen*, [1988] AC 130, 134 (PC); *Palmer v R* [1971] AC 814, 825 (PC), discussed in Ormerod and Laird (n 2) 399; *R v Hinchcliffe* [1823] 168 ER 998; JF Stephen, *A Digest of Criminal Law* 9th edn (Whitefish, Kessinger Publishing, 2010/1950) 251–52. But see *R v Scarlett* [1994] 98 Cr App R 290 (standing for the rather novel proposition that, before self-defence would be unavailable, (a) the force used must have been unreasonable, and (b) the defender must have either believed that the force used was unreasonable or have given the matter absolutely no thought).

[99] [1987] 3 All ER 411 (CA).

[100] [1971] 1 All ER 1077, 1088 (PC).

of *Blackburn v Bowering*,[101] thus has clearly provided that a person may use such force as is *objectively* reasonable in the circumstances as he or she *subjectively* believes them to be.[102]

The Criminal Justice and Immigration Act 2008 now provides that, when determining whether the degree of force used was reasonable, the fact-finder is to consider:

(a) that a person acting for a legitimate purpose may not be able to weigh to a nicety the exact measure of any necessary action; and
(b) that evidence of a person's having only done what the person honestly and instinctively thought was necessary for a legitimate purpose constitutes strong evidence that only reasonable action was taken by that person for that purpose.[103]

Moreover, section 76(4) sets forth that the reasonableness of a defender's force is to be assessed on the facts and circumstances as the defender genuinely believed them to be, *even if* his belief as to the *circumstances* was mistaken and unreasonable.[104] So the question today is whether, when faced with the threat honestly perceived by the defendant, a reasonable person would have used that level of force?[105] Put another way, was the force used reasonable in the circumstances and danger as the defender believed them to be?[106]

The Act notably creates a carve-out for 'householder cases;' in those cases, the degree of force is only regarded as not being 'reasonable in the circumstances as [the defender] believed them to be' if it was 'grossly disproportionate' in those circumstances.[107] This broadening of the law was instituted in response to calls to reform the law so that householders using force to defend themselves in their homes could receive greater legal protections.[108] Presently in householder cases,

[101] [1994] 1 WLR 1324, 1330, 1333.
[102] See generally Ormerod and Laird (n 2) 389–90.
[103] Criminal Justice and Immigration Act 2008, § 76(7).
[104] See generally *R v Chuong* [2013] EWCA Crim 1716; *R v Faraj* [2007] EWCA Crim 1033. See also Ormerod and Laird (n 2) 38–53. Note that expert medical evidence is admissible to help establish a defendant's genuine belief as to the facts that defendant believed existed. See generally *R v Ibrahim* [2014] EWCA Crim 121; *R v Press and Thompson* [2013] EWCA Crim 1849.
[105] See *R v Robinson* [2017] EWCA Crim 923; *R v Riddell* [2017] EWCA Crim 413; *R v Mula* [2013] EWCA Crim 1293. See also Ormerod and Laird (n 2) 381–82.
[106] The circumstances, of course, directly implicate the perceived danger. See generally *R v Harvey* [2009] EWCA Crim 469; *Shaw (Norman) v R* [2002] 1 Cr App R 10.
[107] Criminal Justice and Immigration Act 2008, § 76(5)(A). See also Herring (n 1) 624–25.
[108] See J Collins and AJ Ashworth, 'Householders, Self-Defence and the Right to Life' (2016) 132 *LQR* 377; S Miller, '"Grossly Disproportionate": Home Owners' Legal License to Kill' (2013) 77 *Journal of Criminal Law* 299, cited in Ormerod and Laird (n 2) 388. See also N Wake, 'Battered Women, Startled Householders and Psychological Self-Defence: Anglo-Australian Perspectives' (2013) 77 *Journal of Criminal Law* 433 (contending that the 'grossly disproportionate' standard is confusing and permits 'dangerous' levels of violence).

a defendant is liable if, in the circumstances as he believed them to be, the jury concludes:

1. That he used grossly disproportionate force; or
2. The degree of force he used was disproportionate *and* was unreasonable.[109]

In *non-householder* cases, in contrast, the focus is exclusively on reasonableness; a defendant is liable if the jury concludes that the amount of force he used was unreasonable in the circumstances as he believed them to be.[110]

In householder cases, then, if the force used by the defender was not grossly disproportionate, the focus shifts to whether the degree of force deployed was reasonable. This, in turn, requires the jury to be instructed on the types of circumstances relevant to this inquiry, including the time of day, the vulnerability of the occupants, the conduct of the intruder at the time, the shock of detecting an intruder, the presence and availability of other help, and the desire to protect the home and its occupants (collectively, on what the householder 'instinctively and honestly thought was necessary'[111]).[112]

ii. No 'Half-Way House'

The English common law required that a person who used an unreasonable amount of force be held criminally liable. We have not, however, yet examined the critical question of whether the liability is full, or, instead, is somehow *reduced* to reflect the diminished culpability of the defender.

In *R v Clegg*,[113] the House of Lords confirmed, albeit obiter, *Palmer*'s[114] holding that excessive force can lead to a conviction for murder because the defence of self-defence is only available to those who use proportionate force.[115] The Lords found that the defence of self-defence

> is not a half-way house. There is no rule that a defendant who has used a greater degree of force than was necessary in the circumstances should be found guilty of manslaughter rather than murder.[116]

[109] See *R v Cheeseman* [2019] EWCA Crim 149; *R v Ray* [2017] EWCA Crim 1391 (effectively superseding *R (Collins) v Secretary of State for Justice* [2016] EWHC 33 (Admin)).

[110] *R v Ray* [2017] EWCA Crim 1391.

[111] *R v Hitchens* [2011] EWCA Crim 1626.

[112] See Ormerod and Laird (n 2) 389. It is also important to recognise that 'householder cases' involve not just homeowners, but, rather, involve *non-trespassers*. Ie, the defender must not be a trespasser, and he must believe that the attacker is entering the building (or part of it) as a trespasser. See *R v Cheeseman* [2019] EWCA Crim 149; *R v Day* [2015] EWCA Crim 1646.

[113] [1995] 2 WLR 80 (HL).

[114] *Palmer v R* [1971] AC 814, 824–32.

[115] [1995] 2 WLR 80 (HL). See also *R v McInnes* [1971] 3 All ER 295, 301–03 (CCA).

[116] See generally [1995] 2 WLR 80, 87 (HL); B Krebs, 'Justification and Excuse in Article 31(1) of the Rome Statute' (2013) 2 *Cambridge Journal of International and Comparative Law* 382, 396.

Once again abruptly departing from the earlier common law position,[117] and contrary to the law of most other jurisdictions (though with no discussion of the relative balancing of values justifying the decision),[118] the defence of self-defence in England is in fact 'all or nothing.' Using excessive force in self-defence today (in non-householder-cases) results in the actor being subjected to full criminal liability, regardless of the actor's honest belief.[119] No attempt is, therefore, made by the English cases to follow the value-based model's approach of distinguishing between negligent individuals who at most should be liable in tort and reckless individuals whose irresponsible use of excessive force makes them appropriate for criminal liability.[120] And so a defender who, through mere negligence, makes an unreasonable mistake and uses excessive force may under the English law be guilty of murder, whereas the same actor under the value-based model would only be liable for civil damages.[121]

C. Duty to Retreat and Avoid Conflict

While there historically was some dispute as to whether safe retreat was required in cases of justifying necessity,[122] the dominant view was that actors committing a justifiable homicide were to be 'commended rather than blamed' for their actions.[123] They, therefore, did not have to retreat, but rather could stand their ground and defend themselves 'on the spot.'[124]

Excusable homicide, in turn, was divided into two categories: homicide *per infortunium*, where the defender did a lawful act without the intention to hurt anyone, but through unfortunate chance kills another, and homicide *se defendendo* upon a 'chance medley' or sudden quarrel, where the defender was not considered 'altogether faultless.'[125] The latter case typically involved two combatants who engaged in a quarrel that escalated to a point where one of the them used deadly force.[126]

While *chance-medley* and manslaughter were often not precisely distinguished in the treatises and cases of the day, the difference seems to have been

[117] See, eg, *R v Huntley* [1852] 175 ER 497; *R v Odgers*, [1843] 174 ER 355.
[118] See, eg, Rönnau and Hohn (n 4) side-notes 281–82 (discussing the German position).
[119] See generally *Palmer v R* [1971] AC 814, 824–32.
[120] See ch 2(IV)(C). See also *R v Martin* [2001] EWCA Crim 2245 (holding that, while '[i]t has been suggested that [a defendant mistakenly using excessive force] should be regarded as being guilty of manslaughter and not murder,' such a change 'would have to be made by Parliament').
[121] See ch 2(IV)(C).
[122] See JC Smith and B Hogan, *Criminal Law* 5th edn (London, LexisNexis, 2005/1983) 234c; Bacon (n 57) 776.
[123] See Russell (n 3) 509; 4 Bl Comm 181.
[124] See generally Stephen (n 98) 252; Russell (n 3) 435.
[125] See Wilshere (n 8) 205; Harris (n 8) 147–53; Russell (n 3) 511–15; East (n 8) 219–22; Hawk PC 108–15.
[126] Hawk PC 83, 87; Hale PC 479; RG Singer, 'The Resurgence of Mens Rea: III – The Rise and Fall of Strict Criminal Liability' (1989) 30 *Boston College Law Review* 472.

that in the case of *chance-medley* the defendant, 'before any mortal stroke given … had declined any further combat and retreated as far as he could with safety ….'[127] Once one of the slayers retreated to the wall, any killing during the *chance-medley* was viewed as a homicide *se defendendo*. In such a case, the slayer was not convicted but instead had to forfeit his goods.[128] Blackstone,[129] Foster,[130] Hale,[131] and Hawkins[132] all agreed that, before a killing could qualify as homicide *se defendendo*, the common law required, with some relatively minor caveats,[133] that the defender 'retreat to the wall.'[134] In short, homicide *se defendendo* occurred when the killing resulted from a quarrel or fight, and the killer either did not begin the fight, but later was involved in it; or, having begun the fight, declined any further struggle and tried to retreat before being pressed to kill his attacker in order to protect himself from death or serious bodily harm.[135]

The English law up to this day continues to allow a person being attacked to forcefully repel the attack and does not impose a categorical duty to retreat.[136] A showing that the defender sought to withdraw, however, continues to be potent evidence that the defender acted *reasonably* and that the defensive conduct was, in fact, necessary.[137] In *R v Bird*,[138] for instance, the defendant was convicted after a retrial of unlawful wounding in violation of section 20 of the Offences Against the Person Act 1861. The defendant had been celebrating her 17th birthday when her ex-boyfriend arrived at the party with his new girlfriend. An argument broke out. During the course of the argument, which escalated into physical violence, the ex-boyfriend held the defendant up against a wall. The defendant hit the ex-boyfriend in the face with a glass she was holding, injuring his eye.[139] The Court of Appeal held:

> There were formerly technical rules about the duty to retreat before using force, or at least fatal force. This is now simply a factor to be taken into account in deciding whether it was necessary to use force, and whether the force was reasonable.[140]

[127] M Foster, *Crown Cases* (1809) 277. See also *R v Odgers* [1843] 174 ER 355, 356; Stephen (n 98) 253; 4 Bl Comm 184–85.

[128] For a discussion of when forfeiture of goods was required, see Hale PC 492–96. See also Foster (n 127) 288.

[129] 4 Bl Comm 183–85.

[130] Foster (n 127) 275–78.

[131] Hale PC 479.

[132] Hawk PC 87.

[133] Such as assaults on the 'highway.' When the attacker intends to feloniously rob or murder an individual who is on a highway, the individual 'may justify killing the other without giving back at all ….' Ibid at 84.

[134] Note that homicides in the 'advancement of public justice' (ie, in felony prevention and the detention of fleeing felons) were the only killings that were considered justified; the actor was not viewed as acting *se defendendo*, and as a result, he or she was not required to retreat. See 4 Bl Comm 178–81; Hale PC 478–83; Singer (n 126) 472.

[135] *R v Semini* [1948] 1 KB 405, 407.

[136] See generally Ormerod and Laird (n 2) 399–400; Baker (n 5) 897. See also *R v McInnes* [1971] 3 All ER 295.

[137] See *R v Ray* [2017] EWCA Crim 1391.

[138] [1985] 1 WLR 816.

[139] Ibid at 817.

[140] Ibid at 816, 820.

The Criminal Justice and Immigration Act 2008 reflects this approach, providing that the 'possibility' of retreat is to be considered a 'factor to be taken into account,' but does not 'giv[e] rise to a duty to retreat.'[141] Contrary to the more nuanced approach of the value-based model (discussed in Chapter 2(V)(A)(iv), which differentiates the relevant values implicated by threatened *harming* versus threatened *wronging*), then, the English cases do not distinguish between culpable and innocent attacks in the context of retreat.

D. Intentionally Provoked Attacks and Other Blameworthy Conduct on the Part of the Defender

Self-defence has been, and continues to be, unavailable where the defender purposefully provoked the attack so that he could kill using self-defence.[142] This position accords with the value-based model.[143] While the cases and commentators focus much attention on the intersection between self-defence and provocation, very little has been written by judges or commentators on the extent to which a defender's provocative behaviour limits his right to self-defence. In *R v Brittain*, the Court of Criminal Appeals cited to *Browne* and opined, albeit obiter, that it was 'less than certain' that the defendant in that case, who got out of his car and shouted at the driver of another car before assaulting him, would be able to properly invoke self-defence.[144]

In passing section 54 of the Coroners and Justice Act 2009, Parliament, as noted, abolished the common law defence of provocation and replaced it with the partial defence to murder – 'loss of control.'[145] As discussed, that partial defence is only available if the defender commits the killing (or is party to it) after losing self-control as the result of a 'qualifying trigger.' Additionally required is a showing that a person of the same sex, age, and with a normal amount of tolerance and self-restraint operating under like circumstances, 'might have reacted in the same or in a similar way ….'[146] The loss of control need not be 'sudden,'[147] cannot be the result of a 'considered desire for revenge,'[148] and places the burden on the prosecution to prove beyond a reasonable doubt that the defence is not satisfied once the defendant adduces sufficient evidence to reasonably raise the issue.[149] A defendant who is able to successfully raise the loss of control defence is liable for manslaughter instead of murder.[150] Moreover, self-defence will be available to

[141] Criminal Justice and Immigration Act 2008, § 76(6)(A).

[142] See Coroners and Justice Act 2009, § 56 ('Abolition of the common law defence of provocation'). See also *R v Browne* [1973] NI 96, 107.

[143] See ch 2(II).

[144] No. 3431/C/84, December 6, 1984 transcript.

[145] Coroners and Justice Act 2009, § 54.

[146] Ibid at § 54(1).

[147] Ibid at § 54(2).

[148] Ibid at § 54(4).

[149] Ibid at §§ 54(5) & (6). See also *R v O'Brien* [2004] EWCA Crim 2900; Ormerod and Laird (n 2) 380.

[150] Coroners and Justice Act 2009, § 54(7).

a person who started a fight, provided the person who he attacked goes beyond defending himself and, in fact, goes on the offensive.[151]

V. Evaluating England's Self-Defence Law from a Value-Centric Perspective

The discussion thus far has traced out some significant – and largely unanticipated – changes in England's self-defence law during the past century. Notably, few broader trends or policy shifts could be recognised. Rather, the changes appear quite ad hoc; they seemingly were not driven by any particular logical pattern or progression.[152] This, perhaps, reflects what Horder has described as the more general 'tendency of the English courts to reach for the concepts of reasonableness, without setting out the relevant rights first, [which is] an unfortunate aspect of legal culture.'[153] Horder's observations find support in the instant analysis, and this, as argued, lends further support for the position we are testing.

Perhaps the most noteworthy, and unpredictable, change came in the area of determining when defensive force is 'necessary.' The common law historically provided that an actor's belief in the necessity of his defensive conduct had to be objectively reasonable. Today, in sharp contrast, if an actor can convince a jury that he honestly (subjectively) believed that the threat was imminent and that defensive force was necessary to ward off an unlawful attack, then he is entitled to claim self-defence irrespective of how unreasonable that belief is. By thus allowing even unreasonably (but honestly) mistaken actors to assert self-defence, the English law signals a particular devaluation of the protection of value-based model value #1 (collective reduction of violence) and value #2 (protecting the particular purported 'attacker'), while concurrently potentially overvaluing value #3 (equal standing) and value #4 (protection of the defender's autonomy).[154] Another notable difference is that, departing from the value-based model's approach, English self-defence law does not permit anticipatory self-defence. Under the value-based model, in contrast, self-preferential force is justified only when it is 'immediately necessary.'[155]

[151] See *R v Rashford* [2005] EWCA Crim 3377, discussed in *Marsh v DPP* [2015] EWHC 1022 (Admin). See also *R v Keane* [2010] EWCA Crim 2514; *R v McGrath* [2010] EWCA Crim 2514 (CA)]; *R v Harvey* [2009] EWCA Crim 469.

[152] See generally Ormerod and Laird (n 2) 380 (describing the development of England's self-defence law as 'haphazard,' resulting in 'inconsistencies and anomalies'). Of course, this is a feature of the common law more generally. See generally WN Drake, Jr, 'The Common Law and the Rule of Law: An Uncomfortable Relationship' (2016) 45 *Stetson Law Review* 439, 447.

[153] Horder (n 30) 133. See also M Dyson and B Vogel, 'Reflections on Criminal Law in England and Germany' in M Dyson and B Vogel (eds), *The Limits of Criminal Law: Anglo-German Concepts and Principles* (Cambridge, Intersentia, 2018) 567 (noting that the 'English system [lacks a] clear hierarchy of norms').

[154] See ch 2(IV)(A)–(D).

[155] See ch 4(II)(B).

Largely mirroring the findings in the Chapter 6 analysis of US self-defence law, then, the examination of self-defence in England revealed little discussion over the values that do, or should, animate self-defence doctrine, or how changes in perspective might change self-defence outcomes. This book demonstrates that, in the absence of a shared analytical language of values, the English courts, on what appears to have been a largely ad hoc basis, handed down cases signalling significant changes in self-defence law. The unpredictability of these changes in the English law of self-defence, and the hidden normativity that this lack of transparency encourages, thus lend additional support for the value-based model's underlying value-explicit approach.

8

Parting Observations

We examined the role values play in self-defence doctrine, as well as practice (via an analysis of the subject jurisdictions), as well as through a discussion of some of the in-the-public-consciousness cases that have led to the widespread calls for justice reform. More specifically, we proposed and then scrutinised the claim that a more detailed accounting of the underlying values providing the rationale for self-defence will improve the transparency and quality of decision-making, and, relatedly, will reduce the impact of hidden normativity. The set of values the value-based model proposed, however, were quite explicitly not positioned as the only possible appropriate set of values. Nor was it claimed that there are not some other reasonable ways of ordering the proffered values.[1] Instead, the claim is that this original model provides a reasonable and unique analytical point of departure for examining the thorny theoretical and practical issues involved in self-defence cases. To the extent that future observers conclude the value-based model overlooked certain values, inappropriately included others, or confused the hierarchy or weighting between and among the included values, such criticisms do not undermine the value-based model. To the contrary, they validate the reason for constructing the value-based model in the first place. For such unclouded and pellucid disagreements inherently proceed on a value-centric footing. And so it worries me not at all that others may point out the perceived errors of my ways; provided, to do so, they concede that a proper and fulsome accounting of implicated values does, in fact, matter to the self-defence debate.

The prediction concerning the 'quality' of value-based outcomes, moreover, is not based on individual normative evaluations of end-states and social outcomes. Rather, the prediction tested here is that a common analytical language that is value-explicit will facilitate more democratic, transparent, incremental, and nuanced policy-based and focused decision-making.

The premise underlying the position we are testing is that an array of values drives self-defence decisions. Consequently, unless these values are identified and openly debated, hidden normativity can be expected to take hold so that the values driving self-defence decisions are most likely to be those of the individual scholar, legislator, or judge, rather than those agreed upon in the context of a broader democratic consensus. Based on the foregoing, and the supporting analysis conducted throughout, it is contended that we have persuasively confirmed the position that

[1] See ch 1.

a more value-informed assessment of self-defence doctrine's rationale will help refine and clarify the discourse.

In particular, and as detailed below, the analysis reveals that the value-based model discussed in Chapter 4, and the German criminal justice system discussed in Chapter 5, generally address challenging self-defence issues through careful and explicit discussion of the implicated values. This, in turn, allows them to make more thoughtful choices among the various available perspectives.

In contrast, it was demonstrated that in the US (Chapter 6) and England (Chapter 7), important questions of value tend to be resolved in an ad hoc manner and based on resolution of technical-legal arguments. Rarely did legislators, judges, or scholars with granularity examine the tension between the respective US and English systems' interests in protecting the attacker versus the defender (let alone the values animating these macro-principles). Attempts in the US to cloak trained law enforcement officers with additional protections not available to ordinary citizens who are similarly acting in the heat of the moment, moreover, were suspect when this book was first being penned – and are now doubly so when viewed through today's law reform lens.

A value-centric approach, in short, drives out much of the hidden normativity that inherently and corrosively influences the decision-making seen in the US and England. These notable differences in approach, process, and outcome, therefore, broadly confirm the prediction that a value-explicit approach improves the quality of decision-making (as that term is defined herein).

Moving from the general to the specific, to test the claim first introduced in Chapter 1, Chapter 2 constructed the 'value-based model' of self-defence to serve as a template allowing for an exploration of the proposed value-centric approach. The chapter began by examining the orthodox view that there are only two principles that clash in the self-defence context, namely, the principle of protecting the defender and the principle of protecting the attacker.

The discussion then progressed, concluding that merely recognising these two principles, without more, provides only a minimal analytical foothold. In order to give these broad concepts content, I proposed seven individual values that it is contended provide a reasonable rationale for self-defence: collective violence reduction by protecting the state's collective monopoly on force (value #1), protecting the individual attacker's right to life (value #2), safeguarding the equal standing between people (value #3), protection of the defender's autonomy (value #4), ensuring the primacy of the legal process (value #5), maintaining the legitimacy of the criminal law (value #6), and deterring future attackers (value #7).

Beyond identifying the values, we discussed why each of them deserves to be considered a potential decision-ground in self-defence cases. In so doing, we not only examined the arguments for and against their inclusion, but also focused on how and when they can be in tension with, or support of, each other. We, moreover, reviewed how to approach the relative hierarchical ordering of these values under different self-defence scenarios. It is contended that this uniquely comprehensive array of values, and the discussion of how they may at times 'clash' with each other, went far to establish a defensible rationale for self-defence. And so much the better if future observers are able to refine this effort, for, as was the case with Major Walter Wingfield's enduring efforts, this certainly is not the final, authoritative word on the matter.

The findings in Chapter 2 support the value-based model's central premise, namely, that the proposed values are in fact relevant to self-defence decisions (that is, that they, depending on the circumstance, can function as what have been termed 'decision-grounds'). They also provide a persuasive and much-needed explanation for the doctrine's rationale. Further, Chapter 2 demonstrated that, absent a value-based framework informing an open and value-centric dialogue, the underlying basis for self-defence rulings, as well as changes in self-defence doctrine, will, in an unnecessary deviation from the norm of systemic transparency, remain largely hidden from public view and will be the individual decision-maker's own. Further, by introducing the state-of-mind-based distinction between forfeiting and waiving the right to non-interference, this book added a more nuanced way of thinking about the much-debated 'gap in the right to non-interference' said to occur in self-defence scenarios.

With this value-based template in place, Chapter 3 conducted a thematic literature review. The purpose of the review was two-fold. The first objective was to probe whether the value-based model held up to scholarly scrutiny and, in fact, served as a useful template. Second, we sought to determine whether the value based model was unique, or whether, instead, scholars had already proposed variants of a fully comprehensive, value-centric approach for analysing self-defence cases.

The conclusion reached was that, while some scholars did tether their analyses on what they described as the values undergirding self-defence (and, thereby, recognised that values do in fact 'matter'), they in the main considered only one or two values. For example, Leverick narrowly focuses on the 'right to life' to develop her argument that only threatened death may be met with deadly force. And so even threatened rape or other forms of serious bodily injury at the hands of, say, a fully culpable and sadistic attacker threatening to permanently maim his victim do not justify deadly force in self-defence. Schopp, on the other hand, considers the autonomy of the defender so inviolate that he would sanction deadly force if it was necessary to prevent the theft of property or to ward off a fairly minor assault.

While Leverick and Schopp largely focused on one value, Sangero conducted what I view as the most searching analysis of the 'factors' he believes explain the underlying 'rationale' of self-defence law (namely, the defender's autonomy; the attacker's culpability; and harm to the 'social-legal order'). But Sangero's analysis for no good reason neglected to pay equal attention to other important standalone values, namely, the state's collective violence-reduction role, the attacker's right to life, the importance of equal standing, the primacy and legitimacy of the legal process, and deterrence. Nor did Sangero more closely examine the relationship between the three values he identified or examine what might happen if and when they come into conflict with each other. And so, while Sangero's account comes closest to engaging in a comprehensive value-based discussion about self-defence, the Chapter 3 thematic literature review confirms that the value-based model offers a unique and useful template. It conceptualises self-defence's rationale as being tethered to values that, when implicated, function as self-defence 'decision-grounds.'

Having in Chapter 2 developed the value-based model, and in Chapter 3 determined that the model offers 'something new' when it comes to the important discussion around self-defence, Chapter 4 used the value-based template to drive the value-based analysis further. Specifically, Chapter 4 addressed the central theoretical questions characterising the self-defence debate. In so doing, the book showed how the value-based model allowed for the development of internally consistent, defensible answers to the core theoretical questions. For example, we concluded that: self-defence functions as a justification, not an excuse; a defender must be both internally and externally justified to be able to claim self-defence (and reasonable mistakes of fact, therefore, make the justification of self-defence unavailable); imminence should be evaluated objectively; defensive force must be 'immediately necessary,' making self-defence more available to battered intimate partners; self-defence should be available (though in diminished form) against innocent attackers, as the attack need not be criminal; objectively disproportionate force should preclude self-defence; there should be no duty to retreat when faced with a culpable attack and safe retreat is not an option; passive conduct can constitute an 'attack'; police officers acting objectively unreasonably should not be permitted to hide behind their subjective (but unreasonably mistaken) beliefs as to the threat(s) facing them; unknowingly justified defenders should not be able to claim self-defence; deadly force should not be available to defend property or to ward off trivial threats; and even though there is no strict duty to avoid conflict, individuals must at least attempt to avoid places where they know an attack is likely.

I also conceded that the answers to these important doctrinal questions are very much subject to change as one's normative judgements concerning the implicated values shifts. But from my perspective the model's adaptability serves to confirm, rather than to invalidate, the hypothesis. Consistent with the position we have been testing, by framing the debate from a value-centric perspective, the analysis proceeds by examining whether important values were omitted, or whether the weighting of others was inappropriate. By forcing these inherently normative questions more squarely into the public forum, the value-based approach expands the range of perspectives represented in the debate. It, moreover, encourages more thoughtful and nuanced choices among those perspectives. Stated differently, by refocusing the debate on values, the value-based model makes transparent the types of normative judgements that in the main have been left either un- or under-addressed. The research conducted in Chapter 4, therefore, lends significant support to the position we tested.

To further assess the model, Chapters 5–7 used the value-based approach to evaluate the self-defence laws in Germany, the US, and England. What the book revealed was that in Germany, changes in the law of self-defence were in the main incremental and, relatedly, were accompanied by significant value-focused debate concerning the various alternative courses of action (and reasons for pursuing or rejecting them). In contrast, in the US, and even more so in England, law reforms tended to come about with little notice, and were largely untethered to any particular, explicit moral or value-based framework or discussions concerning alternative outcomes.

For example, English law's abrupt move away from objective reasonableness, so that self-preferential force was considered justified so long as the defender honestly believed the force was necessary, came about with little warning. The change, moreover, surprisingly arrived unaccompanied by a discussion over how this change in the law impacted values such as the state's monopoly on force, the putative 'attacker's' interest, the primacy of the legal process, etc.

Substantively, we also pointed out other notable differences between how England addresses certain central self-defence questions and how they are handled in Germany, the US, and by the value-based model. For example, under English law, there is no objective evaluation of whether an attack is imminent, and there is also no default duty to retreat or to avoid conflict. And in the US, some (but not all) jurisdictions deviate from the objective reasonableness standard when it comes to law enforcement officers, justifying use of defensive force whenever an officer subjectively believes it was necessary.

Proposed Self-Defence Jury Instruction

The defendant has offered evidence of having acted in self-defence.

You are instructed that the use of force is justified when a person reasonably believes that it is necessary for the defence of oneself [or another] against the immediate use of unlawful force. However, a person must use no more force than what, from an objective perspective, was reasonably necessary under the circumstances.

Force likely to cause death or great bodily harm is justified in self-defence only if a person reasonably believes that such force is necessary to prevent death or great bodily harm, and in fact acts as a result of that belief.

The government must prove beyond a reasonable doubt that the defendant did not act in reasonable self-defence. Put another way, in this case the government bears the burden of *disproving* the defendant's self-defence claim.

Comments to the Jury Instruction

When there is evidence of self-defence, this additional element should be added to the instruction on the substantive offence. For example, 'Fourth, the defendant did not act in reasonable self-defence.'

> A defendant is entitled to a self-defence instruction when there is any foundation in the evidence, even though the evidence may be weak, insufficient, inconsistent, or of doubtful credibility.
>
> The jury must unanimously reject the defendant's self-defence theory in order to find the defendant guilty. *United States v Ramirez*, 537 F3d 1075, 1083 (9th Cir 2008).

While the decision to accept these rules may be defensible (or even persuasive to some), there is little detailed, value-based analysis that justifies them. Rather, English cases and law reform proposals, like their US counterparts, tend to be analysed on the basis of technical legal arguments. They, in so doing, largely ignore the important value trade-offs that are inevitably implicated.

In contrast, and as Chapter 5 illustrated, when German law introduced 'socio-ethical' limitations on the once hard-edged law of self-defence, this resulted in significant scholarly debate that persists to the present day. Likewise, German law's permission to use deadly force to defend property has been widely analysed. It is, therefore, much clearer what values the German proponents (and opponents) of authorising deadly force in defence of property view as most directly implicated, and how and why the law may in the future change.

We next in Chapters 5–7 provided real-world illustrations of how a value-based approach leaves less room for hidden normativity by encouraging clarification and refinement of the (value-based) arguments. The chapters, moreover, demonstrate the advantages of having a shared value-centric language with which to identify disagreements, pin-point areas of common ground, and propose alternative constructions. These findings, in short, lend further support for the claim that a value-centric approach to self-defence increases transparency and predictability.

It is, therefore, submitted that we have conclusively confirmed that a broader consideration of the values implicated in self-defence scenarios considerably improves the transparency of decision-making, and, relatedly, reduces the role of hidden normativity. This seems like a fairly uncontroversial (or, at least, very defensible) position; yet it has been largely elusive, never receiving a meaningfully comprehensive examination in any of the volumes of self-defence scholarship. By in this manner demonstrating not only that a value-centric dialogue drives normative questions out of hidden baselines, but also that expanding the range of perspectives represented in the debate facilitates more thoughtful choices among available options, the findings here validate the hypothesis. What is more, the proposed value-centric approach promises to yield outcomes that support, rather than detract from, the legitimacy and creditworthiness of the criminal law generally. For they will have been reached not on the basis of hidden normativity and false dichotomies, but, rather, through an all-things-considered analysis of values deemed relevant in each challenging self-defence case in which competing rights and interests collide.

Table 5 Overview of Comparative, International Value-Based Models

Issue	Value-Based Model	Germany	US	England
Does self-defence function as a justification or an excuse?	Justification. See Chapter 4(I)	Justification. See Chapter 5(III)	Justification. See Chapter 6(II)	Justification. See Chapter 7(I) & (II)
Must circumstances be both internally and externally justified to qualify as self-defence?	Yes. See Chapter 4(I)(B)	Yes. See Chapter 5(III)	Yes. See Chapter 6(II)	No (only internal justification is required). See Chapter 7(II)(B)
Do even reasonable mistakes of fact make self-defence unavailable?	Yes. See Chapter 4(I)(B)	Yes. See Chapter 5(III)(A)	Yes. See Chapter 6(II)(A)	No. See Chapter 7(II)(A)
Is self-defence available against innocent 'attackers'?	Yes. See Chapter 4(V)(A)	Yes. See Chapter 5(IV)(B)	Yes. See Chapter 6(III)(B)	Yes. See Chapter 7(III)(B)
Can an unknowingly justified defender claim self-defence?	No. See Chapter 4(I)(B)(ii) & (iii)	No. See Chapter 5(III)(B)	No. See Chapter 6(II)(B)	No. See Chapter 7(II)(B)
Must the attack be criminal?	No. See Chapter 4(V)(A)(iv)	No. See Chapter 5(IV)(B)	No. See Chapter 6(III)(B)	No. See Chapter 7(III)(B)
Can deadly force be used to protect property?	No. See Chapter 4(III)(B)	Yes. See Chapter 5(IV)(A)	No. See Chapter 6(III)(A)	No. See Chapter 7(III)(A)
Can deadly force be used to ward off trivial threats?	No. See Chapter 4(III)(C)	No. See Chapter 5(IV)(A) & (V)(B)(ii)	No. See Chapter 6(III)(A) & (G)	No. See Chapter 7(III)(A) & IV(B)
Can passive conduct constitute an 'attack' authorising self-defence?	Yes. See Chapter 4(V)(A)(iv)	Yes. See Chapter 5(IV)(D)	Yes. See Chapter 6(III)(D)	Yes. See Chapter 7(III)(D)
Is imminence of the threat objectively evaluated?	Yes. See Chapter 4(II)(B) & (V)(A)(vi)	Yes. See Chapter 5(IV)(E)(ii)	Yes. See Chapter 6(III)(E)(ii)	No. See Chapter 7(III)(E)(ii)

(continued)

Table 5 ***(Continued)***

Issue	Value-Based Model	Germany	US	England
What is the relationship between imminence and necessity?	Defensive force must be 'immediately necessary.' See Chapter 4(II)	Imminence is part of 'justifying necessity.' See Chapter 5(IV)(E) & (V)(A)	Imminence means 'about to occur.' Imminence and necessity are separate concepts (force must be 'necessary' to respond to imminent harm). See Chapter 6(III)(E) & (F)	Imminence is part of the 'necessity calculation.' See Chapter 7(III)(E) & IV(A)
Can a 'battered woman' rely on anticipatory self-defence?	Yes, if force is 'immediately necessary.' See Chapter 4(V)(A)(vi)	No. See Chapter 5(V)(C)(iv)	No. See Chapter 6(III)(E)(iii)	No. See Chapter 7(III)(E)(iii)
Are there special rules for 'attacks' by the police?	Yes – prima facie justification to effectuate arrest. If acting outside of scope of authorisation normal self-defence rules pertain. See Chapter 4(V)(B)	Yes. See Chapter 5(IV)(C)	No. See Chapter 6(III)(C)	No. See Chapter 7(III)(C)
Does objectively disproportionate defensive force preclude a self-defence justification?	Yes. See Chapter 4(B)	Yes. See Chapter 5(V)(B)	Yes. See Chapter 6(III)(G)	Yes. See Chapter 7(IV)(B)
Is there a strict duty to retreat?	No. But retreat may be required if the defender knows attack is by an 'innocent' and/or if safe retreat is an option. See Chapter 4(II)(C)	No, unless defender knows attack is by an 'innocent' or family member. See Chapter 5(V)(C)	Generally, yes (if outside of the home and not in a stand-your-ground state). See Chapter 6(III)(H)	No. See Chapter 7(IV)(C)
Is there a strict duty to avoid conflict?	No. But individuals must at least attempt to avoid places where they *know* an attack is likely. See Chapter 4(II)(C)	No, unless defender knows attack is by an 'innocent' or family member. See Chapter 5(V)(C)	No. See Chapter 6(III)(I)	No. See Chapter 7(IV)(C)

BIBLIOGRAPHY

Aagaard TS, 'Environmental Harms, Use Conflicts, and Neutral Baselines in Environmental Law' (2011) 60 *Duke LJ* 1505

Abanonu R, 'De-Escalating Police-Citizen Encounters' (2018) 27 *S Cal Rev L & Soc Just* 239

Abel RL, 'Should Tort Law Protect Property Against Accidental Loss' (1986) 23 *San Diego L Rev* 79

Ackerman B, *Social Justice in the Liberal State* (New Haven, Yale University Press, 1981)

Ackerman RM, 'Communitarianism and the Roberts Court' (2017) 45 *Fla St U L Rev* 59

Addae AE, 'Challenging the Constitutionality of Private Prisons: Insights from Israel' (2019) 25 *Wm & Mary J Race Gender & Soc Just* 527

Aitken R & Munro VE, 'Domestic Abuse and Suicide Report 2018' *Refuge Publications* (2018)

Alces PA, 'Regret and Contract Science' (2000) 89 *Geo LJ* 143

Alcorn M, 'Setting the Standard: Changing the Use of Force Standard Used by California Police' (2018) 50 *U Pac L Rev* 251

Aleinikoff TA, 'Constitutional Law in the Age of Balancing' (1987) 96 *Yale LJ* 943

Alexander GS, 'Intergenerational Communities' (2014) 7 *Law & Ethics Hum Rts* 21

Alexander L, 'Lesser Evils: A Closer Look at the Paradigmatic Justification' (2005) 24 *Law & Phil* 611

——, 'Unknowingly Justified Actors and the Attempt/Success Distinction' (2004) 39 *Tulsa L Rev* 851

Alexander L et al, *Crime and Culpability* (Cambridge, Cambridge University Press, 2009)

Alexy R, 'Balancing, Constitutional Review, and Representation' (2005) 3 *Int'l J Const L* 572

——, 'Constitutional Rights, Balancing, and Rationality' (2003) 16 *Ratio Juris* 131

Allhoff F, 'Self-Defense Without Imminence' (2019) 56 *Am Crim LR* 1527

Alm D, 'Self-Defense, Punishment and Forfeiture' (2013) 32 *Crim Just Ethics* 91

Aloyo E, 'Just Assassinations' (2013) 5 *Int'l Theory* 347

Altantulkhuur K, 'A Second Rape: Testing Victim Credibility Through Prior False Accusations' [2018] *U Ill L Rev* 1091

Alvarez L & Buckley C, 'Zimmerman Is Acquitted in Trayvon Martin Killing' *NY Times* (New York, 13 July 2013) A1

Amnesty Int'l, *Deadly Force: Police Use of Lethal Force in the United States* (2015)

Anderson JL, 'Playing with Fire: Contemporary Fault Issues in the Enigmatic Crime of Arson' (2016) 39 *UNSW LJ* 950

Angel M, 'Why Judy Norman Acted in Reasonable Self-Defense: An Abused Woman and a Sleeping Man' (2008) 16 *Buff Women's LJ* 65

Arenella P, 'Convicting the Morally Blameless: Reassessing the Relationship Between Legal and Moral Accountability' (1992) 39 *UCLA L Rev* 1511

Irwin T, *Aristotle, Nicomachean Ethics* 2nd edn (Oxford, Oxford University Press, 1999)

Armour JD, 'Race Ipsa Loquitur: Of Reasonable Racists, Intelligent Bayesians, and Involuntary Negrophobes' (1994) 46 *Stan L Rev* 781

Arneson RJ, 'Self-Defense and Culpability: Fault Forfeits First' (2018) 55 *San Diego L Rev* 231

Ashworth AJ, 'Belief, Intent and Criminal Liability' in Eekelaar J and Bell J (eds), *Oxford Essays in Jurisprudence* (Oxford, Oxford University Press, 1987)

——, 'Is the Criminal Law a Lost Cause?' (2000) 116 *LQR* 225

——, *Positive Obligations in Criminal Law* (Oxford, Hart Publishing, 2013)

——, 'Self-Defence and the Right to Life' (1975) 34 *CLJ* 282

Ashworth AJ & Horder J, *Principles of Criminal Law* 5th edn (Oxford, Oxford University Press, 2006)

Azmat AT, 'What Mistake of Law Just Might Be: Legal Moralism, Liberal Positivism, and the Mistake of Law Doctrine' (2015) 18 *New Crim LR* 369

Bacon M, *A New Abridgement of the Law* (Palala Press, 2015/1832)
Bagaric M & Isham P, 'A Rational Approach to the Role of Publicity and Condemnation in the Sentencing of Offenders' (2019) 46 *Fla St U L Rev* 239
Bagaric M et al, 'Trauma and Sentencing: The Case for Mitigating Penalty for Childhood Physical and Sexual Abuse' (2019) 30 *Stan L & Pol'y Rev* 1
Baker DJ, 'Mutual Combat Complicity, Transferred Intention/Defenses and the Exempt Party Defense' (2016) 37 *U La Verne L Rev* 205
——, *Textbook of Criminal Law* 4th edn (Oxford, Oxford University Press, 2015)
Bakircioglu O, 'The Contours of the Right to Self-Defence: Is the Requirement of Imminence Merely a Translator for the Concept of Necessity?' (2008) 72 *J Crim L* 131
Baron M, 'Justifications and Excuses' (2005) 2 *Ohio St J Crim L* 387
Bayles M, 'Reconceptualizing Necessity and Duress' (1986) 33 *Wayne L Rev* 1191
Bazelon DL, 'The Morality of the Criminal Law' in Morawetz T (ed), *Criminal Law* (New York, New York University Press, 1991)
Beale JH, Jr, 'Homicide in Self-Defense' (1903) 3 *Colum L Rev* 526
Beck G, 'The Idea of Human Rights Between Value Pluralism and Conceptual Vagueness' (2007) 25 *Pa St Int'l L Rev* 615
——, 'The Moral Void at the Heart of Human Rights Adjudication' (2013) 8 *J Comp L* 237
Bedau H, 'The Right to Life' (1968) 52 *Monist* 550
Bedi M, 'Excusing Behavior: Reclassifying the Federal Common Law Defenses of Duress and Necessity Relying on the Victim's Role' (2011) 10 *J Crim L & Criminology* 575
Beetham D, *The Legitimation of Power* (MacMillan Education, 2013)
——, *The Legitimation of Power* (Amherst, Prometheus Books, 1991)
Behne K, 'Packing Heat: Judicial Review of Concealed Carry Laws Under the Second Amendment' (2016) 89 *S Cal L Rev* 1343
Behr V, 'Punitive Damages in American and German Law – Tendencies Towards Approximation of Apparently Irreconcilable Concepts' (2003) 78 *Chi-Kent L Rev* 105
Bell KL, 'Toward a New Analysis of the Abortion Debate' (1991) 33 *Ariz L Rev* 907
Bergelson V, 'Duress Is No Excuse' (2018) 15 *Ohio St J Crim L* 395
——, 'Justification or Excuse – Exploring the Meaning of Provocation' (2009) 42 *Tex Tech L Rev* 307
Berman MN, 'Justification and Excuse, Law and Morality' (2003) 53 *Duke LJ* 1
Berman MN & Farrell IP, 'Provocation Manslaughter as Partial Justification and Partial Excuse' (2011) 52 *Wm & Mary L Rev* 1027
Berner A, 'Die Notwehrtheorie' in *Archiv des Criminalrechts* (1884)
——, *Lehrbuch Des Deutschen Strafrechtes* (Wentworth Press, 2018/1989)
Bernsmann K, 'Private Self-Defence and Necessity in German Penal Law and in the Penal Law Proposal – Some Remarks' (1996) 30 *Isr L Rev* 171
——, 'Überlegungen zur tödlichen Notwehr bei nicht lebensbedrohlichen Angriffen' (1992) 104 *ZStW* 290
Bertel C, 'Notwehr gegen verschuldete Angriffe' (1972) 84 *ZstW* 1
Bettelheim B, *Surviving and Other Essays* (London, Thames & Hudson, 1979)
Bettinson V, 'Aligning Partial Defences to Murder with the Offence of Coercive or Controlling Behaviour' (2019) 83 *J Crim L* 71
Bibas S, 'Transparency and Participation in Criminal Procedure' (2006) 81 *NYU L Rev* 911
Bilz K, 'The Puzzle of Delegated Revenge' (2007) 87 *BU L Rev* 1059
Binder G, 'The Rhetoric of Motive and Intent' (2002) 6 *Buff Crim LR* 1
——, 'Victims and the Significance of Causing Harm' (2008) 28 *Pace L Rev* 713
Bishop JP, *Commentaries on the Criminal Law* (Arkose Press, 2015/1858)
Blackstone W, *Commentaries on the Laws of England*, vol 3 (Oxford, Oxford University Press, 2016/1776)
——, *Commentaries on the Laws of England*, vol 4 (Oxford, Oxford University Press, 2016/1776)
Blair JP et al, 'Reasonableness and Reaction Time' (2011) 14 *Police Q* 323
Blinder M, 'The Battered Woman's Syndrome' in *Psychiatry in the Everyday Practice of Law* 5th edn (West Group Publishing, 2019)

Blumenthal JA, 'Who Decides? Privileging Public Sentiment About Justice and the Substantive Law' (2003) 72 *UMKC L Rev* 1

Bock D, *Strafrecht, Allgemeiner Teil* (Berlin, Springer-Verlag Berlin and Heidelberg GmbH & Co KG, 2018)

Boggiani M, 'When Is a Trafficking Victim a Trafficking Victim? Anti-Prostitution Statutes and Victim Protection' (2016) 64 *Clev St L Rev* 915

Bohlander M, 'When the Bough Breaks – Defences and Sentencing Options Available to Battered Women and Similar Scenarios Under German Law' in Reed A and Bohlander M (eds), *Loss of Control and Diminished Responsibility* (Ashgate Publishing, 2016)

Bónis P, 'The Self-Defense in the Tripartitum and the European Ius Commune' (2014) 5 *J on Eur Hist L* 80

Boone M & Kox M, 'Neutrality as an Element of Perceived Justice in Prison: Consistency Versus Individualization' (2014) 10 *Utrecht L Rev* 118

Bottoms AE & Tankebe J, 'Beyond Procedural Justice: A Dialogic Approach to Legitimacy in Criminal Justice' (2012) 102 *J Crim L & Criminology* 119

Bowers J & Robinson PH, 'Perceptions of Fairness and Justice: The Shared Arms and Occasional Conflicts of Legitimacy and Moral Credibility' (2012) 47 *Wake Forest L Rev* 211

Brink DO, 'Retributivism and Legal Moralism' (2012) 25 *Ratio Juris* 496

Bronsther J, 'Torture and Respect' (2019) 109 *J Crim L & Criminology* 423

Brookbanks W & Ekins R, 'The Case Against the "Three Strikes" Sentencing Regime' [2010] *NZ L Rev* 689

Brooks JD, 'Deadly-Force Self-Defense and the Problem of the Silent Subtle Provocateur' (2015) 24 *Cornell JL & Pub Pol'y* 533

Brown DK, 'Democracy and Decriminalization' (2007) 86 *Tex L Rev* 223

Brudner A, 'Agency and Welfare in the Penal Law' in Shute S et al (eds), *Action and Value in Criminal Law* (Oxford, Oxford University Press, 1996)

——, 'Constitutionalizing Self-Defense' (2011) 61 *U Toronto LJ* 867

——, 'The Ideality of Difference: Toward Objectivity in Legal Interpretation' (1989–1990) 11 *Cardozo L Rev* 1133

Buchanan A & Powell R, 'The Limits of Evolutionary Explanations of Morality and Their Implications for Moral Progress' (2015) 126 *Ethics* 1

Burke AS, 'Rational Actors, Self-Defense, and Duress: Making Sense, Not Syndromes, Out of the Battered Woman' (2002) 81 *NC L Rev* 211

Carter JC, *The Provinces of Written and Unwritten Law* (Whitefish, Kissinger Publishing, 2010/1889)

Castillo ME, 'Florida's Stand Your Ground Regime: Legislative Direction, Prosecutorial Discretion, Public Pressures, and the Legitimization of the Criminal Justice System' (2016) 42 *J Legis* 101

Chalfin A & McCrary J, 'Criminal Deterrence: A Review of the Literature' (2017) 55 *J Econ Literature* 5

Chalmers J & Leverick F, 'Fair Labelling in Criminal Law' (2008) 71 *MLR* 217

Chan W & Simester AP, 'Four Functions of Mens Rea' (2011) 70 *CLJ* 381

Chapman FE & MacLean J, 'Pulling the Patches of the Patchwork Defence of Duress: A Comment on R. v. Aravena' (2015) 62 *Crim LQ* 420

Chapman J, 'Doomsday: A Look at the Ethical Issues Behind the Government's Coercive Powers in Response to a Public Health Nightmare' (2008) 9 *JL & Soc Challenges* 24

Chemerinsky E, 'Getting Beyond Formalism in Constitutional Law: Constitutional Theory Matters' (2001) 54 *Okla L Rev* 1

——, 'Rationalizing the Abortion Debate: Legal Rhetoric and the Abortion Controversy' (1982) 31 *Buff L Rev* 107

Cheng C & Hoekstra M, 'Does Strengthening Self-Defense Law Deter Crime or Escalate Violence? Evidence from Expansions to Castle Doctrine' (2013) 48 *J Hum Resources* 821

Chevigny PG, 'The Right to Resist an Unlawful Arrest' (1969) 78 *Yale LJ* 1128

Chiao V, 'Ex Ante Fairness in Criminal Law and Procedure' (2012) 15 *New Crim LR* 277

Chiesa LE, 'The Rise of Spanish and Latin American Criminal Theory' (2008) 11 *New Crim LR* 363

Chin GJ, 'Unjustified: The Practical Irrelevance of the Justification/Excuse Distinction' (2009) 43 *U Mich JL Reform* 79

Ching B, 'Mirandizing Terrorism Suspects? The Public Safety Exception, the Rescue Doctrine, and Implicit Analogies to Self-Defense, Defense of Others, and Battered Woman Syndrome' (2015) 64 *Cath U L Rev* 613
Choudhry S & Herring J, 'Righting Domestic Violence' (2006) 20 *Int'l JL Pol'y & Fam* 95
Christopher RL, 'Exculpation as Inculpation' (2017) 49 *Ariz St LJ* 1141
——, 'Mistake of Fact in the Objective Theory of Justification: Do Two Rights Make Two Wrongs Make Two Rights … ?' (1994) 85 *J Crim L & Criminology* 295
——, 'Self-Defense and Objectivity: A Reply to Judith Jarvis Thomson' (1998) 1 *Buff Crim LR* 537
——, 'Unknowing Justification and the Logical Necessity of the Dadson Principle in Self-Defence' (1995) 15 *OJLS* 229
Cicero MT, *On Invention, Book II* (84 BC)
Clark SE et al, 'Legitimacy, Procedural Justice, Accuracy, and Eyewitness Identification' (2018) 8 *UC Irvine L Rev* 41
Clark WL, *Handbook of Criminal Law* 3rd edn (Charleston, Nabu Press, 2020/1915)
Clarkson CM & Keating HM, *Criminal Law: Text and Materials* 9th edn (London, Sweet & Maxwell, 2017)
CNN Library, 'Trayvon Martin Shooting Fast Facts' *CNN* (5 June 2013)
Coca-Vila I, 'Conflicting Duties in Criminal Law' (2019) 22 *New Crim LR* 34
Cody S & Koenig A, 'Procedural Justice in Transnational Contexts' (2018) 58 *Va J Int'l L* 1
Coffee JC, Jr, 'Hush: The Criminal Status of Confidential Information After McNally and Carpenter and the Enduring Problem of Overcriminalization' (1988) 26 *Am Crim LR* 121
Cohan JA, 'Homicide by Necessity' (2006) 10 *Chap L Rev* 119
Cohen L, 'The "Reasonable Black Child" – Youth, Race, and the Fourth Amendment' (2018) 33 *ABA Crim Just* 37
Coleman JL, *Risks and Wrongs* (Cambridge, Cambridge University Press, 1992)
Collins J & Ashworth AJ, 'Householders, Self-Defence and the Right to Life' (2016) 132 *LQR* 377
Colvin E, 'Ordinary and Reasonable People: The Design of Objective Tests of Criminal Responsibility' (2001) 27 *Monash U L Rev* 197
Cotton M, 'The Necessity Defense and the Moral Limits of Law' (2015) 18 *New Crim LR* 35
Council of Europe & European Court of Human Rights, *Guide on Article 2 of the European Convention on Human Rights: Right to Life* (2019)
Cover R, 'Violence and the Word' (1986) 95 *Yale LJ* 1601
Coyle M, 'The Transformative Potential of the Truth and Reconciliation Commission: A Skeptic's Perspective' (2017) 95 *Can B Rev* 767
Cramer P, '§ 16 Irrtum über Tatumstände' in *Adolf Schönke & Horst Schröder, Strafgesetzbuch* 25th edn (Beck CH, 1997)
Creach DL, 'Partially Determined Imperfect Self-Defense: The Battered Wife Kills and Tells Why' (1982) 34 *Stan L Rev* 615
Criminal Law Policy Unit, Ministry of Justice, *Partial Defences to Murder: Loss of Control and Diminished Responsibility; and Infanticide: Implementation of Sections 52, and 54 to 57 of the Coroners and Justice Act 2009*, Circular 2010/13 (UK)
Crippa LA, 'Multilateral Development Banks and Human Rights Responsibility' (2010) 25 *Am U Int'l L Rev* 531
Crocker L, 'Justification and Bad Motives' (2008) 6 *Ohio St J Crim L* 277
Crocker PL, 'The Meaning of Equality for Battered Women Who Kill Men in Self-Defense' (1985) 8 *Harv Women's LJ* 121
Croquet N, 'Implied External Limitations on the Right to Cross-Examine Prosecution Witnesses: The Tension Between a Means Test and a Balancing Test in the Appraisal of Anonymity Requests' (2010) 11 *Melb J Int'l L* 27
Crump D, 'Deterrence' (2018) 49 *St Mary's LJ* 317
D'Angelo M, 'Merkmal Der Gegenwartigkeit in Notwehrrech Bei Neuen Konfliktmustern Aus Rechtsvergleichender Sicht' (unpublished PhD dissertation, University of Freiburg, 2016)

D'Arcy E, *Human Acts* (Oxford, Oxford University Press, 1963)
Dagan T, 'The Currency of Taxation' (2016) 84 *Fordham L Rev* 2537
Dagger R, 'Communitarianism and Republicanism' in Gaus GF and Kukathas C (eds), *Handbook of Political Theory* (Thousand Oaks, Sage Publications, 2014)
Dan-Cohen M, 'The Value of Ownership' (2001) 1 *Global Jurist Frontiers* 1
Darley JM et al, 'Enacting Justice: The Interplay of Individual and Institutional Perspectives' in Hogg M and Cooper J (eds), *The Sage Handbook of Social Psychology* (Thousand Oaks, Sage Publications, 2003)
De Cremer D & Tyler TR, 'The Effects of Trust in Authority and Procedural Fairness on Cooperation' (2007) 92 *J Applied Psychol* 639
De Pisan C, *The Book of Fayettes of Armes and of Chyvalrye* (Oxford, Oxford University Press, 1932)
Deiters M, *SK-StGB - Systematischer Kommentar Zum Strafgesetzbuch, Band 1* (Luchterhand (Hermann), 2017)
Delaney J, 'Towards a Human Rights Theory of Criminal Law: A Humanistic Perspective' (1978) 6 *Hofstra L Rev* 831
Dempsey MM, 'Public Wrongs and the "Criminal Law's Business" - When Victims Won't Share' in Cruft R et al (eds), *Crime, Punishment, and Responsibility: The Jurisprudence of Anthony Duff* (Oxford, Oxford University Press, 2011)
Dennis IH, 'On Necessity as a Defence to Crime: Possibilities, Problems and the Limits of Justification and Excuse' (2009) 3 *Crim L & Phil* 29
Dervan LE, 'White Collar Overcriminalization: Deterrence, Plea Bargain, and the Loss of Innocence' (2013) 101 *Ky LJ* 723
Desautels-Stein J, 'The Market as a Legal Concept' (2012) 60 *Buff L Rev* 387
Diamond JL, 'The Myth of Morality and Fault in Criminal Law Doctrine' (1996) 34 *Am Crim LR* 111
Dieckmann JA, 'Plädoyer für die eingeschränkte Schuldtheorie beim Irrtum über Rechtfertigungsgründe' (1994) 4 *Jura* 178
Dimock S, 'Criminalizing Dangerousness: How to Preventatively Detain Dangerous Offenders' (2015) 9 *Crim L & Phil* 537
Dobinson I & Elliott E, 'A Householder's Right to Kill or Injure an Intruder Under the Crime and Courts Act 2013: An Australian Comparison' (2014) 78 *J Crim L* 80
Dodge J, '*Porter v. State:* Appropriately Pushing the Limits of the Battered Spouse Syndrome Statute' (2018) 18 *U Md LJ Race Religion Gender & Class* 235
Dölling D et al, *Gesamtes Strafrecht* (Baden-Baden, Nomos Verlagsgesellschaft, 2017)
Drake WN, Jr, 'The Common Law and the Rule of Law: An Uncomfortable Relationship' (2016) 45 *Stetson L Rev* 439
Dressler J, 'Battered Women and Sleeping Abusers: Some Reflections' (2006) 3 *Ohio St J Crim L* 457
——, 'Battered Women Who Kill Their Sleeping Tormenters: Reflections on Maintaining Respect for Human Life While Killing Moral Monsters' in Shute S and Simester AP (eds), *Criminal Law Theory: Doctrines of the General Part* (Oxford, Oxford University Press, 2002)
——, 'New Thoughts About the Concept of Justification in the Criminal Law: A Critique of Fletcher's Thinking and Rethinking' (1984) 32 *UCLA L Rev* 61
——, 'Rethinking Heat of Passion: A Defense in Search of a Rationale' (1982) 73 *J Crim L & Criminology* 421
——, *Understanding Criminal Law* 6th edn (London, LexisNexis, 2012)
——, *Understanding Criminal Law* (London, LexisNexis, 1995)
Driggers A, 'Raj Rajaratnam's Historic Insider Trading Sentence' (2012) 49 *Am Crim LR* 2021
Dsouza M, *Rationale-Based Defences in Criminal Law* (Oxford, Hart Publishing, 2017)
Dubber MD & Hörnle T, *Criminal Law: A Comparative Approach* (Oxford, Oxford University Press, 2014)
Duff A, *Answering for Crime: Responsibility and Liability in the Criminal Law* (Oxford, Hart Publishing, 2007)
——, 'Choice, Character, and Criminal Liability' (1993) 12 *Law & Phil* 345

——, 'A Criminal Law We Can Call Our Own?' (2017) 111 *Nw U L Rev* 1491
——, 'Punishment, Citizenship and Responsibility' in Tam H (ed), *Punishment, Excuses and Moral Development* (Taylor & Francis, 1996)
——, *Punishment, Communication and Community* (New York, Oxford University Press, 2001)
——, *The Realm of Criminal Law* (Oxford, Oxford University Press, 2018)
Dupree T, 'You Sell Molly, I'll Sell Holly: Prosecuting Sex Trafficking in the United States' (2018) 78 *La L Rev* 1025
Duttge G, '§ 16 Irrtum Über Tatumstände' in *Gesamtest Strafrecht* (Baden-Baden, Nomos Verlagsgesellschaft, 2017)
Dutton MA & Goodman LA, 'Coercion in Intimate Partner Violence: Toward a New Conceptualization' (2005) 52 *Sex Roles* 743
Dworkin R, 'Rights as Trumps' in Waldron J (ed), *Theories of Rights* (Oxford, Oxford University Press, 1985)
Dyan H & Gross E, 'Between the Hammer and the Anvil: Battered Women Claiming Self-Defense and a Legislative Proposal to Amend Section 3.04(2)(B) of the US Model Penal Code' (2015) 52 *Harv J on Legis* 17
Dyckman M, 'Bringing the Wild West to Florida' *St Petersburg Times* (St Petersburg, Fla, 27 Mar 2005)
Dyer C & Travis A, 'Hague's law: the whole truth and nothing but?' *The Guardian* (26 April 2000, 20:34 EDT)
Dyson M & Vogel B, 'Reflections on Criminal Law in England and Germany' in Dyson M and Vogel B, *The Limits of Criminal Law: Anglo-German Concepts and Principles* (Cambridge, Intersentia Ltd, 2018)
East EH, *A Treatise of the Pleas of the Crown* (Nabu Press, 2011/1803)
Eckstein R, 'Towards a Communitarian Theory of Responsibility: Bearing the Burden for the Unintended' (1991) 45 *U Miami L Rev* 843
Ehrlich I, 'Participation in Illegitimate Activities: A Theoretical and Empirical Investigation' (1973) 81 *J Pol Econ* 521
Elliott C, 'Interpreting the Contours of Self-Defence Within the Boundaries of the Rule of Law, the Common Law and Human Rights' (2015) 79 *J Crim L* 330
Elsea J, *The Posse Comitatus Act and Related Matters: The Use of the Military to Execute Civilian Law* (Version 7, Congressional Research Service R42659, 2018)
Enker AN, 'In Support of the Distinction Between Justification and Excuse' (2009) 42 *Tex Tech L Rev* 273
Erb V, 'Notwehr als Menschenrecht. Zugleich eine Kritik der Entscheidung des LG Frankfurt am Main im "Fall Daschner"' (2005) 25 *NZSt* 593
——, 'Notwehr und Notstand' in von Heintschel-Heinegg B (ed), *Münchner Kommentar zum Strafgesetzbuch, Band 1* (Beck CH, 2017)
Erdsiek G, 'Umwelt und Recht' [1962] *NJW* 2240
Eser A, 'Justification and Excuse: A Key Issue in the Concept of Crime' in Eser A et al (eds), *Justification and Excuse: Comparative Perspectives*, vol 1 (1987)
Ewert MY, 'One Strike and You're out of Public Housing: How the Intersection of the War on Drugs and Federal Housing Policy Violated Due Process and Fair Housing Principles' (2016) 32 *Harv J Racial & Ethnic Just* 57
Farrell DM, 'The Justification of General Deterrence' (1985) 94 *Phil Rev* 367
Feenstra R, 'Dutch Kantharos Case and the History of Error In Substantia' (1973–1974) 48 *Tulsa L Rev* 846
Fehr C, '(Re-)Constitutionalizing Duress and Necessity' (2017) 42 *Queen's LJ* 99
——, 'Self-Defence and the Constitution' (2017) 43 *Queen's LJ* 85
Feinberg J, *Doing and Deserving: Essays in the Theory of Responsibility* (New Jersey, Princeton University Press, 1970)
——, *Harm to Others* (New York, Oxford University Press, 1984)
——, *Harm to Self* (New York, Oxford University Press, 1986)

Felber R, *Die Rechtswidrigkeit des Angriffs in den Notwehrbestimmungen* (1979)
Fenster M, 'The Opacity of Transparency' (2006) 91 *Iowa L Rev* 885
Ferrante M, 'Deterrence and Crime Results' (2007) 10 *New Crim LR* 1
Ferraro KF, *Fear of Crime: Interpreting Victimization Risk* (Albany, New York University Press, 1995)
Ferzan KK, 'Culpable Aggression: The Basis for Moral Liability to Defensive Killing' (2012) 9 *Ohio St J Crim L* 669
——, 'Defending Imminence: From Battered Women to Iraq' (2004) 46 *Ariz L Rev* 247
——, 'Self-Defense and the State' (2008) 5 *Ohio St J Crim L* 449
Finkelstein CO, 'Responsibility for Unintended Consequences' (2005) 2 *Ohio St J Crim L* 579
——, 'Self-Defense as a Rational Excuse' (1996) 57 *U Pitt L Rev* 621
Fischer T, '§ 32 Vorbemerkungen' in *Strafgesetzbuch* (Heymanns Verlag GmbH, 2019)
Fissell BM, 'Federalism and Constitutional Law' (2017) 46 *Hofstra L Rev* 489
Fletcher GP, *Basic Concepts of Criminal Law* (New York, Oxford University Press, 1998)
——, *A Crime of Self-Defense: Bernhard Goetz and the Law on Trial* (New Jersey, Prentice Hall, 1988)
——, 'Dogmas of the Model Penal Code' (1998) 2 *Buff Crim LR* 3
——, 'Domination in the Theory of Justification and Excuse' (1996) 57 *U Pitt L Rev* 553
——, 'The Individualization of Excusing Conditions' (1974) 47 *S Cal L Rev* 1269
——, 'The Nature of Justification' in Shute S et al (eds), *Action and Value in Criminal Law* (Oxford, Oxford University Press, 1993)
——, 'Paradoxes in Legal Thought' (1985) 85 *Colum L Rev* 1263
——, 'Proportionality and the Psychotic Aggressor: A Vignette in Comparative Criminal Theory' (1973) 8 *Isr L Rev* 367
——, 'Punishment and Self-Defense' (1989) 8 *Law & Phil* 201
——, *Rethinking Criminal Law* (New York, Oxford University Press, 1978)
——, 'The Right and the Reasonable' (1985) 98 *Harv L Rev* 949
——, 'The Right to Life' (1979) 13 *Ga L Rev* 1371
——, 'Should Intolerable Prison Conditions Generate a Justification or an Excuse For Escape?' (1979) 26 *UCLA L Rev* 1355
Fontaine RG, 'An Attack on Self-Defense' (2010) 47 *Am Crim LR* 57
——, 'In Self-Defense Regarding Self-Defense: A Rejoinder to Professor Corrado' (2010) 47 *Am Crim LR* 97
Foohey P, 'Jevic's Promise: Procedural Justice in Chapter 11' (2018) 93 *Wash L Rev Online* 128
Foster M, *Crown Cases* (Forgotten Books, 2018/1809)
Frank R, *Das Strafgesetzbuch für das Deutsche Reich* (Whitefish, Kessinger Publishing, 2010/1931)
Franks MA, 'I Am/I Am Not: On Angela Harris's Race and Essentialism in Feminist Legal Theory' (2014) 102 *Calif L Rev* 1053
Freund G, *Strafrecht: Allgemeiner Teil* (Berlin, Springer-Verlag Berlin and Heidelberg GmbH & Co KG, 2008)
Frey RG, 'Moral Standing, the Value of Lives, and Speciesism' in Russ Shafer-Landau, *The Ethical Life* 4th edn (New York, Oxford University Press, 2017)
Fried C, *Right and Wrong* (Cambridge, Mass, Harvard University Press, 1978)
Frisch W, *Vorsatz Und Risiko* (Heymanns, 1983)
Frister H, 'Die Notwehr im System der Notrechte' [1988] *GA* 291
Frowe H, *Defensive Killing* (Oxford, Oxford University Press, 2014)
——, 'A Practical Account of Self-Defence' (2010) 29 *Law & Phil* 245
Fuller LL, *The Morality of Law* (New Haven, Yale University Press, 1964)
Funk TM, 'Justifying Justifications' (1999) 19 *OJLS* 631
——, 'A Mere Youthful Indiscretion? Reexamining the Policy of Expunging Juvenile Delinquency Records' (1996) 29 *U Mich JL Reform* 885
Gaggioli G, 'Human Rights and Personal Self-Defense in International Law' (2017) 18 *Melb J Int'l L* 460
Gan O, 'Contractual Duress and Relations of Power' (2013) 36 *Harv JL & Gender* 171
Garcia J, 'Defending Self-Defense: Why Florida Should Follow the Eleven States that Already Allow for Campus Carry' (2018) 31 *St Thomas L Rev* 89

Gardner GK, '*Bailey v. Richardson* and the Constitution of the United States' (1953) 33 *BU L Rev* 176
Gardner J, 'Justifications and Reasons' in Simester AP and Smith A (eds), *Harm and Culpability* (Oxford, Oxford University Press, 1996)
——, 'The Mark of Responsibility' (2003) 23 *OJLS* 157
Gauthier D, 'Self-Defense and the Requirement of Imminence' (1996) 57 *U Pitt L Rev* 615
Geilen G, 'Eingeschränkte Notwehr unter Ehegatten?' [1976] *JR* 314
Geilen G, 'Notwehr und Notwehrexzess' [1981] *Jura* 200
Geisser R, 'A Just War Inquiry of Police, Prosecutors & Deadly Force' (2017) 10 *Wash U Juris Rev* 59
Gellner E, *Conditions of Liberty: Civil Society and Its Rivals* (London, Penguin Books, 1994)
Gemmill WN, 'Criminal Procedure (Report of Committee E of the Institute)' (1912) 3 *J Am Inst Crim L & Criminology* 566
George RP, 'The Concept of Public Morality' (2000) 45 *Am J Juris* 17
Ghanayim K & Wattad MS-A, 'Reconsidering the Grounds and the Causing Conditions for the Necessity Defense: Between Justification and Excuse – A Comprehensive Study' (2017) 86 *UMKC L Rev* 111
Gilman ME, 'The Poverty Defense' (2013) 47 *U Rich L Rev* 495
Ginn C, 'Ensuring the Effective Prosecution of Sexually Violent Crimes in the Bosnian War Crimes Chamber: Applying Lessons from the ICTY' (2013) 27 *Emory Int'l L Rev* 565
Golding MP, 'A Note on Discovery and Justification in Science and Law' in Pennock JR and Chapman JW (eds), *Justification: Nomos XXVIII* (1986)
Gorbes EE, 'The Domestic Abuse (Scotland) Act 2018: The Whole Story' (2018) 22 *Edinburgh L Rev* 406
Gossett WT, 'The Rule of Law or the Defiance of Law' (1969) 55 *ABA J* 823
Grabczynska A & Ferzan KK, 'Justifying Killing in Self-Defence' (2009) 99 *J Crim L & Criminology* 235
Graff C, 'The Religious Right to Therapeutic Abortions' (2017) 85 *Geo Wash L Rev* 954
Gray D, 'Retributivism, Confrontation, and the Death Penalty: Some Skepticism About Dan Markel's Skepticism' (2018) 51 *Tex Tech L Rev* 1
Greco L, 'Notwehr und Proportionalität' [2018] *GA* 665
Green DA, 'Indigenous Intellect: Problems of Calling Knowledge Property and Assigning It Rights' (2009) 15 *Tex Wesleyan L Rev* 335
Green SP, 'Castles and Carjackers: Proportionality and the Use of Deadly Force in Defense of Dwellings and Vehicles' [1999] *U Ill L Rev* 1
——, 'Moral Ambiguity in White Collar Criminal Law' (2004) 18 *Notre Dame JL Ethics & Pub Pol'y* 501
Green TA, 'The Jury and the English Law of Homicide 1200–1600' (1976) 74 *Mich L Rev* 413
Greenawalt K, *Conflicts of Law and Morality* (New York, Oxford University Press, 1989)
——, 'The Perplexing Borders of Justification and Excuse' (1984) 84 *Colum L Rev* 1897
Greenstein RK, 'The Three Faces of ORPP: Value Clashes in the Law' (1993) 54 *La L Rev* 95
Grotius H, *On the Rights of War and Peace* (Charleston, Nabu Press, 2009)
Gruber A, 'The Duty to Retreat in Self-Defense Law and Violence Against Women' *Oxford Handbooks Online* (6 July 2017), https://doi.org/10.1093/oxfordhb/9780199935352.013.5
Gusfield JR, 'Moral Passage: The Symbolic Process in Public Designations of Deviance' (1967) 15 *Soc Probs* 175
Haas R, *Notwehr Und Nothilfe: Zum Prinzip Der Abwehr Rechtwidriger Angriffe* (1978)
Habermas J, *Between Facts and Norms: Contributions to a Discourse Theory of Law and Democracy* (Oxford, Polity Press, 1996)
——, *Faktizität und Geltung Beiträge zur Diskurstheorie des Rechts und Des Demokratischen Rechtsstaats* (Suhrkamp, 1992)
——, 'Reply to Symposium Participants, Benjamin N. Cardozo School of Law' in Rosenfeld M and Arato A (eds), *Habermas on Law and Democracy: Critical Exchanges* (Berkeley, University of California Press, 1998)
Haldemann F, 'Another King of Justice: Transitional Justice as Recognition' (2008) 41 *Cornell Int'l LJ* 675
Hale M, *Pleas of the Crown* (Arkose Press, 2015/1736)

Hampton J, 'Correcting Harms Versus Righting Wrongs: The Goal of Retribution' (1992) 39 *UCLA L Rev* 1659

——, 'Forgiveness, Resentment and Hatred and the Retributive Idea' in Murphy JG and Hampton J, *Forgiveness and Mercy* (Oxford, Oxford University Press, 1988)

Harker K & Wright E, 'The HIV Stigma: Duty or Defence' (2015) 4 *UCL J L & Juris* 55

Harrelson J, 'Genocide and the Rape of Armenia' (2010) 4 *U St Thomas JL & Pub Pol'y* 163

Harris SF, *Principles of the Criminal Law* (Hansebooks, 2020/1877)

Hart HL, 'Are There Any Natural Rights?' in Quinton A (ed), *Political Philosophy* (Oxford, Oxford University Press, 1967)

——, *The Concept of Law* (Oxford, Oxford University Press, 1994)

——, *Punishment and Responsibility* (New York, Oxford University Press, 1968)

——, 'Social Solidarity and the Enforcement of Morality' (1967) 35 *U Chi L Rev* 1

Hart HM, Jr, 'The Aims of the Criminal Law' (1958) 23 *Law & Contemp Probs* 401

Hatch OG, 'The Brady Handgun Prevention Act and the Community Protection Initiative: Legislative Responses to the Second Amendment' [1998] *BYU L Rev* 103

Hauhart RC, 'The Involuntary Action Defense to a Criminal Indictment' (1984) 11 *N Ky L Rev* 321

Hawkins WA, *Treatise of the Pleas of the Crown* (Nobel Press, 2011/1787)

Hayek FA, *The Constitution of Liberty* (Chicago, University of Chicago Press, 1990)

——, *The Fatal Conceit: The Errors of Socialism* (London, Taylor & Francis, 1988)

Hegel GWF, *Philosophy of Right* (New York, Dover Publications, 1952)

——, *Phenomenology of Spirit* (Cambridge, Cambridge University Press, 2019/1807)

Heinrich B, *Strafrecht Allgemeiner Teil* (Stuttgart, Kohlhammer, 2016)

Hemmens C & Levin D, '"Not a Law at All": A Call for a Return to the Common Law Right to Resist Unlawful Arrest' (1999) 29 *Sw U L Rev* 1

Henderson LN, 'The Wrongs of Victim's Rights' (1985) 37 *Stan L Rev* 937

Henderson SE & Sorensen K, 'Search, Seizure, and Immunity: Second-Order Normative Authority and Rights' (2013) 32 *Crim Just Ethics* 108

Herring J, *Criminal Law* (Palgrave, 2018)

——, *Law and the Relational Self* (MS on file with author)

——, 'The Serious Wrong of Domestic Abuse and the Loss of Control Defence' in Reed A and Bohlander M (eds), *Loss of Control and Diminished Responsibility: Domestic, Comparative and International Perspectives* (Ashgate Publishing, 2011)

——, 'The Severity of Domestic Abuse' (2018) 30 *Nat'l L Sch India Rev* 37

Herring J & Foster C, 'Welfare Means Relationality, Virtue and Altruism' (2012) 32 *LS* 480

Hessbruegge JA, *Human Rights and Personal Self-Defense in International Law* (New York, Oxford University Press, 2016)

Hessick CB, 'Motive's Role in Criminal Punishment' (2006) 80 *S Cal L Rev* 89

Heyman SJ, 'Foundations of the Duty to Rescue' (1994) 47 *Vand L Rev* 673

Hillman RA, 'The Rhetoric of Legal Backfire' (2002) 43 *BC L Rev* 819

Himmelreich K, 'Erforderlichkeit der Abwehrhandlung, Gebotensein der Notwehrhandlung; Provokation und Rechtsmissbrauch; Notwehrexzeß' [1966] *GA* 129

His R, *Das Strafrecht des deutschen Mittelalters* (Wentworth Press, 2018/1964)

Hobbes T, *Leviathan* (London, Penguin Classics, 1982/1651)

Hoffman ML, 'Moral Internalization: Current Theory and Research' in Berkowitz L (ed), *Advances in Experimental Social Psychology*, vol 10 (San Diego, Elsevier Science Publishing, 1977)

Hogan B, 'The *Dadson* Principle' [1989] *Crim LR* 679

Hohfeld WN, 'Some Fundamental Legal Conceptions as Applied in Judicial Reasoning' (1913) 23 *Yale LJ* 16

Holland TE, 'Introduction' to Legnano GD, *Tractatus De Bello, De Represaliis et de Duello* (Andesite Press, 2015/1917)

Hollander-Blumoff R, 'The Psychology of Procedural Justice in the Federal Courts' (2011) 63 *Hastings LJ* 127

Hollander-Blumoff R & Tyler TR, 'Procedural Justice and the Rule of Law: Fostering Legitimacy in Alternative Dispute Resolution' [2011] *J Disp Resol* 1
Hooker B, 'The Elements of Well-Being' (2015) 3 *J Prac Ethics* 15
Horder J, *Ashworth's Principles of Criminal Law* 8th edn (Oxford, Oxford University Press, 2016)
——, 'Redrawing the Boundaries of Self-Defence' (1995) 58 *MLR* 431
——, 'Self-Defence, Necessity and Duress: Understanding the Relationship' (1998) 11 *Can JL & Juris* 143
Hörnle T, 'Social Expectations in the Criminal Law: The "Reasonable Person" in a Comparative Perspective' (2008) 11 *New Crim LR* 1
Hoyson L, 'Rape Is Tough Enough Without Having Someone Kick You from the Inside: The Case for Including Pregnancy as Substantial Bodily Injury' (2010) 44 *Val U L Rev* 565
Hruschka J, 'Der Gegenstand des Rechtswidrigkeitsurteils nach heutigem Strafrecht' [1980] *GA* 1
——, *Strafrecht Nach Logisch-Analytischer Methode* (Berlin, De Gruyter, 1988)
Hubbard FP, 'The Value of Life: Constitutional Limits on Citizens' Use of Deadly Force' (2014) 21 *Geo Mason L Rev* 623
Husak DN, 'A Liberal Theory of Excuses' (2005) 3 *Ohio St J Crim L* 287
——, 'Partial Defenses' (1998) 11 *Can JL & Juris* 167
Hutchinson DL, '"Continually Reminded of Their Inferior Position": Social Dominance, Implicit Bias, Criminality, and Race' (2014) 46 *Wash U JL & Pol'y* 23
Ikejiaku B-V, 'International Law, the International Development Legal Regime and Developing Countries' (2014) 7 *Law & Dev Rev* 131
Isensee J, 'Die Friedenspflicht der Bürger und das Gewaltmonopol des Staates' in Müller G and Eichenberger K (eds), *Staatsorganisation und Staatsfunktionen im Wandel: Festschrift für Kurt Eichenberger zum 60 Geburtstag* (Duncker & Humblot, 1982)
Jackson J et al, *Just Authority? Trust in the Police in England and Wales* (Cullompton, Taylor & Francis, 2012)
Jähnke B et al, *Strafgesetzbuch (Leipziger Kommentar)* (De Gruyter, 2018)
Jakobs G, *Rechtfertigung Und Entschuldigung IV* (Carlsen Verlag GmbH, 1993)
——, *Strafrecht: Allgemeiner Teil* (Berlin, De Gruyter, 2011)
Jarass HD & Pieroth B, *Grundgesetz für die Bundesrepublik Deutschland* 4th edn (Beck CH, 1997)
Jescheck H-H & Weigend T, *Lehrbuch des Strafrechts, Allgemeiner Teil* 5th edn (Duncker & Humblot GmbH, 1996)
Johnson JJ, 'Why Mississippi Should Reform Its Penal Code' (2019) 37 *Miss C L Rev* 107
Johnson M, *A Typology of Domestic Violence: Intimate Terrorism, Violent Resistance, and Situational Couple Violence* (Boston, Mass, Northeastern University Press, 2008)
Johnson NJ, 'Self-Defense' (2006) 2 *JL Econ & Pol'y* 187
Kadish SH, 'Respect for Life and Regard for Rights in the Criminal Law' (1976) 64 *Calif L Rev* 871
——, 'Excusing Crime' (1987) 75 *Calif L Rev* 257
——, 'Some Observations on the Use of Criminal Sanctions in Enforcing Economic Regulations' (1963) 30 *U Chi L Rev* 423
Kagan M, 'Dubious Deference: Reassessing Appellate Standards of Review in Immigration Appeals' (2012) 5 *Drexel L Rev* 101
Kahan DM, 'Social Influence, Social Meaning, and Deterrence' (1997) 83 *Va L Rev* 349
Kahan DM & Braman D, 'Cultural Cognition and Public Policy' (2006) 24 *Yale L & Pol'y Rev* 149
——, 'The Self-Defensive Cognition of Self-Defense' (2008) 45 *Am Crim LR* 1
Kant I, *The Metaphysics of Morals* (Cambridge, Mass, Hackett Publishing, 1991)
Kantorowicz H, *The Definition of Law* (Cambridge, Cambridge University Press, 2014/1980)
Kargl W, 'Die Intersubjektive Begründung und Begrenzung der Notwehr' (1998) 110 *ZStW* 38
Kasachkoff T, 'Comment and Reply to Suzanne Uniacke's "A Response to Two Critics"' (2000) 19 *Law & Phil* 635
——, 'Killing in Self-Defense: An Un-Questionable or Problematic Defense?' (1998) 17 *Law & Phil* 509
Kasiske P, 'Begründung und Grenzen der Nothilfe' [2004] *Jura* 832

Kates DB, Jr & Engberg NJ, 'Deadly Force Self-Defense Against Rape' (1982) 15 *UC Davis L Rev* 873
Kaufman WRP, 'Is There a "Right" to Self-Defense?' (2004) 23 *Crim Just Ethics* 20
——, 'Self-Defense, Imminence, and the Battered Woman' (2007) 10 *New Crim LR* 342
Kaufmann A, 'Zum Stande der Lehre vom personalen Unrecht' in *Festschrift für Hans Welzel zum 70 Geburtstag am 25 März 1974* (Berlin, De Gruyter, 1974)
Keckler CNW, 'Life v. Death: Who Should Capital Punishment Marginally Deter?' (2006) 2 *JL & Econ* 51
Kennedy H, *Eve Was Framed: Women and British Justice* (London, Vintage Publishing, 1992)
Keren-Paz T, 'Injuries from Unforeseeable Risks Which Advance Medical Knowledge: Restitution-Based Justification for Strict Liability' (2014) 5 *J Eur Tort Law* 275
Kershnar S, 'Forfeiture Theory and Symmetrical Attackers' (2017) 36 *Crim Just Ethics* 224
Kim JY, 'The Rhetoric of Self-Defense' (2008) 13 *Berkeley J Crim L* 261
Kinports K, 'Defending Battered Women's Self-Defense Claims' (1988) 67 *Or L Rev* 393
Klein A, 'Criminal Law and the Counter-Hegemonic Potential of Harm Reduction' (2015) 38 *Dalhousie LJ* 447
Klein LK, 'Rights Clash: How Conflicts Between Gay Rights and Religious Freedoms Challenge the Legal System' (2010) 98 *Geo LJ* 505
Klinger S, 'Youth Competence on Trial' [2007] *NZ L Rev* 235
Klose P, 'Notrecht des Staates aus staatlicher Rechtsnot' (1977) 89 *ZStW* 61
Knapp AT, 'Law's Revolutionary: James Wilson and the Birth of American Jurisprudence' (2014) 29 *JL & Pol* 189
Koch B, 'Prinzipientheorie der Notwehreinschränkungen' (1992) 104 *ZStW* 785
Koller M, *Not Kennt Kein Gebot* (Lit Verlag, 2006)
Kopacz C & Penick E, 'Double-Edge Sword of Victim Survival: Imperfect Self Defense' (2015) 29 *Chi Bar Assoc Rec* 32
Kopel DB et al, 'The Human Right of Self-Defense' (2007) 22 *BYU J Pub L* 43
Kotecha B, 'Necessity as a Defence to Murder: An Anglo-Canadian Perspective' (2014) 78 *J Crim L* 341
Kratzsch D, *Grenzen Der Strafbarkeit Im Notwehrrecht* (Berlin, De Gruyter, 1968)
Krause FW, 'Zur Einschränkung der Notwehrbefugnis' [1979] *GA* 329
Krause S, 'Killing in Defence of Property: A Constitutional Approach' [2012] *J S Afr L* 469
Krebs B, 'Justification and Excuse in Article 31 of the Rome Statute' (2013) 2 *Cambridge J Int'l & Comp L* 382
Kremnitzer M, 'Proportionality and the Psychotic Aggressor: Another View' (1983) 18 *Isr L Rev* 178
Kremnitzer M & Ghanayim K, 'Proportionality and the Aggressor's Culpability in Self-Defense' (2004) 39 *Tulsa L Rev* 875
Kreps DM, *A Course in Microeconomic Theory* (New Jersey, Princeton University Press, 1990)
Krey V, 'Zur Einschränkung des Notwehrrechts bei der Verteidigung von Sachgütern' (1979) 34 *JZ* 702
Kudlich H, 'Praxiskommentar' (2019) 39 *NStZ* 599
Kühl K, 'Die gebotene Verteidigung gegen provozierte Angriffe. Überlegungen aus Anlass der neusten Rechtsprechung des Bundesgerichtshofs zur Notwehrprovokation' in *Joachim Schulz & Gunter Bemmann, Festschrift für Günter Bemmann* (1997)
——, *Strafrecht Allgemeiner Teil* 8th edn (Vahlen Franz GmbH, 2017)
Kühl K & Heger M, 'Vorbemerkung § 32' in *Strafgesetzbuch: Kommentar* (Heymanns Verlag GmbH, 2018)
Kunen SMI, 'Superhuman in the Octagon, Imperfect in the Courtroom: Assessing the Culpability of Martial Artists Who Kill During Street Fights' (2011) 60 *Emory LJ* 1389
La Fond JQ, 'The Case for Liberalizing the Use of Deadly Force in Self-Defense' (1983) 6 *U Puget Sound* 237
Lacey N, *State Punishment: Political Principles and Community Values* (London, Routledge, 1988)
LaFave WR & Scott AW, *Substantive Criminal Law* 2nd edn (West Group Publishing, 2003)
——, *Substantive Criminal Law* (Eagan, Cengage Learning, 1986)
Lagodny O, 'Notwehr gegen Unterlassen' [1991] *GA* 300
Lamond G, 'Coercion and the Nature of Law' (2001) 7 *Legal Theory* 35

——, 'Core Principles of English Criminal Law' in Dyson M and Vogel B (eds), *The Limits of Criminal Law: Anglo-German Concepts and Principles* (Cambridge, Intersentia, 2018)
——, 'What is a Crime' (2007) 27 *OJLS* 609
Langbein JH, 'Controlling Prosecutorial Discretion in Germany' (1974) 41 *U Chi L Rev* 439
Lanham D, 'Larsonneur Revisited' [1976] *Crim LR 276*
Larsen JL, 'State Courts in a Federal System' (2019) 69 *Case W Res L Rev* 525
Law Commission, *Partial Defences to Murder Final Report*, Law Com No 290 (UK)
Lazarus L & Blackbourn J, 'Intelligence and the Criminal Law in England and Wales' in Dyson M and Vogel B (eds), *The Limits of Criminal Law: Anglo-German Concepts and Principles* (Cambridge, Intersentia, 2018)
Lee CKY, 'The Act-Belief Distinction in Self-Defense Doctrine: A New Dual Requirement Theory of Justification' (1998) 2 *Buff Crim LR* 191
——, 'Making Race Salient: Trayvon Martin and Implicit Bias in a Not Yet Post-Racial Society' (2013) 91 *NC L Rev* 1555
——, *Murder and the Reasonable Man: Passion and Fear in the Criminal Courtroom* (New York, New York University Press, 2003)
——, 'Race and Self-Defense: Toward a Normative Conception of Reasonableness' (1996) 81 *Minn L Rev* 367
——, 'Reforming the Law on Police Use of Deadly Force: De-Escalation, Preseizure Conduct, and Imperfect Self-Defense' [2018] *U Ill L Rev* 629
LeFrancois AG, 'The Act of Judging and the Performance of Being Earnest: Responding to Professor Chemerinsky's Informalism' (2001) 54 *Okla L Rev* 26
Leider R, 'Taming Self-Defense: Using Deadly Force to Prevent Escapes' (2018) 70 *Fla L Rev* 971
Lenckner T, '§32 Notwehr' in *Adolf Schönke & Horst Schröder, Strafgesetzbuch* 25th edn (Beck CH, 1997)
——, '"Gebotensein" und "Erforderlichkeit" der Notwehr' [1968] *GA* 1
Leoni B, *Freedom and the Law* 3rd edn (Indianapolis, Liberty Fund, 1991)
Lerner RL, 'The Worldwide Popular Revolt Against Proportionality in Self-Defense Law' (2006) 2 *JL Econ & Pol'y* 331
Lesch H, 'Die Notwehr' in Widmaier G et al (eds), *Festschrift für Hans Dahs* (Schmidt, Dr Otto, 2005)
Levanon L, 'Criminal Punishment as a Restorative Practice' (2015) 18 *New Crim LR* 537
Leverick F, *Killing in Self-Defence* (Oxford, Oxford University Press, 2006)
Levin B, 'The Consensus Myth in Criminal Justice Reform' (2018) 117 *Mich L Rev* 259
Levine K, 'Police Suspects' (2016) 116 *Colum L Rev* 1197
Levy K, 'Does Situationism Excuse – The Implications of Situationism for Moral Responsibility and Criminal Responsibility' (2015) 68 *Ark L Rev* 731
Lim M, 'A New Approach to the Ethics of Life: The Will to Live in Lieu of Inherent Dignity or Autonomy-Based Approaches' (2014) 24 *S Cal Interdisc LJ* 27
Liszt F, *Lehrbuch des Deutschen Strafrechts* 9th edn (Berlin, De Gruyter, 1899)
Loader I & Sparks R, 'Unfinished Business: Legitimacy, Crime Control, and Democratic Politics' in Tankebe J and Liebling A (eds), *Legitimacy and Criminal Justice: An International Exploration* (Oxford, Oxford University Press, 2013)
Locke J, *Second Treatise on Government* (Oxford, Oxford University Press, 2016/1689)
——, *Two Treatises of Government and a Letter Concerning Toleration* (New York, Dover Publications, 1690/2003)
Lorca R, 'The Presumption of Punishment: A Critical Review of Its Early Modern Origins' (2016) 29 *Can JL & Juris* 385
Lott JR, Jr & Mustard DB, 'Crime, Deterrence, and Right-to-Carry Concealed Handguns' (1997) 26 *J LS* 1
Loxton D et al, 'Psychological Health in Midlife Among Women Who Have Ever Lived with a Violent Partner or Spouse' (2006) 21 *J Interpersonal Violence* 1092

Lurigio AJ & Resick PA, 'Healing the Psychological Wounds of Criminal Victimization: Predicting Postcrime Distress and Recovery' in Lurigio AJ et al (eds), *Victims of Crime, Problems, Policies, and Programs*, vol 25 (Thousand Oaks, Sage Publications, 1990)

Macedo S, 'What Self-Governing Peoples Owe to One Another: Universalism, Diversity, and the Law of Peoples' (2004) 72 *Fordham L Rev* 1721

Mandiberg SF, 'Reasonable Officers vs. Reasonable Lay Persons in the Supreme Court's Miranda and Fourth Amendment Cases' (2010) 14 *Lewis & Clark L Rev* 1481

Manikis M & Grbac P, 'Bargaining for Justice: The Road Towards Prosecutorial Accountability in the Plea Bargaining Process' (2017) 40 *Man LJ* 85

Manninen BA, 'Rethinking *Roe v. Wade*: Defending the Abortion Right in the Face of Contemporary Opposition' (2010) 10 *Am J Bioethics* 33

Markel D, 'Retributive Justice and the Demands of Democratic Citizenship' (2012) 1 *Va J Crim L* 1

Matt H & Renzikowski J, *Strafgesetzbuch* (Vahlen Franz GmbH, 2013)

Mayer H, *Das Strafrecht des Deutschen Volkes* (tredition GmbH, 2018/1936)

Mayer M, *Der Allgemeine Teil des Deutschen Strafrechts* (Forgotten Books, 2018/1923)

Mayson SG, 'Collateral Consequences and the Preventative State' (2015) 91 *Notre Dame L Rev* 301

McConnell T, 'The Nature and Basis of Inalienable Rights' (1984) 3 *Law & Phil* 25

McGinley AC, 'Reasonable Men?' (2012) 45 *Conn L Rev* 1

McMahan J, 'Self-Defense Against Morally Innocent Threats' in Robinson PH et al (eds), *Criminal Law Conversations* (New York, Oxford University Press, 2011)

——, 'Self-Defense and the Problem of the Innocent Attacker' (1994) 104 *Ethics* 252

McMahon M & McGorrery P, 'Criminalising Controlling and Coercive Behaviour: The Next Step in the Prosecution of Family Violence?' (2016) 41 *Alternative LJ* 98

Mead GH, *Mind, Self, and Society* (Chicago, University of Chicago Press, 1967)

Meares TL et al, 'Updating the Study of Punishment' (2004) 56 *Stan L Rev* 1171

Meier JS, 'Dangerous Liaisons: A Domestic Violence Typology in Custody Litigation' (2017) 70 *Rutgers U L Rev* 115

Merten D & Arzt G, *Rechtsstaat und Gewaltmonopol (Recht Und Staat in Geschichte Und Gegenwart)* (1975)

Michaelsen C, 'Reforming Australia's National Security Laws: The Case for a Proportionality-Based Approach' (2010) 29 *U Tas L Rev* 31

Mill JS, *On Liberty and Other Writings* (Cambridge, Cambridge University Press, 1989)

——, *On Liberty And Utilitarianism* (New York, Bantam Doubleday Dell Publishing Group, 1993)

Miller AD, 'Two Theories of Criminal Justice' (1981) 79 *Mich L Rev* 904

Miller DAH, 'Retail Rebellion and the Second Amendment' (2011) 86 *Ind LJ* 939

Miller EJ, 'Encountering Resistance: Non-Compliance, Non-Cooperation and Procedural Justice' [2016] *U Chi Legal F* 295

Miller S, '"Grossly Disproportionate": Home Owners' Legal Licence to Kill' (2013) 77 *J Crim L* 299

Mitsch W, 'Nothilfe gegen provozierte Angriffe' [1986] *GA* 533

Mogridge G, 'The Reasonable Man: Negligence and Criminal Capacity' (1980) 97 *S Afr LJ* 267

Montague P, 'Self-Defense and Choosing Between Lives' (1981) 40 *Phil Stud* 207

Montenbruck A, *Deutsche Straftheorie* (Freie Universität Berlin, 2018)

Moon RM, 'An Examination of UK Law as It Pertains to the Unmarried Father: Current Legal Thinking in an International Context' (2010) 6 *Cambridge Student L Rev* 259

Moore JD, 'Reasonable Provocation: Distinguishing the Vigilant from the Vigilante in Self-Defense Law' (2013) 78 *Brook L Rev* 1659

Moore M & Hurd HM, 'Punishing the Awkward, the Stupid, the Weak, and the Selfish: The Culpability of Negligence' (2011) 5 *Crim L & Phil* 147

Moore MH, 'Legitimizing Criminal Justice Policies and Practices' (1997) 66 *FBI L Enforcement Bull* 14

Moore MS, *Act and Crime: The Philosophy of Action and Its Implications for Criminal Law* (Oxford, Oxford University Press, 1993)

Moriarty JC, 'While Dangers Gather: The Bush Preemption Doctrine, Battered Women, Imminence and Anticipatory Self-Defense' (2005) 30 *NYU Rev L & Soc Change* 1

Morris CW, *An Essay on the Modern State* (Cambridge, Cambridge University Press, 2002)

Morris H, 'Persons and Punishment' in Morris H, *On Guilt and Innocence: Essays in Legal Philosophy and Moral Psychology* (University of California Press, 1976)

Mousourakis G, 'Distinguishing Between Justifications and Excuses in the Criminal Law' (1998) 9 *Stellenbosch L Rev* 165

Munzer SR, *New Essays in the Legal and Political Theory of Property* (Cambridge, Cambridge University Press, 2010)

Murdoch JB, 'Is Imminence Really Necessity? Reconciling Traditional Self-Defense Doctrine with the Battered Woman Syndrome' (2000) 20 *N Ill U L Rev* 191

Murphy K et al, 'Motivating Compliance Behavior Among Offenders: Procedural Justice or Deterrence?' (2016) 43 *Crim Just & Behavior* 102

Nader L, 'The Anthropological Study of Law' in Sack P and Aleck J (eds), *Law and Anthropology* (New York, New York University Press, 1992)

Nadler J, 'Flouting the Law' (2005) 83 *Tex L Rev* 1399

Nedelsky J, *Law's Relations: A Relational Theory of Self, Autonomy, and Law* (New York, Oxford University Press, 2013)

Neuborne B, 'Ghosts in the Attic: Idealized Pluralism, Community and Hate Speech' (1992) 27 *Harv CR-CL L Rev* 371

Nourse VF, 'Reconceptualizing Criminal Law Defenses' (2003) 151 *U Pa L Rev* 1691

——, 'Self-Defense and Subjectivity' (2001) 68 *U Chi L Rev* 1235

Nozick R, *Anarchy, State, and Utopia* (New York, Ingram Publisher Services, 1974)

Oldenquist A, 'Loyalties' (1982) 79 *J Phil* 173

Oleson KC & Darley JM, 'Community Perceptions of Allowable Counterforce in Self-Defense and Defense of Property' (1999) 23 *Law & Hum Behav* 629

Omichinski NM, 'Applying the Theories of Justifiable Homicide to Conflicts in the Doctrine of Self-Defense' (1987) 33 *Wayne L Rev* 1447

Ormerod D & Laird K, *Smith, Hogan, and Ormerod's Criminal Law* 15th edn (Oxford, Oxford University Press, 2018)

Osborne E, *Self-Regulation and Human Progress: How Society Gains When We Govern Less* (Palo Alto, Stanford University Press, 2018)

Osiel M, 'The Banality of Good: Aligning Incentives Against Mass Atrocity' (2005) 105 *Colum L Rev* 1751

Packer HL, 'Mens Rea and the Supreme Court' [1962] *Sup Ct Rev* 107

Park I, *The Right to Life in Armed Conflict* (Oxford, Oxford University Press, 2018)

Partlett W, 'Criminal Law and Cooperative Federalism' (2019) 56 *Am Crim LR* 1663

Paternoster R, 'Decisions to Participate in and Desist from Four Types of Common Delinquency: Deterrence and the Rational Choice Perspective' (1989) 23 *Law & Soc'y Rev* 7

Pathinayake A, 'Should We Deter Against General Deterrence?' (2018) 9 *Wake Forest JL & Pol'y* 63

Pavić I, 'Human Dignity in the Context of Prison Privatization' (2018) 8 *Jurid Trib* 6

Pawlik M, 'Die Notwehr nach Kant und Hegel' (2002) 114 *ZStW* 259

Perkins RM, *Criminal Law and Procedure: Cases and Materials* 3rd edn (Minnesota, West Academic, 2017/1966)

Perron W, '§ 32' in Eser A et al (eds), *Schönke/Schröder: Strafgesetzbuch* 30th edn (Beck CH, 2019)

Perry MJ, 'The Morality of Human Rights' (2013) 50 *San Diego L Rev* 775

Pest R, 'Die Erforderlichkeit der Notwehrhandlung' in Stam F and Werkmeister A (eds), *Der Allgemeine Teil des Strafrechts in der aktuellen Rechtsprechung* (Baden-Baden, Nomos Verlagsgesellschaft, 2019)

Petersen N, 'Avoiding the Common-Wisdom Fallacy: The Role of Social Sciences in Constitutional Adjudication' (2013) 11 *Int'l J Const L* 294

Pfuhl EH, Jr, 'Humanistic Criminology: Future Prospects' (1985) 12 *J Soc & Soc Welfare* 604

Phillipson C, 'Introduction' to Gentili A, *De Iure Belli Libri Tres*, vol II (William S Hein & Company, 1995)

Pichhadze A, 'Proposals for Reforming the Law of Self-Defence' (2008) 72 *J Crim L* 409

Picinali F, 'Innocence and Burdens of Proof in English Criminal Law' (2014) 13 *Law Probability & Risk* 243

Pitman T, 'Living with Coercive Control: Trapped Within a Complex Web of Double Standards, Double Binds and Boundary Violations' (2016) 47 *British J Soc Work* 143

Plato, 'The Laws' in Hamilton E et al (eds), *The Collected Dialogues of Plato* (New Jersey, Princeton University Press, 360 BC/1961)

Popper AF, 'In Defense of Deterrence' (2011) 75 *Alb L Rev* 181

Porat B, 'Lethal Self-Defense Against a Rapist and the Challenge of Proportionality: Jewish Law Perspective' (2013) 26 *Colum J Gender & L* 123

Poscher R, 'The Ultimate Force of the Law: On the Essence and Precariousness of the Monopoly on Legitimate Force' (2016) 29 *Ratio Juris* 311

Preub UK, 'Communicative Power and the Concept of Law' (1995) 17 *Cardozo L Rev* 1179

Primoratz I, *Justifying Legal Punishment* (Humanities Press International, 1989)

Prittwitz C, 'Zum Verteidigungswillen bei der Notwehr' [1980] *GA* 381

Punzo A, 'Microstamping: Hot Lead or Dud Round' (2019) 49 *Seton Hall L Rev* 375

Qureshi WA, 'Legal Exceptions to the Inalienable Right to Life' (2019) 53 *USF L Rev* 263

Radice J, 'The Reintegrative State' (2017) 66 *Emory LJ* 1315

Ramsay P, 'The Responsible Subject as Citizen: Criminal Law, Democracy and the Welfare State' (2006) 69 *MLR* 29

Ramsey CB, 'Provoking Change: Comparative Insights on Feminist Homicide Law Reform' (2010) 100 *J Crim L & Criminology* 33

Randles TB, 'Soft-Served Deserts: Soft Retributivism as a Free Will Independent Alternative for the Criminal Justice System' (2018) 67 *Cath U L Rev* 495

Rausch RL, 'Reframing Roe: Property over Privacy' (2012) 27 *Berkeley J Gender L & Just* 28

Rawls J, 'The Basic Liberties and Their Priority' in McMurrin SM (ed), *The Tanner Lectures on Human Values III* (Cambridge, Cambridge University Press, 1982)

——, *Justice as Fairness: A Restatement* (Cambridge, Mass, Harvard University Press, 2001)

——, *Political Liberalism* (New York, Columbia University Press, 2011/1993)

——, *A Theory of Justice* (Cambridge, Mass, Harvard University Press, 1971)

Raymond M, 'Looking for Trouble: Framing and the Dignitary Interest in the Law of Self-Defense' (2010) 71 *Ohio St LJ* 287

Raz J, *Between Authority and Interpretation: On the Theory of Law and Practical Reason* (Oxford, Oxford University Press, 2009)

——, 'Legitimate Authority' in *The Authority of Law: Essays On Law and Morality* (2009)

——, *The Morality of Freedom* (Oxford, Oxford University Press, 1986)

Reed A, 'Self-Defence – Applying the Objective Approach to Reasonable Force' (1996) 60 *J Crim L* 94

Renzikowski J, *Notstand und Notwehr* (Duncker & Humblot GmbH, 1994)

Retzko S, *Die Angriffsverursachung bei der Notwehr* (Lit Verlag, 2001)

Rhoades K, 'Choice & Trafficking' (2018) 64 *St Louis B J* 30

Richards DAJ, 'Rights, Resistance, and the Demands of Self-Respect' (1983) 32 *Emory LJ* 405

Richardson J, *Archbold: Criminal Pleading Evidence & Practice* 67th edn (London, Sweet & Maxwell, 2019)

Richardson LS & Goff PA, 'Self Defense and the Suspicion Heuristic' (2012) 98 *Iowa L Rev* 293

Rietiker D, 'Police Violence and How to Fight It, in Particular when Racially Motivated: The Example of the European Court of Human Rights' (2019) 52 *Suffolk U L Rev* 417

Ripstein A, *Force and Freedom: Kant's Legal and Political Philosophy* (Cambridge, Mass, Harvard University Press, 2009)

——, 'Tort Law in Liberal State' (2007) 1 *J Tort L* 1

Robert JV & de Keijser JW, *Democratising Punishment: Sentencing, Community Views and Values* (2014)

Robinson PH, 'Causing the Conditions of One's Own Defense: A Study in the Limits of Theory in Criminal Law Doctrine' (1985) 71 *Va L Rev* 1
——, 'Competing Theories of Justification: Deeds v. Reasons' in Simester AP and Smith A (eds), *Harm and Culpability* (Oxford, Oxford University Press, 1996)
——, *Criminal Law Defenses* (West Publishing Company, 2019)
——, 'Criminal Law Defenses: A Systematic Analysis' (1982) 82 *Colum L Rev* 199
——, 'Fair Notice and Fair Adjudication: Two Kinds of Legality' (2005) 154 *U Pa L Rev* 335
——, 'Hybrid Principles for the Distribution of Criminal Sanctions' (1987–1988) 82 *Nw U L Rev* 19
——, 'Imputed Criminal Liability' (1984) 93 *Yale LJ* 609
——, 'The Ongoing Revolution in Punishment Theory: Doing Justice as Controlling Crime' (2010) 42 *Ariz St LJ* 1089
——, 'Punishing Dangerousness: Cloaking Preventive Detention as Criminal Justice' (2001) 114 *Harv L Rev* 1429
——, *Structure and Function in Criminal Law* (Oxford, Oxford University Press, 1997)
Robinson PH & Darley JM, 'Does Criminal Law Deter? A Behavioural Science Investigation' (2004) 24 *OJLS* 173
——, 'Intuitions of Justice: Implications for Criminal Law and Justice Policy' (2007) 81 *S Cal L Rev* 1
——, *Justice, Liability, and Blame: Community Views and the Criminal Law* (Taylor & Francis, 1995)
——, 'The Role of Deterrence in the Formulation of Criminal Law Rules: At Its Worst When Doing Its Best' (2003) 91 *Geo LJ* 949
——, 'Testing Competing Theories of Justification' (1998) 76 *NC L Rev* 1095
Robinson PH et al, 'The Disutility of Injustice' (2010) 85 *NYU L Rev* 1940
Rodin D, *War & Self-Defense* (Oxford, Oxford University Press, 2003)
Rodwan G, 'Criminal Law' (1993) 39 *Wayne L Rev* 503
Rönnau T & Hohn K, '§ 32 Notwehr' in Cirener G et al (eds), *Strafgesetzbuch: Leipziger Kommentar Band 3 §§ 32-37*, vol 3, 13th edn (Berlin, De Gruyter, 2019)
Rose A, 'Forfeiture of Confrontation Rights Post-Giles: Whether a Co-Conspirator's Misconduct Can Forfeit a Defendant's Right to Confront Witnesses' (2011) 14 *NYU J Legis & Pub Pol'y* 281
Rosenau H, 'Notwehr und Notstand' in Satzger H and Schluckebier W (eds), *Strafgesetzbuch: Kommentar*, vol 4 (Heymanns Verlag GmbH, 2019)
Rosenbaum DP, 'Community Crime Prevention: A Review and Synthesis of the Literature' (1988) 5 *Just Q* 323
Rousseau J-J, *The Social Contract* (London, Penguin Books, 1947)
Roxin C, 'Die "Sozialethische Einschränkungen" des Notwehrrechts' (1981) 93 *ZStW* 68
——, *Strafrecht, Allgemeiner Teil* 3rd edn (Beck CH, 1997)
——, *Strafrecht: Allgemeiner Teil Band I, Grundlagen, der Aufbau der Verbrechenslehre* (Beck CH, 2006)
Royer CE, 'The Disobedient Jury: Why Lawmakers Should Codify Jury Nullification' (2017) 102 *Cornell L Rev* 1401
Rückert C, *Effektive Selbstverteidigung Und Notwehrrecht* (Tübingen, Mohr Siebeck, 2017)
Rulli LS, 'Seizing Family Homes from the Innocent: Can the Eighth Amendment Protect Minorities and the Poor from Excessive Punishment in Civil Forfeiture?' (2016) 19 *U Pa J Const L* 1111
Russell H, *The Use of Force and Article 2 of the ECHR in Light of European Conflicts* (Oxford, Hart Publishing, 2017)
Russell WO, *A Treatise on Crimes and Indictable Misdemeanours* 2nd edn (Charleston, Gale, 2010/1826)
Ryan CC, 'Self-Defense, Pacifism and the Possibility of Killing' (1983) 93 *Ethics* 508
Sales NA, 'Regulating Cyber-Security' (2013) 107 *Nw U L Rev* 1503
Sandel MJ, *Democracy's Discontent: America in Search of a Public Philosophy* (Cambridge, Mass, Harvard University Press, 1996)
Sandomierski D, 'Tension and Reconciliation in Canadian Contract Law Casebooks' (2017) 54 *Osgoode Hall LJ* 1181
Sangero B, 'Heller's Self-Defense' (2010) 13 *New Crim LR* 449
——, 'A New Defense for Self-Defense' (2006) 9 *Buff Crim LR* 475

——, *Self-Defence in Criminal Law* (Oxford, Hart Publishing, 2006)
Sarat A & Kearns TR, 'A Journey Through Forgetting: Toward a Jurisprudence of Violence' in Sarat A and Kearns TR (eds), *The Fate of Law* (Ann Arbor, University of Michigan Press, 1993)
Schaffstein F, 'Putative Rechtfertigungsgründe und finale Handlungslehre' (1951) 5 *MDR* 196
Schlüchter E, 'Kein Recht zur Beweisvernichtung nach einem potentiellen Selbstbedienungsladendiebstahl' [1987] *JR* 309
Schmidhäuser E, 'Die Begründung der Notwehr' [1991] *GA* 97
——, 'Über Die Wertstruktur Der Notwehr' in *Festschrift Für Richard M Honig* (1970)
Schneider EM, 'Describing and Changing: Women's Self-Defense Work and the Problem of Expert Testimony on Battering' (1986) 9 *Women's Rts L Rep* 195
Schopp RF, *Justification Defenses and Just Convictions* (Cambridge, Cambridge University Press, 1998)
——, 'Justification Defenses and Just Convictions' (1993) 24 *Pac LJ* 1233
——, 'Justifying Capital Punishment in Principle and in Practice: Empirical Evidence of Distortion in Application' (2002) 81 *Neb L Rev* 805
——, 'Multiple Personality Disorder, Accountable Agency, and Criminal Acts' (2001) 10 *S Cal Interdisc LJ* 297
——, 'Reconciling Irreconcilable Capital Punishment Doctrine as Comparative and Noncomparative Justice' (2001) 53 *Fla L Rev* 475
——, 'Self-Defense' in Coleman J (ed), *In Harm's Way* (Cambridge, Cambridge University Press, 1994)
——, 'Sexual Predators and the Structure of the Mental Health System: Expanding the Normative Focus of Therapeutic Jurisprudence' (1995) 1 *Psychol Pub Pol'y & Law* 161
——, 'Verdicts of Conscience: Nullification and Necessity as Jury Responses to Crimes of Conscience' (1996) 69 *S Cal L Rev* 2039
Schopp RF et al, 'Battered Woman Syndrome, Expert Testimony, and the Distinction Between Justification and Excuse' [1994] *U Ill L Rev* 45
Schroth U, 'Notwehr bei Auseinandersetzungen in engen persönlichen Beziehungen' [1984] *NJW* 2562
Schulhofer SJ, 'The Gender Question in Criminal Law' (1990) 7 *Soc Phil & Pol'y* 105
Schulz J & Bemmann G, *Festschrift Für Günter Bemmann* (Beck CH, 1997)
Schünemann B, 'Die deutschsprachige Strafrechtwissenshcaft nach der Strafrechtsreform im Spiegel des Leipziger Kommentars und des Wiener Kommentars' [1985] *GA* 341
Schwarze F, *Das Strafgesetzbuch für den Norddeutschen Bund* (Berlin, De Gruyter, 1870)
Schwirck H, 'Law's Violence and the Boundary Between Corporal Discipline and Physical Abuse in German South West Africa' (2002) 36 *Akron L Rev* 81
Secula MR, 'Particularities of Contraventions Against Other Forms of Legal Liability' [2010] *L Annals Titu Maiorescu U* 159
Seelmann K, 'Grenzen privater nothilfe' (1977) 89 *ZStW* 36
Segev R, 'Fairness, Responsibility and Self-Defense' (2005) 45 *Santa Clara L Rev* 383
Sendor BB, 'Crime as Communication: An Interpretive Theory of the Insanity Defense and the Mental Elements of Crime' (1986) 74 *Geo LJ* 1371
——, 'Mistakes of Fact: A Study in the Structure of Criminal Conduct' (1990) 25 *Wake Forest L Rev* 707
——, 'The Relevance of Conduct and Character to Guilt and Punishment' (1996) 10 *Notre Dame JL Ethics & Pub Pol'y* 99
——, 'Restorative Retributivism' (1994) 5 *J Contemp Legal Issues* 323
Sepinwall AJ, 'Faultless Guilt: Toward a Relationship-Based Account of Criminal Liability' (2017) 54 *Am Crim LR* 521
Shafer-Landau R, *The Ethical Life* 4th edn (New York, Oxford University Press, 2017)
Simester A & von Hirsch A, 'On the Legitimate Objectives of Criminalisation' (2016) 10 *Crim L & Phil* 367
Simester AP, 'Mistakes in Defence' (1992) 12 *OJLS* 295
Simester AP & von Hirsch A, *Crimes, Harms, and Wrongs: On the Principles of Criminalisation* (Oxford, Hart Publishing, 2011)
Simmons R, 'The Role of the Prosecutor and the Grand Jury in Police Use of Deadly Force Cases: Restoring the Grand Jury to Its Original Purpose' (2017) 65 *Clev St L Rev* 519

Simon WH, 'The Organization of Prosecutorial Discretion' in Langer M and Sklansky D (eds), *Prosecutors and Democracy – A Cross-National Study* (Cambridge, Cambridge University Press, 2017)
Simons KW, 'The Relevance of Victim Conduct in Tort and Criminal Law' (2005) 8 *Buff Crim LR* 541
——, 'Self-Defense, Mens Rea, and Bernhard Goetz' (1989) 89 *Colum L Rev* 1179
——, 'Self-Defense: Reasonable Beliefs or Reasonable Self-Control' (2008) 2 *New Crim LR* 51
Singer RG, 'The Resurgence of Mens Rea: III – The Rise and Fall of Strict Criminal Liability' (1989) 30 *BC L Rev* 337
Skolnik T, 'Homelessness and the Impossibility to Obey the Law' (2016) 43 *Fordham Urb LJ* 741
Skopets M, 'Battered Nation Syndrome: Relaxing the Imminence Requirement of Self-Defense in International Law' (2006) 55 *Am U L Rev* 753
Slater J, 'Making Sense of Self-Defence' (1996) 5 *Nottingham LJ* 140
Smith JC, *Justification and Excuse in the Criminal Law* (London, Sweet & Maxwell, 1989)
——, 'The Use of Force in Public or Private Defence and Article 2' [2002] *Crim LR* 961
Smith JC & Hogan B, *Criminal Law* 5th edn (London, LexisNexis, 2005/1983)
Smith SD, 'Is the Harm Principle Illiberal' (2006) 51 *Am J Juris* 1
Soles DE, 'Four Concepts of Loyalty' (1993) 8 *Int'l J Applied Phil* 43
Solum LB, 'Procedural Justice' (2004) 78 *S Cal L Rev* 181
Sparks R et al, *Prisons and the Problem of Order* (Oxford, Oxford University Press, 1996)
Spendel G, '§ 32 Notwehr' in Jähnke B et al (eds), *Strafgessetzbuch: Leipziger Kommentar* 11th edn (Berlin, De Gruyter, 1992)
Stark E, *Coercive Control: How Men Entrap Women in Personal Life* (New York, Oxford University Press, 2007)
——, 'Re-Presenting Woman Battering: From Battered Woman Syndrome to Coercive Control' (1995) 58 *Alb L Rev* 973
Stell LK, 'Close Encounters of the Lethal Kind: The Use of Deadly Force in Self-Defense' (1986) 49 *Law & Contemp Probs* 113
Stephen JF, *A Digest of Criminal Law* 9th edn (Whitefish, Kessinger Publishing, 2010/1950)
Stockdale F, 'Withdrawing a License to Kill: Why American Law Should Jettison Stand Your Ground and Adopt the English Approach to Retreat' (2016) 39 *BC Int'l & Comp L Rev* 453
Stone GR, 'Autonomy and Distrust' (1993) 64 *U Colo L Rev* 1171
Sunstein CR & Thaler RH, 'Libertarian Paternalism Is Not an Oxymoron' (2003) 70 *U Chi L Rev* 1159
Sweeney D, 'Standing Up to "Stand Your Ground" Laws: How the Modern NRA-Inspired Self-Defense Statutes Destroy the Principle of Necessity, Disrupt the Criminal Justice System, and Increase Overall Violence' (2016) 64 *Clev St L Rev* 715
Sytnichenko L, 'Otfried Höffe's Theory of Social Justice' (2015) 44 *Polish Pol Sci YB* 23
Tadros V, 'The Scope and the Grounds of Responsibility' (2008) 11 *New Crim LR* 91
Tankebe J, 'Self-Help, Policing, and Procedural Justice: Ghanaian Vigilantism and the Rule of Law' (2009) 43 *Law & Soc'y Rev* 245
Thomas M, 'Defenceless Castles: The Use of Grossly Disproportionate Force by Householders in Light of *R (Collins) v. Secretary of State for Justice*' (2016) 80 *J Crim L* 407
Thompson K & Cohen J, 'Trayvon Martin case: Poll finds stark racial divide' *Wash Post* (10 April 2012) A3
Thomson JJ, *Rights, Restitution, and Risk: Essays in Moral Theory* (Cambridge, Mass, Harvard University Press, 1986)
——, 'Self-Defense' (1991) 20 *Phil & Pub Aff* 283
Thorburn M, 'Justifications, Powers, and Authority' (2008) 117 *Yale LJ* 1070
Tobler H, *Die Grenzgebiete Zwischen Notstand Und Notwehr* (Whitefish, Kessinger Publishing, 1894)
Tomlinson KD, 'An Examination of Deterrence Theory: Where Do We Stand?' (2016) 80 *Fed Probation J* 33
Trechsel S, 'Comparative Observations on Human Rights Law and Criminal Law' [2000] *St Louis-Warsaw Transatlantic LJ* 1
Trevelyan HM (ed), *The Works of Lord Macaulay*, vol 7 (Hardback Publishing, 2019/1866)
Tsesis A, 'Balancing Free Speech' (2016) 96 *BU L Rev* 1

Tur RHS, 'Justifications of Reverse Discrimination' in Stewart M (ed), *Law, Morality and Rights* (Dordrecht, Springer, 1983)
Tyler TR, 'Procedural Justice, Legitimacy, and the Effective Rule of Law' (2003) 30 *Crime & Just* 283
——, 'Psychological Perspectives on Legitimacy and Legitimation' (2006) 57 *Ann Rev Psychol* 375
——, 'Public Mistrust of the Law: A Political Perspective' (1998) 66 *U Cin L Rev* 847
——, 'Trust and Law Abidingness: A Proactive Model of Social Regulation' (2001) 81 *BU L Rev* 361
——, *Why People Obey the Law* (New Haven, Yale University Press, 1990)
Tyler TR & Fagan J, 'Legitimacy and Cooperation: Why Do People Help the Police Fight Crime in Their Communities?' (2008–2009) 6 *Ohio St J Crim L* 231
UNCHR (Sub-Commission), *Prevention of Human Rights Violations Committed with Small Arms and Light Weapons* (2006), UN Doc A/HRC/Sub.1/58/27 (prepared by Barbara Frey)
Uniacke S, 'In Defense of "Permissible Killing": A Response to Two Critics' (2000) 19 *Law & Phil* 627
——, *Permissible Killing: The Self-Defence Justification of Homicide* (Cambridge, Cambridge University Press, 1994)
——, 'Self-Defense and Natural Law' (1991) 36 *Am J Juris* 73
Van Craen M & Skogan WG, 'Trust in the Belgian Police: The Importance of Responsiveness' (2015) 12 *Eur J Criminology* 129
Verchick RRM, 'Culture, Cognition, and Climate' [2016] *U Ill L Rev* 969
Vogel B, 'The Core Legal Concepts and Principles Defining Criminal Law in Germany' in Dyson M and Vogel B (eds), *The Limits of Criminal Law: Anglo-German Concepts and Principles* (Cambridge, Intersentia, 2018)
von Humboldt W, *The Limits of State Action* (Indianapolis, Liberty Fund, 1993)
von Maurach R & Zipf H, *Strafrecht, Allgemeiner Teil* (Heidelberg, CF Müller, 1992)
von Pufendorf S, *De Officio Hominis et Civis Juxta Legem Naturalem Libri Duo*, vol 2 (Palala Press, 2015/1927)
——, *Of the Law of Nature and Nations*, vol 2 (Wentworth Press, 2016/1710)
——, *On The Duty of Man and Citizen* (Cambridge, Cambridge University Press, 2007/1991)
von Scherenberg C-F, *Die Sozialethischen Einschränkungen der Notwehr* (Bern, Peter Lang AG, 2009)
von Talge J, 'Victimization Dynamics: The Psycho-Social and Legal Implications of Family Violence Directed Toward Women and the Impact on Child Witnesses' (1999–2000) 27 *W St U L Rev* 111
Wagner RE, 'Corporate Criminal Prosecutions and Double Jeopardy' (2019) 16 *Berkeley Bus LJ* 205
——, 'Corporate Criminal Prosecutions and the Exclusionary Rule' (2016) 68 *Fla L Rev* 1119
Wake N, 'Battered Women, Startled Householders and Psychological Self-Defence: Anglo-Australian Perspectives' (2013) 77 *J Crim L* 433
Waldron J, *The Right to Private Property* (Oxford, Oxford University Press, 1989)
——, 'Self-Defense: Agent-Neutral and Agent-Relative Accounts' (2000) 88 *Calif L Rev* 711
Walen A, 'Consensual Sex Without Assuming the Risk of Carrying an Unwanted Fetus; Another Foundation for the Right to an Abortion' (1997) 63 *Brook L Rev* 1051
Walker LE, *The Battered Woman Syndrome* 4th edn (New York, Springer Publishing, 2016)
Wallace S, 'Beyond Imminence: Evolving International Law and Battered Women's Right to Self-Defense' (2004) 71 *U Chi L Rev* 1749
Wallerstein S, 'Justifying the Right to Self-Defense: A Theory of Forced Consequences' (2005) 91 *Va L Rev* 999
Wang C, 'The Police Are Innocent as Long as They Honestly Believe: The Human Rights Problems with English Self-Defense Law' (2017) 49 *Colum Hum Rts L Rev* 373
Wannop AL, 'Battered Woman Syndrome and the Defense of Battered Women in Canada and England' (1995) 19 *Suffolk Transnat'l L Rev* 251
Ward CV, 'Restoring Fairness to Campus Sex Tribunals' (2018) 85 *Tenn L Rev* 1073
Warda G, 'Die Geeignetheit der Verteidigungshandlung bei der Notwehr Strittiges in der aktuellen Diskussion' [1996] *GA* 405
Washburn R, 'The Decline of Authority' (1927) 32 *Com L League J* 229
Wasserman D, 'Justifying Self-Defense' (1987) 16 *Phil & Pub Aff* 356

Watkins LE et al, 'The Longitudinal Impact of Intimate Partner Aggression and Relationship Status on Women's Physical Health and Depression Symptoms' (2014) 28 *J Fam Psychol* 655
Watson CW, 'Justifiable Use of Deadly Force in Law Enforcement' (1973) 78 *Dick L Rev* 115
Weber M, *Economy and Society: An Outline of Interpretive Sociology* (Berkeley, University of California Press, 1978)
——, 'Politics as a Vocation' in Gerth HH and Mills CW (eds), *From Max Weber: Essays in Sociology* (London, Taylor and Francis, 1919/1946)
Weinrib EJ, 'Restitutionary Damages as Corrective Justice' (2000) 1 *Theoretical Inquiries LF* 1
Welzel H, *Das Deutsche Strafrecht* 11th edn (Berlin, De Gruyter, 1969)
Wessels J & Satzger H, *Wessels/Beulke: Strafrecht – Allgemeiner Teil* (Müller Jur Vlg CF 2018)
Westen P, 'Poor Wesley Hohfeld' (2018) 55 *San Diego L Rev* 449
——, 'Reflections on Joshua Dressler's Understanding Criminal Law' (2018) 15 *Ohio St J Crim L* 311
Wexler DB, 'Justice, Mental Health, and Therapeutic Jurisprudence' (1992) 40 *Clev St L Rev* 517
Wharton F, *A Treatise on the Criminal Law of the United States* 3rd edn (Arkose Press, 2015/1855)
——, *A Treatise on the Criminal Law of the United States* 7th edn (Arkose Press, 2015/1874)
White L, 'God, Guns & Money: A Global Perspective on Intentional Homicide' (2016) 44 *W St U L Rev* 47
Whiteman JM, 'Recent Decisions: The Court of Appeals of Maryland' (2002) 61 *Md L Rev* 795
Whitman JQ, 'Between Self-Defense and Vengeance/Between Social Contract and Monopoly of Violence' (2004) 39 *Tulsa L Rev* 901
Williams G, 'Necessity: Duress of Circumstances or Moral Involuntariness?' (2014) 43 *Common L World Rev* 1
——, 'Convictions and Fair Labelling' (1983) 42 *CLJ* 85
——, *Criminal Law: The General Part* 2nd edn (London, 1961)
——, 'The Logic of "Exceptions"' (1988) 47 *CLJ* 261
Wilshere AM, *Principles and Practice of the Criminal Law* (Hardpress Publishing, 1936)
Wilson MF, 'System of Self-Redress' (1879) 7 *Am L Rec* 577
Wilt MP, 'Civil Disobedience and the Rule of Law: Punishing Good Lawbreaking in a New Era of Protest' (2017) 28 *Geo Mason U CR LJ* 43
Winkler A, 'Is the Second Amendment Becoming Irrelevant' (2018) 93 *Ind LJ* 253
Wright AP, 'Resisting Unlawful Arrests: Inviting Anarchy or Protecting Individual Freedom?' (1997) 46 *Drake L Rev* 383
Wright RF, 'Public Defender Elections and Popular Control over Criminal Justice' (2010) 75 *Mo L Rev* 803
Yeager D, 'Decoding the Impossibility Defense' (2018) 56 *U Louisville L Rev* 359
Yeo S, 'Battered Woman Syndrome in Australia' (1993) 143 *New LJ* 13
Young R, 'What is so Wrong with Killing People?' (1979) 54 *Philosophy* 515
Young SB, 'The Moral Basis of American Law: An Hypothesis' (2004–2005) 82 *U Det Mercy L Rev* 649
Zedner L, 'Securing Liberty in the Face of Terror: Reflections from Criminal Justice' (2005) 32 *JL Soc'y* 507
Zgaga S, 'The Defence of Duress in International Criminal Law' (2013) 68 *Pravnik* [*Lawyer*] 95

INDEX

abortion 126–7
action-plans 95, 99
actus reus 50, 53, 102, 103, 194
'ancient right' of self-defence 1, 13, 14
Arbery, A 8, 185
Ashworth, A 76–7, 80, 82
attacker's culpability 28, 29, 30, 33, 34, 35, 37
attacker's right to life *see* **protecting the attacker's individual (presumptive) right to life**
autonomy of the defender v autonomy of the attacker 17–18
avoiding conflict *see* **retreat and avoiding conflict**

balancing the competing values 61, 68–9
  proposed weighted value approach 70–73
  simple priority approach 70
  single-value approach, and 69–70
Barras, F 8, 9
battered intimate partners 129–31
  England 199–202
  Germany 153–5, 161
  United States 179–80
Blackstone, W 13, 207
Bottoms, A 29–30
Braman, D 27
Brooke, Lord Justice 198
Brooks, R 8, 175
Brosnan, D 175

carelessness 60, 104
'castle doctrine' 1
causally-based conceptions of responsibility 63
character theory 34, 36
Cheng, C 87
'clash' between systemic and individual interests 87
collective rights 20, 69, 85
condemnation *see* **criminal conviction**
conditional forfeiture 65
conditional right to life 61, 66
conditional waiver 65–6
conduct-guiding norms 36
contingent threats and innocent shields 127–8
conventional public morality 34
'core' criminal liability 32, 33
criminal conviction
  stages of evaluation 49, 50
    conviction is upheld on appeal and becomes final 56
    defining the 'partially expressed public morality' 50–52
    establishing the defendant's mental fitness to proceed 52–3
    excused defendants 55–6
    fact-finder determines that the particular defendant violated the offence definition 53–4
    justification defences 54–5
    prosecutor's decision to bring charges 52
    sentencing of defendants 56
culpability-based conceptions of responsibility 63
culpable threats 68

deadly force in defence of property
  human rights 122
  proportionality 116–17
decision grounds, values as *see* **value-based decision-grounds**
defence of property 2, 5, 36, 116–17, 122, 135, 164, 195, 216
defender's autonomy *see* **protecting the defender's autonomy**
demand not to be harmed 34
democratic legitimacy 48
deterring (potential) attackers 58
  general deterrence 58, 59–60
  justification for the value 57
  limitations 57
  literature on 86–7
  specific deterrence 58, 60
  tension with, or support for, the other values 57
discretionary competence 35
disproportionate harm *see* **proportionality**

disrespect of others' rights 28, 29, 31, 32, 33, 34, 35, 36
Dressler, J 62, 130
Dsouza, M 36, 65, 82–3, 90–91, 94
duress 95, 97, 106, 108

'eight stages of public condemnation' *see* **criminal conviction**
Engberg, N 82, 84–5
England
- attacks
  - innocent attackers 195
  - passive conduct 196–8
  - police officers 196
  - protected interests 195
- battered intimate partners 199–202
- burden of proof 188
- 'chance medley' 189, 206, 207
- 'Dadson Principle' 193, 194
- excusable homicides 189, 206, 207
- 'half-way house', absence of 205
- homicide *se defendendo* 189, 206, 207
- imminence 198–9
  - subjective / objective evaluation 199
- justifiable homicides 189, 206
- justification
  - 'Dadson Principle' 193, 194
  - mistakes of fact 190, 191, 192–3
  - reasonableness of belief 190, 191, 192
  - subjective / objective standard 190–93
  - unknowing justification 193–5
- law of self-defence 188–9
- necessity 202–3
- *prima facie* case of self-defence 188
- property, defence of 195
- proportionality 203–6
- provocation 208, 209
- retreat and avoiding conflict 206, 207, 208
- value-centric perspectives on English law 190, 209–10, 215

ensuring the primacy of the legal process 43–5
- justification for the value 42
- limitations 42–3
- literature on 85
- tension with, or support for, the other values 42

equal standing *see* **maintaining the equal standing between people**
Erb, V 12, 30, 76, 79–80, 83, 84, 140, 143
erosion of the justice system's popular authority, guarding against 46, 48, 49
European Convention on Human Rights *see* **human rights**
excessive force 116
- *see also* **proportionality**

excuses 94, 95, 96, 97
external justification 98, 99, 100, 103

fault-based forfeiture of rights 62, 64, 65
Fearon, B 8
Fletcher, G 17, 78–9, 88, 94
Floyd, G 1
forced choice theory 63
forfeiture of rights 61, 64–5, 66–8
- conditional forfeiture 65
- conditional right to life 61, 66
- conditional waiver 65–6
- culpable and non-culpable / innocent attackers 63–4, 67, 68
- fault-based forfeiture 62, 64, 65
- forced choice theory 63
- rights theory 62
- temporary suspension of rights 62, 65
- 'unjust threat' 66, 67, 68
- versus waiver of rights 61, 66, 68

Foster, M 207
Frowe, H 90
'fully expressed public morality' 30, 44, 45, 46, 49, 54, 55, 56, 57, 93, 94, 95, 96, 98, 100, 102, 103

Gauthier, D 14
general deterrence 58, 59–60
Gentili, A 14
Germany
- attacks
  - family members 160–61
  - imminence 151–3
  - legally protected interests 147–8
  - non-culpable attackers 155
  - passive conduct 150–51
  - police officers 149–50
  - 'unlawful attack' 148–9
- battered intimate partners 153–5, 161
- defence of property 164
- dualistic justification of self-defence 139, 140
- excessive force 137
- hierarchy of values 134
- imminence 151–3
  - subjective / objective evaluation 152–3

justification 136, 137
'defensive will' 144, 146
mistakes of fact 145–6
objective standard 144, 145
protection of both the legal order and the individual 139–40
protection of the individual 139
protection of the legal order 138
unknowing justification 146, 147
necessity 156–7
permissiveness of self-defence law 135, 142
proportionality 137, 157–8, 159
grossly disproportionate force 158–9
provocation 161–3
putative excessive force 146
retreat and avoiding conflict 159–61
'right need not yield to the wrong' 137, 138, 164
socio-ethical limitations on self-defence 141–3, 163–4
value-driven self-defence regime 135, 137, 140, 163–5, 214–15, 216
Ghanayim, K 85, 87
Goetz, B 15
Goff, P 113
Golding, M 16
Grotius, H 67
'guilty mind' 50

Hale, M 207
Hankison, B 177
harming versus wronging 65, 68, 101, 149, 208
Hart, H 85
Hawkins, W 207
Hegel, G 17
Heger, M 75, 163
Herald of Free Enterprise 197
'hidden normativity' 6, 8, 15, 211, 212, 216
historical conceptions of self-defence 13–14
Hobbes, T 13–14
Hoekstra, M 87
Hohn, K 75, 142
Horder, J 209
hostility towards others' rights 31, 33
human rights 120–21
right to life 121
deadly force in defence of property 122
defensive force must be 'absolutely necessary' 121
mistakes 123
positive obligations 121
strict proportionality 122
'humanitarian' justification for self-defence 2, 6, 76, 88, 106, 119, 124, 142, 143, 164

imminence
England 198–9
Germany 151–3
necessity, and 108–10
United States 178–9
imputation of unequal standing 25, 28, 42, 79, 80, 111
incompatibility thesis 88, 90, 100, 144, 192
incompetence of attacker 33
individual rights, protection of 23, 75
innocent attackers / 'threats' 123–5
abortion 126–7
battered intimate partners 129–31
contingent threats and innocent shields 127–8
England 195
Germany 155
hypothetical well 126
passive threats 128–9, 150–51, 177, 196–8
'plank of Carneades' 129
instrumental concerns 4
internal justification 99, 100, 103
intuitions 6

jury instructions 215–16
justification 93–4, 95, 96, 97, 98, 101, 111
England
mistakes of fact 190, 191, 192–3
unknowing justification 193–5
external justification 98, 99, 100, 103
Germany *see* **Germany**
internal justification 99, 100, 103
legal justification 101, 103, 194
offence-defence distinction 102, 103
paradox of mutual justification 100, 132, 133, 192
United States 169, 170, 171
mistakes of fact 169
unknowing justification 170
unknowing justification 101–2, 103

Kadish, S 22
Kahan, D 27
Kant, I 17
Kantorowicz, H 85
Kasachkoff, T 63
Kates, D 82, 84–5
Kremnitzer, M 37–8, 85, 87
Kühl, K 75, 163

labelling 96–7
Laird, K 32–3
Lee, C 133
legal justification 101, 103, 194
legal legitimacy 48
legitimacy of the legal order *see* **maintaining the legitimacy of the legal order**
Leider, R 106
Lenckner, T 143
Leoni, B 31
Leverick, F 12, 16, 26, 62, 64, 65, 68, 69, 74–5, 77–8, 80–82, 88, 109–10, 112, 113, 114, 213
Leviathan 14
literature on value-based decision-grounds 87–92, 213–14
Locke, J 13

Macaulay, Lord 101
maintaining the equal standing between people 28–37
  attacker's culpability 28, 29, 30, 33, 34, 35, 37
  justification for the value 27–8
  limitations 28
  literature on 79–83
  reciprocity 30
  relationships of restraint 29, 30, 33, 34
  tension with, or support for, the other values 28
maintaining the legitimacy of the legal order 47–9
  democratic legitimacy 48
  justification for the value 45–6
  legal legitimacy 48
  limitations 46
  literature on 86
  normative legitimacy 48
  tension with, or support for, the other values 46
  unjust self-defence outcomes as a threat to law's moral credibility 56–7
Martin, Tony 8–9
Martin, Trayvon 7
Mayer, H 158
McMichael, G 8, 185
McMichael, T 8, 185
mens rea 32, 50, 53, 54, 103, 104, 192, 194
mistakes of fact 103–4
  England 190, 191, 192–3
  Germany 145–6
  United States 169
  unreasonable mistakes 104–5
monopoly on force, state's *see* **reducing overall societal violence by protecting the state's collective monopoly on force**
moral and ethical compasses 5
moral authority of the law 16, 44, 46, 47, 111
moral blameworthiness 94–5
  see also **carelessness; negligence; recklessness**
moral condemnation 32
  see also **criminal conviction**
mutual justification, paradox of 100, 132, 133, 192
mutual recognition of rights 35, 40

necessity 94, 97, 105, 106, 107
  England 202–3
  Germany 156–7
  human rights
    defensive force must be 'absolutely necessary' 121
  imminence, and 108–10
  United States 181
negligence 31, 32, 60, 162, 206
non-compensable values 71–2, 84, 111, 118, 119, 124, 125
normative legitimacy 48
Nourse, V 23, 89
Nozick, R 40, 126

Ormerod, D 32–3

Packer, H 94
paradox of mutual justification 100, 132, 133, 192
passive threats 128–9
  England
    passive conduct 196–8
  Germany
    passive conduct 150–51
  United States
    passive conduct 177
personal characteristics and reasonableness analysis 105, 192
personal domain
  protection of 1, 28, 35, 36, 37, 39, 40, 67, 105, 108, 197
'plank of Carneades' 129
police officers
  special rules 132–3
    England 196
    Germany 149–50
    United States 175–7, 215

popular legitimacy 46, 48, 49
'positionality of blame' 90, 94
presumptive right to life *see* **protecting the attacker's individual (presumptive) right to life**
primacy of the legal process *see* **ensuring the primacy of the legal process**
primacy of the 'right' over the 'wrong' 5
procedural justice 3, 29, 45, 47, 48, 49
property, defence of 2, 5, 36, 116–17, 122, 135, 164, 195, 216
proportionality 94, 115, 116
  deadly force in defence of property 116–17
  dealing with trivial threats 118, 119, 120
  England 203–6
  excessive force 116
  Germany 137, 157–8, 159
    grossly disproportionate force 158–9
  human rights 122
  strict proportionality approach 114–15
  United States 181–2
protecting the attacker's individual (presumptive) right to life 26–7
  justification for the value 25
  limitations 26
  literature on 76–9
  tension with, or support for, the other values 25–6
protecting the defender's autonomy 39–42
  justification for the value 39
  limitations 39
  literature on 83–5
  tension with, or support for, the other values 39
protection of the socio-legal order 37–8
provocation 95
  England 208, 209
  Germany 161–3
  United States 183, 184, 185

Raz, J 40, 41
reasonableness
  mistakes of fact 104–5
reciprocity 30
recklessness 60, 125, 161, 162
reducing overall societal violence by protecting the state's collective monopoly on force 21–5
  justification for the value 19–20
  limitations 21
  literature on 74–6
  subsidiary right 23
  tension with, or support for, the other values 20–21
'relationships of restraint' 29, 30, 33, 34
restorative retributivism 29
retreat and avoiding conflict 112–14
  England 206, 207, 208
  Germany 159–61
  United States 182, 183
retributivism 29, 45
Richardson, L 113
right to life 121
  see also **human rights**
right to non-interference 31, 35, 36, 39, 62, 64, 65, 66, 67, 68, 213
rights as absolute ends 31
rights theory 62
Robinson, P 86
Rolfe, G 8, 175
Rönnau, T 75, 142
Rousseau, J-J 30

Sangero, B 12, 37, 38, 82, 84, 86, 87, 91–2, 213–14
Schmidhäuser, E 143
scholarly neglect of values as decision-grounds *see* **literature on value-based decision-grounds**
Schopp, R 16, 24, 64, 69, 76, 83, 84, 89, 118, 119, 213
'self-help' 43, 85, 141, 180
Simester, A 101
Simon, Lord 191
Simons, K 65
'sliding scale' approach to resolving tension between rights 21, 29, 108, 113, 124, 128
Smith, J 103
socio-ethical limitations on self-defence 141–3, 163–4
socio-legal order, protection of 37–8
sovereignty of individuals 39, 64, 83, 84, 112, 118, 119
specific deterrence 58, 60
'stages of systemic condemnation' *see* **criminal conviction**
'stand-your-ground' law 1, 7
  United States 182
Stark, E 131
state's collective monopoly on force *see* **reducing overall societal violence by protecting the state's collective monopoly on force**

Stell, L 87
strict proportionality approach 114–15
'subsidiary right', self-defence as 23
'supreme value of human life' 27
systemic condemnation *see* **criminal conviction**

Tankebe, J 29–30
Taylor, B 177
temporary forfeiture of rights 62, 65
'tough on crime' approaches 1
'traditional' criminal liability 32, 33
trivial threats
proportionality 118, 119, 120
subjective / objective evaluation of 119–20
'two principles in tension' view of self-defence 17–18, 212
Tyler, T 47

unequal standing, imputation of 25, 28, 42, 79, 80, 111
Uniacke, S 62, 64, 66, 67, 68, 85, 89–90
unique threat posed by culpable attacks 28, 37
United States
attacks
criminal conduct 175
passive conduct 177
police officers 175–7, 215
protected interests 171–5
avoid conflict, duty to 183
battered intimate partners 179–80
blameworthy conduct by defender 168
'castle doctrine' 1
defence of property 116–17
imminence 178–9
subjective / objective evaluation of 178–9
imperfect self-defence 168
justification 169, 170, 171
mistakes of fact 169
subjective / objective standard 169, 170
unknowing justification 170
killing to prevent a felony 168
legal system 166
Model Penal Code (MPC) 167
necessity 181
perfect self-defence 168
proportionality 181–2
provocation 183, 184, 185
reasonableness 169, 170, 176
retreat, duty to 182, 183
'right to self-preservation' 167
'stand-your-ground' 182
value-centric perspectives on US law 185–7
universal demands 30, 34
'unjust' self-defence outcomes 56–7
'unjust threat' 66, 67, 68
unknowing justification 101–2, 103
England 193–5
Germany 146, 147
United States 170
unreasonable mistakes 104–5
utilitarianism 41

value-accommodation methods *see* **balancing the competing values**
value-based decision-grounds 4, 5, 6, 212–13
balancing the competing values 61, 68–9
proposed weighted value approach 70–73
simple priority approach 70
single-value approach, and 69–70
see also **forfeiture of rights**
broadening the self-defence justification 15
deterring (potential) attackers 57–60, 86–7
ensuring the primacy of the legal process 42–5, 85
limiting the right to self-defence 16
literature on 87–92, 213–14
maintaining the equal standing between people 27–37, 79–83
maintaining the legitimacy of the legal order 45–9, 56–7, 86
monistic approach 5, 77, 78
protecting the attacker's individual (presumptive) right to life 25–7, 76–9
protecting the defender's autonomy 39–42, 83–5
protection of the socio-legal order 37–8
reducing overall societal violence by protecting the state's collective monopoly on force 19–25, 74–6
value-based model of self-defence 13, 18, 19
balance of values 18
benefits of 10, 12, 74, 211–12, 214, 216
Germany
value-driven self-defence regime 135, 137, 140, 163–5, 214–15, 216
overview of comparative, international value-based models 217–18
value-centric perspectives on English law 190, 209–10, 215
value-centric perspectives on US law 185–7

value-judgements 2
violation of the 'sacredness' of the body 13
von Pufendorf, S 67

waiver-versus-forfeiture of rights 61, 66, 68
Walker, K 177
Walker, Lord Justice 198
Wallerstein, S 62
Ward, Lord Justice 198
Wasserman, D 63
'well hypothetical' 126
Wingfield, Major 213
wronging versus harming 65, 68, 101, 149, 208

Zedner, L 70
Zimmerman, G 7

RETHINKING SELF-DEFENCE

Self-defence – the 'ancient right' – has never been more relevant than in the present era of widespread calls for criminal justice reform. This book substantially advances the patinaed discussion by introducing for the first time a comprehensive value-centric approach to thinking about the deeper rationale of the defence. It tackles core issues such as the relative importance of the State's claimed monopoly on force, procedural justice and the need to shore up the justice system's legitimacy and creditworthiness, everyone's presumptive 'right to life', and the importance of ensuring equal standing between citizens. In so doing, the book breaks ground by addressing public perceptions of 'just' and 'right' outcomes, as well as the emphasis legal systems place (and should place) on State power.

www.ingramcontent.com/pod-product-compliance
Ingram Content Group UK Ltd.
Pitfield, Milton Keynes, MK11 3LW, UK
UKHW020244290926
15470UKWH00002B/726

9 781509 934171